N○○T ™

Not For Tourists Guide to
SEATTLE

Get more on
notfortourists.com

Keep connected with:
**Twitter:
twitter/notfortourists**

**Facebook:
facebook/notfortourists**

**iPhone App:
nftiphone.com**

Not For Tourists, Inc

Skyhorse Publishing

designed by:
Not For Tourists, Inc
NFT$_{TM}$—Not For Tourists$_{TM}$ Guide to Seattle
www.notfortourists.com

Publisher
Skyhorse Publishing

Creative Direction &
Information Design
Jane Pirone

Director
Stuart Farr

Managing Editor
Scott Sendrow

Production Manager
Aaron Schielke

City Editor
Jessica Baxter

Writing and Editing
Jessica Baxter
Frank Chiachiere
Scott Sendrow

Research
Nalini Ramautar

Graphic Design and
Production
Aaron Schielke

Information Systems
Manager
Juan Molinari

Printed in China
Print ISBN#: 978-1-63450-206-1 $21.99
Ebook ISBN: 978-1-5107-0025-3
ISSN 2163-9191
Copyright © 2015 by Not For Tourists, Inc.
7th Edition

Every effort has been made to ensure that the information in this book is as up-to-date as possible at press time. However, many details are liable to change—as we have learned.
Not For Tourists cannot accept responsibility for any consequences arising from the use of this book.

Not For Tourists does not solicit individuals, organizations, or businesses for listings inclusion in our guides, nor do we accept payment for inclusion into the editorial portion of our book; the advertising sections, however, are exempt from this policy. We always welcome communications from anyone regarding ANYTHING having to do with our books; please visit us on our website at www. notfortourists.com for appropriate contact information.

Skyhorse Publishing books may be purchased in bulk at special discounts for sales promotion, corporate gifts, fund-raising, or educational purposes. Special editions can also be created to specifications. For details, contact the Special Sales Department, Skyhorse Publishing, 307 West 36th Street, 11th Floor, New York, NY 10018 or specialsales@skyhorsepublishing.com.

www.skyhorsepublishing.com

10 9 8 7 6 5 4 3 2 1

Dear NFT User:

Ever since the city's humble beginnings, we've been a transient's town, full of sailors on leave, gold rush/dot-com/grunge rock hopefuls, and gentlemen loafers sleeping beneath the stars. Microsoft, Starbucks, Amazon, and Sub Pop changed all that, and suddenly the city's reputation changed in the eyes of the world and itself, becoming an international hub of commerce, technology, and youth culture. The dot-com bust punctured the economy but not Seattle's upwardly mobile self-image, so we steadfastly cling to the notion that we can reclaim our former glory (even if many of us are working in bars or writing code instead of selling out the Paramount or playing golf with Bezos and Gates).

You might need to be a millionaire to buy a house here, but you only need a couple of bucks to buy this book. So while you wait for whatever big break you seek, there is a vibrant music scene, great food, amazing art, incredible libraries, quirky landmarks, and thousands of eccentric panhandlers willing to accept any spare change that's weighing you down. And NFT is here to help you navigate it all!

So whether you were born in Ballard or just moved from Boston, beginning a start-up venture or squandering your venture capital, you need this book. You'll find each and every one of Seattle's neighborhoods represented within, with full details on all the essential nightlife, restaurants, shopping spots, and coffee shops—hell, we've even included a whole section on…gulp…the Eastside.

NFT Seattle is full of new listings and updates, but if there's still something amiss or missing, by all means let us know. Your feedback is essential in helping us make this the ultimate guide to Seattle. Dig www.notfortourists.com to give us pro or con feedback. We can take it! And check out our nifty mobile app, for the latest up-to-date information on the go.

—Jane, Scott, Jessica, Frank, et al.

Table of Contents

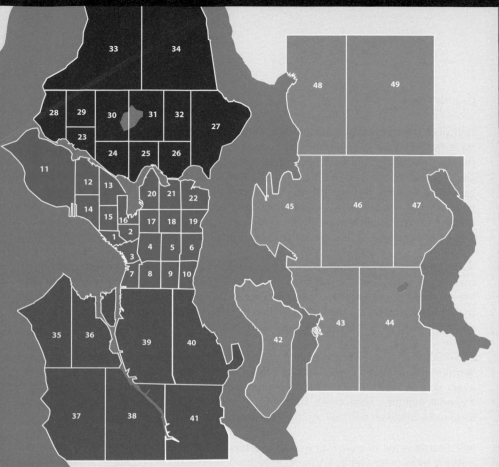

Map 1 • Belltown

Map 1

The formerly seedy Belltown now bursts with condos, boutique eateries, and noisy nightlife destinations. But don't fret, heroin can still be scored on the proper street corners. Homeless shelters and public health centers neighbor the rock clubs, art galleries, and sushi joints, making for an occasionally jarring mix of people. To escape the craziness, take a stroll through SAM's fabulous **Olympic Sculpture Park.**

○ Landmarks

- **Cinerama** · 2100 4th Ave
  206-448-6680
  One of three theaters in the world showing three-panel Cinerama films. Amazing.
- **The Edgewater Hotel** · 2411 Alaskan Way
  206-728-7000
  Yes, Virginia, you really can fish from your hotel window.
- **Olympic Sculpture Park** · 2901 Western Ave
  206-654-3100
  Ambitious venue for the SAM's sculpture collection.
- **Seattle P.I. Globe** · 101 Elliott Ave W
  800-542-0820
  Is it the Post-Intelligencer or the Daily Planet?

🖳 Coffee

- **Bedlam Coffee** · 2231 2nd Ave
  206-910-2300
  Coffeehouse or community center: you decide.
- **Cherry Street Coffee House** · 2719 1st Ave
  206-441-5489
  Good coffee, nice staff, but the owner added a sick leave surcharge to protest a city mandate. Not cool.
- **Cherry Street Coffee House** · 2621 5th Ave
  206-812-1298
  Good coffee, nice staff, but the owner added a sick leave surcharge to protest a city mandate. Not cool.
- **Dimitrou's Jazz Alley Coffee** · 2203 6th Ave
  206-441-9729
  They'll get you jazzed, alright.
- **Midtown Espresso** · 2133 5th Ave
  206-443-9070
  Best breakfast sandwiches in town.
- **Street Bean Espresso** · 2702 3rd Ave
  206-708-6803
  Good coffee for a great cause: Helping kids get off the streets.

- **Uptown Espresso** · 2801 Alaskan Way
  206-770-7777
  Self-proclaimed "Home of the Velvet Foam" but the coffee underneath is just so-so.
- **Uptown Espresso** · 2504 4th Ave
  206-441-1084
  Self-proclaimed "Home of the Velvet Foam" but the coffee underneath is just so-so.
- **Wheelhouse Coffee** · 2113 Westlake Ave
  206-467-0160
  Serving Lighthouse coffee with a smile is totally in their wheelhouse.

🍸 Nightlife

- **101 Restaurant & Lounge** · 101 Denny Way
  206-448-3035
  Emphasis on the word "lounge."
- **The 5 Point Café** · 415 Cedar St
  206-448-9991
  Start and finish your Belltown adventure at this all-night joint.
- **Amber** · 2214 1st Ave
  206-728-8500
  If Maxim Magazine owned a bar.
- **Black Bottle** · 2600 1st Ave
  206-441-1500
  Damned if it ain't noisy, though the list is decent, and the flatbreads rule.
- **The Crocodile** · 2200 2nd Ave
  206-441-4618
  Legendary venue where some of Seattle's biggest names got their start.
- **Cyclops Café and Lounge** · 2421 1st Ave
  206-441-1677
  A tip of the fedora to old Belltown lounge days.
- **Far Eats** · 2301 5th Ave
  206-770-3287
  Above-average Indian tucked away in the quiet part of Belltown.
- **Foundation Nightclub** · 2218 Western Ave
  206-535-7285
  Top 40 and blurred lines galore.

Map 1

Belltown

- **Hula Hula** · 106 1st Ave N
206-284-5003
Drink BOWLS full of rum in this ultra tiki lounge.
- **Lava Lounge** · 2226 2nd Ave
206-441-5660
Free shuffleboard and a great '80s jukebox offer a refuge from Belltown yuppies.
- **List** · 2226 1st Ave
206-441-1000
Terrific weeknight happy hour. Typical B-Town douchery on weekends.
- **Palace Kitchen** · 2030 5th Ave
206-448-2001
Just getting started at midnight? Eat fine grub until 1 am, drink 'til 2 am.
- **Queen City Grill** · 2201 1st Ave
206-443-0975
Decent Northwest fare and loud Belltown crowd.
- **Rabbit Hole** · 2222 2nd Ave
206-956-4653
Worth jumping down, depsite squandered theme potential. Hush puppies.
- **Rendezvous** · 2322 2nd Ave
206-441-5823
Dive bar with a touch of old Hollywood class.
- **Rob Roy** · 2332 2nd Ave
206-956-8423
Linda's rather impressive attempt at swank. Two-fist Cristal with High Life.
- **Rocco's** · 2228 2nd Ave
206-448-2625
Pizza and cocktails from the crazy alcoholics who brought you Noc Noc.
- **Sarajevo Lounge** · 2332 1st Ave
206-448-9000
Party like the Bosians and/or Herzegovinians.
- **Shorty's** · 2222 2nd Ave
206-441-5449
Pinball, hot dogs, and booze: the Holy Trinity of Awesome.

- **Some Random Bar** · 2604 1st Ave
206-745-2185
Inventive menu, gorgeous decor, WORST NAME EVER.
- **Spitfire** · 2219 4th Ave
206-441-7966
"Urban sports bar" pleases all sorts with awesome happy hour.
- **Spur Gastropub** · 113 Blanchard St
206-728-6706
Another notable notch on the McCracken/Tough empire's fancy-ass bed post.
- **Tia Lou** · 2218 1st Ave
206-733-8226
Happy hour patio: Muy bonita. Night crowd: El Douche.
- **Tini Bigs** · 100 Denny Way
206-284-0931
Be so very new millennium by heading back to the '50s at this martini lounge.
- **Twist** · 2313 1st Ave
206-448-9478
The twist is that you're the meat.
- **Umi Sake House** · 2230 1st Ave
206-374-8717
Late-night sushi happy hour in indoor zen garden!
- **The Upstairs** · 2209 2nd Ave
206-441-4013
A Hipstamatic wet dream.
- **Vittles Neighborhood Bistro & Bar** ·
2330 2nd Ave
206-448-3348
Decadent happy hour menu served twice nightly.
- **Wasabi** · 2311 2nd Ave
206-441-6044
"Bistro" is Japanese for "Yuppie."
- **The Whisky Bar** · 2122 2nd Ave
206-443-4490
Guess what their specialty is.

Belltown

Map 1

Shorty's is the closest thing to heaven in Seattle with pinball, booze, and hot dogs. **Cinerama** is a close second, offering one of the best movie-going experiences in the world. Other highlights include the Polynesian-tastic happy hour at **Ohana**, the Rat Pack drink experience at the **Rendezvous**, and a rock show at the legendary **Crocodile**.

🍴 Restaurants

- **The 5 Point Café** · 415 Cedar St
206-448-9991 · $
24-hour bar/diner with decent food. Just don't piss off the wait staff.
- **Anthony's Bell Street Diner** · 2201 Alaskan Way
206-448-6688 · $$$
Casual (and affordable) offshoot of the popular Anthony's chain.
- **Anthony's Pier 66** · 2201 Alaskan Way
206-448-6688 · $$$$
Pacific Northwest chain on Elliott Bay.
- **Assaggio Ristorante** · 2010 4th Ave
206-441-1399 · $$$$
If you don't mind the tourists, some of the food is pretty good.
- **Bell Thai** · 2211 4th Ave
206-441-8488 · $$
Great lunch deals. Otherwise uninspiring.
- **Bellini Italian Bistro** · 2302 1st Ave
206-441-4480 · $$
Napoli-style pizza and pasta with the full Italian dining experience. You're too skinny.
- **Biscuit Bitch Belltown** · 2303 3rd Ave
206-728-2219 · $
Southern hospitality and buttery goodness behind a resting bitch face.
- **Black Bottle** · 2600 1st Ave
206-441-1500 · $$
Fill your jowls with flatbread and wine to drown out the noise.
- **Buffalo Deli** · 2123 1st Ave
206-728-8759 · $
Pretty much determined to have the best French dip in town.
- **Cantina Lena** · 2105 5th Ave
206-519-5723 · $$$
Tom Douglas does Mexican (and it's pretty bueno). Also, CHURROS.
- **CJ's Eatery** · 2619 1st Ave
206-728-1648 · $$
Delicious omelettes and amazing homemade chicken noodle soup.
- **The Crocodile** · 2200 2nd Ave
206-441-4618 · $
Serving wood-fired pizza late in the Back Bar.
- **Dahlia Lounge** · 2001 4th Ave
206-682-4142 · $$$$
Another gem in Tom Douglas's juggernaut. Great for dates.
- **El Camion** · 1021 Occidental Ave S
206-659-0236 · $
Amazing truck tacos and tamales you can trust.
- **El Gaucho** · 2505 1st Ave
206-728-1337 · $$$$
Super-luxurious surf and turf, best for impressing the pants off someone.
- **Far Eats** · 2301 5th Ave
206-770-3287 · $$
Above-average Indian tucked away in the quiet part of Belltown.
- **Flying Fish** · 2234 1st Ave
206-728-8595 · $$$$
Fish for the fresh-faced younger set.
- **The Grill from Ipanema** · 2313 1st Ave
206-457-4885 · $$$
A carnivore's paradise if you can get past the name and annoying website.
- **Holy Cannoli** · 2720 3rd Ave
206-841-8205 · $
Your Italian pastry & stromboli prayers have been answered.
- **Hook & Plow** · 2100 Alaskan Way
206-256-1040 · $$
Lackluster hotel (Marriott) restaurant disguised as a trendy gastropub.
- **Icon Grill** · 1935 5th Ave
206-441-6330 · $$$
Kitchsy-crazy interior and familiar favorites bumped up a notch.
- **The Innkeeper** · 2510 1st Ave
206-441-7817 · $$
You don't have to go home, but you can't stay here.
- **La Fontana Siciliana** · 120 Blanchard St
206-441-1045 · $$
Much-loved Sicilian spot.
- **La Vita E Bella** · 2411 2nd Ave
206-441-5322 · $$
Among the most deliciousest pizza crusts in town—crisp, chewy, perfect.

24 25 26
12 13
20 21 22
14 15 16 17 18 19
1 2
3 4 5 6
7 8 9 10

Map 1

Belltown

- **Local 360** · 2234 1st Ave
  206-441-9360 · $$
  Appealing to any degree of Seattlite, from kid to drunken foodie.
- **Lola** · 2000 4th Ave
  206-441-1430 · $$
  Always hoppin', so service can be spotty. Food's a little Greek and a lot delicious.
- **The Lucky Diner** · 2630 1st Ave
  206-805-0133 · $$
  Ultra-modern diner. Just a little too clean to be a greasy spoon.
- **Macrina Bakery & Café** · 2408 1st Ave
  206-448-4032 · $$
  Macrina's baked goods will make breakfast your most important meal.
- **Mama's Mexican Kitchen** · 2334 2nd Ave
  206-728-6262 · $$
  Kitschy Mexican cooking with a thing for Elvis (and cheese).
- **Marrakesh Moroccan Restaurant** · 2334 2nd Ave
  206-956-0500 · $$$
  Belly Dancer Had a Little Lamb.
- **Ohana** · 2207 1st Ave
  206-956-9329 · $$
  Pu-pus that are far from poo poo.
- **Palace Kitchen** · 2030 5th Ave
  206-448-2001 · $$$
  Gourmet late-night dining in Seattle? This is your spot.
- **Queen City Grill** · 2201 1st Ave
  206-443-0975 · $$$$
  Seafood's the focus, unless you count the horndogs hoping to score.
- **Restaurant Zoe** · 2137 2nd Ave
  206-256-2060 · $$$
  The brown butter-bathed ricotta gnudi is now officially Seattle legend.
- **Rocco's** · 2228 2nd Ave
  206-448-2625 · $$
  Pizza and cocktails from the crazy alcoholics who brought you Noc Noc.
- **Serious Pie** · 316 Virginia St
  206-838-7388 · $$$
  Truly amazing crust in tiny quarters.

- **Shaker and Spear** · 2000 2nd Ave
  206-826-1700 · $$$
  Fancy hotel restaurant seafood.
- **Shiro's Sushi** · 2401 2nd Ave
  206-443-9844 · $$$
  Wait to sit at the bar, chat with Shiro, be utterly delighted.
- **Six Seven** · 2411 Alaskan Way
  206-269-4575 · $$$$
  Northwest seafood classics.
- **Some Random Bar** · 2604 1st Ave
  206-745-2185 · $$
  Inventive menu, gorgeous decor, WORST NAME EVER.
- **Spur Gastropub** · 113 Blanchard St
  206-728-6706 · $$$
  Multiple award-winning cuisine in a vaguely western bar and the crowds to prove it.
- **Tavolata** · 2323 2nd Ave
  206-838-8008 · $$
  Fantastically sexy space with handmade pastas to match.
- **Tilikum Place Café** · 407 Cedar St
  206-282-4830 · $$
  Euro flavors with a delightfully NW twist. Also sexy waitstaff.
- **Top Pot Doughnuts** · 2124 5th Ave
  206-728-1966 · $
  Top Pot is tops!
- **Two Bells** · 2313 4th Ave
  206-441-3050 · $$
  A rare old soul in trendy Belltown. Tasty burgers.
- **Vittles Neighborhood Bistro & Bar** ·
  2330 2nd Ave
  206-448-3348 · $$$
  Comfort food for grownups.
- **Wasabi** · 2311 2nd Ave
  206-441-6044 · $$$$
  Sushi rolls usually involving avocado or cream cheese. Not for purists.
- **The Yellow Leaf Cupcake Co.** · 2209 4th Ave
  206-441-4240 · $
  The next evolution of cupcakes.
- **Zeek's Pizza** · 419 Denny Way
  206-285-8646 · $$
  Pizzas with pizzazz, like the Thai version with peanut sauce.

Eating-wise, indulge on tasty baked goods at **Macrina**. For something a little more upscale, try the cozy and inventive flavors of **Tilikum Place Cafe**. And of course there are all those Tom Douglas places: **Dahlia Lounge**, **Lola**, **Serious Pie**, and **Palace Kitchen**—it seems like the list goes on and on. For more in the Top Chef vein, visit Ethan Stowell's **Tavolata**. Elsewhere, all the romance and intrigue of Morocco comes alive in the mysterious-looking **Marrakesh Moroccan Restaurant** And if 24-7 greasy grub is all you're after, try **The 5 Point Café**.

Shopping

- **Boston St** · 1902 Post Alley
  206-634-0580
  The children's (somewhat smart ass, sometimes endearing) everything store.
- **Champion Party Supply** · 124 Denny Way
  206-284-1980
  From slutty nurse costumes to slutty werewolf costumes. And party supplies!
- **Dahlia Bakery** · 2001 4th Ave
  206-441-4540
  Take a hot steaming loaf of Tom Douglas home with you.

- **Kuhlman** · 2419 1st Ave
  206-441-1999
  Your friends Ben Sherman and Fred Perry live here.
- **Peter Miller Books** · 2326 2nd Ave
  206-441-4114
  Top-notch selection of architecture and design books.
- **Rudy's Barbershop** · 89 Wall St
  206-448-8900
  Absolute best cheap haircut.
- **Singles Going Steady** · 2219 2nd Ave
  206-441-7396
  Terrific range of new/used punk and indie music sold by friendly crusties.

Map 2 · **South Lake Union**

N

1

South
Lake
Union
Park

Lake Union

Ward St

**Fairview
& Campus Drive**

Aloha St

Minor Ave N

Yale Ave N

Valley St

Aurora Av Ramp

N Broad St

**Westlake
& Mercer**

**Terry
& Mercer**

Valley St

Fairview N

Lake Union Park

Mercer St

E Roy St

Roy St

Roy St

E Roy St

A

N Broad St

Republican St

8th Ave N

E Mercer St

E Repu

16

E Harrison St

1100

1300

Harrison St

15

Aurora Ave N

99

Dexter Ave N

8th Ave N

9th Ave N

Westlake Ave N

**Westlake
& Thomas**

**Terry
& Thomas**

E Harrison St

Boren Ave N

Thomas St

Fairview Ave N

Cascade
Playground

Yale Ave N

Pontius Ave N

17

Eastlake Ave E

Exit 166

5

Melrose Ave E

800

1100

E Harrison St

1300

Denny Park

John St

1100

B

**Elephant
Car Wash**

Battery St

Aurora Ave N

Bell St

Westlake Ave

**Westlake
& 9th**

Blanchard St

**Westlake
& Denny**

Denny Way

1100

100

Denny Way

Court Pl

Howell St

1300

**DENNY
TRIANGLE**

Lenora St

Minor Ave

Boren Ave

Yale Ave

4

E Olive Pl

6th Ave N

Bell St

Virginia St

Terry Ave

9th Ave

Stewart St

Minor Ave

Yale Ave

Bellevue Ave

C

Blanchard St

**Westlake
& 7th**

1

8th Ave

7th Ave

6th Ave

Howell St

Olive Way

Pine St

3

Pike St

Melrose Ave

Minor Ave

Lenora St

Virginia St

Stewart St

Terry Ct

Union St

Hubbell Pl

Terry Ave

DOWNTOWN

Western Ave

E Pine St

E Pike St

9th Ave S

University St

Boren Ave

Connecticut Pl

Seneca St

| 1/4 mile | .25 km |

What do you get the man who has everything? How about a neighborhood? For years, Paul Allen sought to make this warehouse wasteland into a destination. Once Amazon.com moved in, he finally succeeded. Tom Douglas followed with a handful of restaurants and condos sprung up to house the young professionals the 'hood is designed to ensnare. Naturally, these people will shop at Whole Foods. However, you still won't catch anyone local riding the S.L.U.T.

○ Landmarks

- **Elephant Car Wash** · 616 Battery St
  206-441-6776
  That giant pink elephant in the sky.

Coffee

- **Espresso Vivace** · 227 Yale Ave N
  206-388-5164
  Coffee so good it makes you purr.
- **Zoka Coffee Roaster & Tea Company** ·
  351 Boren Ave
  206-545-4277
  A true Seattle original.

Nightlife

- **13 Coins** · 125 Boren Ave N
  206-682-2513
  Sometimes you just gotta blow $50 on steak and lobster at 3 am.
- **Brave Horse Tavern** · 310 Terry Ave N
  206-971-0717
  Get blotto the Tom Douglas way.
- **Dimitriou's Jazz Alley** · 2033 6th Ave
  206-441-9729
  Seattle's longstanding jazz venue. Let them entertain you.
- **El Corazon** · 109 Eastlake Ave E
  206-262-0482
  If you like your punk and metal with a little teenager.
- **Feierabend** · 422 Yale Ave N
  206-340-2528
  Grab a bier and make new friends. Prost.
- **Lo-Fi** · 429 Eastlake Ave E
  206-254-2824
  A dance club for grownups and young folks with refined musical taste.
- **Re-Bar** · 1114 Howell St
  206-233-9873
  Fringe theater, live music, and decidedly drag-friendly. Experience the unexpected.

Map 2

Map 2

South Lake Union

🍴 Restaurants

- **13 Coins** · 125 Boren Ave N
206-682-2513 · $$$
Sometimes you just gotta blow $50 on steak and lobster at 3 am.
- **314 Pie** · Boren Ave
206-701-9233 · $$
Aussie pies by locally based Aussiephiles will ensure you a g'day.
- **The Berliner Döner Kebab** · 428 Westlake Ave N
206-838-5032 · $
A very Seattle gyrocery with tofu instead of falafel.
- **Cactus** · 350 Terry Ave N
206-913-2250 · $$
Legendary local chain, serving outstanding mojitos and Mexican.
- **Café Suisse** · 2008 Westlake Ave
206-633-3876 · $
This bona fide Swiss cafe is not to be missed.
- **Caffe Torino** · 422 Yale Ave N
206-682-2099 · $
Helping Seattle to keep its superior coffee reputation.
- **Cuoco** · 301 Terry Ave N
206-971-0710 · $$$
Italian food with bellissimo results.
- **FareStart** · 700 Virginia St
206-267-7601 · $$
Eat well, feel great: FareStart trains the disadvantaged to launch new lives as chefs.
- **Happy Grillmore** · Harrison & Boren Ave N
206-486-0797 · $
Fatty burgers that are way better than Adam Sandler's last 10 movies.
- **Hot Dog King** · 400 Westlake Ave
206-327-4847 · $
Long live the king!
- **Kaosamai Thai Cook Truck** · 970 Denny Way
206-349-6533 · $
Exactly what you would expect: Thai food out of a truck.
- **La Lot** · 925 Stewart St
206-682-8812 · $$
If you're into Vietnamese fusion, you'll like this place la lot.
- **La Toscanella Bakery & Paninoteca** · 116 Westlake Ave N
206-682-1044 · $
An authentic-as-hell Italian bakery and cafe with cannoli and everything!
- **Lunchbox Laboratory** · 1253 Thomas St
206-621-1090 · $
Stunning burger specimens—the "dork" is a thing of beauty.
- **Marination Mobile** · 132 N Canal St
$
Giving Seattle what they didn't know they wanted: Mexikoreanysian.
- **Mio Sushi** · 120 Westlake Ave N
206-971-0069 · $$
Franchise sushi that will do in a pinch.
- **Mistral Kitchen** · 2020 Westlake Ave
206-623-1922 · $$$
Got cash? Splurge for the 8 course menu.
- **Off the Rez** · Boren Ave N & Harrison St
206-414-8226 · $
The Native American flatbread tacos that will change your life. Fatter, maybe. But blissfully satiated.
- **Outside the Box** · 411 Fairview Ave S
425-272-5361 · $$
Since that Paleo thing doesn't seem to be going away, here's a food truck that parks outside Crossfit gyms.
- **Petra Mediterranean Bistro** · 1933 7th Ave
206-448-2604 · $
A stand-out gem in the vast sea of Mediterranean food in Seattle.
- **PlayDate SEA** · 1275 Mercer St
206-623-7529 · $
An 8,500 sqft indoor playground with numerous vantage points for parents to relax with their Stumptown coffee and smartphones.

If you like Tom Douglas restaurants (and what's not to like?), you'll be pleased as hand-crafted locally made punch to dine here. Experience a welcome re-invention of Italian cuisine at **Cuoco**, take in a sporting match at the **Brave Horse Tavern** or brunch with the family at **Portage Bay Cafe**. **Petra** is a stand-out gem in the vast sea of Mediterranean food in Seattle.

- **Portage Bay Cafe** · 391 Terry Ave N
  206-462-6400 · $$
  Local organic breakfasts and lunches.
- **Re:public** · 429 Westlake Ave N
  206-467-5300 · $$$
  A republic worth standing for.
- **Serious Pie** · 401 Westlake Ave N
  206-436-0500 · $$
  It's worth the potentially long wait. SERIOUSLY.
- **Serious Pie & Biscuit** · 401 Westlake Ave N
  206-436-0050 · $
  Leave it to Tom Douglas to make the breakfast sandwich more decadent.
- **Shilla Restaurant** · 2300 8th Ave
  206-623-9996 · $$
  Menu is a crash-course in Korean Food 101. Impressive panchan.
- **Skinny Phoenix** · Harrison St & Boren Ave N
  253-293-9296 · $
  I don't know how the phoenix stays so skinny eating breakfast pizza.
- **Top Pot Doughnuts** · 590 Terry Ave N
  206-995-8296 · $
  Top Pot is tops!
- **Tutta Bella** · 2200 Westlake Ave
  206-624-4422 · $$
  Excellent pizza for new condo owners.
- **Veggie Grill** · 446 Terry Ave N
  206-623-0336 · $$
  Santa Monica-based chain offers up the ultimate in vegetarian comfort food.
- **Xplosive Mobile Food Truck** · 425 Terry Ave
  206-612-4739 · $$
  Asian fusion taste explosions.
- **Zaw** · 434 Yale Ave N
  206-623-0299 · $$
  It's not delivery. It's artisan take-and-bake.

Shopping

- **Eurostyle Your Life** · 2008 Westlake Ave
  206-633-3876
  Cool products from Europe and the US.
- **Play it Again Sports** · 1304 Stewart St
  206-264-9255
  Used sports equipment, check here before walking the block to REI.
- **REI** · 222 Yale Ave N
  206-223-1944
  The granola flagship store with an impressive rock wall.

Map 3 · **Downtown**

Ⓝ

1 Denny Park

2 Denny Way

Howell St · Exit 16

Clay St

Vine St

Court Pl
Yale Ave

Wall St

Battery St

Bell St

9th Ave

Blanchard St

Minor Ave

Boren Ave

E O

Lenora St

Terry Ave

Minor Ave

1st Ave

Battery St

A

5th Ave

4th Ave

3rd Ave

Virginia St

9th Ave

8th Ave

Stewart St

Howell St

Olive Way

Pine St

Melrose Ave

Pike St

7th Ave

6th Ave

Westlake Ave

Paramount Theatre ○

PAGE 268

9th Ave W

2 ▲

Exit 166

Union St

Regrade Park

Blanchard St

1st Ave

2nd Ave

Lenora

Bell St

Western Ave

Giant Rotating Shuttlecock

Western Ave ○

Victor Steinbrueck Park

Virginia St

Stewart St

Pine St

Moore Theater

PAGE 267

1 ●

Pine St

5th Ave

6th Ave

E Pine St

E Pike St

Convention and Trade Center

Union St

7th Ave W

Hubbel Pl

Convention Pl

University St

9th Ave W

Exit 165A

Starbucks ○

Pike St

Virginia St

Pike Pl

Post Aly

Newis Ln

Post Alley

Pine St

Pike St

The Blade ○

5th Avenue Theatre ○

Rainier Tower ○

PAGE 177

Freeway Park

8th Ave

7th Ave

PAGE 188

Pike Place Market

Rachel the Pig ○
Gum Wall ○

1st Ave

Union St ○

PAGE 265

Benaroya Hall

4th Ave

3rd Ave

University St

4 ▶

Exit 164

B

Waterfront Park

Seattle Art Museum ○

The Hammering Man ○

Seneca St

Spring St

Seattle Central Library

5

6th Ave

5th Ave

The Great Wheel ○

99

Alaskan Way

Madison St

PAGE 195

Marion St

Elliott Bay

1st Ave

2nd Ave

Post Ave

Western Ave

Columbia St

Cherry St

James St

4th Ave

3rd Ave

5th Ave

6th Ave

Columbia Center ○

Jefferson St

C

Western Ave

7 ▼

Pioneer Square Park

Yesler Way

2nd Avenue Ext S

City Hall Park

Dilling Way

Prefontaine Pl S

Terrace St

S Washington St

S Main St

3rd Ave S

2nd Ave S

3rd Ave S

S Jackson St

| 1/4 mile | .25 km |

S King St

Map 3

Like most downtowns, Seattle's mainly caters to tourists, consumers, and the work-a-day crowd. Therefore department stores, happy hours, and Starbucks are plentiful. But fancy condos are starting to spring up on every block, and more people are calling this 'hood home. You can get your culture on at **Benaroya Hall** or the **Seattle Art Museum**. Westlake Center is flavor country in terms of colorful characters, religious zealots, and the occasional "Personality Test" booth.

o Landmarks

- **5th Avenue Theatre** · 1308 5th Ave
  206-625-1900
  Lavish Chinese-inspired interior. Cheesy shows.
- **Benaroya Hall** · 200 University St
  206-215-4747
  Seattle Symphony's state-of-the-art performance hall.
- **The Blade** · 2nd Ave & Pike St
  Used to be crack and coke. Now it's condos and coffee.
- **Columbia Center** · 701 5th Ave
  Tallest building in Seattle with an observation deck on the 73rd floor.
- **Freeway Park** · 700 Seneca St
  206-684-4075
  Architecturally stunning park built over I-5.
- **Giant Rotating Shuttlecock** ·
  Western Ave & Lenora St
  Officially known as Angie's Umbrella.
- **The Great Wheel** · 1301 Alaskan Way
  206-623-8600
  Buy tickets online to save yourself an hour's wait before you wait some more. And keep in mind it's just a ferris wheel.
- **The Hammering Man** · 100 University St
  206-654-3100
  Jonathan Borofsky's mechanized sculpture looms over the SAM.
- **Moore Theatre** · 1932 2nd Ave
  206-682-1414
  Historic, architecturally stunning performance hall.
- **Paramount Theatre** · 911 Pine St
  206-682-1414
  Former vaudeville theater houses a rare Wurlitzer organ.
- **Pike Place Market** · 1501 Pike Pl
  206-682-7453
  So authentic even locals shop here!
- **Pike Place Market Gum Wall** ·
  Lower Post Alley & Pike St
  The most unlikely public art created by thousands of wads of masticated gum.

- **Rachel the Piggy Bank** · Pike St & Pike Pl
  Meeting point for internet daters.
- **Rainier Tower** · 1301 5th Ave
  Architect Minoru Yamasaki also designed the World Trade Center in NYC.
- **Seattle Art Museum Downtown** · 1300 1st Ave
  206-654-3100
  A museum named SAM.
- **Seattle Central Library** · 1000 4th Ave
  206-386-4636
  Koolhaas designed. Stunning inside and out. Free tours.
- **Starbucks** · 1912 Pike Pl
  206-448-8762
  Original store (but not original location); where it all began.

🖥Coffee

- **Ancient Grounds** · 1220 1st Ave
  206 749-0747
  Part art gallery, part coffee joint.
- **Caffe Appassionato** · 801 Alaskan Way
  206-264-2500
  Classic Seattle coffee shop vibe at this small-ish local chain. Frasier would love it here.
- **Caffe D'Arte** · 1625 2nd Ave
  206-728-4468
  Italian-style espresso.
- **Caffe Ladro** · 108 Union St
  206-267-0600
  Strong coffee for the strong coffee drinker.
- **Caffe Ladro** · 801 Pine St
  206-405-1950
  Strong coffee for the strong coffee drinker.
- **Cherry Street Coffee House** · 1212 1st Ave
  206-264-9372
  Good coffee, nice staff, but the owner added a sick leave surcharge to protest a city mandate. Not cool.
- **Cherry Street Coffee House** · 103 Cherry St
  206-621-9372
  Good coffee, nice staff, but the owner added a sick leave surcharge to protest a city mandate. Not cool.

Map 3

Downtown

- **Cherry Street Coffee House** · 808 3rd Ave
206-442-9372
Good coffee, nice staff, but the owner added a sick leave surcharge to protest a city mandate. Not cool.
- **Diva Espresso** · 401 5th Ave
206-682-2173
Local chain with unpredictable service. I guess it's kind of like ordering coffee from a diva.
- **Espresso Caffe Dior** · 725 Pike St
206-624-0814
Also sandwiches.
- **Ghost Alley Espresso** · 1499 Post Alley
206-805-0195
Have a spiritual coffee experience next to the infamous wall of masticated gum corpses.
- **Monorail Espresso** · 520 Pike St
206-625-0449
Their product is a whole hell of a lot more useful than the actual monorail. Tastier too.
- **Moore Coffee Shop** · 1930 2nd Ave
206-728-5668
Nutella latte. Need I say Moore?
- **Nordstrom eBar** · 500 Pine St
206-628-2111
Nothing special, but hey, it's right there.
- **Pegasus Coffee Bar** · 711 3rd Ave
206-682-3113
Bainbridge Island roasters' downtown location.
- **Pegasus Coffee Bar** · 1218 3rd Ave
206-292-3013
Bainbridge Island roasters' downtown location.
- **Phoenix Cafe** · 1017 3rd Ave
206-466-1906
Serving Fonte coffee with their own fiery twist.
- **Seattle Coffee Works** · 107 Pike St
206-340-8867
To these guys, making coffee is not work.
- **Simon's Espresso Cafe** · 925 4th Ave
206-957-4545
The best thing going in this particular office building. May even some of the surrounding ones.
- **Voxx Coffee** · 1200 6th Ave
206-682-1242
A welcoming shop with tons of outlets. Take off your coat and stay a while.

ⓨ Nightlife

- **Alibi Room** · 85 Pike St
206-623-3180
Dark, underground bar with a lounge feel.
- **Athenian** · 1517 Pike Pl
206-624-7166
Drink with other Pike Place Market alcoholics.
- **BOKA** · 1010 1st Ave
206-357-9000
Terrific happy hour food. Otherwise a boka bore.
- **Can Can** · 94 Pike St
206-652-0832
1940s cabaret is alive and well. Make reservations EARLY.
- **Carlile Room** · 820 Pine Street
206-946-9720
T-Doug gets into the nightlife business.
- **Contour** · 807 1st Ave
206-447-7704
Ongoing mix 'em up of live and DJ'd music.
- **The Diller Room** · 1224 1st Ave
206-467-4042
Cozy booths and cozier food with an Italian flare.
- **Fado Irish Pub** · 801 1st Ave
206-264-2700
More like Frat-O.
- **The Forge Lounge** · 65 Marion St
206-623-5107
Grab a sandwich and a drink to help you stomach ferry travel.
- **GameWorks** · 1511 7th Ave
206-521-0952
Another dateless Friday night.
- **Kells** · 1916 Post Alley
206-728-1916
Where everybody gets a little Irish in them.
- **Moore Theatre** · 1932 2nd Ave
206-682-1414
Architecturally stunning performance hall.
- **Nitelite Lounge** · 1926 2nd Ave
206-443-0899
Lethal drinks and Johnny Cash comfort lonely hearts and ironic hipsters.

No national telecast is complete without the requisite fish-flinging shot from **Pike Place Market**. Less heralded, but just as impressive, is the mastication celebration of the **Gum Wall** there. If you're going to patronize a Starbucks, it might as well be the coffee behemoth's original Pike Place store. Rem Koolhaas' **Seattle Central Library** is as advertised, and provides a satisfying architectural counterpoint to the Space Age nostalgia just north of here.

- **Oliver's Lounge** · 405 Olive Way
  206-623-8700
  Feel wealthier and classier by buying overpriced martinis in a posh hotel scene.
- **The Owl & Thistle** · 808 Post Ave
  206-621-7777
  In true Irish fashion, you'll probably witness a fight.
- **Paramount Theatre** · 911 Pine St
  206-682-1414
  Opulent theater showcasing big-name musicals, concerts, and events.
- **Purple Café & Wine Bar** · 1225 4th Ave
  206-829-2280
  Dramatic in size, selection, and ambiance. Suits abound.
- **Showbox at the Market** · 1426 1st Ave
  206-628-3151
  Superb sight lines and crystalline sound on the city's biggest nightclub stage.
- **Suite 410** · 410 Stewart St
  206-682-4101
  For those who miss pretentious LA bars.
- **Trace Bar** · 1112 4th Ave
  206-264-6060
  A bit of New York swank, if you're into that.
- **The Triple Door** · 216 Union St
  206-838-4333
  Live music venue with a Vegas nightclub slant.
- **Virginia Inn** · 1937 1st Ave
  206-728-1937
  A one-drink destination.
- **Von's Gustobistro** · 1225 1st Ave
  206-621-8667
  Red meat, Manhattans, and Martinis.
- **White Horse Trading Company** · 1908 Post Alley
  206-441-7767
  Top-secret English pub and bookstore. Enjoy a hearthside ale.
- **Yard House** · 1501 4th Ave
  206-682-2087
  Cheesecake Factory-themed pub tries to be all things to all people and falls short.
- **Zig Zag Cafe** · 1501 Western Ave
  206-625-1146
  These guys make getting cocktails into the main event.

Restaurants

- **Andaluca** · 407 Olive Way
  206-382-6999 · $$$$
  Tasty upscale tapas will have you exclaiming "¡Qué sabroso!"
- **Bakeman's** · 122 Cherry St
  206-622-3375 · $
  The plump turkey sandwiches are dirt-cheap, and damn tasty.
- **Belle Epicurean** · 1206 4th Ave
  206-262-9404 · $
  Inspired French pastries served with snooty attitude.
- **Biscuit Bitch** · 1909 1st Ave
  206-441-7999 · $
  Southern hospitality and buttery goodness behind a resting bitch face.
- **Blueacre Seafood** · 1700 7th Ave
  206-659-0737 · $$$
  Steelhead proprietor successfully branches out to the water.
- **The Brooklyn** · 1212 2nd Ave
  206-224-7000 · $$$$
  Gulp down the oysters (the specialty here) in old-Seattle elegance.
- **Brown Bag Baguette** ·
  $
  Finger-licking bahn-mi-ish sandwiches.
- **Café Campagne** · 1600 Post Alley
  206-728-2233 · $$$
  Campagne's more laid-back sister. And the absolute best brunch downtown.
- **Cafe Fonté** · 1321 1st Ave
  206-777-6193 · $$
  Lovely cafe across from the SAM serving locally sourced everything.
- **Cafe Zum Zum** · 823 3rd Ave
  206-622-7391 · $
  Giant affordable lunch that is yum yum.
- **Caffe Lieto** · 1909 1st Ave
  206-441-7999 · $
  Weekend nights, mannered Lieto becomes the Biscuit Bitch. And that's a bitch you DO want to trifle with.

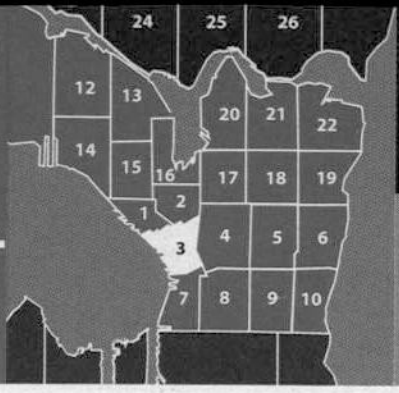

Map 3

Downtown

- **Calozzi's Cheesesteaks** · 1306 4th Ave
206-623-1330 · $$
Tough-to-please Chicago ex-pats say these are ALMOST as good as the real thing.
- **Campagne** · 86 Pine St
206-728-2800 · $$$$
Frenchified Northwest loved for 20 years by tourists and locals alike.
- **Carlile Room** · 820 Pine Street
206-946-9720 · $$
Tom Douglas' version of a fan letter to Brandi Carlile. Creative bar bites and a DJ booth.
- **Coffee and...A Specialty Bakery** ·
1500 Western Ave
206-280-7946 · $$
The ellipsis stands for gluten free baked goods galore.
- **Copacabana Cafe** · 1520 Pike Pl
206-622-6359 · $$$
Bolivian food but the real draw is the balcony.
- **Country Dough** · 1916 Pike Pl
206-728-2598 · $
Chinese carbs heaven.
- **The Crumpet Shop** · 1503 1st Ave
206-682-1598 · $
Fresh, buttery crumpets with sweet or savory toppings. Not just for Brits!
- **Dilettante Mocha Café** · 1300 5th Ave
206-223-1644 · $$
Just skip dinner and indulge in a chocolate dessert orgy. You deserve it.
- **Dragonfish** · 722 Pine St
206-467-7777 · $$
Pop-culture Asian that takes a ride around the Pacific Rim.
- **El Borracho** · 1521 1st Ave
206-538-0040 · $$
Mellow Mexican cafe with plenty of tequila to get you borracho. (There's a family section too).
- **Elliot's Oyster House** · 1201 Alaskan Way
206-623-4340 · $$$
Get messy with the cioppino.
- **Emmett Watson's Oyster Bar** · 1916 Pike Pl
206-448-7721 · $$
Seattle's very first oyster bar, appropriately shabby—in a good way.

- **Etta's** · 2020 Western Ave
206-443-6000 · $$$
Fresh seafood from Tommy D.
- **Fonte Cafe & Wine Bar** · 1321 1st Ave
206-777-6193 · $$
Fontastic coffee and gourmet eats.
- **Fusion on the Run** · 4th Ave & Madison St
206-957-3724 · $
Kalua pork tacos, bra.
- **Gelatiamo** · 1400 3rd Ave
206-467-9563 · $
Some tasty pastries and heavenly gelato.
- **The Georgian** · 411 University St
206-621-7889 · $$$$$
For impressing the spouse, the in-laws, or your boss.
- **Hard Rock Cafe** · 116 Pike St
206-204-2233 · $$
Party like it's 1994.
- **Il Bistro** · 93 Pike St
206-682-3049 · $$$$
Decent Italian off the Market; nice scotch selection.
- **Il Fornaio** · 600 Pine St
206-264-0994 · $$
If you must eat in a mall, this place has edible Italian.
- **Italian Family Pizza** · 1206 1st Ave NW
206-538-0040 · $
You'll think you've died and gone to east coast pizza heaven.
- **Jack's Fish Spot** · 1514 Pike Pl
206-467-0514 · $
No-nonsense counter that embodies the soul of the Market—for better or worse.
- **Japonessa Sushi Cocina** · 1400 1st Ave
206-971-7979 · $$$
If you've ever wondered what Asian Tapas tasted like, mystery solved.
- **Jemil's Big Easy** · 2nd Ave & Pike St
206-930-8915 · $$
Jemil claims to be "the real thing" in terms of Cajun cuisine. And he's absolutely right.
- **Katsoori Grill** · 94 Stewart St
206-441-5456 · $$
A lunch buffet that tastes like fine dining.

Grab a bar stool at the **Zig Zag** for a stiff cocktail. **The Showbox** and the **Moore** have top-notch music calendars, and the **Paramount Theatre** hosts all things to all people, big and small. Jazz it up with the cool kats at **Can Can**. Disregard the hipsters and glass-gaze the lethal drinks at the **Nitelite**.

- **La Creperie Voila** · 707 Pike St
206-447-2737 · $$
In the eating wasteland that is the Convention Center, Voila is your warm, buttery salvation.
- **Le Panier** · 1902 Pike Pl
206-441-3669 · $$
Win popularity by doling out their macaroons—they will blow you away.
- **Le Pichet** · 1933 1st Ave
206-256-1499 · $$
Eat roast chicken. Drink beaujolais. Pretend you're in Paris. Save airfare.
- **Lecosho** · 89 University St
206-623-2101 · $$
If you like eating pig, they provide numerous ways to do it.
- **Long Provincial Vietnamese Restaurant** · 1901 2nd Ave
206-443-6266 · $$
Modern Vietnamese cuisine in a dark, posh hole.
- **Lowell's** · 1519 Pike Pl
206-622-2036 · $$$
Seafood at Pike Place Market, with breakfast and cocktails, too.
- **Lumpia World** · 4th Ave & Pine St
206-371-7995 · $
Lumpia are basically Filipino taquitos/egg rolls. You probably want to eat that.
- **Mae Phim Thai Restaurant** · 94 Columbia St
206-624-2979 · $
Enormous portions of slightly authentic Thai for not much more than a fiver.
- **Market Grill** · 1509 Pike Pl
206-682-2654 · $
Homemade chowder and blackened salmon sandwiches are worth the wait.
- **Matt's in the Market** · 94 Pike St
206-467-7909 · $$$
Market-fresh produce and fish tossed up to the second floor window? It's magic.
- **Maximilien** · 81 Pike St
206-682-7270 · $$$
Classic French in all its butter-sauced glory; classy and cheap happy hour.

- **Maximus Minimus** · 2nd Ave & Pike St
206-601-5510 · $
Yummy BBQ served out of a giant metal pig.
- **McCormick's Fish House & Bar** · 722 4th Ave
206-682-3900 · $$$
Corporate club vibe with weekly oyster specials.
- **Mee Sum Pastry** · 1526 Pike Pl
206-682-6780 · $
Marvelous buns.
- **Metropolitan Grill** · 820 2nd Ave
206-624-3287 · $$$$$
Martinis, mahogany and meat.
- **Morton's The Steakhouse** · 1511 6th Ave
206-223-0550 · $$$$$
Yet another dark-wood, clubby, pricey steakhouse. Tableside service.
- **Mr. D's Greek Delicacies** · 1518 Pike Pl
206-622-4881 · $
Gyros to go, wrapped in a cone.
- **Osaka Grill** · 128 Pike St
206-340-1793 · $
Worth braving the grime for tasty teriyaki.
- **The Pink Door** · 1919 Post Alley
206-443-3241 · $$
Acceptable Italian, cranky servers. And sometimes people swing from trapezes.
- **Place Pigalle** · 81 Pike St
206-624-1756 · $$$$
Great views highlight a nice seafood menu.
- **Plum Vegan Burgers + More** · 2nd Ave & Pike St
$
The geniuses behind vegan fine dining bring their unbelievably delicious show on the road.
- **Potbelly Sandwich Shop** · 1429 4th Ave
206-623-0099 · $
Decent sandwich chain, giving Specialities a run for their money.
- **Potbelly Sandwich Shop** · 1111 3rd Ave
206-204-0079 · $
Decent sandwich chain, giving Specialities a run for their money.
- **Purple Café & Wine Bar** · 1225 4th Ave
206-829-2280 · $$$
Tome-like wine list can be intimidating; food is upscale café fare.

Map 3

- **Rachel's Ginger Beer** · 1530 Post Alley
206-467-4924 · $
A craft soda fountain with a booze option. Finally, something that's truly fun for the whole family.
- **RN74** · 1433 4th Ave
206-456-7474 · $$$
The highway to fancy pants.
- **Sazerac** · 1101 4th Ave
206-624-7755 · $$$$
Trendy twists on Southern classics. Upscale-tacky interior.
- **Seatown** · 2010 Western Ave
206-436-0390 · $$
Snacks a la Tom Douglas: You either love him or are an idiot.
- **Shuckers** · 411 University St
206-621-1984 · $$$$
Slick business-y types slurp oysters and sign deals.
- **Skillet** ·
206-512-2000 · $
Seasonal, local bistro food…out of a traveling Airstream trailer.
- **Sky View Cafe** · 701 5th Ave
206-860-7449 · $
Ravishing Radish catering's 73rd floor club house in Columbia Tower.
- **Steelhead Diner** · 95 Pine St
206-625-0129 · $$
Pitch-perfect dishes exude the essence of Seattle and the Northwest.
- **Street Donuts** ·
206-414-7410 · $
Donuts made fresh in front of your face! On the street!
- **Street Treats** · 6th Ave & Pike St
206-714-9535 · $
Custom ice cream sandwiches…duuuuuuuuude.
- **Sullivan's Steakhouse** · 621 Union St
206-494-4442 · $$$
Steaks, martinis, and jazz…if you're into that sort of thing.
- **Sweet Iron Waffles** · 1200 3rd Ave
206-682-3336 · $$
Like the waffle house. But only waffles.

- **Tap House Grill** · 1506 6th Ave
206-816-3314 · $$
160 beers on tap. We repeat: 160 beers. On tap.
- **Three Girls Bakery** · 1514 Pike Pl
206-622-1045 · $
The sandwiches are classic, no frills, and the hands-down favorite.
- **Top Pot Doughnuts** · 720 3rd Ave
206-454-3694 · $
Top Pot is tops!
- **Trace** · 1112 4th Ave
206-264-6060 · $$$$
Find your culinary center piled high and gorgeous on the plate. Renowned.
- **Tulio Ristorante** · 1100 5th Ave
206-624-5500 · $$$$
Fancified Italian dishes loved by businesspeople. Great service.
- **Turkish Delight** · 1930 Pike Pl
206-443-1387 · $
Brave the Market crowd for the 3-buck lentil soup.
- **Urbane** · 1639 8th Ave
206-676-4600 · $$$$
Hit the happy hour or convince the boss to bring the corporate card.
- **Von's Gustobistro** · 1225 1st Ave
206-621-8667 · $$
Red meat, Manhattans, and Martinis.
- **Wild Ginger** · 1401 3rd Ave
206-623-4450 · $$$
Wildly overrated, but still remains an eternal favorite.
- **Wild Rye Cafe Bakery** · 806 Pike St
206-694-5049 · $
Where you can find quiet neighborhood feeling right smack in downtown.
- **Yard House** · 1501 4th Ave
206-682-2087 · $$
Cheesecake Factory-themed pub tries to be all things to all people and falls short.
- **Zig Zag Cafe** · 1501 Western Ave
206-625-1146 · $$
You would have no idea that the food gets second billing at this cocktail bar.

As far as seafood goes, and as far as highbrow is concerned, **Matt's in the Market** gives a true taste of Pike Place while Tom Douglas serves up calamari and Copper River salmon for his adoring fans at **Etta's Seafood**. If thy lower brow, gorge thee at **Emmett Watson's** or **Jack's**. For the landlubber, the best ginger beer you ever tasted, guaranteed, is at **Rachel's**.

Shopping

- **American Apparel** · 1504 6th Ave
  206-381-3400
  Soft t-shirts and free porn!
- **Baby and Company** · 1936 1st Ave
  206-448-4077
  Want to pay to dress like you live in Manhattan? Try here.
- **Bavarian Meats** · 1920 Pike Pl
  206-441-0942
  German-style meat products; more than just brats and wursts.
- **BB Ranch** · 94 Pike St
  206-299-8486
  Where happy farm animals died for your dinner.
- **Beecher's Handmade Cheese** · 1600 Pike Pl
  206-956-1964
  Stop in everyday for a free sample and then buy the place out.
- **Bergman Luggage** · 1901 3rd Ave
  206-448-3000
  Serious baggage for serious travelers.
- **BLMF Literary Saloon** · 1501 Pike Pl
  206-621-7894
  Used and rare books in Pike Place Market.
- **Bottega Italiana** · 1425 1st Ave
  206-343-0200
  Seattle's best gelato.
- **Chocolate Box** · 108 Pine St
  206-443-3900
  Think Willy Wonka's Chocolate Factory.
- **City Fish Co.** · 1535 Pike Pl
  800-334-2669
  Oldest fish market at Pike Place.
- **The Confectional** · 1530 Pike Pl
  206-257-6597
  The real sin is skipping dessert.
- **DeLaurenti Specialty Food & Wine** · 1435 1st Ave
  206-622-0141
  Euro-snacks that you craved during that summer abroad.

- **Diva Dollz** · 624 1st Ave
  206-652-2299
  Bettie Page would have loved this place.
- **Don & Joe's Meats** · 85 Pike St
  206-682-7670
  Old-school butcher shop.
- **First and Pike News** · 93 Pike St
  206-624-0140
  Classic Pike Place Market newstand.
- **Gian DeCaro Sartoria** · 2025 1st Ave
  206-448-2812
  Gian transforms your Polartek boy into a suave Italian lover.
- **Golden Age Collectibles** · 1501 Pike Pl
  206-622-9799
  Essential geek merchandise.
- **The Good Coffee Company** · 818 Post Ave
  206-622-5602
  Stock up on your at-home caffeinated needs.
- **Hair Fair Wig Shop** · 124 Pike St
  206-623-9430
  The Blade's best and only wig shop. RIP Wigland.
- **Ian** · 1919 2nd Ave
  206-441-4055
  I don't know who this Ian person is, but he must be loaded.
- **Isadora's** · 1601 1st Ave
  206-441-7711
  The queen of vintage. Prices to match.
- **Lamplight Books** · 1514 Pike Pl
  206-652-5554
  Charming second-hand book seller.
- **Left Bank Books Collective** · 92 Pike St
  206-622-0195
  Anarchist, revolution, Chomsky—everything that made the '60s great.
- **Leroy Mens' Wear** · 201 Pike St
  206-682-1033
  Classy duds for classy dudes.
- **Market Magic** · 1501 Pike Pl
  206-624-4271
  Make your social life magically disappear.

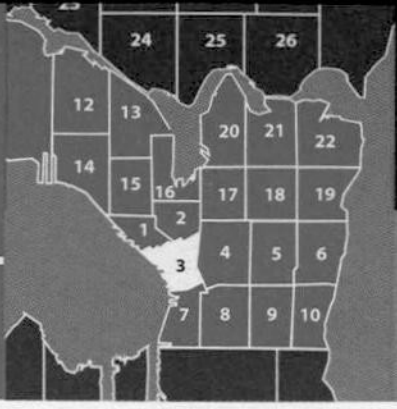

Map 3

- **Market Optical** · 1906 Pike Pl
  206-448-7739
  Contact lenses are so yesterday. Whack out with really expensive frames.
- **Marketspice** · 85 Pike St
  206-622-6340
  This is one of those times when you should believe the hype. Marketspice Tea is the shiz.
- **Metsker Maps** · 1511 1st Ave
  206-623-8747
  A geographer's paradise.
- **Mt. Townsend Creamery** · 89 Pike St
  206-743-9059
  You'll need to climb a mountain to burn off all that cheesy goodness.
- **Nordstrom** · 500 Pine St
  206-628-2111
  It all began here: The legendary customer service, the fine designer goods.
- **Nordstrom Rack** · 400 Pine St
  206-448-8522
  Nordstrom stuff, a half season later and much cheaper. Go for the shoes.
- **Old Seattle Paperworks** · 1501 Pike Pl
  206-623-2870
  Vintage ads, posters, magazines, and newspapers.
- **Paris Grocery** · 1418 Western Ave
  206-682-0679
  That's a baguette in my pocket AND I'm glad to see you.

- **Perennial Tea Room** · 1910 Post Alley
  206-448-4054
  All tea all the time. Stock up for your favorite tea addict.
- **Pike Place Fish Market** · 86 Pike Pl
  206-682-7181
  Purveyors of flying fish and Seattle-area B-roll.
- **Pike Place Market Creamery** · 1514 Pike Pl
  206-622-5029
  Who can resist Nancy Nipples' dairy products?
- **Piroshky Piroshky** · 1908 Pike Pl
  206-441-6068
  Russian piroshkies, both sweet and savory.
- **Polish Pottery Place** · 1501 Pike Pl
  206-903-1285
  Hand-crafted pottery with Polish designs.
- **Pure Food Fish Market** · 1515 Pike Pl
  206-622-5765
  No flying fish, just great seafood and service.
- **Rachel's Ginger Beer** · 1530 Post Alley
  206-467-4924
  It's a tad pricey, but guaranteed to be the best ginger beer you've ever tasted.
- **Sandylew** · 1408 1st Ave
  206-903-0303
  Clothes for offbeat cougars and independent ladies.
- **Schmancy** · 1932 2nd Ave
  206-728-8008
  Coolest stuffed animals ever.

Get up early, brave the tourists, and shop like a local at **Pike Place Market**. The fresh food and flowers are all worth sticking out the crowds. That said, if you really can't bear the thought of seeing your dinner marched on the aquacultural perpwalk that is the **Pike Place Fish Market**, go to **Harry at Pure Food Fish**. Raise your cholesterol levels at **Beecher's Handmade Cheese**. And return your old car tires at the original **Nordstrom**.

- **Seattle Art Museum Shop** · 1300 3rd Ave
  206-654-3100
  Rent art for your new condo. Reasonable prices on contemporary art for rent.
- **Seattle Mystery Bookshop** · 117 Cherry St
  206-587-5737
  It's all here. Detective fiction, suspense, thrillers, true crime.
- **Sephora** · 415 Pine St
  206-624-7003
  All the make-up you can dream-up in one store.
- **Sneaker City** · 110 Pike St
  206-621-7923
  Fill your proverbial wazoo full of sneakers.
- **The Spanish Table** · 1426 Western Ave
  206-682-2827
  Catherine sends you home with fine sherries and fixings for tapas.
- **Sur La Table** · 84 Pine St
  206-448-2244
  National upmarket kitchen chain; stop in for fish bone tweezer.
- **Sway & Cake** · 1631 6th Ave
  206-624-2699
  Fun, flirty LA labels for the ladies. Cake not included.
- **Teavana** · 600 Pine St
  206-623-3581
  Come as you are. But bring your credit card.

- **Tenzing Momo** · 93 Pike St
  206-623-9837
  Herbs, teas, incense, tarot readings. Get your hippie supplies here.
- **Top Ten Toys** · 600 Pine St
  206-623-1370
  Classic, teaching, affordable toys that won't bum a kid out either.
- **Twist** · 600 Pine St
  206-315-8080
  Gorgeous jewelry, eclectic ceramics, and other fine, expensive breakables.
- **Uli's Famous Sausage** · 1511 Pike Pl
  206-839-1712
  Tasty sausagefest.
- **Vain** · 2018 1st Ave
  206-441-3441
  Hair. Shop. Art.
- **Watson Kennedy Fine Home** · 1022 1st Ave
  206-652-8350
  Their largest shop dedicated to an eclectic mix of fun goods.
- **Watson Kennedy Fine Living** · 86 Pine St
  206-443-6281
  Swanky Frenchy things your lady friends will like.
- **Zanadu Comics** · 1923 3rd Ave
  206-443-1316
  The best place to satisfy the new comics Wednesday jones.

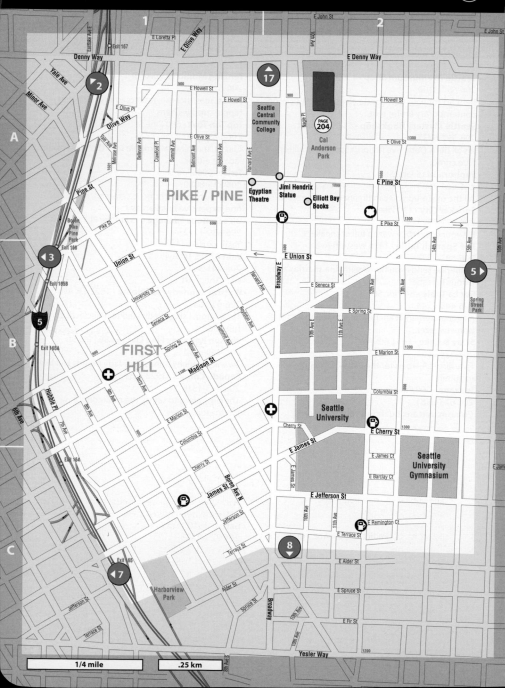

Map 4 · **First Hill / Pike / Pine**

Map 4

If you absolutely have to get sick, try to do it on "Pill Hill," where numerous hospitals, medical centers, and private practices make having a heart attack or getting injured downright convenient. Meanwhile, the nearby Pike/Pine corridor is the epicenter of Seattle hipster culture, where twenty-something bohemians waste their youth in assorted tattoo parlors, carefully-designed dive bars, and vintage clothing stores. Stop by **Stumptown**, **Victrola**, or **Bauhaus** for your caffeine fix.

o Landmarks

• **Cal Anderson Park** • 1635 11th Ave
206-684-4075
Capitol Hill's Central Park.
• **The Elliott Bay Book Company** • 1521 10th Ave
206-624-6600
Flagship establishment of the Seattle literary scene.
• **Jimi Hendrix Statue** • Broadway & E Pine St
Tribute to the wailing guitar god.
• **SIFF Cinema Egyptian** • 805 E Pine St
206-324-9996
Built in 1915, filmhouse with Masonic Temple trimmings.

Coffee

• **Bauhaus Books & Coffee** • 414 E Pine St
206-625-1600
A little pretentious but so worth it.
• **Broadcast Coffee** • 1623 Bellevue Ave
206-467-4717
Broadcasting the best of Seattle products including Stumptown, Mighty O, and Macrina.
• **Caffe Vita** • 1005 E Pike St
206-709-4440
The best of the local chains.
• **Cherry Street Coffee House** • 1223 E Cherry St
206-454-3592
Good coffee, nice staff, but the owner added a sick leave surcharge to protest a city mandate. Not cool.
• **Cupcake Royale/Verite Coffee** • 1111 E Pike St
202-883-7656
Coffee and cupcakes go well together.
• **Diva Espresso** • 502 9th Ave
206-724-0658
Local chain with unpredictable service. I guess it's kind of like ordering coffee from a diva.
• **Kaladi Brothers Coffee** • 517 E Pike St
206-388-1700
Alaskan coffee pioneers behind something amazing called the Sivetz Air Roasting method.
• **Pettirosso** • 1101 E Pike St
206-324-2233
Gem of a coffeehouse.

• **Porchlight Coffee & Records** • 1318 E Pike St
206-329-5461
Herkimer Coffee and new & used vinyl.
• **Stumptown Coffee Roasters** • 616 E Pine St
206-329-0115
Puddletown favorite heads north.
• **Stumptown Coffee Roasters** • 1115 12th Ave
206-323-1544
Puddletown favorite heads north.
• **Victrola Roastery and Cafe** • 310 E Pike St
206-624-1725
From a time before coffee was good.

Nightlife

• **95 Slide** • 722 E Pike St
206-328-7666
A sports bar for socially conscious hipsters who love their M's and S's.
• **Artusi** • 1535 14th Ave
206-678-2516
Small food menu & disappointing beer selection. As the Italians say, "Meh."
• **Auto Battery** • 1009 Union St
206-322-2886
Sports and drink where car batteries were once sold.
• **Baltic Room** • 1207 Pine St
206-625-4444
Fashionable dance spot with the big velvet drapes.
• **Bar Ferd'nand** • 1531 Melrose Ave
206-623-5882
Geek out about biodynamics at the wine bar.
• **Barboza** • 925 E Pike St
206-709-9442
A live music club in the basement of Neumos. Password not required.
• **Barca** • 1510 11th Ave
206-325-8263
Bitchy wait staff serve you drinks in the dark.
• **Canon: Whiskey & Bitters Emporium** •
928 12th Ave
A canon you'll want to shoot yourself INTO.

Map 4

First Hill / Pike / Pine

- **Century Ballroom** · 915 E Pine St
206-324-7263
Lindy, swing, salsa, tango anyone? Do it here in style, lessons available for klutzes.
- **Cha Cha Lounge** · 1013 E Pike St
206-322-0703
High-attitude tiki bar for hipsters.
- **The Chieftain Irish Pub** · 908 12th Ave
206-324-4100
Dime-a-dozen Irish pub.
- **Chop Suey** · 1325 E Madison St
206-324-8005
Alt-rock club with the ethnically insensitive moniker.
- **Clever Dunne's Irish House** · 1501 E Olive Way
206-709-8079
Best pub quiz ever.
- **Comet Tavern** · 922 E Pike St
206-322-9272
Order an Oly and get into a fight!
- **Crescent Lounge** · 1413 E Olive Way
206-726-1774
Divey gay bar with karaoke seven nights a week.
- **The Cuff** · 1533 13th Ave
206-323-1525
Try (or try not) to get cuffed in the men's room.
- **Elysian Brewing Company** · 1221 E Pike St
206-860-1920
Super food and micros but lacks atmosphere. Bring interesting company.
- **Fireside Room** · 900 Madison St
206-622-6400
Where Thurston Howell, III would hang if he weren't stuck on that island.
- **Garage Billiards & Bowl** · 1130 Broadway
206-322-2296
Getting drunk and bowling is obviously a wise combination.
- **Grim's** · 1512 11th Ave
206-324-7467
Fancy pub food specifically designed for the inebriated palate.
- **Havana** · 1010 E Pike St
206-323-2822
Kick it like Castro.

- **The Hideout** · 1005 Boren Ave
206-903-8480
Drink tasty cocktails amidst paintings inspired by fever dreams.
- **John John's Game Room** · 1351 E Olive Way
206-696-1613
Pinball and alcohol. What's not to like?
- **Knee High Stocking Co** · 1356 E Olive Way
206-979-7049
A pioneer of the post-prohibition speakeasy movement.
- **Linda's Tavern** · 707 E Pine St
206-325-1220
Hipsters vie for seniority.
- **Lost Lake Cafe & Lounge** · 1505 10th Ave E
206-323-5678
Seattle's own Twin Peak's style diner complete with damn fine coffee and pie 24 hours a day.
- **Madison Pub** · 1315 E Madison St
206-325-6537
Eat, drink, and be gay.
- **Manhattan** · 1419 12th Ave
206-325-6574
Apparently, Manhattanites are addicted to bourbon and $50 steak.
- **Marjorie** · 1412 E Union St
206-441-9842
Fresh cocktails in a Euro-style ambiance.
- **Mercury @ Machinewerks** · 1009 E Union St
Private club for people who know goth people.
- **Moe Bar** · 1425 10th Ave
206-709-9951
Convenient for shows at Neumo's. Inconvenient for fun.
- **Montana** · 1506 E Olive Way
206-422-4647
Much like its namesake, it's a place for drinking.
- **Narwhal** · 1118 E Pike St
206-325-6492
The Unicorn's basement-dwelling cousin. Same carnival decor + video games.
- **Neighbours** · 1509 Broadway
206-324-5358
Straight-friendly all-night dance parties for the fabulous people.

Map 4

If you're under 30 (or never stopped partying), you'll have a blast at the bars along Pike and Pine. **Linda's** has a great jukebox and a heated back patio. Over 30? Try the awesome **Melrose Market** for all your foodie needs. Meet some ladies at the **Wild Rose**, take a date to **Anchovies & Olives**, score some late night tacos (**Rancho Bravo**) or fish n' chips (**Pike Street Fish Fry**), or kick it old school grungy at the **Comet**.

- **Neumos** • 925 E Pike St
  206-709-9442
  Music club that welcomes Seattle's legions of hip-hoppers and punk rockers.
- **Oddfellows Cafe & Bar** • 1525 10th Ave
  206-325-0807
  The odds are good and the goods are also good.
- **The Old Sage** • 1410 12th Ave
  206-557-7430
  Smoked meats galore by the speakeasy gurus behind Tavern Law.
- **Pie Bar** • 1361 E Olive Way
  206-257-1459
  Two great words that taste great together. Everything pie from drink to dessert.
- **The Pine Box** • 1600 Melrose Ave
  206-588-0375
  With 34 microbrew taps, it just may be your funeral.
- **Poco Wine + Spirits** • 1408 E Pine St
  206-322-9463
  Intimate and contemporary; Northwest emphasis with traveling international list.
- **Pony** • 1221 E Madison St
  206-324-2854
  The stallion of gay bars.
- **Purr** • 1518 11th Ave
  206-325-3112
  Martini bar for classy cats.
- **Quarter Lounge** • 909 Madison St
  206-332-0772
  Cheap drinks and pool. Not much else. You get what you pay for.
- **R Place** • 619 E Pine St
  206-322-8828
  Karaoke, dancing, and all-male underwear contests.
- **Redwood** • 514 E Howell St
  206-329-1952
  Hunting lodge chic. Vegetarians and Nuge fans come together!
- **Rhein Haus**• 912 12th Ave
  206-325-5409
  Indoor bocce court, a bazillion beers and brats and a line out the door every weekend.
- **Richard Hugo House** • 1634 11th Ave
  206-322-7030
  Pretend you like poetry, get laid.

- **Rock Box** • 1603 Nagle Pl
  206-302-7625
  For those about to rock…behind closed doors.
- **The Saint** • 1416 E Olive Way
  206-323-9922
  Cleanse your soul with 80 different tequilas and super-fresh fare.
- **Saint John's Bar and Eatery** • 719 E Pike St
  206-245-1390
  Rock n' roll restaurateurs head up a hard rock cafe that's worthwhile.
- **Seattle Eagle** • 314 E Pike St
  206-621-7591
  Quintessential leather bar.
- **Six Arms** • 300 E Pike St
  206-223-1698
  Dude. They have tater tots.
- **Still Liquor** • 1524 Minor Ave
  206-467-4075
  Another Seattle speakeasy provides that old-timey drunk feeling.
- **Sun Liquor Distillery** • 514 E Pike St
  206-720-1600
  A micro boozery from the wonderful folks at Sun Liquor.
- **Tango** • 1100 Pike St
  206-583-0382
  Awesome if you're not paying.
- **Tavern Law** • 1406 12th Ave
  206-322-9734
  Speakeasy Chic: Cos Seattle's alcohol laws aren't puritanical enough.
- **Trove** • 500 E Pike St
  206-457-4622
  Creative cocktails in a crimson-drenched lounge.
- **Unicorn** • 1118 E Pike St
  206-325-6492
  A peek inside the dreams of hipsters.
- **Vito's** • 929 9th Ave
  206-397-4053
  The historic lounge of ill-repute is back and classier than ever.
- **Wild Rose** • 1021 E Pike St
  206-324-9210
  Friendly and fun lesbians. $1 Taco Tuesdays aren't (just) a euphemism.

🍴Restaurants

- **8 Oz. Burger Bar** · 1401 Broadway
  206-466-5989 · $$
  Micro-chain that sells…guess what…8 oz burgers.
- **Anchovies & Olives** · 1550 15th Ave
  206-838-8080 · $$$$
  Ethan Stowell's fishy enterprise. So fresh and so clean clean.
- **Annapurna Café** · 1833 Broadway
  206-320-7770 · $$
  Warm, nourishing food from Nepal, Tibet, and India served in a cozy basement.
- **Ayutthaya Thai Cuisine** · 727 E Pike St
  206-324-8833 · $$
  Unbelievably fresh and satisfying Thai. Dubious musical accompaniment.
- **Ba Bar** · 550 12th Ave
  206-328-2030 · $$
  Enjoy Vietnamese street food indoors and pretty much whenever you want.
- **Baguette Box** · 1203 Pine St
  206-332-0220 · $
  Amazing, super-fresh sandwiches. The tofu 'wich, especially delish.
- **Ballet** · 914 E Pike St
  206-328-7983 · $
  Cheap Asian fusion with a vast selection.
- **Bar Ferd'nand Coffee** · 1531 Melrose Ave
  206-623-5882 · $$
  A snack bar, Sitka & Spruce style.
- **Big Mario's NY Style Pizza** · 1009 E Pike St
  206-922-3875 · $
  East Coast expats, here's your precious NY pizza. Now shut up.
- **Bimbo's Cantina** · 1013 E Pike St
  206-322-9950 · $
  If Hunter S. Thompson opened a burrito joint.
- **Boom Noodle** · 1121 E Pike St
  206-701-9130 · $$
  Japanese izakaya spot with flavors that explode in your mouth. Boom!
- **Café Presse** · 1117 12th Ave
  206-709-7674 · $$
  Authentic French bistro serving food until 2 am. Très magnifique!

- **Cascina Spinasse** · 1531 14th Ave
  206-251-7673 · $$$$
  Definitely occasion dining, but a meal you won't soon forget.
- **Cedars on Broadway** · 500 Broadway
  206-325-3988 · $
  Indian food that's naan-stop delicious. Many claim its dominance.
- **Chatterbox Café** · 1100 12th Ave
  206-324-2324 · $
  Dubious service, but there aren't a whole lot of other Singaporean cuisine options in town.
- **Chavez** · 1734 12th Ave
  206-695-2588 · $$$$
  Excellent Mexican street food without that pesky discount.
- **Chungee's Drink & Eat** · 1830 12th Ave
  206-323-1673 · $$
  Self-explanatory late-nite Chinese.
- **Coffee Tree** · 905 8th Ave
  206-387-7545 · $
  Maybe they should look into finding a good service tree to go along with that coffee.
- **Cure** · 1641 Nagle Pl
  206-568-5475 · $$
  The cure for the common meat, cheese and booze deficiency.
- **Fogón Cocina Mexicana** · 600 E Pine St
  206-320-7777 · $$
  This sweet Mexican family is kind enough to share their transcendent food with Seattleites. Gracias!
- **Freddy Junior's** · 1513 Broadway Ave
  206-323-1413 · $
  Freddy of Rancho Bravo fame tries his hand at a slider joint. He does tacos better.
- **High 5 Pie** · 1400 12th Ave
  206-695-2284 · $
  Move over, cupcakes. Pies are the new It Dessert.
- **Hot Mama's Pizza** · 700 E Pine St
  206-322-6444 · $
  Everything looks hotter with beer goggles on.
- **Hunt Club** · 900 Madison St
  206-343-6156 · $$$$
  Doesn't the name just ooze pretension? So do the setting and the prices.

Map 4

Go casually upscale with the farm-to-plate genius of **Terra Plata**. Matt Dillon's **Sitka & Spruce** and **Bar Ferd'nand** lend a Toply Cheffed gravitas to the 'hood. Impress vegetarian friends—or those who love them—at **Plum Bistro**. Elsewhere, Hill trolls swear by **Hot Mama's Pizza**, and **Mamnoon** will hook you on their Syrian and Lebanese flavors.

- **In the Bowl Vegetarian Noodle Bistro** •
1554 E Olive Way
206-568-2343 • $
Another example of fake meat made delicious. And they deliver.
- **Jimmy John's** • 1221 Madison St
206-812-1043 • $
Like Subway but with delivery.
- **juicebox** • 1517 12th Ave
206-607-7866 • $$$
Gwyneth Paltrow's idea of a good time.
- **Kafe Berlin** • 613 9th Ave
206-623-4242 • $
Vaguely German cafe which serves pretzels alonside panini.
- **Kedai Makan** • 1510 E Olive Way
$
Insanely good Malaysian grub served out of a tiny room.
- **La Cocina Oaxaquena** • 1216 Pine St
206-623-8226 • $$
The Bizzaro cousin of the insanely popular Carta de Oaxaca in Ballard. Same great food, different crowd.
- **La Spiga Osteria** • 1429 12th St
206-323-8881 • $$$
Gorgeous pastas and sandwiches. Emilia-Romagna comes to Seattle.
- **Lark** • 926 12th Ave
206-323-5275 • $$$$
Little plates never had it so good. Casual elegance epitomized.
- **Little Uncle** • 1509 E Madison St
206-329-1503 • $
The best Thai food you can get from a little window. Online ordering!
- **Lost Lake Cafe & Lounge** • 1505 10th Ave E
206-323-5678 • $$
Seattle's own Twin Peak's style diner complete with damn fine coffee and pie 24 hours a day.
- **Machiavelli** • 1215 Pine St
206-621-7941 • $$$
Canoodle over some noodles in this hip, affordable Italian favorite.
- **Mamnoon** • 1508 Melrose Ave
206-906-9606 • $$$
This ain't your daddy's seasonal Middle Eastern food (unless your daddy is Lebanese).

- **Marination Station** • 1412 Harvard Ave
$
The stationary version of the food truck.
- **Marjorie** • 1412 E Union St
206-441-9842 • $$$
Eclectic is an understatement. Nice patio.
- **Mediterranean Express** • 1417 Broadway
206-860-3989 • $$$
Garlicky Greek goodness.
- **Mediterranean Kitchen** • 1009 Boren Ave
206-467-5046 • $
Garlicky Greek goodness.
- **Mesob** • 1325 E Jefferson St
206-860-0403 • $
Arguably the best Ethiopian joint in Seattle. Ignore the sketchy exterior.
- **Momiji** • 1522 12th Ave
206-457-4068 • $$$
You'll want to make a night of their speciality sushi rolls and cocktails.
- **My Sweet Lil Cakes** • 1208 Pine St
206-351-0356 • $
MF-ing waffles on a stick! Sweet AND savory; meat AND veg; gluten AND not. Nailed it.
- **Nue** • 1519 14th Ave
206-257-0312 • $$
Gastropub meets Asian street food.
- **Octo Sushi** • 1621 12th Ave
206-805-8998 • $$$
Sushi sushi joy joy.
- **The Old Sage** • 1410 12th Ave
206-557-7430 • $$
Smoked meats galore by the speakeasy gurus behind Tavern Law.
- **The Other Coast Cafe** • 721 E Pike St
206-257-5927 • $
A proudly Northwestern delicatessen.
- **Pho Le's** • 720 E Pike St
206-322-1818 • $
More pho for your salty soup satisfaction.
- **Pie Bar** • 1361 E Olive Way
206-257-1459 • $$
Two great words that taste great together. Everything pie from drink to dessert.
- **Piecora's** • 1401 E Madison St
206-322-9411 • $$
The best NY-style pizza in town, whole or by the slice.

Map 4

- **Pike Street Fish Fry** · 925 E Pike St
206-329-7453 · $$
Unbelievably fresh fish and chips: a revelatory, late-night godsend on Cap Hill.
- **Pinto Thai Bistro & Sushi Bar** · 408 Broadway
206-724-0559 · $$
All your Asian favs under one roof, plus extra special specials.
- **Plum Vegan Bistro** · 1429 12th Ave
206-838-5333 · $$$
Vegan food doesn't have to be made by crusty punks. It can get dressed up once in a while!
- **Poco Wine + Spirits** · 1408 E Pine St
206-322-9463 · $$
Small plates of cold duck and local cheeses pair exquisitely with the top-notch wines.
- **Poquitos** · 1000 E Pike St
206-453-4216 · $$
Accessible, authentic Mexican using high-quality ingredients.
- **Primo** · 1106 8th Ave
206-547-7466 · $
Italian carb heaven.
- **Quinn's** · 1001 E Pike St
206-325-7711 · $$
Farm food meets fine dining. Get the wild boar sloppy joes and leave the vegetarians at home.
- **Rancho Bravo Tacos** · 1001 E Pine St
206-322-9399 · $
The popular taco truck has finally found a permanent home.
- **Regent Bakery & Cafe** · 1404 E Pine St
206-743-8866 · $$
Family-run Chinese bakery well known for their massive selection of cakes.
- **Restaurant Zoë** · 1318 E Union St
206-256-2060 · $$$
A gastropub without the pub.
- **Rhein Haus**· 912 12th Ave
206-325-5409 · $$
Indoor bocce court, a bazillion beers and brats and a line out the door every weekend.
- **Saley** · 800 Olive Way
206-405-3444 · $
A sweet, small one-woman crepe shop.
- **Sitka & Spruce** · 1531 Melrose Ave
206-324-0662 · $$$
The freshest local ingredients. Tiny, busy, worth it.
- **Skillet Diner** · 1400 E Union St
206-512-2000 · $$
Now you don't have to chase their food truck to score some bacon jam.
- **Slab Sandwiches + Pie** · 1201 10th Ave
206-323-5275 · $
Rotating menu of inspired sandwich creations (+ pie) served in a tiny, tiny room.
- **Sushi Kanpai** · 900 8th Ave
206-588-2769 · $$
Superior sushi happy hour.
- **Tacos Guaymas** · 1415 Broadway
206-860-3871 · $$
Cheap and filling.
- **Tango** · 1100 Pike St
206-583-0382 · $$$$
Posh yet cozy; come for the half-price wine bottles on Mondays.
- **Terra Plata** · 1501 Melrose Ave
206-325-1501 · $$
Mindblowing local, seasonal and sustainable fare, some from the restaurant's rooftop.
- **Trove** · 500 E Pike St
206-457-4622 · $$$
Small but solid selection of Korean-influenced vittles.
- **Via Tribunali** · 913 E Pike St
206-322-9234 · $$
One bite of the pizza will transport you back to Napoli.
- **Vostok Dumpling House** · 1416 Harvard Ave
206-687-7865 · $$
The Russians really know how to eat. Fortunately, they're willing to share.
- **Zaw** · 1424 E Pine St
206-325-5528 · $$
It's not delivery. It's artisan take-and-bake.
- **zpizza** · 1620 Broadway
206-432-9158 · $
Organic toppings and vegan/GF options. Seattle hipster pizza heaven.

Shopping is plentiful in the Pike/Pine Corridor. For retro gear, or if you are looking for pieces for a Halloween costume, try **Atlas Clothing Co.** After you're dudded up, hit **Rain Shadow** for the best in locally farmed meatware. And **The Elliott Bay Book Company** is the favorite son of Puget Sound literati.

Shopping

- **35th North** • 1100 E Pike St
  206-320-1252
  Comprehensive selection of goods for co-ed skaters.
- **Atlas Clothing Co.** • 1419 10th Ave
  206-323-0960
  Retro treasures, new and used.
- **Babeland** • 707 E Pike St
  206-328-2914
  A sex shop you can be proud to visit, staffed by enlightened women.
- **The Calf & Kid** • 1531 Melrose Ave
  206-467-5447
  Artisan cheese on Cap Hill. I kid you not.
- **City Market** • 1722 Bellevue Ave
  206-323-1715
  Thanks to South Park, everyone calls it Shitty Market. It's anything but.
- **Edge Of The Circle Books** • 701 E Pike St
  206-726-1999
  Find your fourth corner and do some spells.
- **Le Frock** • 613 E Pike St
  206-623-5339
  Swanky vintage clothing for dudes and dolls.
- **Lifelong Thrift Store** • 1017 E Union St
  206-957-1655
  Proceeds help people affected by AIDS.
- **Lucky Devil Tattoo Parlor** • 1407 E Madison St
  206-323-1637
  Personable, versatile artists help you piss off your parents for a reasonable price!
- **Marigold and Mint** • 1531 Melrose Ave
  206-682-3111
  Organic flowers end edible plants from a Snoqualmie farm. So quaint!
- **Melrose Market** • 1501 Melrose Ave
  Indoor farmer's market. Why didn't we think of that before?

- **Molly Moon's** • 917 E Pine St
  206-708-7947
  Fresh, local, sustainably organic ice cream.
- **NuBe Green** • 921 E Pine St
  206-402-4515
  Sustainable gifts for the friend with more than one dreamcatcher.
- **Oola Distillery** • 1314 E Union St
  206-709-7909
  Local booze-makers offer samples of their goods. And the goods are good.
- **Rain Shadow Meats** • 1531 Melrose Ave
  206-467-6328
  Making Cap Hill feel even smaller with locally farmed meats.
- **Rudy's Barbershop** • 614 E Pine St
  206-329-3008
  Absolute best cheap haircut!
- **SugarPill** • 900 E Pine St
  206-322-7455
  An old timey apothecary for all your chocolate and tonic needs.
- **Throwbacks Northwest** • 1205 E Pike St
  206-402-4855
  Look dope in old-school Sonics, Mariners, and Seahawks gear.
- **Twice Sold Tales** • 1833 Harvard Ave
  206-324-2421
  Buy and sell used books whilst petting kitties.
- **Wall of Sound** • 315 E Pine St
  206-441-9880
  An honest to god record store. With records and everything!
- **Westlake Center** • 400 Pine St
  206-467-1600
  Maybe, if every other store in Seattle goes out of business. Maybe.
- **Zero Zero Hair** • 1525 Summit Ave
  206-568-3996
  The best hipster hairstyling bang for your buck.
- **Zion's Gate Records** • 1100 E Pike St
  206-568-5446
  Turntables, wide range of vinyl, smoking accessories.

Map 5 • **Central District (North)**

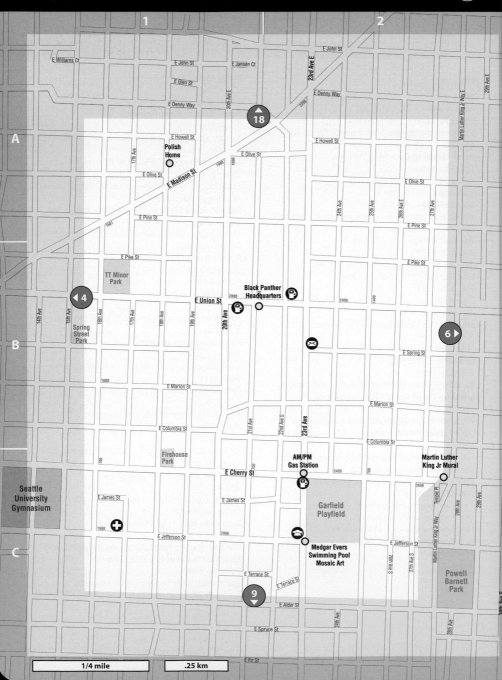

N

1

2

E Williams Ct

E John St

E John St

E Jansen Ct

E Glen St

E Denny Way

E Denny Way

23rd Ave E

29th Ave E

Martin Luther King Jr Way E

A

E Howell St

Polish Home

E Olive St

E Howell St

18

E Olive St

E Madison St

17th Ave

E Olive St

E Pine St

24th Ave

25th Ave

26th Ave E

27th Ave

E Pine St

E Pike St

E Pike St

TT Minor Park

E Union St

Black Panther Headquarters

4

14th Ave

15th Ave

16th Ave

17th Ave

18th Ave

19th Ave

20th Ave

6

B

Spring Street Park

E Spring St

1600

E Marion St

E Marion St

E Columbia St

21st Ave S

22nd Ave S

23rd Ave

E Columbia St

Firehouse Park

AM/PM Gas Station

Martin Luther King Jr Mural

Seattle University Gymnasium

E James St

E Cherry St

E James St

Garfield Playfield

2400

Martin Luther King Jr Way

Temple Pl

28th Ave

29th Ave

C

1600

E Jefferson St

2000

Medgar Evers Swimming Pool Mosaic Art

E Jefferson St

Powell Barnett Park

E Terrace St

E Terrace St

9

E Alder St

26th Ave

27th Ave S

S 20th Ave

28th Ave

E Spruce St

1/4 mile

.25 km

E Fir St

Map 5

The north side of the Central District is an Ethiopian and African-American community being swallowed by new developments. Family-owned groceries and restaurants sit quietly between the busy streets of Adler, 23rd Avenue, MLK, and Union where the Garfield Community Center and the **Martin Luther King, Jr. Mural** are located.

○ Landmarks

- **AM/PM Gas Station** • E Cherry St & 23rd Ave
  Panhandlers' address.
- **Black Panther Headquarters** • 2111 E Union St
  Power to the people.
- **Martin Luther King Jr. Mural** • 2726 E Cherry St
  A painting of his contemplation.
- **Medgar Evers Swimming Pool Mosaic Art** •
  500 23rd Ave
  Beautiful child-like art.
- **Polish Home** • 1714 18th Ave
  206-322-3020
  Pierogies and bison grass vodka every Friday night.

☕ Coffee

- **Cortona Cafe** • 2425 E Union St
  206-327-9728
  Serving espresso, waffles and beer. It's up to you whether or to order all 3 at once.
- **Tougo Coffee Co.** • 1410 18th Ave
  206-860-3518
  Stick your kids in the play area and get a coffee ToStay.

🍸 Nightlife

- **CC Attle's** • 1701 E Olive Way
  206-726-0565
  Feed the bears!
- **Central Cinema** • 1411 21st Ave
  206-328-3230
  Drink beer and watch a cult or classic film. So simple yet so brilliant.
- **The Neighbor Lady** • 2308 E Union St
  206-695-2072
  Vegetarian bar and grill with a sexy brothel vibe.
- **The Twilight Exit** • 2514 E Cherry St
  206-324-7462
  Where hipsters go to avoid other hipsters.

🍴 Restaurants

- **Assimba Ethiopian Cuisine** • 2722 E Cherry St
  206-322-1019 • $
  Ethiopian utopia.
- **Bannister** • 1408 18th Ave
  206-860-3518 • $$$$
  Part of your complete romantic night out in the Central District.
- **The Barbeque Pit** • 2515 E Cherry St
  206-724-0005 • $
  Sometimes a "pit" isn't a bad place to eat lunch.
- **Cafe Selam** • 2715 E Cherry St
  206-328-0404 • $
  This hole-in-the-wall Ethiopian is a favorite with cabbies.
- **Catfish Corner** • 2726 E Cherry St
  206-323-4330 • $
  Like fried bottom feeders? This is the place.
- **Central Cinema** • 1411 21st Ave
  206-328-3230 • $
  Forget popcorn. Pair a movie with good beer and decent grub.
- **El Gallito** • 1700 20th Ave
  206-329-8088 • $
  Easy to overlook, but so perfect before a night of boozin'. Huge portions.
- **Ezell's Famous Chicken** • 501 23rd Ave
  206-324-4141 • $
  Oprah's had Ezell's chicken FedExed straight from Seattle to her mouth. Really.
- **Meskel Ethiopian Restaurant** • 2605 E Cherry St
  206-860-1724 • $
  You'll need lots of napkins. And beer.
- **The Neighbor Lady** • 2308 E Union St
  206-695-2072 • $$
  Vegetarian bar and grill with a sexy brothel vibe.
- **Tougo Coffee Co.** • 1410 18th Ave
  206-860-3518 • $
  Stick your kids in the play area and get a coffee ToStay.

🛍 Shopping

- **Uncle Ike's Pot Shop** • 2310 E Union St
  206-420-4537
  The uncle you actually want at Thanksgiving dinner. They know their shit.

Map 6 · **Madrona**

N

19

5

10

Howell Park

Madrona Playground

Madrona Park

Spectrum Dance Theater

Powell Barnett Park

Lake Washington

A

B

C

1

2

E John St

E Denny Blaine Pl

E Denny Way

E Florence Ct

E Denny Way

E Howell St

E Schubert Pl

E Olive St

E Olive Ln

E Pine St

E Pine St

E Pike St

E Pike St

E Union St

E Spring St

E Marion St

E Marion St

E Columbia St

E Columbia St

E Arlington Pl

E Cherry St

E James St

E James St

E Conover Ct

E Jefferson St

E Jefferson St

E Terrace St

E Terrace St

E Spruce St

E Alder St

Lake Dell Ave

E Spruce St

E Superior St

Martin Luther King Jr Way E

28th Ave E

27th Ave

28th Ave

33rd Ave E

34th Ave E

35th Ave E

38th Ave

37th Ave

Madrona Pt E

Madrona Ln E

Madrona Dr

39th Ave E

Evergreen Pl

40th Ave

Grand Ave

Madrona Dr

38th Ave

37th Ave

Newport Way

Lake Washington Blvd E

39th Ave

Randolph Pl

Norwood Pl

38th Ave

Wellington Ave

Lake Washington Blvd E

Fairview Ave

Randolph Ave

Erie Ave

35th Ave

34th Ave

Martin Luther King Jr Way

Temple Pl

27th Ave

28th Ave

29th Ave

30th Ave

31st Ave

32nd Ave

33rd Ave

34th Ave

35th Ave

36th Ave

Howell Pl

3000

3400

1600

3000

3400

3000

3498

3400

3000

3400

1100

1100

700

700

1/4 mile

.25 km

What's steeper? Madrona's rising home values or the walk from the lake? A short bus ride from downtown Seattle, this lovely area on Lake Washington is home to staid matriarchs, gay couples, artists, and multi-generational families residing in everything from Seattle big-money mansions to shabby cottages. Locals covet life on the beach with astounding views of Mount Rainier, but it's the variety of food and drink on 34th Avenue that's the real draw.

○ Landmarks

- **Spectrum Dance Theater** •
  800 Lake Washington Blvd
  206-325-4161
  Beautiful old brick building is a rare waterfront venue for dance performances

Coffee

- **Cupcake Royale/Verite Coffee** • 1101 34th Ave
  206-883-7656
  Cupcakes and coffee go well together.
- **Hi Spot Café** • 1410 34th Ave
  206-325-7905
  Locals love this place.

Nightlife

- **Bottlehouse** • 1416 34th Ave
  206-708-7164
  A house party of a higher calibre.
- **Madrona Eatery & Ale House** • 1138 34th Ave
  206-323-7807
  Great bar food. Bring the whole family.
- **Red Cow** • 1423 34th Ave
  206-454-7932
  When you like a steak with your happy hour.

Restaurants

- **Bistro Turkuaz** • 1114 34th Ave
  206-324-3039 • $$$
  Awesome Turkish food.
- **Café Soleil** • 1400 34th Ave
  206-325-1126 • $$
  Laid-back breakfast mornings and spicy Ethiopian nights.
- **Hi Spot Café** • 1410 34th Ave
  206-325-7905 • $$
  Locals love this place.
- **Lalibela** • 2800 E Cherry St
  206-322-8565 • $
  Standard Ethiopian; great combo platter.
- **Madrona Eatery & Ale House** • 1138 34th Ave
  206-323-7807 • $$
  Great bar food. Bring the whole family.
- **Red Cow** • 1423 34th Ave
  206-454-7932 • $$$$
  Ethan Stowell's tribute to all things bovine.
- **St. Clouds** • 1131 34th Ave
  206-726-1522 • $$$
  Upscale neighborhood joint with style and late-night dining.

Shopping

- **Conley Hats** • 913 27th Ave
  206-322-1868
  Made to order hats. Now that's old-school.
- **Décor on 34th** • 1421 34th Ave
  206-571-0094
  Stylish home décor shop.
- **Hitchcock Madrona** • 1406 34th Ave
  206-838-7173
  Cool little store: jewelry, clothes, etc.
- **Juniper** • 3314 E Spring St
  206-838-7496
  The very definition of boutique.
- **Molly Moon's** • 1408 34th Ave
  206-324-0753
  Organic ice cream with unusual flavors that sells like…cold ice cream.

Map 6

Map 7 · **Pioneer Square / SoDo**

Seneca St
Spring St
Madison St
Marion St
Columbia St
Columbia St
Cherry St
James St
3rd Ave
4th Ave
2nd Ave
Jefferson St
8th Ave

PIONEER SQUARE

Elliott Bay

Bainbridge Island
Bremerton

Pioneer Sq
Park
Western Ave

Smith
Tower

City Hall
Park

The Underground
Tour

Yesler Way

S Washington St

Occidental
Park

Fallen
Firefighters'
Memorial

Waterfall
Garden

S Main St

2nd Ave

3rd Ave

S Washington St

Kobe
Terrace
Park

S Main St

Alaskan Way

4th Ave

S Jackson St

S Jackson St

5th Ave S

6th Ave S

S King St

S King St

King
Street
Station
PAGE 220

S Weller St

S Lane St

B

S Railroad Way

1st Ave S

Occidental Ave S

S Dearborn St

99

Alaskan Way S

CenturyLink Field
PAGE 216

CenturyLink Field
Events Center

S Dearborn St

Airport Way S

S Vermont St

S Royal Brougham Way

Utah Ave S

1st Ave S

Occidental Ave S

3rd Ave S

4th Ave S

6th Ave S

SODO

Safeco
Field
PAGE 271

S Atlantic St

Edgar Martinez Dr

S Atlantic St

Colorado Ave S

S Massachusetts St

S Massachusetts St

S Massachusetts St

1/4 mile   .25 km

Map 7

As the city's oldest neighborhood, there's a mystique about Pioneer Square, the nation's original "Skid Road" where the early settlers toiled through harsh conditions. Today, Pioneer Square entertains a tenuous mix of tourists, art galleries, and frat bars around its community living room, Occidental Square. Start your day at **Grand Central Bakery** for homemade pastries.

○ Landmarks

- **CenturyLink Field** · 800 Occidental Ave S
  206-381-7555
  Get tossed in the CLink while you cheer on the Sounders or Seahawks.
- **Fallen Firefighters' Memorial** ·
  Occidental Ave S & S Main St
  Bronze firemen amid the pigeons and the homeless.
- **Safeco Field** · 1250 1st Ave S
  206-628-0888
  Lovable M's keep losing here, but you can drown your sorrows in $11 pints of beer.
- **Smith Tower** · 506 2nd Ave
  206-622-4004
  View from 1914 tower is cheaper (and maybe better) than the Space Needle.
- **Tashiro Kaplan Artists Lofts** · 115 Prefontaine Pl S
  Affordable live-work spaces supporting Pioneer Square artists.
- **Waterfall Garden** · S Main St & 2nd Ave S
  This tranquil urban haven commemorates the birth of UPS.

☕ Coffee

- **Caffe Umbria** · 320 Occidental Ave S
  206-624-5847
  Big-time roaster's Pioneer Square flagship.
- **Caffe Vita** · 125 Prefontaine Pl S
  206-652-8331
  The best of the local chains.
- **Grand Central Bakery** · 214 1st Ave S
  206-622-3644
  Caffe Vita brew served here.
- **Trabant Coffee & Chai** · 602 2nd Ave
  Dude. This chai rocks.
- **Zeitgeist** · 171 S Jackson St
  206-583-0497
  Not as revolutionary as they'd have you believe, but not bad.

🍸 Nightlife

- **Central Saloon** · 207 1st Ave S
  206-622-0209
  Frat boys have been drinking here since 1892.
- **Collins Pub** · 526 2nd Ave
  206-623-1016
  Craft and Belgian beers to the nth degree.
- **Cowgirls Inc.** · 421 1st Ave S
  206-340-0777
  Like Coyote Ugly, but sluttier.
- **Damn the Weather** · 116 1st Ave S
  206-946-1283
  A Decemberists song that became a restaurant.
- **Double Header** · 407 2nd Ave S
  206-464-9918
  Friendly old dudes who like dudes.
- **Easy Joe's American Pub** · 704 1st Ave
  206-623-3440
  It's like if one of the cool Top Chef guys opened a diner.
- **Elysian Fields** · 542 1st Ave S
  206-382-4498
  Stadium-size brewery a home-run shot from Safeco Field.
- **Good Bar** · 240 2nd Ave S
  206-624-2337
  Streamlined spirits list and a syrup-based breakfast cocktail. I'd call that better than good.
- **Pyramid Alehouse** · 1201 1st Ave S
  206-682-3377
  Get sh*t-faced like the Egyptians used to do.
- **Quality Athletics** · 121 S King St
  206-420-3015
  A sports bar for the refined palate by Josh Henderson.
- **Temple Billiards** · 126 S Jackson St
  206-682-3242
  Great pizza and very little competition for a table.
- **Triangle Pub** · 553 1st Ave S
  206-628-0474
  Great spot for a Rainier before you watch the M's lose again.
- **Trinity Nightclub** · 111 Yesler Way
  206-447-4140
  Different action in three spacious rooms. Be twenty something, wear less, enjoy more.

Map 7

Pioneer Square / SoDo

🍴Restaurants

- **Al Boccalino** · 1 Yesler Way
  206-622-7688 · $$$$
  Nice Southern Italian in a historic building.
- **Bar Sajor** · 323 Occidental Ave S
  206-682-1117 · $$$
  Famed Chef Matt Dillon's attempt at classing up Pioneer Square.
- **The Berliner DÃ¶ner Kebab** · 221 1st Ave S
  206-838-0339 · $
  A very Seattle gyrocery with tofu instead of falafel.
- **Café Paloma** · 93 Yesler Way
  206-405-1920 · $
  Lovingly made meze-style food and delicious pita.
- **Casco Antiguo** · 115 Occidental Ave S
  206-538-0400 · $$$$
  Street tacos inside a building.
- **Damn the Weather** · 116 1st Ave S
  206-946-1283 · $$$
  A Decemberists song that became a restaurant.
- **Delicatus** · 103 1st Ave S
  206-623-3780 · $$
  Latin for Seattle Deli. Sea-town themed sandwiches.
- **Easy Joe's American Pub** · 704 1st Ave
  206-623-3440 · $$
  It's like if one of the cool Top Chef guys opened a diner.
- **Good Bar** · 240 2nd Ave S
  206-624-2337 · $$$
  Milk braised pork, Ploughman's plates, and a breakfast cocktail. I'd say that's better than good.
- **Grand Central Bakery** · 214 1st Ave S
  206-622-3644 · $
  Great lunch spot with amazing pastries.
- **Green Leaf Vietnamese Restaurant** ·
  418 8th Ave S
  206-340-1388 · $
  Fresh, fantastic Vietnamese. One of the best and busiest in town.

- **Il Corvo Pasta** · 217 James St
  206-538-0999 · $
  Nothing like a pasta lunch to get you through the rest of your work day.
- **Il Terrazzo Carmine** · 411 1st Ave S
  206-467-7797 · $$$
  Classic, well-executed Italian.
- **Jimmy John's** · 102 1st Ave S
  206-621-9500 · $
  Like Subway but with delivery.
- **The London Plane** · 322 Occidental Ave S
  206-624-1374 · $$
  A brilliant combo of foodie shop and wine cafe. Possibly too classy for Pioneer Square.
- **Marcela's Creole Cookery** · 106 James St
  206-223-0042 · $$
  Down-home grub, N'awlins style. Try the muffuletta.
- **The People's Burger** · 922 Occidental Ave S
  206-471-5781 · $
  A burger revolution.
- **Pizzeria Napoletana** · 125 Prefontaine Pl S
  206-652-8331 · $$
  A tiny taste of Napoli conveniently located inside a coffee shop.
- **Quality Athletics** · 121 S King St
  206-420-3015 · $$$
  A sports bar for the refined palate by Josh Henderson.
- **Rain Shadow Meats Squared** ·
  404 Occidental Ave S
  206-467-4854 · $$
  Enjoy your acquisitions straight away in the deli portion of this unmatched butcher shop.
- **Salumi Artisan Cured Meats** · 309 3rd Ave S
  206-621-8772 · $
  Mario Batali's dad makes damn good salami.
- **Tat's Delicatessen** · 159 Yesler Way
  206-264-8287 · $
  Big, sloppy sammies to stink up your big meeting or office party.
- **Thai Curry Simple** · 406 5th Ave S
  206-327-4838 · $
  Simply amazing curry and breakfast. (Yes, breakfast!)

It has old-fashioned charm in spades, even if it's hidden under the grimy veil of homelessness, petty crime, and drunken revelers. It's also a refuge for men's men seeking cheap booze and thrills at bars like **Central Saloon**, while Mariners and Seahawks fans crowd into **Triangle Pub**. Meanwhile, Matt Dillon classes things up at **Bar Sajor** and foodies flock to **Salumi** to indulge in heavenly pork products. **Rain Shadow Meats Squared** is the quintessential Northwest meat emporium with a deli so that you don't have to wait till you get home to chow down.

Shopping

- **Arundel Books** · 209 Occidental Ave S
  206-624-4442
  New, used, and rare books in former Wessel & Lieberman space.
- **Ebbets Field Flannels** · 408 Occidental Ave S
  206-382-7249
  Finest maker of historic and authentic baseball uniforms.
- **The Globe Bookstore** · 218 1st Ave S
  206-682-6882
  Books: Shakespeare and beyond.

- **Magic Mouse Toys** · 603 1st Ave
  206-682-8097
  We think it's run by elves.
- **Rain Shadow Meats Squared** ·
  404 Occidental Ave S
  206-467-4854
  Even the drunks of Pioneer Square like farm fresh meat.
- **Salumi Artisan Cured Meats** · 309 3rd Ave S
  206-621-8772
  Mario Batali's dad makes damn good salami. Take home some gnocchi on Tuesdays.

Map 8 · **International District**

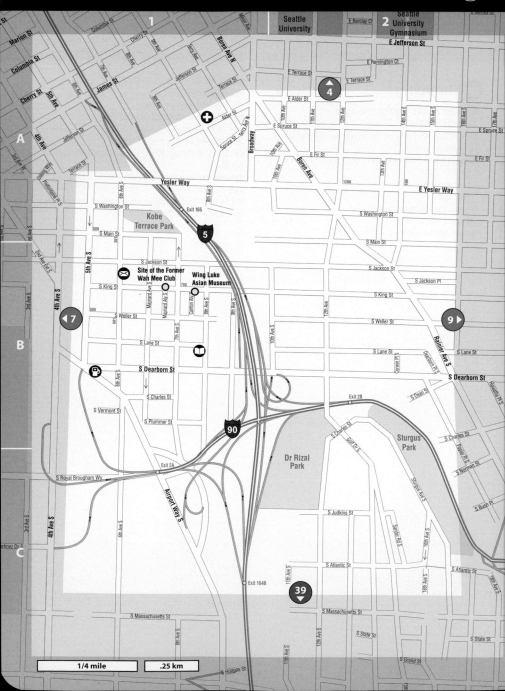

Map 8

This historic neighborhood has provided a cultural hub for Seattle's sizable Asian-American population since the 19th century. Home to Filipino, Vietnamese, Cambodian, Japanese, and Chinese businesses of every stripe, the International District truly feels, well, international. It's hardly the most glamorous area of the city, but strolling through the ID is highly recommended.

o Landmarks

- **Site of the Former Wah Mee Club** •
  S King St & Maynard Alley S
  Site of 1983 gang massacre.
- **Wing Luke Museum** • 719 S King St
  206-623-5124
  A gem of a museum in the heart of the ID.

Coffee

- **Gossip Espresso & Tea** • 651 S King St
  206-624-5402
  Bubble tea.
- **Oasis Tea Zone** • 519 6th Ave S
  206-447-8098
  Bubble tea and other Asian junk food. In other words, delicious.
- **Panama Hotel Tea & Coffee House** • 607 S Main St
  206-515-4000
  Lavazza beans.

Nightlife

- **Bush Garden** • 614 Maynard Ave S
  206-682-6830
  Drunken late-night karaoke. Beware of bachelorettes.
- **Fort St. George** • 601 S King St
  206-382-0662
  Japan meets the UK at this pub that also serves decent food.
- **Venus Karaoke** • 601 S King St
  206-264-1779
  Rent a room and get lost in translation.

🍴 Restaurants

- **663 Bistro** • 663 S Weller St
206-667-8760 • $
Chinese with a rare, incomparably light touch. A shining highlight in the ID.
- **Fuji Bakery** • 526 S King St
206-623-4050 • $
Gorgeous Asian-inspired patries, which shame the entire nation of France.
- **Hing Loon** • 628 S Weller St
206-682-2828 • $$
The smoked duck: primal, carnivorous pleasure.
- **Honey Court Seafood Restaurant** •
516 Maynard Ave S
206-292-8828 • $$
Late night Chinese for your drinking and dumpling pleasure.
- **House of Hong** • 409 8th Ave S
206-622-7997 • $$
Great food, even better name.
- **Hue Ky Mi Gia** • 1207 S Jackson St
206-568-1268 • $
Ooddles of tasty noodles.
- **Jade Garden** • 704 S King St
206-622-8181 • $$
Some argue it's Seattle's best dim sum; honestly, it probably is.
- **Loving Hut** • 1226 S Jackson St
206-299-2219 • $
Comfort food just like your militant vegan Grandma used to make.

- **Malay Satay Hut** • 212 12th Ave S
206-324-4091 • $$
Three cuisines unite under one roof, with delicious results.
- **Maneki** • 304 6th Ave S
206-622-2631 • $$
Tasty traditional Japanese food. A Seattle institution.
- **Mikado Teppanyaki** • 1306 S King St
206-860-1556 • $$$
Like Benihana, but classier.
- **Phnom Penh** • 660 S King St
206-748-9825 • $
Cambodian noodle joint.
- **Pho Bac** • 415 7th Ave S
206-621-0532 • $
A reliable pho filling station. Try the banh mi and spring rolls too.
- **Ping's Dumpling House** • 508 S King St
206-623-6764 • $
If a house full of dumplings sounds good to you, it's hard to go wrong here.
- **Saigon Vietnam Deli** • 1200 S Jackson St
206-328-2357 • $$
Some of the best banh mi you'll find. Cheap, fast, and so good.
- **Samurai Noodle** • 606 5th Ave S
206-624-9321 • $
If your experience has been more Top Ramen than top notch, prepare to get your mind blown.

International District

Map 8

Uwajimaya Village features an awesome food court, a bookstore, apartments, and even a bank—you could move in and never leave. But hit the streets of the ID for the real eats. **Maneki**, a Seattle gem, has been dishing up sushi and traditional Japanese for over 100 years. If you want to try Cambodian, head to**Phnom Penh**. Or grab a super cheap bahn mi at **Saigon Deli**. Meanwhile, **Momo** is a unique boutique.

- **Shanghai Garden** • 524 6th Ave S
206-625-1688 • $$
Delicious hand-shaved barley noodles and at least 100 other options.
- **Spring Garden** • 1032 S Jackson St
206-859-6998 • $
Chow down and pretend you can get vitamin D from a sky-painted ceiling.
- **Szechuan Noodle Bowl** • 420 8th Ave S
206-623-4198 • $
Perfect scallion pancakes. Perfect noodle soups. Perfect dumplings.
- **Tai Tung** • 655 S King St
206-622-7372 • $$
Sit at the counter with the regulars and soothe yourself with one of many comforting soups.
- **Tamarind Tree** • 1036 S Jackson St
206-860-1404 • $
Exotically droolworthy Vietnamese cuisine.
- **Tea Garden** • 708 Rainier Ave S
206-709-9038 • $$
The dim sum flows freely, and it is fantastic. One of Seattle's best.
- **Tsukushinbo** • 515 S Main St
206-467-4004 • $
Hidden Japanese gem is a favorite of local chefs.
- **Uwajimaya** • 600 5th Ave S
206-624-6248 • $
Hawaiian, Filipino, Korean, and more. All food courts should be this tasty.
- **World Pizza** • 672 S King St
206-682-4161 • $
Bringing a little vegetarian Italian flair to the I.D.

Shopping

- **Big John's Pacific Food Importers** •
1001 6th Ave S
206-682-2022
Primarily Mediterranean grocery. Bulk and otherwise.
- **International Model Toys** • 601 S King St
206-682-8534
Pac Man belt buckles for the kids…or, ya know, you.
- **Kinokuniya Bookstore** • 525 S Weller St
206-587-2477
If NFT was available in Japanese, it would be sold here.
- **Momo** • 600 S Jackson St
206-329-4736
Your new favorite boutique, and truly unique.
- **Pink Gorilla** • 601 S King St
206-264-2434
You'll love this place if you played video games in the 80's…or still do.
- **RE-PC** • 1565 6th Ave S
206-623-9151
Bins and bins of computer stuff.
- **Star Tea Shop** • 616 S Jackson St
206-382-7827
A beautiful collection of tea and tea accessories. Sample before you buy.
- **Tsue Chong Company** • 800 S Weller St
206-623-0801
Giant bags of fortune cookies.
- **Uwajimaya** • 600 5th Ave S
206-624-6248
Asian superstore with groceries, gifts, restaurants, even apartments.

Map 9 · **Central District (South)**

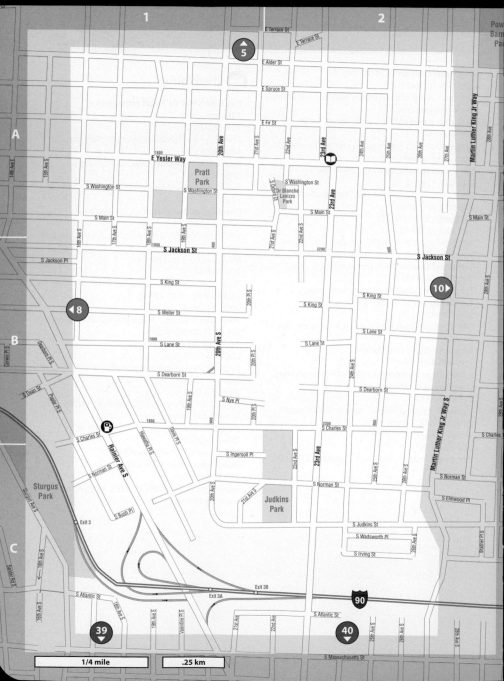

N

1 2

Pow
Barn
Pa

E Terrace St
E Terrace St
5
E Alder St

E Spruce St

E Fir St

A

20th Ave
21st Ave S
22nd Ave
23rd Ave
24th Ave
25th Ave
26th Ave
27th Ave

Martin Luther King Jr Way

16th Ave S
15th Ave S
1800
E Yesler Way

Pratt
Park
S Washington St
S Washington St
S Washington St
S Washington St
Dr Blanche
Lavizzo
Park
Davis Ct

S Dakota Ct

23rd Ave

S Main St
S Main St
S Main St
S Main St

16th Ave S
17th Ave S
18th Ave S
19th Ave S
1800
480
21st Ave S
22nd Ave S
2298
4th

S Jackson St
S Jackson St
S Jackson St

S Jackson Pl

28th Ave S

S King St
S King St
S King St
10

B

8
S Weller St
20th Pl S

S Lane St
S Lane St

20th Ave S
S Lane St
24th Ave S

Oaborn Pl S
Corwell Pl S

S Dearborn St
20th Pl S
S Dearborn St

S Dean St
Poplar Pl S

19th Ave S
S Nye Pl
20th Pl S
2300
S Charles St
S Charles St
900
S Charles St

1800
P

Magnolia Pl S
Davis Pl S

S Charles St
S Ingersoll Pl
22nd Ave S
23rd Ave

Sturgus
Park

Rainier Ave S
S Norman St
25th Ave S
26th Ave S
S Norman St
S Norman St

Sturgus Ave S

20th Ave S
21st Ave S
Judkins
Park
S Elmwood Pl
Bradner Pl S

S Bush Pl

S Judkins St
S Wadsworth Pl

Martin Luther King Jr Way S

C
Exit 3
16th Ave S
26th Ave S
S Irving St

Exit 3B
S Atlantic St
Exit 3A
90
S Atlantic St

16th Ave S
18th Ave S
19th Ave S
Valentine Pl S
21st Ave
22nd Ave
S Atlantic St
25th Ave S
26th Ave S
28th Ave S
39
40
Sartier Pl S
S Massachusetts St

| 1/4 mile | .25 km |

Map 9

Can you say gentrification? Well, promenade along the main streets of CD's south side and experience the word itself. The high traffic streets of Martin Luther King, 23rd Avenue, Massachusetts, and Yesler contain a regurgitated version of Pleasantville. But at least parks are pretty green respites from the irreality.

Coffee

- **Broadcast Coffee** • 1918 E Yesler Way
  206-322-0807
  Broadcasting the best of Seattle products
  including Stumptown, Mighty O, and Macrina.
- **Café Weekend** • 851 Hiawatha Pl S
  206-860-0727
  Have your weekend between Monday and
  Saturday, because they're closed Sundays.

Restaurants

- **Cheeky Cafe** • 1700 S Jackson St
  206-322-9895 • $
  International comfort food to fill out those cheeks.
- **Judkins Street Cafe** • 2608 S Judkins St
  206-322-1091 • $
  Quintessential quaint neighborhood cafe.
- **Moonlight Cafe** • 1919 S Jackson St
  206-322-3378 • $
  Good vegan Vietnamese options in a shabby
  setting.
- **San Fernando Roasted Peruvian Chicken** •
  900 Rainier Ave S
  206-331-3763 • $
  Lynnwood favorite comes to Seattle. Guess what
  they serve.
- **Taco del Mar** • 2309 S Jackson St
  206-329-8383 • $
  Fast food tacos that suffice—they're fresher than
  most.
- **Umai-Do Japanese Sweets** • 1825 S Jackson St
  206-325-7888 • $
  Delectable Japanese treats for happy mouth-
  making.

Shopping

- **Africa Braids and Jewelry** • 2506 S Jackson St
  206-860-7235
  Your hair will thank you.
- **Flowers Just For You** • 2216 S Jackson St
  206-324-1440
  Family owned, friendly, and helpful staff.
- **Two Big Blondes** • 2501 S Jackson St
  206-762-8620
  Phat shirts, phat pants, phat skirts, etc. for those
  livin' large.
- **Western Beauty Supply** • 2301 S Jackson St
  206-329-2582
  Disney World for beauticians.

Map 10 · Leschi

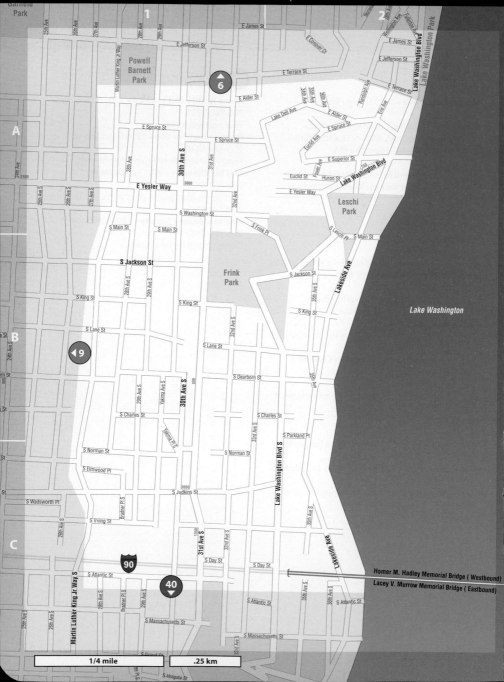

Map 10

Gee, Toto, there's no place like Leschi. The neighborhood rises quietly above the shores of Lake Washington, boasting spectacular views of Mt. Rainier, the Cascade Range, Mt. Baker, the screaming Blue Angels in August, and decorated Christmas ships during December. The packed retail core is home to throngs of weekend cyclists, kayakers, and boaters, but there's plenty of room to toss Frisbees and chase kids in the spacious parks.

Restaurants

- **A La Bonne Franquette** • 1421 31st Ave S
  206-568-7715 • $$$
  As French as French can be.
- **Bluwater Bistro** • 102 Lakeside Ave
  206-328-2233 • $$
  Pricey but perfect seafood and meat for appeasing the carnivore in your life.
- **Daniel's Broiler** • 200 Lake Washington Blvd
  206-329-4191 • $$$$
  Fancy folk (or those whose parents are paying) head here for decent steak.
- **Pert's Deli** • 120 Lakeside Ave
  206-325-0277 • $
  Pick up a turkey and swiss before heading to the park.
- **That's Amore** • 1425 31st Ave S
  206-322-3677 • $$
  A real gem in the restaurant doldrums of Mt. Baker, despite the clichéd name.

Shopping

- **Leschi Market** • 103 Lakeside Ave
  206-322-0700
  Amazing wine selection.

Map 11 • **Magnolia / Interbay**

Map 11

Since it's on a peninsula, Magnolia residents rely on a trio of bridges to connect them to the rest of the city (unless landslides or earthquakes interfere). However, the relative isolation suits this quiet, family-friendly community. Dominated by the 500-acre **Discovery Park** and surrounded by Shilshole Bay and Puget Sound, Magnolia is prime real estate, boasting some of Seattle's most expensive homes. Interbay is an industrial strip useful mostly for getting to and from other neighborhoods.

○ Landmarks

• **Discovery Park** • 3801 Discovery Park Blvd
206-386-4236
534 acres of honest-to-goodness nature.

☕ Coffee

• **Caffe Appassionato** • 4001 21st Ave W
206-281-8040
Classic Seattle coffee shop vibe at this small-ish local chain. Frasier would love it here.
• **Discovery Espresso & Juice** • 3103 W Jameson St
206-286-1481
Neighborhood joint convenient to Discovery Park.
• **Gilman Ave Coffee & Doughnuts** •
4211 Gilman Ave W
206-397-3784
Conduit coffee and a bevy of local doughnuts to go with your bevy-erage.
• **Uptown Espresso** • 3223 W McGraw St
206-285-5663
Self-proclaimed "Home of the Velvet Foam" but the coffee underneath is just so-so.

🍴 Restaurants

• **Bay Café** • 1900 W Nickerson St
206-282-3435 • $$
Waterfront diner doin' it right: breakfast all day and malted milkshakes.
• **Caffe Appassionato** • 4001 21st Ave W
206-281-8040 • $$
Classic Seattle coffee shop vibe at this small-ish local chain. Frasier would love it here.
• **Chinook's at Salmon Bay** • 1900 W Nickerson St
206-283-4665 • $$
Perfect for getting out of the halibut/salmon rut.
• **The Highliner** • 3909 18th Ave W
206-216-1254 • $
Historic pub with new, fishy veneer.
• **Josefina's Mexican Grill** • 2818 Thorndyke Ave W
206-216-1078 • $$
The commercial-style Mexican restaurant that Magnolia has been waiting for.

• **Mondello Ristorante** • 2435 33rd Ave W
206-352-8700 • $$
Real Sicilian trattoria, run by merry Mamma Enza.
• **Palisade** • 2601 W Marina Pl
206-285-1000 • $$$$$
Fancy seafood dishes that range from so-so to spectacular.
• **Queen Margherita** • 3111 W McGraw St
206-548-4908 • $
Pizza ovens made from Mount Vesuvius bricks = Bona fide.
• **Red Mill Burgers** • 1613 W Dravus St
206-284-6363 • $
The undisputed best burger in Seattle. And possibly, the best onion rings.
• **Serendipity Cafe** • 3222 W McGraw St
206-282-9866 • $$
Stick your kids in the back play area while you take a load off.
• **Szmania's** • 3321 W McGraw St
206-284-7305 • $$$$
Colorful, kind of crazy-looking food. Bring the platinum card.
• **Tanglewood Supreme** • 3216 W Wheeler St
206-708-6235 • $$
Seafood date night for Magnolians who can't be bothered to leave the hood.
• **Where Ya At Matt** • W Dravus St & 16th Ave W
$
If you find them, you'll eat po boys & beignets. Fridays in Interbay.

🛍 Shopping

• **Wild Salmon Seafood Market** •
1900 W Nickerson St
206-283-3366
How fresh is this? Dockside store gets fish right off the boats.

Map 12 · **Queen Anne (North)**

Map 12

This neighborhood perched atop Queen Anne Hill, the highest point in Seattle, is a magnet for yuppie families, millionaires, and thrifty octogenarians. Dead people also love Queen Anne North, as the Mt. Pleasant Cemetery's booming business conclusively proves.

Coffee

- **Bustle** • 535 W McGraw St
  206-453-4285
  Serving unusual twists on traditional coffee drinks. Get the Spanish mocha.
- **Java Jazz** • 3457 15th Ave W
  206-282-2321
  Drive thru.
- **Muse Coffee Co.** • 1907 10th Ave W
  206-282-2711
  They didn't write the book on coffee, but they do teach a class.
- **Q Café** • 3223 15th Ave W
  206-352-2525
  Brewing Stumptown Coffee beans.

Restaurants

- **Cheese Wizards** • 210 Nickerson St
  $
  The best way to level up your grilled cheese intake.
- **La Palma** • 3456 15th Ave W
  206-284-1001 • $$
  Delicious and cheap Mexican of the lardy, salty, cheesy variety.
- **Macrina Bakery** • 615 W McGraw St
  206-283-5900 • $$
  Macrina's baked goods will make breakfast your most important meal.
- **Yasuko's Teriyaki** • 3200 15th Ave W
  206-283-9152 • $
  Seattleites love teriyaki. Go figure.

Shopping

- **Flora & Fauna Books** • 3212 W Government Way
  206-623-4727
  Books about botany and horticulture (appointment only).

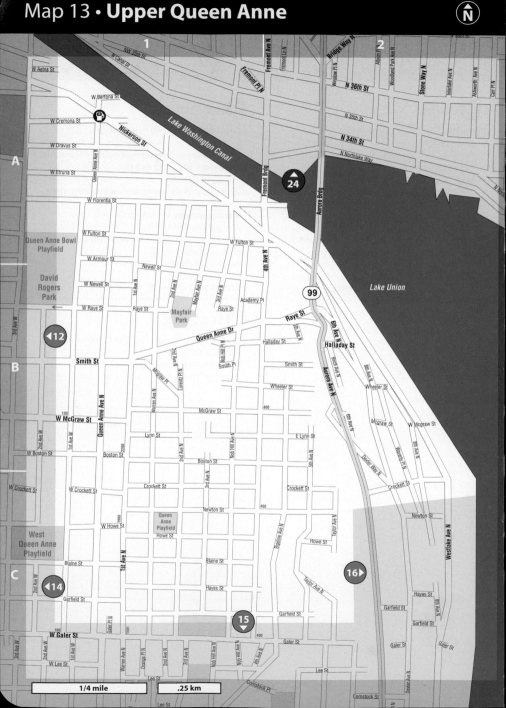

Map 13 • **Upper Queen Anne**

Ⓝ

1

2

NW 35th St
N Canal St
W Aetna St
Fremont Ave N
Fremont Ln N
Fremont Pl N
Bridge Way N
Winslow Pl N
Albion Pl N
Woodland Park Ave N
Stone Way N
Interlake Ave N
Ashworth Ave N
Carr Pl N
N Jot St

W Bertona St
Ⓟ
W Cremona St
Nickerson St
N 36th St

W Dravus St
N 35th St

A

W Etruria St
Queen Anne Way N
N 34th St
N Northlake Way
N North

W Florentia St
Fremont Brdg
▲ **24**
Aurora Brdg

Queen Anne Bowl Playfield
W Fulton St
W Fulton St
4th Ave N

W Armour St
Newell St
99
Lake Union

David Rogers Park
W Newell St
1st Ave N
2nd Ave N
McGraw Ave N
3rd Ave N
Academy Pl
5th Ave N
6th Ave N

◄ **12**
W Raye St
Raye St
Mayfair Park
Raye St
Raye St
8th Ave N

3rd Ave W
Queen Anne Dr
Halladay St
Halladay St

Nob Hill Pl N
Smith Pl
Birch Ave N

B
Smith St
Lorentz Pl N
Smith St
Wheeler St
Wheeler St

Queen Anne Ave N
McGraw Pl
Warren Ave N
McGraw St
400
Aurora Ave N
McGraw St
W Mcgraw St

W McGraw St
100
1st Ave N
2nd Ave N
3rd Ave N
Waverly Pl N
8th Ave N

Lynn St
E Lynn N
9th Ave N

W Boston St
2nd Ave N
Boston St
Nob Hill Ave N
5th Ave N
Dexter Way N

W Crockett St
W Crockett St
Crockett St
Crockett St
Crockett St

3rd Ave W
W Crockett St
3rd Ave N
520
Newton St

West Queen Anne Playfield
Newton St
Queen Anne Playfield
Howe St
400
Taylor Ave N
Westlake Ave N

W Howe St
Howe St
Bigelow Ave N
Howe St

C
Blaine St
1st Ave N
Blaine St
16 ▶
Hayes St

◄ **14**
2nd Ave W
Hayes St
Taylor Ave N
Garfield St
8th Ave N

Garfield St
Galer Pl N
1601
Garfield St
Garfield St
Galer St

W Galer St
Galer Pl N
15 ▼
Galer St
Dexter Ave N
Galer St

3rd Ave W
2nd Ave W
1st Ave W
Warren Ave N
Orange Pl N
2nd Ave N
3rd Ave N
Nob Hill Ave N
5th Ave N
400
Lee St

W Lee St
Lee St
Comstock St

Lee St
Comstock Pl
Comstock St

| 1/4 mile | | .25 km |

Map 13

When the young urban professionals of LQA decide to marry and breed, they buy a house here. When you're deep inside this little suburban chimera, you can easily forget how close you are to the unsavory big city. There aren't many ways for kids or adults to get into trouble in these parts, unless your idea of trouble is having one-too-many mimosas with brunch. Make sure to grab a Mexican hot chocolate from the lovely ladies at **El Diablo**.

Coffee

- **Caffe Appassionato** • 1417 Queen Anne Ave N
  206-270-8760
  Classic Seattle coffee shop vibe at this small-ish local chain. Frasier would love it here.
- **Caffe Ladro** • 2205 Queen Anne Ave N
  206-282-5313
  Strong coffee for the strong coffee drinker.
- **Cederberg Tea House** • 1417 Queen Anne Ave N
  206-285-1352
  South African tea house that offers a passport to deliciousness. Get the malva pudding if it's not sold out.
- **El Diablo Coffee Company** •
  1811 Queen Anne Ave N
  206-285-0693
  The devil must be in their amazing Mexican hot chocolate.
- **Vienna Mae Coffee** • 318 Nickerson St
  206-769-5333
  Cute drive-thru that specializes in hemp milk lattes.

Nightlife

- **Hilltop Ale House** • 2129 Queen Anne Ave N
  206-285-3877
  Neighborhood pub.

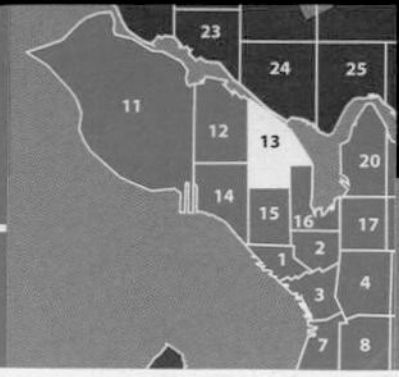

Map 13

Upper Queen Anne

🍴Restaurants

- **5 Spot** • 1502 Queen Anne Ave N
206-285-7768 • $$
Rotating, regional experiments with spotty results, but the fans are die-hard.
- **The Book Bindery** • 198 Nickerson St
206-283-2665 • $$$
An instant classic.
- **Café de Lion** • 1629 Queen Anne Ave N
206-913-2125 • $$
French-inspired pastries which are (almost) too beautiful to eat. Rowr!
- **Canlis** • 2576 Aurora Ave N
206-283-3313 • $$$$
Sure, it'll cost you. But the food is as astounding as the legendary view.
- **Cederberg Tea House** • 1417 Queen Anne Ave N
206-285-1352 • $$
If you're not already familiar with South African baked goods and coffee, you're about to have your mind blown.
- **China Harbor** • 2040 Westlake Ave N
206-286-1688 • $$
Lakeside dining.
- **Chinoise Café** • 12 Boston St
206-284-6671 • $$
Modern sushi joint with a Pan-Asian flair and a heap of noodle dishes.
- **Elliott Bay Pizza Co.** • 2115 Queen Anne Ave N
206-285-0500 • $$
Combining meat, sauce, cheese and bread in nearly endless combinations.
- **Grub** • 7 Boston St
206-216-3628 • $$
A fine dining diner with dishes like lamb burgers and…get ready…an eggs benedict biscuit breakfast sandwich. Whuuuut?
- **Hilltop Ale House** • 2129 Queen Anne Ave N
206-285-3877 • $$
Not your average pub grub. Baked goat cheese salad and curry cashews!
- **Homegrown Sustainable Sandwich Shop** •
2201 Queen Anne Ave N
206-217-4745 • $
It is what it is.
- **Hommage** • 198 Nickerson St
206-283-2665 • $$$$
Solid, inventive French cuisine.
- **How to Cook a Wolf** • 2208 Queen Anne Ave N
206-838-8090 • $$$
Another iteration of Ethan Stowell's clean, composed dishes.
- **La Luna** • 2 Boston St
206-282-2511 • $$
Serving Seattle-style Mexican to the Queen Anne boozers of the night.
- **Le Rêve Bakery & Cafe** • 1805 Queen Anne Ave N
206-623-7383 • $$
Dreamy Parisian pastries and sandwiches. Feel free to pinch yourself.
- **LloydMartin** • 1525 Queen Anne Ave N
206-420-7602 • $$
It sounds like a bank, but it's a restaurant. A really good one, at that.

Upper Queen Anne

This neighborhood is designed for people who plan to be in bed by 11 and like to pay too much for groceries. The **Hilltop Ale House** is decent and your only real nightlife option. **How to Cook a Wolf** will blow you away at dinner time, and for breakfast you can't do better than the **5 Spot**. If it's a special occasion, impress your date with an amazing view of Lake Union at the worth-every-penny **Canlis**.

- **Mezcaleria Oaxaca** • 2123 Queen Anne Ave N
  206-216-4446 • $$
  Sister to La Carta in Ballard and every bit as pretty.
- **Orrapin Thai Cuisine** • 10 Boston St
  206-283-7118 • $
  Mellow, candlelit Thai.
- **Ponti Seafood Grill** • 3014 3rd Ave N
  206-284-3000 • $$$$
  A very good seafood restaurant, and not
  overflowing with tourists.
- **Portage** • 2209 Queen Anne Ave N
  206-352-6213 • $$$
  Worthy of respect. Reservations recommended.
- **Queen Anne Café** • 2121 Queen Anne Ave N
  206-285-2060 • $
  Absolutely superb breakfast dishes; dinner,
  however, is spotty.
- **Six Coins Japanese Food Truck** • 2121 8th Ave
  206-395-5785 • $
  They serve something called a "rice box" that you
  definitely want to eat.
- **Twirl Cafe** • 2111 Queen Anne Ave N
  206-283-4552 • $$
  For moms who want to relax and kids who don't.
- **Zaw** • 1635 Queen Anne Ave N
  206-787-1198 • $$
  It's not delivery. It's artisan take-and-bake.
- **Zeek's Pizza** • 41 Dravus St
  206-285-8646 • $$
  Pizzas with pizzazz, like the Thai version with
  peanut sauce.

Shopping

- **A & J Meats & Seafood** • 2401 Queen Anne Ave N
  206-284-3885
  Great neighborhood butcher and fish monger.
- **Blue Highway Games** • 2203 Queen Anne Ave N
  206-282-0540
  RPGs plus beer; what could go wrong?
- **Chocolopolis** • 1527 Queen Anne Ave N
  206-282-0776
  Over 220 bars of chocolate from 20 different
  countries. Yep.
- **Eat Local** • 2400 Queen Anne Ave N
  206-328-3663
  Local, organic health market.
- **Menchie's** • 2101 Queen Anne Ave N
  206-216-1650
  Serving approximated candy bars & cheesecake
  for housewives by the pound.
- **Queen Anne Book Company** •
  1811 Queen Anne Ave N
  206-284-2427
  Contemporary literature and children's books.

Map 14 • Queen Anne (West)

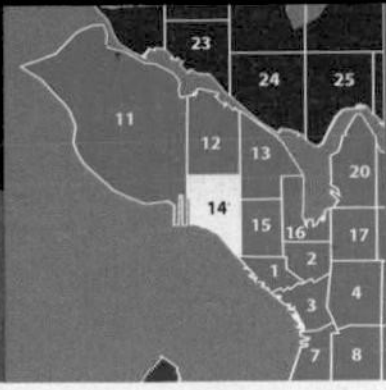

Map 14

Like the rest of Queen Anne, this section caters to the upwardly mobile—meaning condos and attractive views. Speaking of which, Kinnear Park provides fine views of the Seattle skyline and Puget Sound from its upper tier, while the lower section appears welcoming until you stumble upon overgrown shrubs and the makeshift hobo camp.

o Landmarks

- **Kerry Park** • 211 W Highland Dr
  206-684-4075
  All those scenic Seattle postcards? This is the
  vantage point.
- **Parsons Garden** • 7th Ave W & W Highland Dr
  206-684-4081
  Secret garden for non-tourists.

Coffee

- **Caffe Fiorè** • 224 W Galer St
  206-282-1441
  Makes the bold claim of being Seattle's first
  organic coffee.
- **Gourmet Latté** • 540 Elliott Ave W
  206-352-2633
  Gourmet is a relative term, but the coffee at this
  unassuming roadside shack is A-OK.

Nightlife

- **Holy Mountain Brewing Company Taproom** •
  1421 Elliott Ave W
  Big up-and-comers in the Seattle microbrew scene.
- **Targy's** • 600 W Crockett St
  206-352-8882
  Time travel back to the old Queen Anne. Lovely.

Restaurants

- **Betty** • 1507 Queen Anne Ave N
  206-352-3773 • $$
  Comforting bistro dishes, not-so-cozy space. Still,
  locals are adoring.
- **Chopstix** •
  425-610-7388 • $
  Food truck that combines Asian flavors in inspired
  ways. Peking duck taco!
- **Top Pot Doughnuts** • 325 W Galer St
  206-631-2120 • $
  Top Pot is tops!

Shopping

- **Icebox Grocery** • 1903 10th Ave W
  206-708-6742
  A really nice fridge that charges you for raiding it.
- **Molly Moon's** • 321 W Galer St
  206-457-8854
  Organic ice cream with unusual flavors that sells
  like…cold ice cream.

Map 15 • **Lower Queen Anne / Seattle Center**

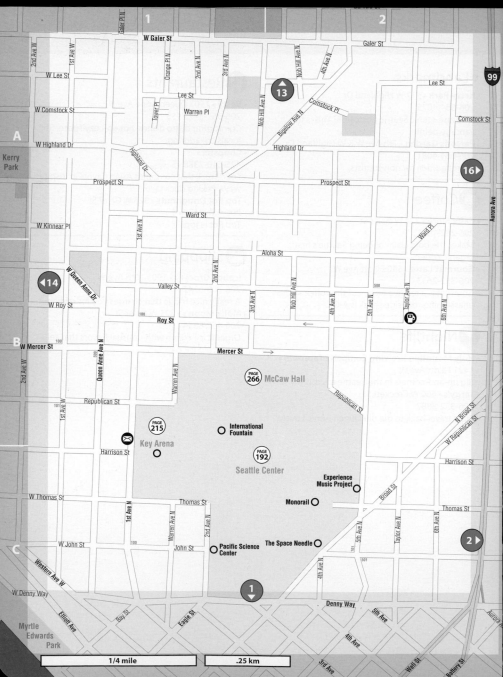

1

2

W Galer St

Galer St

W Lee St

Lee St

W Comstock St

Comstock Pl

13

Comstock St

A

W Highland Dr

Highland Dr

Kerry Park

16▶

Prospect St

Prospect St

W Kinnear Pl

Ward St

Ward Pl

Aloha St

◀14

Valley St

W Roy St

Roy St

B

W Mercer St

Mercer St

Warren Ave N

PAGE 266 McCaw Hall

Republican St

Republican St

PAGE 215

International Fountain

N Republican St

W Republican St

Key Arena

Harrison St

Harrison St

PAGE 192

Seattle Center

W Thomas St

Thomas St

Experience Music Project

Thomas St

Monorail

2▶

W John St

Pacific Science Center

The Space Needle

C

W Denny Way

Denny Way

Myrtle Edwards Park

1

1/4 mile

.25 km

Map 15

The residents of the LQA are mostly single, urban professionals in their mid-twenties to early thirties who enjoy a healthy nightlife and unassuming upscale residences. The neighborhood retains a slightly more economical Belltown vibe. Plus, sometimes they have an express train (some call it a "Monorail") to Westlake Center.

○ Landmarks

- **Experience Music Project** • 325 5th Ave N
206-770-2700
A billionaire's rock memorabilia collection and a public eyesore.
- **International Fountain** • 305 Harrison St
206-684-7200
Water show set to music.
- **Key Arena** • 305 Harrison St
206-281-5800
The former home of the Seattle Sonics is now dominated by ladies sports.
- **McCaw Hill** • 321 Mercer St
206-733-9725
Seattle Center home of the Pacific Northwest Ballet and Seattle Opera.
- **Pacific Science Center** • 200 2nd Ave N
206-443-2001
You're never too old for a Floyd or Zeppelin laser show.
- **Seattle Center** • 305 Harrison St
206-684-7200
Site of the 1962 World's Fair. Also, the Monorail terminus.
- **Seattle Monorail** • 5th Ave & Pine St
206-905-2620
90 thrilling seconds zipping through Seattle (if it's actually running).
- **Space Needle** • 400 Broad St
206-905-2100
Like so many things in life, it's not as big as you'd expect.

Coffee

- **Caffe Ladro** • 600 Queen Anne Ave N
206-282-1549
Strong coffee for the strong coffee drinker.
- **Caffe Vita** • 813 5th Ave N
206-285-9662
The best of the local chains.
- **Caffe Zingaro** • 127 Mercer St
206-352-2861
Lighthouse Roasters plus food.
- **Espresso Elegance** • 122 Elliott Ave W
206-282-8155
Worth a trip off the beaten path for their $2 espresso happy hour.
- **Forza Coffee Company** • 100 4th Ave N
206-404-3679
Come for the coffee. Leave for the food.
- **Uptown Espresso** • 525 Queen Anne Ave N
206-285-3757
Self-proclaimed "Home of the Velvet Foam" but the coffee underneath is just so-so.

Map 15

Lower Queen Anne / Seattle Center

🍸 Nightlife

- **Buckley's On Queen Anne** • 232 1st Ave W
206-691-0232
A fine, friendly neighborhood pub with tasty eats.
- **Crow Restaurant and Bar** • 823 5th Ave N
206-283-8800
Good food and cocktails, but make a reservation or don't bother.
- **Jabu's Pub** • 174 Roy St
206-284-9093
A friendly, comfortable place to get drizunk.
- **Mecca Café** • 526 Queen Anne Ave N
206-285-9728
Visit the Queen Anne of olden days.
- **Ozzie's** • 105 W Mercer St
206-284-4618
Where frat boys go to sing karaoke and bust the occasional head.
- **Peso's** • 605 Queen Anne Ave N
206-283-9353
If you like your meat market with a side of guac.
- **Plaza Garibaldi** • 129 1st Ave N
206-397-4088
Veg-friendly Mex turns LQA karaoke bar on weekends, becomes less friendly.
- **The Sitting Room** • 108 W Roy St
206-285-2830
Warm and orange. You'll see what I mean.
- **Solo Bar** • 200 Roy St
206-213-0080
Faith No More (remember them?) serves up some cocktails.
- **Spectator Bar & Grill** • 529 Queen Anne Ave N
206-599-4263
Typical sports bar transforms into epic punk rock karaoke party at week's end.
- **Sport** • 140 4th Ave N
206-404-7767
A place where intellectuals debate existential theory. Just kidding!
- **Teatro Zinzanni** • 222 Mercer St
206-802-0015
A fine night out. If someone else is paying.
- **Ten Mercer** • 10 Mercer St
206-691-3723
You'll think you've died and gone to a Bret Easton Ellis novel.
- **The Tin Lizzie Lounge** • 600 S 244th St
206-282-7407
The MarQueen's gorgeous hotel bar might want to see the Wizard for a heart.
- **The Vera Project** • 305 Harrison St
206-956-8372
Keeping the kids out of trouble in the coolest way possible.

🍴 Restaurants

- **Bamboo Garden** • 364 Roy St
206-282-6616 • $$
Chinese vegetarian spot that makes fake meat taste unnaturally good.
- **Bigfood** • 305 Harrison St
206-719-5549 • $
Mobile S'quatch-themed food truck now has a stationary spot in the Armory.
- **Blue Water Taco Grill** • 515 Queen Anne Ave N
206-352-2407 • $
Cheap Ameri-Mexican that's at least pretty fresh.
- **Citizen** • 706 Taylor Ave N
206-284-1015 •
Delicious crepes and sandwiches that'll make you count as two citizens.
- **Collections Cafe** • 305 Harrison St
206-753-4935 • $$
The Chihuly Museum's highfalutin eatery decorated with crap from Dale's attic.
- **Crow Restaurant and Bar** • 823 5th Ave N
206-283-8800 • $$
Scoff at the small plate trend and indulge in hearty, sausage-stuffed lasagna.
- **Dick's Drive-In** • 500 Queen Anne Ave N
206-285-5155 • $
A local obsession, specializing in cheap burgers and shakes. Perfect at 1 am.
- **Kidd Valley** • 531 Queen Anne Ave N
206-284-0184 • $
Like a slightly fancier Burger King with not much more to offer.

The hub of LQA is contained in the several blocks near the Seattle Center that are packed with restaurants and bars. Relish delectable Indian at **Roti**. Even carnivores appreciate the faux-meat delights at **Bamboo Garden**. In terms of nightlife, **Ozzie's** and **Peso's** draw the biggest crowds and chiefly deal in meat-marketing. Start or end your night at the classic dive **Mecca Café**.

- **Laredos Grill** • 555 Aloha St
  206-218-1040 • $$
  Queso and tacos till 1am. Ole!
- **Mecca Café** • 526 Queen Anne Ave N
  206-285-9728 • $
  Your taste buds will thank you. Your heart and liver will disown you.
- **The Melting Pot** • 14 Mercer St
  206-378-1208 • $$$$
  Gimmicky and retro, perhaps, but dipping things in cheese can never be bad.
- **New York Pizza & Bar** • 500 Mercer St
  206-913-2565 • $$
  A family house of junk food where mom and dad can also get plastered.
- **Obasan** • 11 Mercer St
  206-282-2333 • $$
  Casual Japanese spot.
- **Oskar's Kitchen** • 621 Queen Anne Ave N
  206-402-3375 • $$
  Shawn Kemp's sexy-fish-themed barstraunt.
- **Pagliacci Pizza** • 550 Queen Anne Ave N
  206-726-1717 • $
  Local favorite pizza chain makes crispy-chewy delights with seasonal ingredients.
- **Peso's** • 605 Queen Anne Ave N
  206-283-9353 • $$$
  Mexican with substance. Same can be said for the margaritas but not the patrons.
- **Pie** • 305 Harrison St
  206-428-6312 • $
  This sweet/savory hand pie-oneer (sorry) now has a stall at Seattle Center.
- **Plaza Garibaldi** • 129 1st Ave N
  206-397-4088 • $$
  Vast and varied Mexican menu made from "family recipes."
- **Plum Juice Bar** • 305 Harrison St
  206-428-6337 • $
  Contributing to the classing up of the Armory with vegan lunch food.
- **Racha** • 23 Mercer St
  206-281-8883 • $$$
  Safe bet for pad thai, once you get past the yuppies.

- **Roti Cuisine of India** • 530 Queen Anne Ave N
  206-216-7684 • $$
  Tasty, reasonably priced lunch buffet. Guaranteed food coma.
- **Shiki Japanese** • 4 W Roy St
  206-281-1352 • $$
  One of the only places in the state to get fugu. Non life-threatening dishes available, too.
- **Skillet Counter** • 305 Harrison St
  206-428-6311 • $$
  Great organic meal if you can withstand their cutesy menu and city prices.
- **SkyCity** • 400 Broad St
  206-905-2100 • $$$
  Ridiculously overpriced, mediocre food—but what a view. For tourists.
- **Solo Bar** • 200 Roy St
  206-213-0080 • $$
  ItalEthioSpaBulgarian cuisine. And tapas.
- **Spectator Bar & Grill** • 529 Queen Anne Ave N
  206-599-4263 • $$
  Typical sports bar transforms into epic punk rock karaoke party at week's end.
- **Sushi Land** • 803 5th Ave N
  206-267-7621 • $
  Fun, cheap sushi.
- **Ten Mercer** • 10 Mercer St
  206-691-3723 • $$$$
  Hip bar and romantic upstairs area—heavy on the meat options.
- **Toulouse Petit** • 601 Queen Anne Ave N
  206-432-9069 • $$
  From the guy who brought you Peso's. Different food, same attitude.
- **Uptown China** • 200 Queen Anne Ave N
  206-285-7710 • $$
  Efficient, spice-a-licious Chinese, best complemented by a Tsingtao.

Shopping

- **Mercer Street Books** • 7 Mercer St
  206-282-7687
  Indie bookstore with used stock.

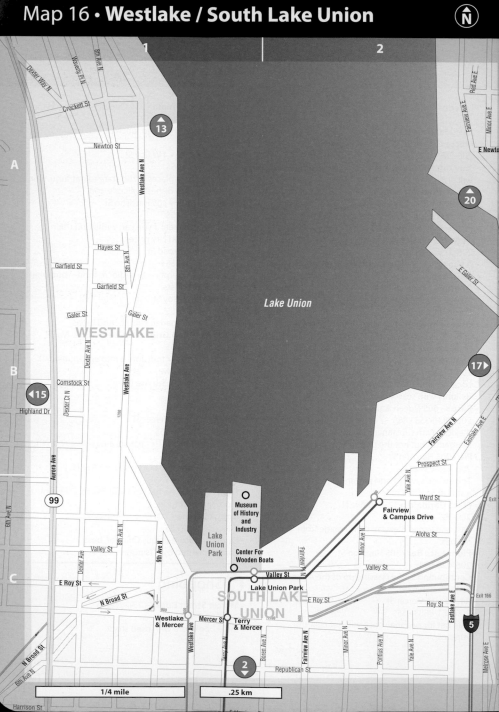

Map 16 · **Westlake / South Lake Union**

N

1   2

▲ 13

A

E Newto

▲ 20

Dexter Way N
Waverly Pl N
8th Ave N
Crockett St
Newton St
Westlake Ave N

Red Ave E
Fairview Ave E

Hayes St
8th Ave N
Garfield St
Dexter Ave N
Garfield St
Galer St
Galer St
Westlake Ave
Dexter Cn N

E Galer St

Lake Union

WESTLAKE

B

◄ 15

Highland Dr
Comstock St

17 ►

Fairview Ave N
Eastlake Ave E

Aurora Ave

Prospect St
Yale Ave N
Ward St

99

Exit

6th Ave N

○
Museum
of History
and
Industry

Fairview
& Campus Drive

Minor Ave N

Aloha St

8th Ave N
Valley St
Dexter Ave
9th Ave N

Lake
Union
Park

Center For
Wooden Boats

Fairview Pl N

Valley St

C

E Roy St

N Broad St

Valley St
Lake Union Park

Exit 166

Roy St

Eastlake Ave E

Exit 166

**SOUTH LAKE
UNION**

E Roy St

Westlake
& Mercer

Westlake Ave

Mercer St

Terry
& Mercer

Terry Ave N

Boren Ave N

Fairview Ave N

Minor Ave N

Pontius Ave N

Yale Ave N

Melrose Ave E

5

N Broad St
6th Ave N

▼ 2

Republican St

Harrison St

1/4 mile	.25 km

Once a light industrial area on sweet little Lake Union, Paul Allen is still putting the finishing touches on the top half of his pet 'hood. The jewel at the center is the spectacular 12-acre **Lake Union Park** on the waterfront. Completed in 2010, plans for the park were originally proposed in the early 1900s; Seattleites don't like to rush into anything. Beware the novelty streetcar that ends its tedious two-mile journey here.

Map 16

○ Landmarks

- **The Center for Wooden Boats** • 1010 Valley St
  206-382-2628
  Free boat rides on Lake Union every Sunday!
- **Lake Union** •
  Connecting Puget Sound with Lake Washington;
  houseboats, pleasurecraft and biotech.
- **Lake Union Park** • 860 Terry Ave N
  Former Naval site now 12-acre urban waterfront
  masterpiece.
- **Museum of History and Industry** •
  860 Terry Ave N
  206-324-1126
  Experience all of Seattle's history from inception to
  present day.

🖥 Coffee

- **Uptown Espresso** • 500 Westlake Ave N
  206-621-2045
  Self-proclaimed "Home of the Velvet Foam" but the
  coffee underneath is just so-so.

🍸 Nightlife

- **Jillian's Billiard Club** • 731 Westlake Ave N
  206-223-0300
  A club that only frat boys want to be a part of.

🍴 Restaurants

- **1Hundred Bistro & Bar** • 1001 Fairview Ave N
  425-455-4278 • $$
  A little bit of Bellevue in South Lake Union.
- **Buca di Beppo** • 701 9th Ave N
  206-244-2288 • $$
  Where your friends have their birthday party if
  they hate you (and themselves).
- **Chandler's Crabhouse** • 901 Fairview Ave N
  206-223-2722 • $$$$
  Not-bad crabs with an excellent view of Lake
  Union.
- **Compass Café** • 860 Terry Ave N
  206-324-1126 • $
  This excellent cafe upstages the Museum of
  History & Industry in which it resides.
- **Daniel's Broiler** • 809 Fairview Ave N
  206-621-8262 • $$$$
  Fancy folk (or those whose parents are paying)
  head here for decent steak.
- **I Love My GFF** • 1016 Republican St
  $
  Piles of healthy goodness. Arch nemesis of the
  Famous Bowl.
- **I Love Sushi** • 1001 Fairview Ave N
  206-625-9604 • $$
  Sushi with a water view.
- **McCormick & Schmick's Harborside** •
  1200 Westlake Ave N
  206-270-9052 • $$$
  Corporate club vibe and an unparalleled $1.95
  happy hour burger.
- **Raney Brothers BBQ** •
  206-371-5078 • $
  Suicide food at its most suicidal.

Map 17 • **Capitol Hill (West)**

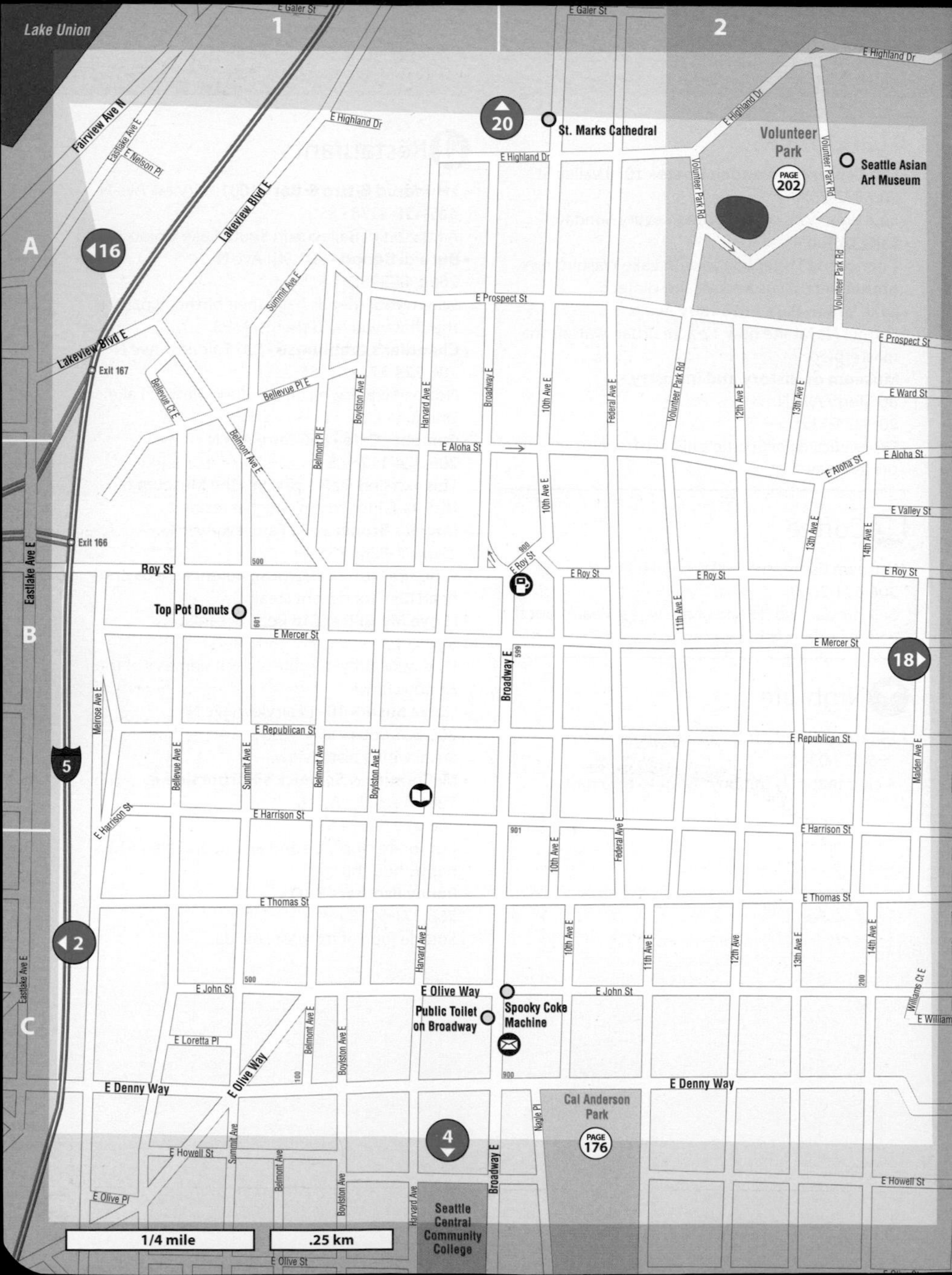

Lake Union

1   2

E Galer St

E Galer St

E Highland Dr

Fairview Ave N

E Nelson Pl

Eastlake Ave E

E Highland Dr

20   ○ St. Marks Cathedral

E Highland Dr

E Highland Dr

Volunteer Park Rd

Volunteer Park

PAGE **202**

○ **Seattle Asian Art Museum**

Lakeview Blvd E

◄16

A

Summit Ave E

Lakeview Blvd E

Exit 167

E Prospect St

E Prospect St

Bellevue Pl E

Bellevue Ct E

Belmont Ave E

Boylston Ave E

Belmont Pl E

Harvard Ave E

Broadway E

10th Ave E

Federal Ave E

Volunteer Park Rd

12th Ave E

13th Ave E

E Ward St

E Aloha St

E Aloha St

E Aloha St

E Valley St

Exit 166

10th Ave E

E Roy St

E Roy St

13th Ave E

14th Ave E

E Roy St

Roy St

Ⓟ Roy St

900

E Roy St

18►

B

Top Pot Donuts ○

E Mercer St

Broadway E 900

11th Ave E

E Mercer St

Melrose Ave E

Bellevue Ave E

Summit Ave E

Belmont Ave E

Boylston Ave E

E Republican St

E Republican St

Maiden Ave E

5

E Harrison St

📖

901

10th Ave E

Federal Ave E

E Harrison St

E Thomas St

E Thomas St

E Thomas St

◄2

E John St

500

Harvard Ave E

10th Ave E

11th Ave E

12th Ave E

13th Ave E

14th Ave E

Williams Ct E

E William

E Loretta Pl

Belmont Ave E

Boylston Ave E

E Olive Way ○

Public Toilet on Broadway ○

Spooky Coke Machine ✉

E John St

E Denny Way

Nagle Pl

E Denny Way

C

E Denny Way

E Olive Way

Summit Ave

Belmont Ave

Boylston Ave

900

Cal Anderson Park

PAGE **176**

E Howell St

E Olive Pl

4
▼

Broadway E

E Howell St

Harvard Ave E

Nagle Pl

Seattle Central Community College

E Olive St

| 1/4 mile | | .25 km |

Map 17

Seattle's a gay-friendly city and there's no neighborhood pinker than Capitol Hill, particularly along the main drag, Broadway. Rainbow flags festoon the lampposts, bold displays of affection are commonplace, and leather daddies can be spotted strolling grocery store aisles in full regalia. Meanwhile, runaway street urchins make themselves at home and no one seems to care about vowels anymore. Get an espresso at **Espresso Vivace** and contemplate it all.

o Landmarks

- **Public Toilet on Broadway** • 115 Broadway E
  A crap capsule of sex and drugs.
- **Saint Mark's Cathedral** • 1245 10th Ave E
  206-323-0300
  Colossal cathedral on the hill; compline choir attracts yuppies, grannies, and street kids alike.
- **Seattle Asian Art Museum** • 1400 E Prospect St
  206-654-3100
  Gorgeous Art Deco building with a superb collection of Asian art.
- **Spooky Coke Machine** • E John St & Broadway E
  Press the mystery button if you dare.
- **Top Pot Doughnuts** • 609 Summit Ave E
  206-323-7841
  The planet's best donut shop.

Coffee

- **Analog Coffee** • 235 Summit Ave E
  A sweet little neighborhood coffee joint that, luddite moniker aside, totally allows laptops.
- **Espresso Vivace** • 532 Broadway E
  206-860-2722
  The ultimate coffee hut.
- **Espresso Vivace** • 321 Broadway E
  206-324-8861
  Watch the beautiful Broadway freak show stroll by.
- **Joe Bar** • 810 E Roy St
  206-324-0407
  Solid joe from Joe.
- **Roy Street Coffee & Tea** • 700 Broadway Ave E
  206-325-2211
  Another incognito Starbucks.
- **TNT Espresso** • 324 Broadway Ave E
  206-323-9151
  You could get better coffee, but probably not as fast.

Nightlife

- **Bait Shop** • 606 Broadway E
  206-420-8742
  Linda Derschang brings her hipster revolution to the Seafood world.
- **Captain Black's** • 129 Belmont Ave E
  206-327-9549
  Here be booze, chicken, waffles, and a patio.
- **Dilettante Mocha Café** • 538 Broadway E
  206-329-6463
  Premium chocolate orgy.
- **Highline** • 210 Broadway E
  206-328-7837
  Valhala for vegan punks. Plus Cake-aroke!
- **The Stumbling Monk** • 1635 E Olive Way
  206-860-0916
  Discuss the waning political climate over Belgian beers. NFT fav.
- **Summit Public House** • 601 Summit Ave E
  206-324-7611
  The quintessential neighborhood pub.
- **Sun Liquor** • 607 Summit Ave E
  206-860-1130
  What's better than freshly-juiced cocktails and warm nuts? Not a damn thing.
- **Theory Vodka Lounge** • 715 Olive Way
  206-915-2852
  Theorize about which of their 75+ vodkas gets you the drunkest.

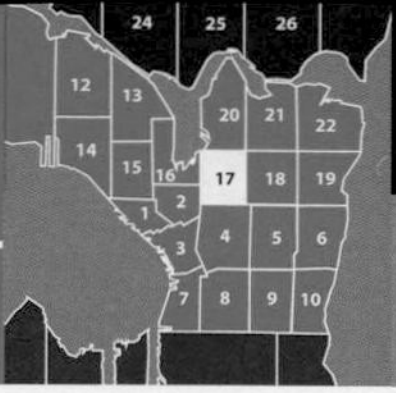

Map 17

Capitol Hill (West)

🍴 Restaurants

- **Altura** • 617 Broadway E
  206-402-6749 • $$$$
  Occasion dining with the full Italian treatment,
  from aperitif to dolce.
- **Aoki Japanese Grill & Sushi Bar** • 621 Broadway E
  206-324-3633 • $$$
  Japanese owned, Japanese served.
- **Bait Shop** • 606 Broadway E
  206-420-8742 • $$
  Linda Derschang brings her hipster revolution to
  the Seafood world.
- **Barriga Llena** • 219 Broadway E
  206-782-1220 • $
  Tortas are Mexican food in sandwich form. These
  are really good versions of that concept.
- **Charlie's Bar & Grill** • 217 Broadway E
  206-323-2535 • $$
  Bar food that tastes like home cookin'. Or tries to.
- **Crumble & Flake Patisserie** • 1500 E Olive Way
  206-329-1804 • $$
  Aptly-named bakery which sells out of its popular
  treats every single day.
- **Deluxe Bar & Grill** • 625 Broadway E
  206-324-9697 • $$
  Kitchen stays open late, and the fries will leave you
  begging for mercy.
- **Dick's Drive-In** • 115 Broadway E
  206-323-1300 • $
  A local obsession, specializing in cheap burgers
  and shakes. Perfect at 1 am.

- **Dilettante Mocha Café** • 538 Broadway E
  206-329-6463 • $$
  Just skip dinner and indulge in a chocolate dessert
  orgy. You deserve it.
- **Glo's** • 1621 E Olive Way
  206-324-2577 • $
  Almost puts Grandma's biscuits and gravy to
  shame. Great on a rainy morning.
- **Irwin's Cafe Hydro House** • 1201 Eastlake Ave E
  206-623-1510 • $$
  Quaint cafe with great pastries and a carb-heavy
  lunch menu.
- **Jai Thai** • 235 Broadway E
  206-322-5781 • $
  Consistently good Thai; the curries are always
  kickin', and the happy hour menu is tops.
- **Noah's Bagels** • 220 Broadway E
  206-720-2925 • $
  Better to wait for your next trip to New York.
- **Pagliacci Pizza** • 426 Broadway E
  206-324-0730 • $$
  Local favorite pizza chain makes crispy-chewy
  delights with seasonal ingredients.
- **Panevino Trattoria** • 416 Broadway E
  206-328-7187 • $$
  A good Italian joint.
- **Pho Cyclo** • 406 Broadway E
  206-329-9256 • $
  Super-tasty bowls of pho. Not the cheapest, but
  one of the yummiest.
- **Pho Than Brothers'** • 516 Broadway E
  206-568-7218 • $
  Three words: free cream puff.

Capitol Hill (West)

Map 17

For Vietnamese pho, try **Pho Cyclo** or the Capitol Hill **Than Brothers**. **Aoki** pulls off good quality sushi and a wide selection of sakes. Feed your Broadway posse at **Dick's Drive-In** late Friday night after sipping a divine cocktail at **Sun Liquor**. **The Stumbling Monk** is a comfy spot for Belgian beers and good conversation. **Glo's** is the place for breakfast (also open late), but be prepared to wait.

- **Poppy** • 622 Broadway E
  206-324-1108 • $$$
  Fine dining in an IKEA show room.
- **Queen Sheba** • 916 E John St
  206-322-0852 • $
  Finger-lickin' spicy goodness to mop up with injera bread. Bring friends.
- **Rom Mai Thai** • 613 Broadway E
  206-726-9058 • $
  Friendly people and top-notch Thai; one of the best on Broadway.
- **Stateside**• 300 E Pike St
  206-557-7273 • $$$$
  Duck duck good.
- **Table 219** • 219 Broadway E
  206-328-4604 • $$
  Same brunch classics from the El Greco days; dinner's got new creative touches.
- **Tacos Chukis** • 219 Broadway E
  206-328-4447 • $
  What they do to your meat with a pinepple is illegal several states.
- **Thomas Street Bistro** • 421 E Thomas St
  206-323-0914 • $$
  Euro dining without the need to learn a foreign language.
- **Top Pot Doughnuts** • 609 Summit Ave E
  206-323-7841 • $
  Top Pot is tops!
- **Zhivago's Café** • 416 Broadway E
  206-328-0500 • $
  Delicious piroshkies. No Bolshevik.

🛍 Shopping

- **American Apparel** • 200 Broadway E
  206-709-8100
  Soft t-shirts and free porn!
- **Broadway Video** • 512 Broadway E
  206-328-5023
  With five-day specials and reservations, who needs Netflix?
- **Castle Megastore** • 206 Broadway E
  206-204-0126
  An adult mega-store.
- **The Confectional** • 618 Broadway E
  206-282-4422
  The real sin is skipping dessert.
- **Crossroads Trading Co.** • 325 Broadway E
  206-328-5867
  Buys and sells only fashionable designer clothing.
- **Metro Clothing Company** • 231 Broadway E
  206-726-7978
  Goth Wear. Costumes for some. Business Casual for others.
- **Mishu Boutique II** • 321 Broadway E
  206-802-8022
  Unique, affordable clothing made by folks in Asia who get lunch breaks.
- **Pretty Parlor** • 119 Summit Ave E
  206-405-2883
  Vintage and locally designed couture that make you feel pretty.
- **Red Light Vintage Clothing** • 312 Broadway E
  206-329-2200
  Vintage clothing for people with 10-inch waists.
- **Spin Cycle** • 321 Broadway Ave E
  206-971-0267
  As lovingly stocked as that shop in *High Fidelity* but without all the attitude.
- **Urban Outfitters** • 401 Broadway E
  206-322-1800
  Fashionable and affordable clothes for faux-city dwellers.
- **Vino Verite** • 208 Boylston Ave E
  206-324-0324
  These guys love wine even more than you do.

Map 18 · **Capitol Hill (East) / Madison Valley**

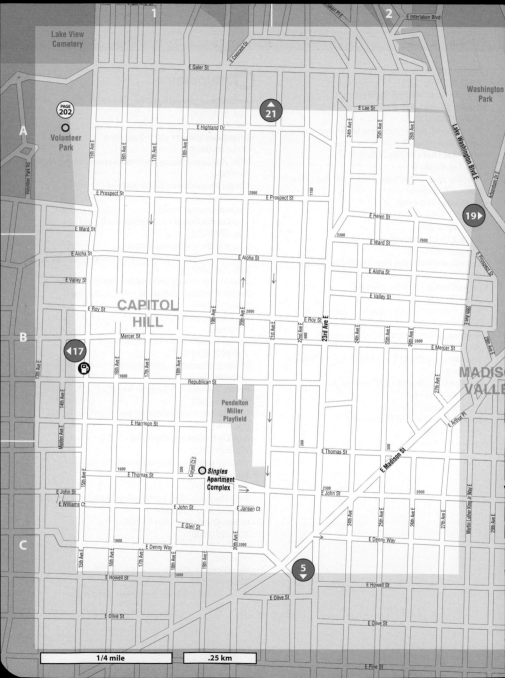

Map 18

While the western side of Capitol Hill caters directly to the young and decadent, the eastern portion of the neighborhood is more of a, well, neighborhood. Still, there's no shortage of pink pride or nightlife, so it's not utter culture shock. Nearby Madison Valley is even homier, with numerous parks, public schools, and escalating real estate values—a far cry from the down-and-out neighborhood it once was.

○ Landmarks

- **Singles Apartment Complex** • 1820 E Thomas St
No, Matt Dillon doesn't live here anymore.
- **Volunteer Park** • 1247 15th Ave E
206-684-4075
Climb to the top of this Victorian-era conservatory and water tower.

Coffee

- **Caffe Ladro** • 435 15th Ave E
206-267-0551
Strong coffee for the strong coffee drinker.
- **Coffee Pronto** • 312 15th Ave E
206-322-9693
Breakfast, too.
- **El Portal Coffee Roasters** • 2310 E Madison St
206-860-6923
El portal goes to Mexico where the coffee is muy bueno.
- **Fuel** • 610 19th Ave E
206-329-4700
Now this is a type of fuel that actually has a future.
- **Victrola Coffee & Art** • 411 15th Ave E
206-325-6520
From a time before coffee was good.

Nightlife

- **The BottleNeck Lounge** • 2328 E Madison St
206-323-1098
Come meet your new neighbors at this cozy spot.
- **Hopvine Pub** • 507 15th Ave E
206-328-3120
100% Pacific Northwest right down to the beer and fleece.
- **Liberty** • 517 15th Ave E
206-323-9898
Sushi and cocktails served by people who are more hip than you.
- **Single Shot** • 611 Summit Ave E
206-420-2238 • $$
You'll want at least a double from these cocktail artisans.
- **Smith** • 332 15th Ave E
206-709-1900
Linda's winning combination of animal heads and hipster pub fare.

Map 18

Capitol Hill (East) / Madison Valley

🍴Restaurants

- **Bamboo** • 345 15th Ave E
  206-567-3399 • $$
  Pho house with veggie-loaded menu.
- **Coastal Kitchen** • 429 15th Ave E
  206-322-1145 • $$$
  A quarterly rotating menu focusing on a different
  global cuisine. And blunch!
- **Crush** • 2319 E Madison St
  206-302-7874 • $$
  Gorgeous food pops against the modern, sexy
  interior. Service to write home about.
- **The Essential Baking Company** •
  2719 E Madison St
  206-328-0078 • $
  You'll think you're in a European bakery.
- **Gyro Cafe** • 107 15th Ave E
  206-324-6435 • $
  Hit-or-miss gyrocery.
- **The Harvest Vine** • 2701 E Madison St
  206-320-9771 • $$
  Gorgeous, perfect tapas.

- **Hello Robin** • 522 19th Ave E
  206-735-7970 • $
  The cookie bakery of your Pinterest dreams.
- **Jamjuree** • 509 15th Ave E
  206-323-4255 • $
  Another competent Thai restaurant.
- **Monsoon** • 615 19th Ave E
  206-325-2111 • $$$
  Sublimely elegant Vietnamese, and oh-so-
  affordable. Great dim sum brunch.
- **NuFlours** • 518 15th Ave E
  206-395-4623 • $$$
  No flour is the nu flour.
- **The Patio Fine Thai** • 524 15th Ave E
  206-328-2406 • $
  Doing their part to keep Thai food ubiquitous in
  Sea-town.
- **Queen Bee Cafe** • 2200 E Madison St
  206-757-6314 • $
  You won't know how you ever lived without
  Crumpwiches.
- **Remedy Teas** • 345 15th Ave E
  206-323-4832 • $$
  150 incredible loose teas, the friendliest staff,
  lovely treats, and a clean, modern interior.

Capitol Hill East is home to plenty of laid-back restaurants and pubs. If Linda's is the hipster starter bar, Derschang's **Smith**, with its rotating taps and charcuterie plates, is where they graduate to once they've settled into steady-paycheck adulthood. Try **Liberty** for sushi in a stylish setting. **Single Shot** serves good food and even better cocktails. Madison Valley is known for fancy four-star eateries like **Crush** and **The Harvest Vine** for folks in ties and polished shoes.

- **Rione XIII** • 401 15th Ave E
  206-838-2878 • $$
  Ethan Stowell brings you wood fired pizza, 13th District Rome style.
- **Single Shot** • 611 Summit Ave E
  206-420-2238 • $$
  Upscale food at dirt cheap prices by a Super Group of Seattle chefs.
- **Smith** • 332 15th Ave E
  206-709-1900 • $$
  Perfect sweet potato fries and brunch make for elegantly eclectic pub fare.
- **Tallulah's** • 550 19th Ave E
  206-860-0077 • $$
  Linda's found a way to get everyone to eat their vegetables: season with meat.
- **Vios Café & Marketplace** • 903 19th Ave E
  206-329-3236 • $
  Beautiful Greek dishes. Wines for the adults, play area for the kiddies.
- **The Wandering Goose** • 403 15th Ave E
  206-323-9938 • $$
  A great place to wander into, goose or otherwise.

Shopping

- **Henrietta's Hats** • 2707 E Madison St
  206-322-8169
  Need a custom Kentucky Derby hat? Here you go.
- **North Hill Bakery** • 518 15th Ave E
  206-325-9007
  Popular local bakery.
- **Shoprite** • 432 15th Ave E
  206-328-5138
  Sort of like a dollar store, but better—and more random.

Map 19

Polar opposite extremes of wealth and health. Families living in mansions on Lake Washington recreate at the Seattle Tennis Club's waterfront courts and privately educate prodigal youth at the elite Bush School. Nearby, at a gritty city intersection, Seattle's Bailey-Bouche provides housing for people living with terminal diseases and public schools get the axe due to budget cuts. Gotta love the commonalities— Seattle Tennis Club, Bush School, and Bailey-Bouche House all have exclusive admission criteria.

o Landmarks

- **Japanese Garden** • 1075 Lake Washington Blvd E
  206-684-4725
  Renowned formal Japanese garden; check out the periodic tea ceremonies.
- **Seattle Tennis Club** • 922 McGilvra Blvd E
  206-324-3200
  A venerable Madison Park institution. Country clubbish.

Restaurants

- **Belle Epicurean** • 3109 E Madison St
  206-466-1320 • $
  Inspired French pastries served with approriately snooty attitude.
- **Café Flora** • 2901 E Madison St
  206-325-9100 • $$
  Eat fancy vegetarian (one of the country's best) in a Zen garden.
- **Nishino** • 3130 E Madison St
  206-322-5800 • $$$
  One of the premier sushi places in town. Reservations requisite.
- **Voilà ! Bistrot** • 2805 E Madison St
  206-322-5460 • $$$
  Classic French in a classy setting. Stupid name.

Shopping

- **City People's Garden Store** • 2939 E Madison St
  206-324-0737
  Yes, you too can have flowers blooming and veggies growing year round in Seattle.
- **Fury Extraordinary Women's Consignment** •
  2810 E Madison St
  206-329-6829
  Got-bucks women consign clothing onto the racks of Fury.
- **The Lavender Heart** • 2812 E Madison St
  206-568-4441
  Walk into the store, breathe in the creative mind of owner Holly Henderson, exhale.

Map 20 • **Eastlake / Montlake / Portage Bay**

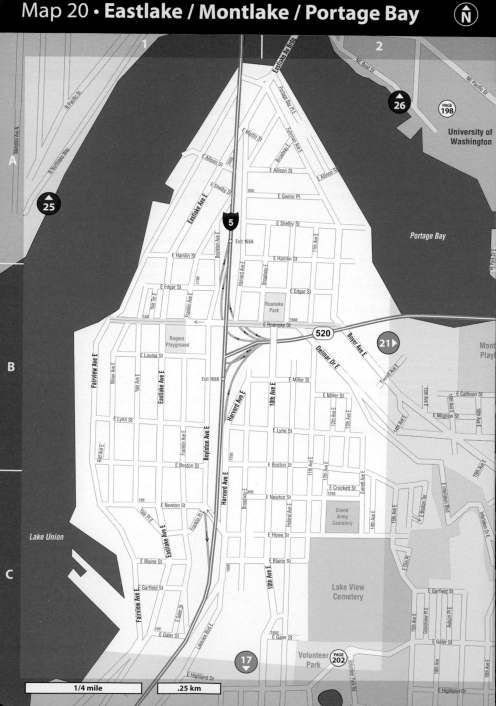

N Pacific St

NE Boat St

NE Pacific St

Eastlake Av Brdg

Portage Bay Pl E

1

2

26

PAGE
198

University of
Washington

N Northlake Way

Meridian Ave N

E Martin St

E Allison St

Fairview Ave E

Broadway E

A

E Allison St

E Allison St

E Shelby St

900

E Gwinn Pl

25

Eastlake Ave E

Boylston Ave E

5

E Shelby St

11th Ave E

Portage Bay

Exit 168A

E Hamlin St

E Hamlin St

E Hamlin St

Harvard Ave E

Broadway E

W Park Dr E

E Edgar St

2700

E Edgar St

Yale Ter E

Franklin Ave E

100

Roanoke
Park

1000

E Roanoke St

520

Boyer Ave E

Rogers
Playground

Delmar Dr E

21

Mont
Playf

B

Fairview Ave E

Minor Ave E

Yale Ave E

E Louisa St

Eastlake Ave E

Exit 168B

Harvard Ave E

10th Ave E

E Miller St

Everett Ave E

19th Ave E

16th Ave E

E Calhoun St

E Miller St

18th Ave E

E Mcgraw St

Reid Ave E

E Lynn St

Franklin Ave E

E Lynn St

11th Ave E

12th Ave E

13th Ave E

14th Ave E

18th Ave E

Boylston Ave E

2200

E Boston St

E Boston St

100

E Newton St

Franklin Pl E

Harvard Ave E

Broadway E

2000

E Newton St

Federal Ave E

E Crockett St
1200

Everett Ave E

E Howe St

14th Ave E

15th Ave E

E Boston Dr

Interlaken Blvd

E Howe St

Grand
Army
Cemetery

Lake Union

Eastlake Ave E

Yale Pl E

E Blaine St

E Blaine St

10th Ave E

Interlaken Dr E

C

Fairview Ave E

E Garfield St

1800

Lake View
Cemetery

E Garfield St

15th Ave E

Grandview Pl E

Auburn Pl E

E Galer St

Galer St

100

E Galer St

E Galer St

Lakeview Blvd E

Volunteer
Park

PAGE
202

16th Ave E

E Highland Dr

17

Volunteer Park Rd

E Highland Dr

1/4 mile

.25 km

Map 20

Eastlake is one gem of a neighborhood with an ideal location—a short bus ride from the U District and a hop-skip-jump from downtown. Being nuzzled up to Lake Washington makes the 'hood that much more desirable. It's old, funky, and a touch European, with its brightly painted homes and homespun shops. Once a more industrial section of town, residential buildings have sprung up near Eastlake's idyllic and thriving houseboat community.

Coffee

- **Voxx Coffee** • 2245 Eastlake Ave E
  206-324-2778
  A welcoming shop with tons of outlets. Take off your coat and stay a while.

Nightlife

- **Eastlake Zoo Tavern** • 2301 Eastlake Ave E
  206-329-3277
  Those grizzled old bartenders also own the joint.
- **Roanoke Park Place** • 2409 10th Ave E
  206-324-5882
  Drown another Husky football loss in their good beer selection.
- **Ship Canal Grill** • 3218 Eastlake Ave E
  206-588-8885
  Nautical-themed sports bar. Nothing says "football" like "fish n' chips."

Restaurants

- **14 Carrot Café** • 2305 Eastlake Ave E
  206-324-1442 • $$
  Typical breakfast fare that's, well, typical. Popular anyway.
- **Abay Ethiopian Cusine** • 2359 10th Ave E
  206-257-4778 • $$
  Probably the best Ethiopian food you've ever tasted, unless your mother is Ethiopian.
- **Blind Pig at Eastlake Teriyaki** •
  2236 Eastlake Ave E
  206-329-2744 • $
  Day-time lunch annex for the unassuming but decadent Blind Pig Bistro serving seasonal sandwiches from multiple genres.
- **Blind Pig Bistro** • 2238 Eastlake Ave E
  206-329-2744 • $$
  Chalkboard foodie place, classing up that weird Eastlake mini strip mall.

- **Le Fournil** • 3230 Eastlake Ave E
  206-328-6523 • $
  The best bakery in town with shockingly humble prices.
- **Little Water Cantina** • 2865 Eastlake Ave E
  206-397-4940 • $$
  Mediocre, overpriced "modern" Mexican. And such small portions.
- **Loulsa's Café & Bakery** • 2379 Eastlake Ave E
  206-325-0081 • $
  Baked goods, espresso, counter service.
- **Mammoth** • 2501 Eastlake Ave E
  206-946-1065 • $$$
  Eat like a caveman who has never heard of the Paleo diet.
- **Ravish** • 2956 Eastlake Ave E
  206-913-2497 • $$
  Wine bar with small plates.
- **Sebi's Bistro** • 3242 Eastlake Ave E
  206-420-2199 • $$
  Did you hear the one about the Polish restaurant?
- **Serafina** • 2043 Eastlake Ave E
  206-323-0807 • $$
  Rustic and charming Italian. A very loyal Eastlake following.
- **Sushi Kappo Tamura** • 2968 Eastlake Ave E
  206-547-0937 • $$$
  Fancy pants sushi that's worth conning someone into paying for.

Shopping

- **Everyday Music** • 1520 10th Ave E
  206-568-3321
  Two floors of used CDs, DVDs, and LPs. Your wallet is screwed.
- **The Flower Lady** • 3230 Eastlake Ave E
  206-325-5751
  Finally out of the parking lot and into her own shop—delightful flowers within budget.

Map 21 • Montlake

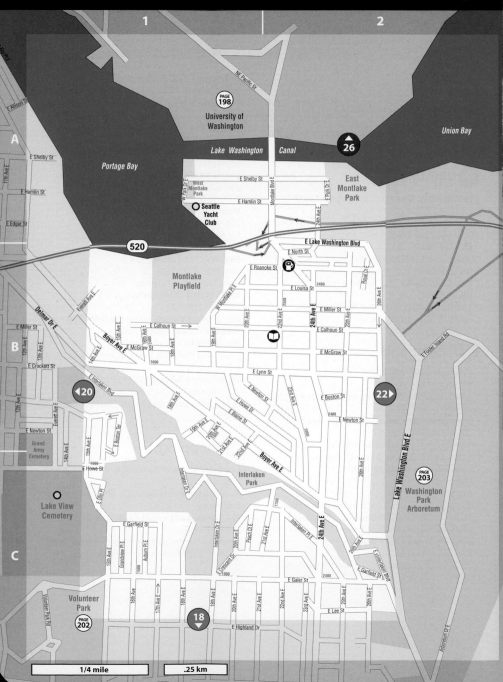

Map 21

This classy, educated neighborhood borders the bucolic Arboretum, the wooded ravines of Interlaken Park, and the Montlake Cut connecting Lake Union and Lake Washington. The venerable **Seattle Yacht Club** presides west of the bridge. The spiffy **Montlake Branch Library** attracts local brainiacs, and regattas draw rowers to May's raucous first day of boating season. Beware—traffic chokes Montlake on Husky game days and during drawbridge openings.

○ Landmarks

- **Lake View Cemetery** • 1554 15th Ave E
  206-322-1582
  Bruce Lee for Kung Fu enthusiasts. Brandon Lee for the Goths.
- **Seattle Yacht Club** • 1807 E Hamlin St
  206-325-1000
  Sorry little buddy. Members only.

Coffee

- **Fuel** • 2300 24th Ave E
  206-405-3835
  Now this is a type of fuel that actually has a future.

Restaurants

- **Café Lago** • 2305 24th Ave E
  206-329-8005 • $$$
  Heartbreakingly wonderful neighborhood Italian.
- **Volunteer Park Cafe and Marketplace** •
  1501 17th Ave E
  206-328-3155 • $
  Stop by after a stroll through Volunteer Park to grab a light-as-air scone.

Shopping

- **Mont's Market** • 2350 24th Ave E
  206-860-7876
  Gourmet goods for the 'hood.
- **Montlake Bicycle Shop** • 2223 24th Ave E
  206-329-7333
  Used bikes rentals, and sales. Knowledgeable staff.
- **Mr. Johnson's Antiques** • 2315 24th Ave E
  206-322-6033
  Fair prices, some negotiable.

Map 22 • **Madison Park**

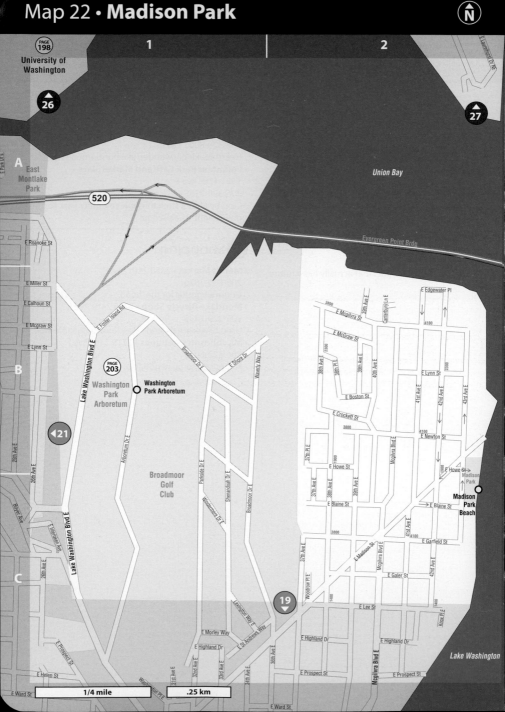

Map 22

Transferred here from Connecticut and miss the East Coast? Move to Madison Park and fork over serious dough for a cozy bungalow. Or for a few million more, you'll feel right at home in Broadmoor, a gated community established long before anyone knew gates from Gates. Waterfront condos have mountain and lake views, and the Madison Park hub will offer you those trendy little shops and cliquey, smug, safe neighborhood feel you've been missing since moving from Darien.

○ Landmarks

- **Washington Park Arboretum** •
  2300 Arboretum Dr E
  206-543-8800
  A haven for tree-huggers, bird-watchers, and botanists.

Coffee

- **East Madison Street Coffee Bar & Deli** •
  2818 E Madison St
  206-327-9242
  You'll go here because you have little other choice.
- **Harbour Pointe Coffeehouse** • 2818 E Madison St
  206-420-1187
  It's totally one of your options in Madison Park!

Nightlife

- **Attic Ale House & Eatery** • 4226 E Madison St
  206-323-3131
  Serving up the brews since '53.

Restaurants

- **Arosa Cafe** • 3121 E Madison St
  206-405-0605 • $
  It's a waffle cafe. I'll let that sink in…
- **Bing's** • 4200 E Madison St
  206-323-8623 • $$
  Madison Park's go-to burger joint. Mainly because it's there.
- **Cactus** • 4220 E Madison St
  206-324-4140 • $$$
  Outstanding mojitos and Mexican.
- **Cafe Parco** • 1807 42nd Ave E
  206-328-4757 • $$
  Up-and-comer in the generally lacking upscale Italian scene.
- **The Independent Pizzeria** • 4235 E Madison St
  206-860-6110 • $
  A classy family pizza joint with a DIY attitude.
- **Madison Kitchen** • 4122 E Madison St
  206-557-4640 • $$
  A decent lunch counter conveniently located near one of the prettiest parks in Seattle.
- **Madison Park Conservatory** • 1927 43rd Ave E
  206-324-9701 • $$$
  A culinary celebration of those animals unlucky enough to be lower on the food chain.

Shopping

- **Madison Cellars** • 4227 E Madison St
  206-323-9333
  Artistic postcard of a wine store—the tiny cellar boasts an eclectic selection.
- **Scoop du Jour** • 4029 E Madison St
  206-325-9562
  32 flavors of ice cream and a deli!

Map 23 · **Ballard**

Map 23

A Scandinavian fishing village at the turn of the 20th century and until relatively recently considered a nice place for seniors, Ballard has reinvented and reinvigorated itself as one of Seattle's most desirable 'nabes. Life's necessities are never hard to track down in this triangle-shaped hub hugging Salmon Bay, and a recent boom in condo development certainly doesn't hurt.

o Landmarks

- **Bergen Place Park** · 5420 22nd Avenue Northwest
  206-684-4075
  Seuss-like tree sculptures and Scandinavian flags.

Coffee

- **Anchored Ship Coffee Bar** · 5306 Ballard Ave NW
  206-484-5143
  Hole-in-the-wall that will keep you anchored.
- **Ballard Coffee Works** · 2060 NW Market St
  206-340-8867
  The coffee here definitely works.
- **Caffè Fiorè** · 5405 Leary Ave NW
  206-706-0421
  Makes the bold claim of being Seattle's first organic coffee.
- **Cupcake Royale/Verite Coffee** ·
  2052 NW Market St
  206-883-7656
  Cupcakes and coffee go well together.
- **Equal Exchange Espresso Bar** · 1400 NW 56th St
  206-783-4955
  They're all about the free trade, so you can feel extra smug about your latte.
- **Java Bean** · 5819 24th Ave NW
  206-788-9677
  Since 1989: organic, shade grown, fair trade.
- **Java Jahn** · 1428 NW Leary Way
  206-789-9441
  They'll be your Jahnny on the spot for your caffeine fix.
- **Sip & Ship** · 1752 NW Market St
  206-789-4488
  Like a home office with an espresso bar.
- **Slate Coffee Bar** · 5413 6th Ave NW
  206-240-7174
  The perfect place for a clean slate.
- **The Way Station** · 336 NW 40th St
  206-789-5900
  When you're short on will, try the Way.

Map 23

Ballard

🍸 Nightlife

- **Ballard Annex Oyster House** ·
5410 Ballard Ave NW
206-783-5410
The fun seafood party that Red Lobster ads promised and couldn't deliver.
- **Ballard Loft** · 5105 Ballard Ave NW
206-420-2737
The place in Ballard to watch the game. Any game.
- **Ballard Smoke Shop** · 5439 Ballard Ave NW
206-784-6611
A smokey taste of Old Ballard.
- **Ballard Station Public House** · 2236 NW Market St
206-906-9040
Super chill Ballard scene specializing in local brews and spirits.
- **BalMar** · 5449 Ballard Ave NW
206-486-5449
Plenty of places to sit to avoid some of the more annoying clientele.
- **The Bergschrund** · 4818 17th Ave NW
206-981-0887
Tap room for the NW Peaks brewery.
- **Hattie's Hat** · 5231 Ballard Ave NW
206-784-0175
Still gritty, but we're no longer afraid to eat there.
- **Hazelwood** · 2311 NW Market St
206-783-0478
Classy but not snooty, with two levels of dimly-lit ambiance.
- **Jolly Roger Taproom** · 1111 NW Ballard Way
206-782-6181
Bigger location with a subdued pirate theme. Fried pickles: Aarr!
- **Kangaroo & Kiwi** · 2026 NW Market St
206-297-0507
Where homesick Australians get pissed with New Zealand ex-pats.
- **Kickin' Boot Whiskey Kitchen** ·
5309 22nd Ave NW
206-783-2668
Ballardites can get their kicks with whiskey and modern southern cuisine.

- **King's Hardware** · 5225 Ballard Ave NW
206-782-0027
Uber-hip bar with unhip crowd on weekends. Brought to you by Linda.
- **The Leary Traveler** · 4354 Leary Way NW
206-783-4805
Frites and beer! Rest your barking dogs here.
- **Lock & Keel Tavern** · 5144 Ballard Ave NW
206-781-8023
A boat graveyard with booze.
- **The Market Arms** · 2401 NW Market St
206-789-0470
Fine footie pub from the blokes behind the George & Dragon.
- **Matador** · 2221 NW Market St
206-297-2855
Lots of tequila. Lots.
- **Ocho** · 2325 NW Market St
206-784-0699
Like having an office party in your walk-in closet.
- **The People's Pub** · 5429 Ballard Ave NW
206-783-6521
Like grandma's dining room, with late-night schnitzel and wurst.
- **The Sexton** · 5327 Ballard Ave NW
206-829-8645
Southern comfort tapas and comfort booze to match.
- **Shelter Lounge** · 4910 Leary Ave NW
206-829-8568
An urban ski lodge.
- **The Sunset** · 5433 Ballard Ave NW
206-784-4880
Opium den-themed bar and concert venue for local bands.
- **The Tractor Tavern** · 5213 Ballard Ave NW
206-789-3599
Live alt twang.
- **Urban Family Public House** · 5329 Ballard Ave NW
206-861-6769
25 taps for people who consider beer their family.
- **Zayda Buddy's** · 5405 Leary Ave NW
206-783-7777
Fhaux-dive with Leinenkugel's!

Spots like **Hattie's Hat**, **Tractor Tavern**, **King's Hardware**, and the **People's Pub** have the bases covered for great neighborhood nightlife. The **Tractor Tavern** is your home for live alt-country. Discover your new favorite band at the **Sunset**.

Restaurants

- **Ann's Teriyaki** · 2246 NW Market St
  206-789-5838 · $
  Huge menu, gigantic portions, quick. And cheap!
- **Ballard Annex Oyster House** ·
  5410 Ballard Ave NW
  206-783-5410 · $$$
  The fun seafood party that Red Lobster ads promised and couldn't deliver.
- **Ballard Mandarin Chinese Restaurant** ·
  5500 8th Ave NW
  206-782-5531 · $$
  I wouldn't do it…unless it were on a bet.
- **Ballard Pizza Company** · 5107 Ballard Ave NW
  206-659-6033 · $$
  Ethan Stowell furthers his Ballard conquest with pizza & gnocchi.
- **Bastille Cafe & Bar** · 5307 Ballard Ave NW
  206-453-5014 · $$
  The French invade Little Norway with haute cuisine. Hipsters rejoice.
- **Bitterroot BBQ** · 5239 Ballard Ave NW
  206-588-1577 · $$
  Even vegetarians don't have much to be bitter about at this transcendent BBQ spot.
- **Café Besalu** · 5909 24th Ave NW
  206-789-1463 · $
  Beautifully crafted pastries, quiches, cookies, brioches…
- **Cafe Mox** · 5105 Leary Ave NW
  206-436-0540 · $
  Gamer cafe with way better food than your D.M. would provide.
- **Cafe Munir** · 2408 NW 80th St
  206-783-4190 · $$
  A nice family Lebanese restaurant that also serves liquor. We don't have enough of these.
- **Cupcake Royale/Verite Coffee** ·
  2052 NW Market St
  206-883-7656 · $
  Cupcakes and coffee go well together.
- **The Dish** · 4358 Leary Way NW
  206-782-9985 · $$
  Probably one of the best tofu scrambles of all the local hippie-dippies.

- **El Camion** · 5314 15th Ave NW
  206-297-1124 · $
  Amazing truck tacos and tamales you can trust.
- **El Camión Adentro** · 6416 15th Ave NW
  206-784-5411 · $
  Brick-and-mortar version of Tom Douglas' (understandably) favorite taco truck.
- **Fez on Wheels** · 1550 NW 49th St
  206-432-0415 · $
  The hummus is a must.
- **Floating Leaves Tea** · 1704 NW Market St
  206-276-9542 · $
  Tea is the new coffee.
- **The Gerald** · 5210 Ballard Ave NW
  206-432-9280 · $$
  Upscale comfort fare perfect for the inebriated foodie.
- **Golden Beetle** · 1744 NW Market St
  206-706-2977 · $$
  An exotic flavor excursion brought to you by Maria Hines of Tilth fame.
- **Hale's Ales Pub** · 4301 Leary Way NW
  206-706-1544 · $$
  Seattle's oldest microbrewery with unfortunate corporate-like atmosphere.
- **The Hi-Life** · 5425 Russell Ave NW
  206-784-7272 · $$
  Breakfast, lunch, dinner, and quart-sized Bloody Marys in a 1911 firehouse.
- **Hot Cakes Molten Chocolate Cakery** ·
  5427 Ballard Ave NW
  206-420-3431 · $$
  Decadent dessert cafe. Known for molten cakes and boozy milkshakes.
- **India Bistro** · 2301 NW Market St
  206-783-5080 · $$
  Perfectly spiced entrees with excellent seafood.
- **Jolly Roger Taproom** · 1111 NW Ballard Way
  206-782-6181 · $$
  Yes, it's a brewery, but to call it pub food would be sacrilegious.
- **Kickin' Boot Whiskey Kitchen** ·
  5309 22nd Ave NW
  206-783-2668 · $$
  Ballardites can get their kicks with whiskey and modern southern cuisine.

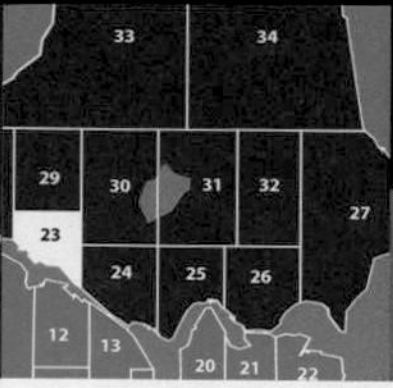

Map 23

Ballard

- **La Carta de Oaxaca** · 5431 Ballard Ave NW
  206-782-8722 · $$
  Authentic Oaxacan—think deep, dark sweet mole—at bargain prices.
- **La Isla** · 2320 NW Market St
  206-789-0516 · $$
  A half-dozen Puerto Rican platos that are addictive and satisfying.
- **Louie's Cuisine of China** · 5100 15th Ave NW
  206-782-8855 · $$
  Chinese comfort food since 1930-something.
- **Matador** · 2221 NW Market St
  206-297-2855 · $$
  If you can't get a table at Oaxaca.
- **Mr. Gyros** · 5522 20th Ave NW
  206-782-7777 · $
  It's almost like he was born to make Gyros.
- **Nick's Off Market** · 1556 NW 56th St
  206-783-0131 · $$
  Local everything served in a casually upscale living room.
- **No Bones About It** ·
  $
  Uniting the world's dietary preferences with their fried avocado tacos.
- **The Other Coast Café** · 5315 Ballard Ave NW
  206-789-0936 · $
  Sloppy sammies and super subs like they slather up way out east.
- **Pasta Bella** · 5913 15th Ave NW
  206-789-4933 · $$$
  Your run-of-the-mill romantic Italian restaurant.
- **Pho Big Bowl** · 2248 NW Market St
  206-588-1249 · $
  Pho-tastic. And big as advertized.
- **Pho Thân Brothers** · 2021 NW Market St
  206-782-5715 · $
  Cheap, fast, and filling, with a free cream puff to boot.
- **Plaka Estiatorio** · 5407 20th Ave NW
  206-829-8934 · $$
  Opa! Hands down best Greek food in town.

- **Raclette** · NW Market St
  206-369-3488 · $$
  They only serve their titular cheesey potato dish. But isn't that enough?
- **Root Table** · 2213 NW Market St
  206-420-3214 · $$
  Menage-a-Thai.
- **Senor Moose** · 5242 Leary Ave NW
  206-784-5568 · $
  Ballard breakfast institution. The guac is already legend.
- **Staple & Fancy Mercantile** · 4739 Ballard Ave NW
  206-789-1200 · $$$
  For a special night out, try the supper in 4 courses.
- **Stoneburner** · 5214 Ballard Ave NW
  206-695-2051 · $$
  Upscale pizza that you don't have to be a stoned burner to enjoy.
- **Streetzeria** ·
  206-755-5433 · $
  Their diverse salad menu might be better than the pizza.
- **Tall Grass Bakery** · 5907 24th Ave NW
  206-706-0991 · $
  Bring extra bread to pay for these award-winning loaves.
- **Top Pot Doughnuts** · 1416 NW 46th St
  206-728-1986 · $
  Top Pot is tops!
- **Vera's** · 5417 22nd Ave NW
  206-782-9966 · $
  Good old breakfast with crusty regulars.
- **Volterra** · 5411 Ballard Ave NW
  206-789-5100 · $$$
  Lovely Italian specialties with contemporary flair.
- **The Walrus and The Carpenter** ·
  4743 Ballard Ave NW
  206-395-9227 · $$$
  Stylish and transcendent oyster bar tucked behind a bike shop.
- **Zayda Buddy's** · 5405 Leary Ave NW
  206-783-7777 · $$
  Midwestern comfort food and Schlitz. Burn in hell, Wisconsin, for sending us more hipsters.

The two main and navigable drags—vibrant Market Street and historic Ballard Avenue—feature tons of restaurants. **La Carta de Oaxaca** is well worth the wait, while **Vera's** is one of the last true old-school dining spots left in the city. Go big at Ethan Stowell's **Staple & Fancy** or Maria Hines' **Golden Beetle**. Have an oyster-gasm at **The Walrus and the Carpenter**. Finally, don't miss the **Ballard Market** every Sunday.

🛍 Shopping

- **Anchor Tattoo** · 2313 NW Market St
  206-784-4051
  You'll be in good, (and clean) hands here.
- **Arcane Comics and More** · 5809 15th Ave NW
  206-781-4875
  Comics, games, and more (but not a lot more).
- **Ballard Farmers Market** · 5330 Ballard Ave NW
  Organic farmers, restauranteurs, and sidewalk buskers.
- **Ballard Town & Country Market** ·
  1400 NW 56th St
  206-783-7922
  Local produce, wine and desserts.
- **Bop Street Records** · 5219 Ballard Ave NW
  206-297-2232
  Huge basement full of vinyl. Certain piles off limits.
- **Buffalo Exchange** · 2232 NW Market St
  206-297-5920
  Second-hand clothes for girls who drink Zima.
- **Card Kingdom** · 5105 Leary Ave NW
  206-523-2273
  The ultimate destination for Lawful Good times.
- **Dutch Bike Co.** · 4741 Ballard Ave NW
  206-789-1678
  Super fancy bikes and espresso. Only in Seattle.
- **Electric & Folding Bikes Northwest** ·
  4810 17th Ave NW
  206-547-4621
  Electric bicycle sales and repairs.
- **Fred Meyer** · 915 NW 45th St
  206-297-4300
  Just like Target but with groceries too!
- **Full Tilt Ice Cream** · 5453 Leary Ave NW
  206-297-3000
  Ice cream, beer & pinball. Sweet.
- **Greener Lifestyles** · 5317 Ballard Ave NW
  206-545-4405
  Interesting, eco-friendly (re: expensive) goods. Appointment Only.
- **Hilliard's Taproom** · 1550 NW 49th St
  206-257-4486
  Taste the local craft beer that has become an instant classic.
- **Horseshoe** · 5344 Ballard Ave NW
  206-547-9639
  Lucky in shopping, unlucky in bank balances.
- **Jo Ann Fabrics** · 2217 NW 57th St
  206-782-6242
  Fabrics supplies and fun decorations at excellent prices.
- **NW Peaks Brewery** · 4912 17th Ave NW
  206-853-0525
  Limited-edition micro-brews inspired by the ice-cold Cascades.
- **Pink Ginger** · 5334 Ballard Ave NW
  206-285-2629
  Fashionable clothes for the ladies Mix-A-Lot sang about.
- **The RE Store** · 1440 NW 52nd St
  206-297-9119
  Funky reused building material and all the cheap knick-knacks you could possibly want.
- **Re-Soul** · 5319 Ballard Ave NW
  206-789-7312
  Where one goes to blow a paycheck on a pair of shoes.
- **Second Ascent** · 5209 Ballard Ave NW
  206-545-8810
  New and used sporting equipment.
- **Secret Garden Bookshop** · 2214 NW Market St
  206-789-5006
  Neighborhood indie with a great kid's section.
- **Sonic Boom Records** · 2209 NW Market St
  206-297-2666
  National and international acts perform free live sets at the Ballard location.
- **Space Oddity Vintage Furniture** ·
  5318 22nd Ave NW
  206-322-6704
  Ground control to major deals.
- **Sweet Mickey's** · 2230 NW 57th St
  206-402-6272
  Old fashioned sweets shop serving shakes, malts and candy rarities.
- **Trove Vintage Boutique** · 2202 NW Market St
  206-297-6068
  Treasures galore (if your treasure is dresses and 60s casserole dishes).
- **Vain** · 5401 Ballard Ave NW
  206-706-2707
  Hair. Shop. Art.
- **Velouria** · 2205 NW Market St
  206-788-0330
  Friendly boutique featuring indie designers.

Map 24 · **Fremont**

Map 24

Once a haven for counterculture in Seattle, Fremont has gentrified in recent years. Getty Images, Adobe, and Google all have offices near the ship canal and the famous naked cyclists of the Solstice Parade now bike past high-end boutiques. **Vladimir Lenin** still glowers in mute disdain over yuppies and hippies alike.

○ Landmarks

- **Archie McPhee** · 1300 N 45th St
  206-297-0240
  Legendary novelty toy shop filled with bacon and mustache-emblazoned items.
- **Aurora Bridge** · Aurora Ave N & N 34th St
  Affectionately known as "Suicide Bridge."
- **Fremont Rocket** · 601 N 35th St
  1950s rocket fuselage bearing the motto, "De Libertas Quirkas," or Freedom to Be Peculiar.
- **Fremont Troll** · N 36th St & Troll Ave N
  Monstrous public art, crushing a real VW.
- **Vladimir Lenin Statue** · 600 N 36th St
  The irony grows stronger with every new condo.
- **Waiting for the Interurban** ·
  Fremont Ave N & N 34th St
  The 1979 sculpture of commuters is the victim of frequent "art attacks" by locals.
- **Woodland Park Zoo** · 5500 Phinney Ave N
  206-548-2500
  Too much fun despite the cute animals behind bars.
- **Woodland Skatepark** · 5201 Green Lake Way N
  You know…for kids!

Coffee

- **Caffe Ladro** · 452 N 36th St
  206-675-0854
  Strong coffee for the strong coffee drinker.
- **Caffe Vita** · 4301 Fremont Ave N
  206-632-3535
  The best of the local chains.
- **Diva Espresso** · 4615 Stone Way N
  206-632-7019
  Local chain with unpredictable service. I guess it's kind of like ordering coffee from a diva.
- **ETG Coffee** · 3512 Fremont Pl N
  206-633-3685
  These people treat coffee like a fine wine. And you'll feel classier drinking it.
- **Fremont Coffee Company** · 459 N 36th St
  206-632-3633
  Fair trade roasters.
- **Lighthouse Roasters** · 400 N 43rd St
  206-634-3140
  Well-liked roasters' cafe.
- **Lucca Espresso** · 3623 Leary Way NW
  206-297-7752
  For coffee-addicted statuary enthusiasts.
- **Milstead & Co.** · 770 N 34th St
  206-659-4814
  Hipster coffee, but in the best possible way.

Map 24

Fremont

Nightlife

- **Backdoor at Roxy's** · 462 N 36th St
  206-632-7322
  Finally! A hipster speakeasy with an all-you-can-eat prime rib special.
- **The Barrel Thief** · 3417 Evanston Ave N
  206-402-5492
  Party like a grown-up with fancy wines, cocktails and truffle-infused snacks. Wine and beer tastings to boot.
- **Brimmer & Heeltap** · 425 NW Market St
  206-420-2534
  Honoring the memory of Le Gourmand by serving comparable food and keeping the sign.
- **Brouwer's Café** · 400 N 35th St
  206-267-2437
  Could double as an S&M dungeon; amazing selection of beer but the food is torture.
- **El Camino** · 607 N 35th St
  206-632-7303
  Mexican frou-frou with covered outdoor seating.
- **George & Dragon Pub** · 206 N 36th St
  206-545-6864
  They call it football here.
- **High Dive** · 513 N 36th St
  206-632-0212
  BBQ and bands.
- **LTD Bar & Grill** · 309 N 36th St
  206-632-7876
  Every sporting event on TV plus Golden Tee.
- **Nectar Lounge** · 412 N 36th St
  206-632-2020
  Good cheap happy hour pizza. Terrible piped-in music.
- **Norm's Eatery and Ale House** · 460 N 36th St
  206-547-1417
  Enjoy a beer with your dog after eating dinner elsewhere.
- **Pacific Inn Pub** · 3501 Stone Way N
  206-547-2967
  When you need a break from the Fremont yuppies.
- **Smash** · 1401 N 45th St
  206-547-3232
  Accessible wine bar operated by former sommelier; international list.
- **Woodsky's** · 303 N 36th St
  206-547-9662
  Ski lodge-themed bar.

Restaurants

- **Agrodolce** · 709 N 35th St
  206-547-9707 · $$$
  Maria Hines' inspired Italian food will make you anything but agro.
- **Art of the Table** · 1054 N 39th St
  206-282-0942 · $$$$
  A true culinary experience with harmonic pairings and intimate company. You won't forget it.
- **Bamboo Village** · 4900 Stone Way N
  206-632-8888 · $$
  With the addition of this Dim Sum place, this 'hood is finally complete.
- **The Barrel Thief** · 3417 Evanston Ave N
  206-402-5492 · $$
  Upscale bar bistro with a weekend waffle brunch and tons of local alcohol.
- **Bizzarro Italian Café** · 1307 N 46th St
  206-632-7277 · $$
  Tasty pasta dishes in a funky, yet intimate, setting.
- **Blue C Sushi** · 3411 Fremont Ave N
  206-633-3411 · $
  What's cooler than a selection of cheap sushi on a conveyer belt?
- **Blue Moon Burgers** · 703 N 34th St
  206-547-1907 · $
  Tremendous burgers that might make you fat, but certainly not blue.
- **Blue Star Café** · 4512 Stone Way N
  206-548-0345 · $$
  Stellar breakfast menu.
- **Brad's Swingside Café** · 4212 Fremont Ave N
  206-633-4057 · $$
  Very Seattle. Very Italian. Very NFT.
- **Brimmer & Heeltap** · 425 NW Market St
  206-420-2534 · $$$
  Honoring the memory of Le Gourmand by serving comparable food and keeping the sign.
- **Brouwer's Café** · 400 N 35th St
  206-267-2437 · $$
  Belgian cuisine and a staggering beer menu.
- **Chillies Paste** · 119 N 36th St
  206-633-1433 · $
  Delicious curries, wide noodle dishes, and a fantastic seafood soufflé.

Fremont

Map 24

Though it lacks quite a few practical amenities, Fremont has more cool shops than you have fingers and seemingly more Thai restaurants per capita than Bangkok. Rare and precious, however, are the meaty Cuban sandwiches at **Paseo** and the low-brow Britishness of the **George & Dragon**. Have a beer with the canine townies and the people who love them at dog-friendly **Norm's Eatery & Alehouse**.

- **Chiso** · 3520 Fremont Ave N
  206-632-3430 · $$$
  Sushi served up chic.
- **Dot's Delicatessen** · 4262 Fremont Ave N
  206-687-7446 · $$
  Local meats and cheeses that really hit the dot.
- **El Camino** · 607 N 35th St
  206-632-7303 · $$
  Flavorful Mexican food with patio dining. Few veg options.
- **Flair Taco** · 66 N 36th St
  206-356-2475 · $
  Feeding Fremont's drunk zombies till 4 am on weekends.
- **Homegrown Sustainable Sandwich Shop** ·
  3416 Fremont Ave N
  206-453-5232 · $
  Sustainable sandwich shop with killer updates of old favs.
- **Jai Thai** · 3423 Fremont Ave N
  206-632-7060 · $
  The curries are always kickin', and the happy hour menu is tops.
- **Joule** · 3506 Stone Way N
  206-632-5685 · $$$
  Inspired small plates pack a punch, fusing Korean spice with French precision.
- **Kidd Valley** · 4910 Greenlake Way N
  206-547-0121 · $
  Hey, at least they have veggie burgers.
- **Kwanjai Thai** · 469 N 36th St
  206-632-3656 · $
  Cheap, reliable, lightning-fast.
- **Mama's Brown Bags** · 770 N 34th St
  206-633-2247 · $$
  Let Mama bring the office lunch! Of course, you'll have to pay her…
- **Manolin** · 3621 Stone Way N
  206-294-3331 · $$$$
  Walrus & Carpenter peeps lavish you with lovingly prepared seafood.
- **Musashi's** · 1400 N 45th St
  206-633-0212 · $$
  Cozy up to the Japanese regulars and chow down on a bento box.

- **Paseo** · 4225 Fremont Ave N
  206-545-7440 · $
  Restaurant the size of a garage, and so is the pork sandwich. So damn good.
- **Pecado Bueno** · 4307 Fremont Ave N
  206-457-8837 · $
  Celebrating the naughtiness of good Mexican food and tequila.
- **Pel'Meni** · 3516 Fremont Pl N
  206-588-2570 · $
  In Center of Universe, Russian Dumplings eat you.
- **Perche No Pasta & Vino** · 1319 N 49th St
  206-547-0222 · $
  Housemade pasta (!); high on faux brick and friendliness.
- **Pie** · 3515 Fremont Ave N
  206-436-8590 · $
  Pie till 2am on weekends! Like that dream you had, without the mama issues.
- **pomerol** · 127 N 36th St
  206-632-0135 · $$$$
  French cuisine that even Snobby McSnobberson would love.
- **Qazis Indian Curry House** · 473 N 36th St
  206-632-3575 · $$
  All-you-can eat lunch buffet! Trust me, you can eat a lot of this stuff.
- **Red Door** · 3401 Evanston Ave N
  206-547-7521 · $
  A better class of pub grub.
- **Restaurant Roux** · 4201 Fremont Ave N
  206-547-5420 · $$
  Let the good times (and excellent food) roll at Where Ya At Matt's highly anticipated brick n' mortar joint.
- **Revel** · 403 N 36th St
  206-547-2040 · $$
  All the mindblowingness of a food truck without the pesky traveling.
- **RockCreek Seafood & Spirits** · 4300 Fremont Ave N
  206-557-7532 · $$$
  Ex-Toulouse Petit chef nails it with this daring local/import seafood hybrid.

Map 24

Fremont

- **Rocking Wok** · 4301 Interlake Ave N
  206-545-4878 · $
  Not the prettiest place to look at, but the bargain-priced dim sum is true Taiwanese.
- **RoRo BBQ & Grill** · 3620 Stone Way N
  206-954-1100 · $$
  A dozen ways to eat BBQd meat, including piled into a bowl.
- **Roxy's Diner** · 462 N 36th St
  206-632-3963 · $
  As close to Katz's as Seattle's going to get. The best is the pastrami on rye.
- **Royal Grinders** · 3526 Fremont Pl N
  206-545-7560 · $
  Giving your belly the royal treatment whether or not you eat meat.
- **Silence-Heart-Nest** · 3508 Fremont Pl N
  206-633-5169 · $
  Delectable vegetarian dishes made with love by Sri Chinmoy devotees.
- **Simply Desserts** · 3421 Fremont Ave N
  206-633-2671 · $
  Simply the best chocolate cake. Anywhere.
- **Sinbad Express** · 3526 Fremont Pl N
  206-632-7426 · $
  Cheap middle-eastern grub to keep you sated on "high" seas.
- **Smash** · 1401 N 45th St
  206-547-3232 · $$
  Accessible wine bar operated by former sommelier; international list.
- **Solsticio** · 1100 N Northlake Way
  206-547-0404 · $
  Nice atmosphere and extensive menu. for a coffee shop.
- **Tacos Guaymas** · 100 N 36th St
  206-547-5110 · $
  Delicious tacos of all kinds including braaaaiiiins for your zombie friends.
- **Tilth** · 1411 N 45th St
  206-633-0801 · $$$
  The definition of seasonal, organic, local cooking. And it's delicious to boot.

- **Trattoria Roma** · 4705 Aurora Ave N
  206-547-9992 · $$
  Pizza place that does better with the sides than the pizza.
- **Tutta Bella Neopolitan Pizzeria** ·
  4411 Stone Way N
  206-633-3800 · $$
  Their pizza has been certified by the Italian government. 'Nuff said.
- **Uneeda Burger** · 4302 Fremont Ave N
  206-547-2600 · $$
  Ted Nugent's dream upscale burger joint.
- **Vif** · 4401 Fremont Ave N
  206-557-7357 · $
  Locally-conscious cafe and wine bar with an Sea-town-tastic organic menu.
- **Zaw** · 4612 Stone Way N
  206-297-1334 · $$
  It's not delivery. It's artisan take-and-bake.

Shopping

- **Alphabet Soup** · 1406 N 45th St
  206-547-4555
  Fun children's bookstore; limited hours so check before going.
- **Archie McPhee** · 1300 N 45th St
  206-297-0240
  For all your potato gun and monster finger puppet needs.
- **B. Brown & Associates** · 3534 Stone Way N
  206-634-1481
  Used and rare books.
- **Bliss** · 3501 Fremont Ave N
  206-632-6695
  Small clothing boutique with designer duds mixed in.
- **Bluebird Ice Cream** · 3515 Fremont Ave N
  206-588-1079
  Beer ice cream? Yes you can.

Get your pastrami fix at **Roxy's Diner**; it's as close to Katz's as Seattle's going to get. On the other end of the spectrum, Maria Hines' **Agrodolce** and **Tilth** both make for destination dining. Meanwhile, **Chiso** takes sushi for a spin in a hip, modern setting. And what started out as a weekend supper club has grown into a hospitable and unforgettable celebration of food at **Art of the Table**.

- **Book Larder** · 4252 Fremont Ave N
  206-397-4271
  Specialty cookbook store for Top Chefing it in your home kitchen.
- **Destee Nation Shirt Co.** · 3412 Evanston Ave N
  206-632-7874
  T-shirts emblazoned with logos of local bars and record shops.
- **Flying Apron Bakery** · 3510 Fremont Ave N
  206-442-1115
  Vegan, gluten-free, wheat-free, funny-tasting bakery.
- **Fremont Sunday Street Market** ·
  Phinney Ave N & N 34th St
  206-781-6776
  The world's most fabulously bizarre bazaar.
- **Fremont Vintage Mall** · 3419 Fremont Pl N
  206-329-4460
  Huge antique store where you're sure to find your next favorite piece.
- **Fusion Beads** · 3830 Stone Way N
  206-782-4595
  A well-organized bead store that also offers classes.
- **Hashtag Recreational Cannabis** ·
  3540 Stone Way N
  206-946-8157
  All about providing the 411 for your 420.
- **The Indoor Sun Shoppe** · 160 N Canal St
  206-634-3727
  When you don't have a garden, they'll help you create one, inside.
- **Jive Time Records** · 3506 Fremont Ave N
  206-632-5483
  Rare vinyl, used CDs, 99Â¢ bins.
- **Les Amis** · 3420 Evanston Ave N
  206-632-2877
  Out-of-this-world clothes at astronomical prices.
- **Marketime Foods** · 4416 Fremont Ave N
  206-632-8958
  The TARDIS of convenience stores. It's bigger on the inside!

- **Mishu Boutique** · 465 N 36th St
  206-802-8022
  Unique, affordable clothing made by folks in Asia who get lunch breaks.
- **Not a Number Cards & Gifts** · 720 N 35th St
  206-784-0965
  Fun, random stuff you never knew you needed.
- **Ophelia's Books** · 3504 Fremont Ave N
  206-632-3759
  Large collection of books for the non cat allergic.
- **PCC Natural Markets** · 600 N 34th St
  206-632-6811
  One-stop shopping for overpriced organic groceries.
- **Piece of Mind** · 315 N 36th St
  206-675-0637
  It's a water pipe…for tobacco.
- **Portage Bay Goods** · 621 N 35th St
  206-547-5221
  Eclectic gifts for babies, children, and adults in a range of prices.
- **Rudy's Barbershop** · 475 N 36th St
  206-547-0818
  Absolute best cheap haircut!
- **Sea Ocean Book Berth** · 3534 Stone Way N
  206-675-9020
  Used and rare maritime books.
- **Show Pony** · 702 N 35th St
  206-706-4188
  Pretty things for your pony. Or, you know, yourself.
- **Theo Chocolate** · 3400 Phinney Ave N
  206-632-5100
  Delicious free-trade, organic chocolate, without the ramped up price.
- **Vintage Angel Company** · 3519 Fremont Pl N
  206-499-1811
  Your childhood is considered vintage now, so you may as well get used to it.

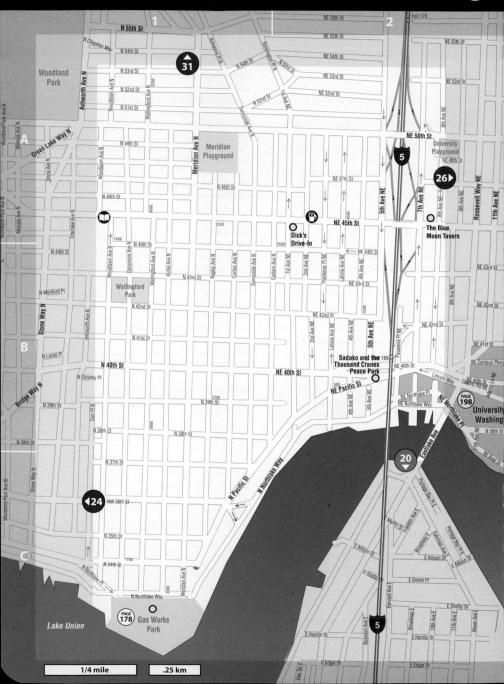

Map 25 · **Wallingford**

Map 25

Thanks to the enormous sign atop the local QFC supermarket (a nod to the old Food Giant sign), visitors know when they reach Wallingford. With Woodland Park and Green Lake to the north and **Gas Works Park** to the south, the neighborhood has a Sunday afternoon vibe all week long. This somewhat sleepy residential neighborhood hosts multiple summer food festivals and is home to the original **Dick's Drive-In**.

○ Landmarks

- **Blue Moon Tavern** • 712 NE 45th St
  206-675-9116
  Countless artistic luminaries have passed out there.
- **Dick's Drive-In** • 111 NE 45th St
  206-632-5125
  A little bit nostalgia, a little bit cholesterol.
- **Gas Works Park** • 2101 N Northlake Way
  206-684-4075
  Industrial site turned America's strangest park. Amazing view.
- **Sadako and the Thousand Cranes Peace Park** • NE 40th St & NE Pacific St
  A tribute to a young girl that died of leukemia after the atomic bombing of Nagasaki.

🖵 Coffee

- **Caffe Appassionato** • 1218 N 45th St
  206-549-9149
  Classic Seattle coffee shop vibe at this small-ish local chain. Frasier would love it here.
- **Chocolati Cafe** • 1716 N 45th St
  206-633-7765
  Coffee, yes. But it's really more about the chocolate.
- **Fuel** • 1705 N 45th St
  206-634-2700
  Now this is a type of fuel that actually has a future.
- **Mosaic Coffeehouse** • 4401 2nd Ave NE
  206-369-0326
  Community coffee shop with a pay-what-you-can business model and an amazing indoor playground.
- **Palazzo** • 1906 N 34th St
  206-634-0922
  Plus baked goods.
- **Seattle Espresso** • 4405 Wallingford Ave N
  206-632-7178
  Fortunately, they put a lot more effort into their coffee than they did their name.
- **Teahouse Kuan Yin** • 1911 N 45th St
  206-632-2055
  Bulk tea plus cafe.
- **Uptown Espresso** • 2300 N 45th St
  206-812-0404
  Self-proclaimed "Home of the Velvet Foam" but the coffee underneath is just so-so.

🍸 Nightlife

- **Al's Tavern** • 2303 N 45th St
  206-545-9959
  Divey and lovable.
- **Blue Moon Tavern** • 712 NE 45th St
  206-675-9116
  Kerouac, Roethke, and other artists have fallen over drunk here.
- **The Grizzled Wizard** • 2317 N 45th St
  206-395-4749
  At last, a place for the cool gothy gamer geeks.
- **The Iron Bull** • 2121 N 45th St
  206-453-3901
  The place to get your sports on in Wallingford.
- **Kate's Pub** • 309 N 45th St
  206-547-6832
  Hidden gem. Specials and games galore. Easy on the Jaeger.
- **May Restaurant and Lounge** • 1612 N 45th St
  206-675-0037
  Pricey but delicious Thai bar food served late and sluggishly.
- **Moon Temple** • 2108 N 45th St
  206-633-4280
  Everyone loves stiff drinks.
- **Murphy's Pub** • 1928 N 45th St
  206-634-2110
  Drinks for Hibernians.

Map 25

Wallingford

Restaurants

- **Boulangerie** • 2200 N 45th St
206-634-2211 • $
Even a Frenchman would admit les croissants sont authentiques.
- **Chocolati Cafe** • 1716 N 45th St
206-633-7765 • $$
You haven't lived till you've eaten a chocolate-covered potato chip.
- **Chutney's Bistro** • 1815 N 45th St
206-634-1000 • $$
Curry cuts across the socioeconimc divide.
- **Dick's Drive-In** • 111 NE 45th St
206-632-5125 • $
A local obsession, specializing in cheap burgers and shakes. Perfect at 1 am.
- **Djan's Modern Thai Restaurant** • 264 NE 45th St
206-633-3526 • $$
Solid Thai delivery.
- **The Essential Baking Company** • 1604 N 34th St
206-545-0444 • $
You'll think you're in a European bakery.
- **Fainting Goat Gelato** • 1903 N 45th St
206-327-9459 • $
Don't tell the Italians, but the Turks can make a damn good gelato.
- **Irwin's Neighborhood Bakery & Cafe** •
2123 N 40th St
206-675-1484 • $$
Quaint cafe with great pastries and a carb-heavy lunch menu.
- **Ivar's Salmon House** • 401 NE Northlake Way
206-632-0767 • $$
It's all about the chowdah at this Seattle seafood institution.
- **Julia's** • 4401 Wallingford Ave N
206-633-1175 • $$
Quirky space, awesome breakfast. And your mom will like it, too.
- **Kabul Afghan Cuisine** • 2301 N 45th St
206-545-9000 • $$
Warm family setting with a traditional Afghan menu.
- **May Restaurant and Lounge** • 1612 N 45th St
206-675-0037 • $$
Refreshing, subtly balanced Thai dishes that are utterly devoid of ketchup.

- **Miyabi 45th** • 2208 N 45th St
206-632-4545 • $$$
A soba restaurant you can take your date to without looking cheap.
- **Molly Moon's** • 1622 N 45th St
206-547-5105 • $
Fresh, local, sustainably organic ice cream—down to the dairy and the compostable dishes.
- **Pinky's Kitchen** • 210 NE 45th St
206-257-5483 • $
Bravo for a late-night BBQ truck (with veggie options).
- **Rancho Bravo Tacos** • 211 NE 45th St
206-830-2657 • $
Mexican served out of a silver trailer. Locals are fanatical for the tacos.
- **Satay** • 1711 N 45th St
206-547-0597 • $
Simple menu. Complex food.
- **Shima** • 4429 Wallingford Ave N
206-632-2583 • $$
Classically trained sushi chef serves it up, Hawaiia style.
- **Sutra** • 1605 N 45th St
206-547-1348 • $$$$
High-end prix-fixe vegetarian.
- **Tiny Ninja Cafe** • 3510 Stone Way N
206-632-0647 • $
Named after the shop's mascot: a diminutive woo ninja who apparently likes live music.
- **TNT Taqueria** • 2114 N 45th St
206-322-0124 • $
Dino-mite tacos made from local, happy farm animals. Plus churros for breakfast!
- **Varsity Inn** • 1801 N 34th St
206-547-2161 • $
Friendly, unassuming diner that becomes a delicious taco place by night.
- **Westward** • 2501 N Northlake Way
206-552-8215 • $$$
Go Westward. There is seafood there. In the open air. A lakeside view for me and you.
- **The Whale Wins** • 3506 Stone Way N
206-632-9425 • $$
A great addition to Seattle's slow food movement

While Wallingford's portion of 45th Street isn't much of a weekend destination, there are more than enough bars, restaurants, and cafes to make a night of it. **Miyabi 45th** is a fine-dining soba noodle house. **Al's** is our favorite little hole in the wall. Happily spend your entire paycheck at **Bottleworks**-- the beer selection is incredible. Or fill your backpack at **Wide World of Books & Maps**, a Seattle institution since the '70s.

Shopping

- **Art of Confections** • 2323 N 45th St
206-633-9984
Amazing cake sculptures that taste as good as they look.
- **Bottleworks** • 1710 N 45th St
206-633-2437
The world's finest beers ripe for the six-packing.
- **Bootyland** • 1815 N 45th St
206-328-0636
Because your baby really needs a Ramones t-shirt.
- **Comics Dungeon** • 319 NE 45th St
206-545-8373
Preventing geeks from getting girlfriends since the early '90s!
- **The Erotic Bakery** • 2323 N 45th St
206-545-6969
What a lovely flower cake…er…oh MY!
- **Fainting Goat Gelato** • 1903 N 45th St
206-327-9459
Don't tell the Italians, but the Turks can make a damn good gelato.
- **Golden Oldies Records Tapes & CDs** •
201 NE 45th St
206-547-2260
45s like mad and 99 cent CDs.
- **Hawaii General Store** • 258 NE 45th St
206-633-5233
For all your next luau needs.
- **I Do Bridal** • 2206 N 45th St
206-633-7926
Small bridal shop with a broad range of dress sizes and prices.

- **Molly Moon's** • 1622 N 45th St
206-547-5105
Fresh, local, sustainably organic ice cream—down to the dairy and the compostable dishes.
- **Open Books: A Poem Emporium** • 2414 N 45th St
206-633-0811
One of the few poetry-only bookstores in the nation.
- **Sugar on Top Salon** • 1601 N 45th St
206-427-9377
You'll be pretty pleased.
- **Trophy Cupcakes** • 1815 N 45th St
206-632-7020
The perfect combo: cute & tasty.
- **Wide World Books & Maps** •
4411 Wallingford Ave N
206-634-3453
The nation's first travel-only bookstore is now 30 years old.
- **Wine World and Spirits** • 400 NE 45th St
206-402-6086
Show me more, spirits!
- **Yogurtland** • 2320 N 45th St
206-634-2900
Rule over your own froyo fairy tale with endless flavor/topping combos.

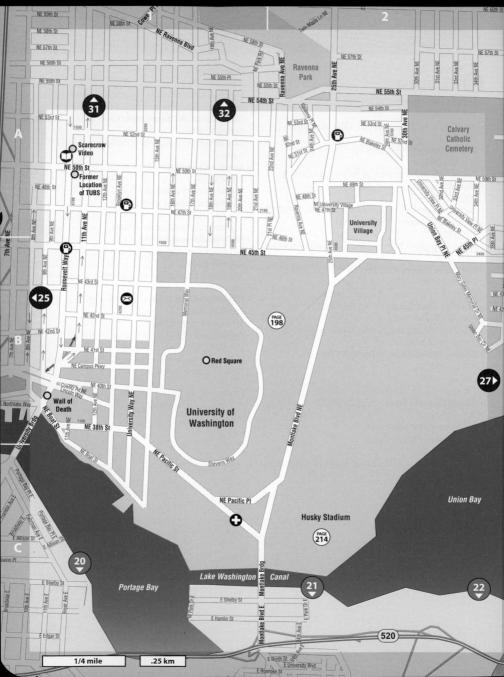

Map 26 · U District

2

NE 60th St
NE 59th St
NE 58th St
NE 58th St
NE 57th St
NE 56th St
NE 55th St

Cowe Pl
NE Ravenna Blvd
18th Ave NE
NE 58th St
Park Rd
NE 55th St
55th Pl

Ravenna Ave NE
25th Ave NE
30th Ave NE
31st Ave NE
33rd Ave NE
34th Ave NE

NE 60th St
NE 57th St
NE 55th St

Ravenna Park

NE 57th St

NE 54th St

31

NE 53rd St

32

1000

NE 52nd St
15th Ave NE

NE 53rd Pl
NE 52nd Ave NE
24th Ave NE
NE 51st St

NE 54th St
NE 53rd St
NE Blakeley St
NE 52nd St

Federal Ave NE
30th Ave NE

Calvary
Catholic
Cemetery

Scarecrow
Video

NE 50th St

Former
Location
of TUBS

NE 48th St

4700

8th Ave NE
9th Ave NE
11th Ave NE
12th Ave NE
Brooklyn Ave NE
15th Ave NE
16th Ave NE
17th Ave NE
18th Ave NE
19th Ave NE
20th Ave NE
21st Ave NE

NE 50th St
NE 47th St

1500

2100
4500

22nd Ave NE
21st Ave NE
NE 46th St
NE 45th St

25th Ave NE

NE 49th St
NE University Village
NE 47th St

University
Village

University View Pl NE
NE University View Pl NE
32nd Ave NE
33rd Ave NE
34th Ave NE
35th Ave NE

NE 50th St
NE Blakeley St

Union Bay Pl NE
NE 45th Pl

3400

◄25

7th Ave NE
8th Ave NE
9th Ave NE
Roosevelt Way NE

NE 43rd St

4200

4500

NE 42nd St

Memorial Way

NE 45th St

PAGE
198

Mary Gates Memorial Dr NE

NE 42nd

Union Bay Pl NE

NE 41st St

B

NE 42nd St

○ Red Square

27►

Cowlitz Rd NE
Lincoln Way
NE 40th St

NE Campus Pkwy

University Way NE

Montlake Blvd NE

NE 38th St

12th Ave NE

○ Wall of
Death

1100

University of
Washington

NE Boat St

University Brdg

11th Ave NE

NE Boat St

NE Pacific St

Stevens Way

Union Bay

NE Pacific Pl

C

Portage Bay Pl E
Franklin Ave E
Fairman Ave E
Broadway E
Brooklyn E

Northlake Way

E Allison St
E Allison St

○ ✚

Husky Stadium

PAGE
214

20

21

22

E Shelby St

Broadway E
10th Ave E
11th Ave E
Boyer Ave E

Montlake Blvd E

Lake Washington Canal

Portage Bay

N Park Dr E
NE Park Dr

Gwinn Pl

Franklin E

E Edgar St

E Shelby St

E Hamlin St

24th Ave E

520

1/4 mile   .25 km

E North St
E University Blvd
E Roanoke St

U-Dub boasts an impeccable reputation as a bastion of higher learning—after all, Bruce Lee once studied here. The campus is as charming as enrollment brochures suggest, but the surrounding area is an unlikely collision of thug-lifers, rah-rah collegiate types, meth-damaged street hustlers, and stubborn eccentrics. The U District has been designated an "alcohol impact zone," banning certain types of beverages from package stores, so plan ahead if you need some fortified wine for a sorority party.

○ Landmarks

- **Former Location of TUBS** •
  4750 Roosevelt Way NE
  Who knew bathing could be so dirty?
- **Husky Stadium** • 3800 Montlake Blvd NE
  206-543-2210
  Loud, picturesque home of Husky football.
- **Red Square** • NE Pacific St
  Home of the Barnett Newman's sculpture, *Broken Obelisk*.
- **Scarecrow Video** • 5030 Roosevelt Way NE
  206-524-8554
  Best video store in the universe.
- **University of Washington** •
  1410 NE Campus Parkway
  206-543-2100
  Beautiful campus, with dramatic views of Mt. Rainier.
- **Wall of Death** • Burke Gilman Trail Under the University Bridge
  A tribute to the carnival motor domes of the early 20th century.

Coffee

- **Burke Museum Cafe** • NE 45th St & 17th Ave NE
  206-543-9854
  Nimble, young coed pick-up bar, er, cafe.
- **Café Allegro** • 4214 University Way NE
  206-633-3030
  Since 1975.
- **Café on the Ave** • 4201 University Way NE
  206-632-6001
  Serving Caffé Vita; lunch and dinner options.
- **Oasis Tea Zone** • 4508 University Way NE
  206-547-9967
  Bubble tea and other Asian junk food. In other words, delicious.
- **Sureshot Cafe** • 4505 University Way NE
  206-632-3100
  Vegan pastries and paninis accompany competent beverages.
- **Trabant Coffee & Chai** • 1309 NE 45th St
  206-675-0668
  Dude. This chai rocks.
- **VHSpresso** • 5030 Roosevelt Way NE
  206-524-8554
  Enjoy a fresh cup of coffee whilst perusing the dusty film selection of Scarecrow Video.
- **Yunnie Bubble Tea** • 4511 University Way NE
  206-547-9648
  Bubble tea on the Ave.

Map 26

33 34
29 30 31 32
27
23
24 25 26
12 13
20 21 22

U District

🍸 Nightlife

- **Big Time Brewery & Alehouse** •
  4133 University Way NE
  206-545-4509
  Laid back college pub for a brew and a slice of pizza.
- **College Inn Pub** • 4006 University Way NE
  206-634-2307
  Best thing about the College Inn: You get older, they stay the same age.
- **Dante's** • 5300 Roosevelt Way NE
  206-525-1300
  Seattle's only Satanic college-themed sports bar.
- **The District** • 4507 Brooklyn Ave NE
  206-634-2000
  Great for a romantic date. Especially if you aren't the one paying.
- **Earl's on the Ave** • 4333 University Way NE
  206-535-4493
  Pints of liquor at closeout prices. Don't make any plans after that.
- **Finn MacCool's** • 4217 University Way NE
  206-675-0885
  Great if you like hanging with loud co-eds. Awful if you don't.
- **Flowers Bar & Restaurant** •
  4247 University Way NE
  206-633-1903
  Vegetarian buffet by day, laid back bar by night.
- **The Kraken Bar & Lounge** •
  5257 University Way NE
  206-522-5334
  Let loose at the Kraken. You'll be glad you did.
- **Monkey Pub** • 5305 Roosevelt Way NE
  206-523-6457
  Frat-free oasis in U District.
- **Neptune Theatre** • 1303 NE 45th St
  206-781-5755
  Indie concerts and comedy shows in a theater worthy of the gods.

🍴 Restaurants

- **50 North** • 5001 25th Ave NE
  206-397-3939 • $$
  Vashon's Hardware Store brings its delicious island secret to the big city.
- **Agua Verde** • 1303 NE Boat St
  206-545-8570 • $$
  Eat authentic Baja-style Mexican cuisine. Then rent a kayak.
- **Aladdin Falafel Corner** • 4541 University Way NE
  206-548-9539 • $
  Perfect for those times when you're too drunk to stumble the extra 2 blocks to Aladdin Gyro-Cery.
- **Aladdin Gyro-Cery** • 4541 University Way NE
  206-632-5253 • $
  Best falafel on the Ave. Standing room only.
- **Araya's Vegetarian Place** •
  5420 University Way NE
  206-524-4332 • $$
  We can't believe it's not meat.
- **Blue C Sushi** • 4601 26th Ave NE
  206-525-4601 • $
  Enjoy the same fast sushi as the Fremont location, but with yuppies.
- **Burger & Kabob Hut** • 4142 University Way NE
  206-632-0324 • $
  A good place to stumble into for onion rings after the bars kick you out.
- **Burke Museum Cafe** • NE 45th St & 17th Ave NE
  206-543-9854 • $
  Nimble, young coed pick-up bar, er, cafe.
- **Cafe Solstice** • 4116 University Way NE
  206-675-0850 • $
  Overrun with students but worth getting food to go.
- **Cedars on Brooklyn** • 4759 Brooklyn Ave NE
  206-527-4000 • $$
  Indian food that's naan-stop delicious. Plus, a nice view of the Safeway parking lot.
- **Chaco Canyon Organic Café** • 4757 12th Ave NE
  206-522-6966 • $
  An amazing voyage into the raw-food universe; the mocha shakes rock!

Kai's makes the best Manhattan in the city, but for serious drinking, head over to Earl's, that place with the black facade and chicken wire instead of windows; during their happy hour, a PINT of well booze is unconsciously cheap. The Kraken Bar & Lounge is very metal, very dirty and your best bet on the Ave for avoiding students. Also try the karaoke at Monkey Pub, a beloved dive with the gritty, punk rock vibe.

- **China Village** • 3224 NE 45th St
206-523-0772 • $$
Above average. Don't let the stock Chinese
Restaurant name fool you.
- **Coffee Drop Cafe** • 4915 25th Ave NE
206-525-5442 • $
Neighborhood coffee goodness. Have a drop of
sandwich while you're at it.
- **Delfino's Chicago Style Pizzeria** •
2631 NE University Village St
206-522-3466 • $$
You may have to wait, but the thickly gooey
Chicago-style 'zas are worth it.
- **Flowers Bar & Restaurant** •
4247 University Way NE
206-633-1903 • $$
Mediterranean veggie buffet may be the best
lunch deal in Seattle.
- **Guanaco's Tacos Pupuseria** •
4106 Brooklyn Ave NE
206-547-2369 • $
There's nothing funny about a good pupuseria.
- **Jimmy John's** • 4141 University Way NE
206-548-9500 • $
Fast sandwiches that can be delivered within the
U District.
- **Kai's Bistro & Lounge** • 1312 NE 43rd St
206-547-2784 • $
Side-street bistro with quality cocktails and great
happy hour.
- **Memo's Mexican Food** • 4743 University Way NE
206-729-5071 • $
If a 24-hour Taco Bell had real Mexican names for
food.
- **Morsel** • 4754 University Way NE
206-268-0154 • $
Picking up where the beloved Nook left off with
genius biscuit dishes and perfect espresso.
- **Orange King** • 1411 NE 42nd St
206-632-1331 • $
A UW student's wet dream. Burgers and teriyaki
under one roof.

- **Pagliacci Pizza** • 4529 University Way NE
206-726-1717 • $
Local favorite pizza chain makes crispy-chewy
delights with seasonal ingredients.
- **Pam's Kitchen** • 5000 University Way NE
206-696-7010 • $
A taste of the Caribbean arrives on The Ave.
- **Pasta & Co** • 4622 26th Ave NE
206-523-8594 • $$
One-stop gourmet chain has fresh bread, wine,
and risotto cakes to go.
- **Pho Thân Brothers'** • 4207 University Way NE
206-632-7272 • $
Cheap, fast, and filling, with a free cream puff to
boot.
- **Pho Vietnam** • 4235 University Way NE
206-547-1709 • $
Lots of love for the noodle soup here, pho good
reason.
- **Pizza Ragazzi** • 5201 University Way NE
206-525-1700 • $
At 4 am, who cares what the pizza tastes like?
- **Portage Bay Café** • 4130 Roosevelt Way NE
206-547-8230 • $$
Local organic breakfasts and lunches.
- **Ristorante Doria** • 4759 Roosevelt Way NE
206-466-2380 • $$
A little bit of Italy in the U.D. Stuff yourself silly and
regret nothing.
- **Samurai Noodle** • 4138 University Way NE
206-547-1774 • $
Top notch Top Ramen.
- **Shultzy's Sausage** • 4114 University Way NE
206-548-9461 • $
Purveyors of fine encased meats, plus a great beer
menu.
- **Starlife on the Oasis Cafe** • 1405 NE 50th St
206-729-3542 • $
A cozy oasis for the long lap-top lunch.
- **Tandoor Indian Restaurant** •
5024 University Way NE
206-523-7477 • $
Consistently excellent, and the best pakora $2.50
can buy.

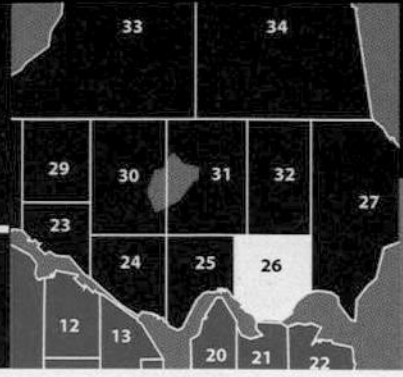

Map 26

U District

- **Tea Republik** • 4527 University Way NE
206-745-2310 • $
More tea than you can shake a stik at.
- **Thai 65** • 4214 University Way NE
206-632-6542 • $
Another of the U District Thai favorites. Lots of seating.
- **Thai Tom** • 4543 University Way NE
206-548-9548 • $
Come for the best open kitchen show in Seattle. Always busy.
- **Thaiger Room** • 4228 University Way NE
206-632-9299 • $
If by Thaigers they mean cockroaches.
- **Ugly Mug Cafe** • 1309 NE 43rd St
206-547-3219 • $
"Ugly" is an ironic name. Oh, and the sandwiches aren't bad either.
- **Veggie Grill** • 2681 NE University Village St
206-523-1961 • $$
Santa Monica-based chain offers up the ultimate in vegetarian comfort food.
- **Village Sushi** • 4741 12th Ave NE
206-985-6870 • $$
Amazing sushi, funky jazz, and weird paintings.
- **Wing Central** • 4524 University Way NE
206-634-9464 • $
Ellensburg's beloved college wing joint goes to the Dawgs.

🛍 Shopping

- **American Apparel** • 4345 University Way NE
206-547-0399
Non-sweatshop basics.
- **Anthropologie** • 2520 NE University Village St
206-985-2101
Higher end clothing and home accessories.
- **Buffalo Exchange** • 4530 University Way NE
206-545-0175
Second-hand clothes for girls who drink Zima.
- **Bulldog News** • 4208 University Way NE
206-632-6397
Pick up a copy of *Obscure French Cinema Monthly* and *People* simultaneously.
- **Cinema Books** • 4753 Roosevelt Way NE
206-547-7667
Reel literature.
- **The Confectionary** • 4608 26th Ave NE
206-523-1443
If this place doesn't make you happy, you have no soul.
- **Crossroads Trading Co.** • 4300 University Way NE
206-632-3111
Vintage. Cheap.
- **The Dreaming** • 5226 University Way NE
206-525-9394
Comics, graphic novels, role playing games.
- **Fireworks** • 2617 NE Village Ln
206-527-2858
Eclectic gift shop.

Thai food reigns supreme, with seemingly dozens of joints on every block varying wildly in quality and price. **Thai Tom** is worth the long wait for a seat, but check out the slightly less delicious **Thai 65** if you're in a hurry. **Memo's** slings burritos 24/7. **Pho Thàn Brothers'** namesake soup blows away the copious competition. **Village Sushi** and **Blue C Sushi** are both dependable—the latter even features one of those silly-but-fun conveyor belt systems.

- **Full Tilt Ice Cream** • 4759 Brooklyn Ave NE
206-524-4406
No pinball or beer at this half-tilt location. But still ice cream!
- **Gargoyles Statuary** • 4550 University Way NE
206-632-4940
For all your gothic, home decorating needs.
- **Half Price Books** • 4709 Roosevelt Way NE
206-547-7859
Books, music, video, magazines.
- **Hardwick's** • 4214 Roosevelt Way NE
206-632-1203
An adventure in hardware.
- **Lucky Vintage** • 4742 University Way NE
206-523-6621
Come in looking like Hilary Clinton, leave like Bettie Page.
- **Magus Books** • 1408 NE 42nd St
206-633-1800
Used bookstore with a friendly, helpful, and knowledgeable staff.
- **Menchie's** • 4609 Village Court NE
206-525-4445
Serving approximated candy bars & cheesecake for housewives by the pound.
- **Recycled Cycles** • 1007 NE Boat St
206-547-4491
Comprehensive bike store specializing in used and DIY bikes.
- **Red Light Vintage Clothing** •
4560 University Way NE
206-545-4044
Vintage clothing for people with 10-inch waists.
- **Rudy's Barbershop** • 4738 University Way NE
206-527-5267
Absolute best cheap haircut!

- **Scarecrow Video** • 5030 Roosevelt Way NE
206-524-8554
Best video store in Seattle? No, best in the world.
- **Sephora** • 2618 NE University Village St
206-526-9110
All the make-up you can dream-up in one store.
- **Shiga's Imports** • 4306 University Way NE
206-633-2400
Decorate your dorm room like an opium den.
- **Something Silver** • 4628 Village Ct NE
206-523-7545
Unique silver jewelry.
- **Trophy Cupcakes** • 2612 Village Ln
206-632-7020
The perfect combo: cute & tasty.
- **University Book Store** • 4326 University Way NE
206-634-3400
Huge bookstore and gift shop. Don't go there the first week of any quarter.
- **University Village** • 2623 NE University Village St
206-523-0622
What the rich housewives do with their husband's money.
- **Valley of Roses** • 4748 University Wy NE
206-522-6887
You don't need a lot of green to shop in this valley.
- **Weaving Works, Inc** • 4717 Brooklyn Ave NE
206-524-1221
Complete explosion of colors and textures, skilled advice for Seattle's needleworkers.
- **The Woolly Mammoth** • 4303 University Way NE
206-632-3254
Sensible shoes for the masses.
- **Yogurtland** • 4334 University Way NE
206-547-2900
Rule over your own froyo fairy tale with endless flavor/topping combos.

Map 27 • **Laurelhurst / Wedgwood / Sand Point** Ⓝ

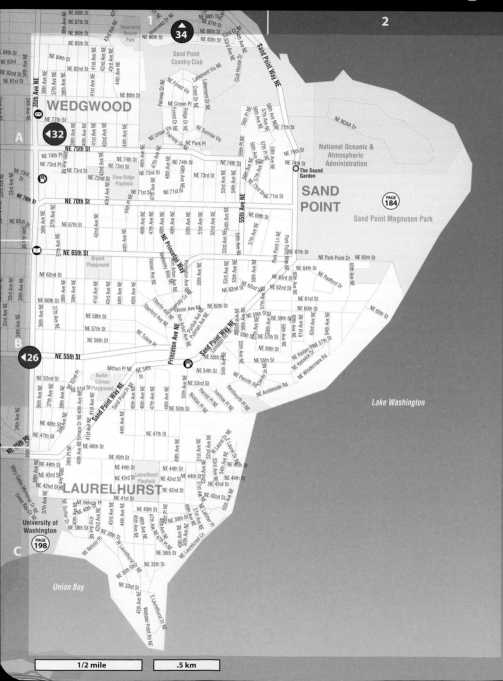

Map 27

The half-dozen 'hoods northeast of UW make up "Seattle's First Suburb": a nice, quiet family-friendly place. UW profs settle here, and the neighborhood is home to one of Seattle's largest Jewish communities. The area is residential, but for nature enthusiasts, **Magnuson Park** offers a universe of entertainment.

Landmarks

• **Sound Garden** • 7400 Sand Point Way NE
Sonorous art installation from which a certain grunge band lifted its name.
• **Warren G. Magnuson Park** •
7400 Sand Point Way NE
206-684-4946
50-acre former military installation turned fantastic public park.

Coffee

• **Cafe Javasti** • 8617 35th Ave NE
206-204-0255
It's all about the crepes.
• **Coffee Crew** • 3614 NE 45th St
206-525-2883
Solid morning option.
• **Gretchen's Place** • 5432 Sand Point Way NE
206-403-1426
Brewing Caffé Vita beans.
• **Van Gogh Coffeehouse** • 8210 35th Ave NE
206-523-1466
Unmatched coffee and customer service from cutie pies.

Nightlife

• **Wedgwood Alehouse** • 8515 35th Ave NE
206-527-2676
Everyone who frequents this place went to high school together.

Restaurants

• **Black Pearl** • 7347 35th Ave NE
206-526-5115 • $$
Great housemade noodles and noticeably ungreasy food.
• **Cafe Javasti** • 8617 35th Ave NE
206-204-0255 • $
It's all about the crepes.
• **Jak's Grill** • 3701 NE 45th St
206-985-8545 • $$$$
Best place for a classy, meaty, potatoey night out.
• **Top Pot Doughnuts** • 6855 35th Ave NE
206-525-1966 • $
Top Pot is tops!
• **Wedgwood Broiler** • 8230 35th Ave NE
206-523-1115 • $$$
Classic dining: Steaks, martinis, and captain's chairs.
• **Zaw** • 7320 35th Ave NE
206-658-2929 • $$
It's not delivery. It's artisan take-and-bake.

Shopping

• **City People's Mercantile** •
5440 Sand Point Way NE
206-524-1200
Yes, you too can have flowers blooming and veggies growing year round in Seattle.
• **Metropolitan Market** • 5250 40th Ave NE
206-938-6600
High end groceries, high end prices.
• **PCC Natural Markets** • 6514 40th Ave NE
206-526-7661
A great natural market that will leave your wallet unnaturally empty.

Map 28 · **Ballard (West)**

33

PAGE
179

Golden
Gardens
Park

NW 85th St

NW 83rd St

Puget Sound

Loyal Ave NW

NW 80th St

A

3000   2600

7700

NW 77th St

Sunset
Hill
Park

29th Ave NW
28th Ave NW
Earl Ave NW
27th Ave NW
26th Ave NW
25th Ave NW
24th Ave NW
Jones Ave NW
23rd Ave NW

32nd Ave NW

NW 75th St

NW 74th St

29

Seaview Ave NW

NW 73rd St

NW 72nd St

7300

NW 73rd St

33rd Ave NW

3400

NW 71st St

Leif Erikson Statue

36th Ave NW

33rd Pl NW

30th Ave NW

NW 70th St

NW 69th St

35th Ave NW

NW 68th St

NW 69th St

NW 68th St

NW 67th St

37th Ave NW
36th Ave NW

35th Ave NW

33rd Ave NW

NW 68th St

NW 67th St

B

NW 67th St

37th Ave NW

NW 67th St

NW 66th St

NW 66th St

NW 65th Ct

NW 65th St

8600

*Shilshole
Bay*

37th Ave NW - Parker Ct

NW 64th St

NW 64th St

2600

34th Ave NW

3200

NW 63rd St

22nd Ave NW

NW 62nd St

NW 62nd St

38th Ave NW

35th Pl NW

35th Ave NW

NW 61st St

Ballard
Playground

NW 61st St

3600

NW 61st St NW

NW 60th St

NW 60th St

NW Brygger Pl

NW 60th St

49th Ave W

W Hooker St

39th Ave W

41st Ave W

NW 59th St

NW 59th St

NW 59th St

5600

45th Ave W

42nd Ave W

W Sheridan St

32nd Ave NW

NW 58th St

NW 57th St

NW 58th St

NW 57th St

28th Ave NW

24th Ave NW

Shilshole Ave NW

Ballard Ave NW

Leary

C

23

W Cramer St

PAGE
180

Discovery
Park

40th Ave NW

36th Ave NW

NW Market St

NW Market St

3000

NW 54th St

NW 54th St

34th Ave NW

W Commodore Way

11

Hiram M. Chittenden Locks

Salmon Bay

| 1/4 mile | | .25 km |

Map 28

○ Landmarks

- **Hiram M. Chittenden Locks** • 3015 NW 54th St
  Industrial-age marvel; watch the local salmon
  populations dwindle before your very eyes!
- **Leif Erikson Statue** • Seaview Ave NW
  Famous viking explorer surrounded by rune-
  stones in the shape of a Viking ship.

Coffee

- **Caffè Fiorè** • 3125 NW 85th St
  206-706-7580
  Makes the bold claim of being Seattle's first
  organic coffee.
- **Firehouse Coffee** • 2622 NW Market St
  206-784-2911
  Kid and dog friendly just like a real firehouse.

Nightlife

- **Percy's & Co** • 5233 Ballard Ave NW
  206-420-3750
  An Apothecary style restaurant and bar with food
  and cocktails to cure what ails you.
- **Sloop Tavern** • 2830 NW Market St
  206-782-3330
  Get drunk cheaply with enormous beers.

Restaurants

- **Anthony's HomePort Shilshole Bay** •
  6135 Seaview Ave NW
  206 783-0780 • $$$
  Pacific Northwest chain with an impressive view.
- **Caffè Fiorè** • 3125 NW 85th St
  206-706-7580 • $$
  Makes the bold claim of being Seattle's first
  organic coffee.
- **Percy's & Co** • 5233 Ballard Ave NW
  206-420-3750 • $$
  An Apothecary style restaurant and bar with food
  and cocktails to cure what ails you.
- **Portage Bay Cafe** • 2821 NW Market St
  206-783-1547 • $$
  Local organic breakfasts and lunches.
- **Ray's Café** • 6049 Seaview Ave NW
  206-782-0094 • $$$
  Venerable institution that's been doing seafood
  right for decades. Watch out for tourists.
- **Red Mill Totem House** • 3058 NW 54th St
  206-784-1400 • $
  Fish & chips by the locks in an awesome Totem
  House! How can you go wrong?
- **The Scoop @ Walter's** • 6408 32nd Ave NW
  206-782-3920 • $
  Walter serves the best of the local ice creams.

Shopping

- **Kick It Boots & Stompwear** • 2607 NW Market St
  206-784-3399
  These boots are made for stompin'.

Map 29 · **Ballard / Loyal Heights**

Map 29

The residential focus of Loyal Heights means family green areas like Salmon Bay and Baker Parks and a half-dozen learning institutions, including Seattle's coolest, Ballard High School. But one blockbuster drive from 85th Street (where Mt. Rainier looms over the city like a giant ice cream cone) down the ever-active 15th Avenue Northwest, and Ballard's long-lost neighborhood brother is found again.

Coffee

- **Grumpy D's Coffee House** • 7001 15th Ave NW
206-783-4039
If you're still grumpy after their coffee, you might be a D.
- **Jumpin' Jimmy's** • 6501 15th Ave NW
206-783-7786
Solid drive-through espresso in a jumpin' jim flash!

Nightlife

- **Chuck's Hop Shop** • 656 NW 85th St
206-297-6212
With 38 beers ON TAP and rotating food trucks outside, its the only convenience store that makes sense as a hangout.
- **The Dray** • 708 NW 65th St
206-453-4527
Beer on tap. Beer to go in growlers. Beer soaked raisins on the grilled cheese.
- **Waterwheel Lounge** • 7034 15th Ave NW
206-784-5701
A rumpus room where you have to pay for drinks.

Restaurants

- **Delancey** • 1415 NW 70th St
206-838-1960 •
Orangette blogger's Ballard pizza venture.
- **The Fat Hen** • 1418 NW 70th St
206-782-5422 • $$
Enough delicious pastries and sammies to turn you into a big fat hen.
- **Honore Artisan Bakery** • 1413 NW 70th St
206-706-4035 • $
Their macaroons will make you swoon.
- **Kasbah Authentic Moroccan** • 1471 NW 85th St
206-788-0777 • $$
Your heart will be still for the b'stilla. And belly dancers are always fun.
- **The Original Pancake House** • 8037 15th Ave NW
206-781-3344 • $$
Homemade batter! A dozen types of flapjacks! It's breakfast heaven.

- **Smokin' Pete's BBQ** • 1918 NW 65th St
206-783-0454 • $$
All meat, all the time. Stacks of napkins requisite.
- **Thai Siam** • 8305 15th Ave NW
206-784-5465 • $
Skip the pad thai; go for the huge, drool-worthy steak salad.
- **Un Bien** • 7302 15th Ave NW
206-588-2040 • $$
The pulled pork Phoenix rising from the ashes of Paseo.
- **Wild Mountain Café** • 1408 NW 85th St
206-297-9453 • $$$
Tasty, funky, spirited home-grown food.

Shopping

- **Cascioppo Bros. Meats** • 2364 NW 80th St
206-784-6121
You can't beat their meat!
- **Chuck's Hop Shop** • 656 NW 85th St
206-297-6212
The convenience store of your dreams with 38 rotating beer taps and plenty of reasons to stay a while.
- **Fresh Fish Company** • 2364 NW 80th St
206-782-1632
Truth in naming conventions.
- **Goodwill** • 6400 8th Ave NW
206-957-5544
Make sure to check for stains.
- **Herb's House** • 716 NW 65th St
206-557-7388
Your family can drink smoothies while you shop for your post-bedtime treats.
- **Larsen's Danish Bakery** • 8000 24th Ave NW
206-782-8285
Danish bakery with all the Scandinavian flavor you've come to expect!
- **Laura Bee Designs** • 6418 20th Ave NW
206-789-4044
If you're gonna pay $80 for a purse, it may as well be made locally.
- **Top Banana** • 6501 15th Ave NW
206-783-7786
This cheap, family-owned produce vendor is more than just bananaz.

Map 30 · **Greenwood / Phinney Ridge**

GREENWOOD

PHINNEY RIDGE

Green Lake

Woodland
Park Zoo

Woodland
Park

1/4 mile   .25 km

The tree-lined corridor at Phinney and Greenwood Avenues is one of the better places to raise a family in Seattle, while the blocks along Aurora will show your kids what will happen to them if they don't stay in school. Right around Green Lake the area turns downright affluent, but all the best shopping, eating, and drinking can be found where the regular folk live.

○ Landmarks

- **Woodland Park** • Aurora Ave N & N 59th St
206-684-4075
Here you'll find a zoo, a rose garden, and a veritable metropolis of bunny rabbits.

🖥Coffee

- **Cafe Bambino** • 405 NW 65th St
206-706-4934
Look for the buddha and charming neon sign.
- **Caffe Vita** • 7402 Greenwood Ave N
206-588-1519
The best of the local chains.
- **Diva Espresso** • 7916 Greenwood Ave N
206-781-1213
Local chain with unpredictable service. I guess it's kind of like ordering coffee from a diva.
- **Green Bean Coffeehouse** •
8515 Greenwood Ave N
206-706-4587
A community coffeehouse with tons of events and a pay-what-you-will menu.
- **Herkimer Coffee** • 7320 Greenwood Ave N
206-784-0202
Roasting their own. Awesome space.
- **Makeda Coffee** • 153 N 78th St
206-782-1489
Asian-inspired and artsy vibe make this a cool stop during Greenwood Art Walk.
- **Monkey Grind Espresso Bar** • 518 N 85th St
206-782-6100
Le Fournil & Alki bakery pastries go perfectly with their no-monkey-business coffee drinks.
- **Neptune Coffee** • 8415 Greenwood Ave N
206-599-8822
Trivia theme nights + coffee + alcohol = out-of-this-world good time.

🍸Nightlife

- **418 Public House** • 418 NW 65th St
206-783-0418
Apparently, "pub" can now mean Mexican food and vegan options.
- **Alibi Room** • 10406 Holman Rd NW
206-623-3180
Equally dark sister lounge to Pike Place Market's clandestine DJ spot.
- **The Angry Beaver** • 8412 Greenwood Ave N
206-782-6044
Poutine flights and hockey for Canucks and those who love them.
- **Barking Dog Alehouse** • 705 NW 70th St
206-782-2974
The dog barks for Belgian beer.
- **The Cozy Nut Tavern** • 123 N 85th St
206-784-2240
If Wes Anderson's *Fantastic Mr. Fox* were a bar.
- **Duck Island Ale House** • 7317 Aurora Ave N
206-783-3360
The friendliest beer connoisseurs in Seattle.
- **El Chupacabra** • 6711 Greenwood Ave N
206-706-4889
Frighteningly delicious Mexican munchies and margaritas.
- **Molly Maguire's** • 610 NW 65th St
206-789-9643
Requisite neighborhood Irish pub, only with real Irish people!
- **The Park Public House** • 6114 Phinney Ave N
206-789-8187
Extra pubbish Public House with friendly service and delicious grub.
- **Prost!** • 7311 Greenwood Ave N
206-706-5430
Small German-themed bar with a friendly attitude.
- **Sully's Snow Goose Saloon** • 6119 Phinney Ave N
206-782-9231
Quaint country pub.
- **Sweet Lou's** • 851 N 85th St
206-782-9690
Formerly the Sundown. Lou's got BBQ, beer, and local flavor for yous.

Map 30

33   34

29   30   31   32   27
23
24   25   26

Map 30

Greenwood / Phinney Ridge

- **Tin Hat Bar & Grill** • 512 NW 65th St
206-782-2770
Even the jukebox has tattoos.
- **Uber Tavern** • 7517 Aurora Ave N
206-782-2337
Enjoy a cold brew at this small hangout.
- **The Yard Cafe** • 8313 Greenwood Ave N
206-588-1746
As comfortable as your own back yard, but with way more booze.

🍴 Restaurants

- **74th St Ale House** • 7401 Greenwood Ave N
206-784-2955 • $$
Serious about food and beer.
- **A La Mode Pies** • 5821 Phinney Ave N
206-383-3796 • $$
Fresh, seasonal pie delivered directly to your face.
- **Barking Dog Alehouse** • 705 NW 70th St
206-782-2974 • $$
Cozy dinners, weekend brunch, and generous beer selection.
- **Beth's Café** • 7311 Aurora Ave N
206-782-5588 • $
12-egg omelets, all-u-can eat hashbrowns. You'll die and go to heaven, or just…die.
- **The Blue Glass** • 704 NW 65th St
206-420-1631 • $$
Upscale pub food that will make you feel superior about getting fat.
- **El Chupacabra** • 6711 Greenwood Ave N
206-706-4889 • $
Hearty Mexican, loud music, wacky interior.
- **Coyle's Bakeshop** • 8300 Greenwood Ave N
206-257-4736 • $
Former Herbfarm pastry apprentice gets her own place! Believe the hype.
- **Four Spoons Cafe** • 850 N 85th St
206-297-6384 • $
French bistro atmosphere.
- **Gorditos** • 213 N 85th St
206-706-9352 • $
Burritos bigger than a newborn baby.

- **Gorgeous George's Mediterranean Kitchen** •
7719 Greenwood Ave N
206-783-0116 • $$
Even if the food sucked (it doesn't) you'd still come back for George.
- **Kalbi Grill Express** • 8202 Greenwood Ave N
206-457-5930 • $$
A fam-friendly introduction to Korean food (grilled fast).
- **Mr. Gyros** • 8411 Greenwood Ave N
206-706-7472 • $
It's almost like he was born to make gyros.
- **Now Make Me a Sandwich** • 85th St NW
206-714-5090 • $
Finally, a way to carry out your misogynistic food fantasies without jail time.
- **The Olive and Grape** • 8516 Greenwood Ave N
206-724-0272 • $$
They have other stuff too.
- **Pete's Egg Nest** • 7717 Greenwood Ave N
206-784-5348 • $
Sure, it's just breakfast. But it is SOLID.
- **Phinney Market Pub & Eatery** •
5918 Phinney Ave N
206-219-9105 • $$
The pub for the fancy NW family. The kids menu features risotto.
- **Pho Thân Brothers'** • 7714 Aurora Ave N
206-527-5973 • $
Cheap, fast, and filling, with a free cream puff to boot.
- **Picnic : A Food & Wine Boutique** •
6801 Greenwood Ave N
206-453-5867 • $$
Buy gourmet items for your fancy-pants picnic or have your picnic right there in the store if it's raining.
- **Razzi's Pizzeria** • 8523 Greenwood Ave N
206-782-9005 • $
A pizza joint the whole, dietary-restricted family can enjoy.
- **Red Mill Burgers** • 312 N 67th St
206-783-6362 • $
The undisputed best burger in Seattle. And possibly, the best onion rings.
- **The Ridgeback Cafe** • 500 NW 65th St
206-783-4073 • $
Cafe and market featuring crepes.

Stumbling Goat Bistro brings casual elegance to the neighborhood, while Gorditos, Beth's Café, and Red Mill feed the happy masses. The crack-house chic of Aurora gives way to two of the most comprehensive beer bars in Seattle—Duck Island Ale House and Über Tavern. Wash your pint down with some good eats at 74th Street Ale House. The younger, grungier crowd is at Tin Hat.

- **Stacia's** • 305 NW 85th St
  206-781-0292 • $$
  Free cookies with your pizza!
- **Stumbling Goat Bistro** • 6722 Greenwood Ave N
  206-784-3535 • $$$
  As a bistro should be: Simple, uncomplicated, romantic.
- **Taquería Tequila Authentic Mexican Food** •
  301 NW 85th St
  206-784-4699 • $
  99 cent tacos, dudes.
- **Thaiku** • 6705 Greenwood Ave N
  206-706-7807 • $$
  Aphrodisiac drinks the are main draw—limit one per person.
- **Yanni's** • 7419 Greenwood Ave N
  206-783-6945 • $$$
  Great place to convert Greek food naysayers. Exceptional dolmathes.
- **Zeek's Pizza** • 6000 Phinney Ave N
  206-285-8646 • $$
  Pizzas with pizzazz, like the Thai version with peanut sauce.

🛍 Shopping

- **Better Meat Co.** • 305 NW 82nd St
  206-783-0570
  Old-timey, new-timey meat.
- **Couth Buzzard Books** • 8310 Greenwood Ave N
  206-436-2960
  General used books.
- **Dreamstrands Comics** • 115 N 85th St
  206-297-3737
  Comics…and such.
- **Fred Meyer** • 100 NW 85th St
  206-784-9600
  Just like Target but with groceries too!
- **Frock Shop** • 6500 Phinney Ave N
  206-297-1638
  Prepare yourself for loads of compliments on whatever you buy here.
- **Greenwood Hardware** • 7201 Greenwood Ave N
  206-783-2900
  Makes you really, really, really hate Home Depot.
- **Greenwood Space Travel Supply Co.** •
  8414 Greenwood Ave N
  206-725-2625
  Space travel (and raising money to benefit 826 Seattle) is all they do!
- **Insurrection** • 8403 Greenwood Ave N
  206-782-5752
  Leather gear for riding horses, steel otherwise.
- **Ken's Market** • 7231 Greenwood Ave N
  206-784-3470
  Last of the old-fashioned neighborhood markets.
- **Lil Paisley** • 6500 Phinney Ave N
  206-784-5255
  Accessorize like Liz Taylor and find the jewels that will always bring you luck.
- **New Roots Organics** • 4544 Leary Way NW
  206-261-2500
  Fruits and vegetables till the cows come home. Recipe suggestions, too.
- **PCC Natural Markets** • 7504 Aurora Ave N
  206-525-3586
  One-stop shopping for overpriced organic groceries.
- **Picnic : A Food & Wine Boutique** •
  6801 Greenwood Ave N
  206-453-5867
  Specialty meats and cheese for your fancy-pants picnic. Plus 400 wines to get your date nice and sloppy.
- **Rudy's Barbershop** • 6415 Phinney Ave N
  206-782-9861
  Absolute best cheap haircut!
- **The Sneakery** • 612 NW 65th St
  206-297-1786
  Hipsters will notice your cool shoes, not your jacked-up ingrown toenail.
- **Top Ten Toys** • 124 N 85th St
  206-782-0098
  Classic, teaching, affordable toys that won't bum a kid out either.
- **Violet Sweet Shoppe** • 6410 Phinney Ave N
  206-297-4441
  Vegans deserve beautiful treats too!
- **Zuma Grocery** • 129 NW 85th St
  206-781-8600
  These Ethiopian foods and ingredients are ZOMG good!

Map 31 • **Green Lake / Roosevelt**

Map 31

Seattle's singletons and families alike flock to Green Lake on rare sunny days for outdoor fun and frolic, jogging, rollerblading, and paddle boat rentals. The pedestrian-friendly lake and surrounding park are true gems for those without private waterfront access or million-dollar houseboats. Nearby Roosevelt, smaller and less popular than its sister 'hood, is a quiet, tree-lined residential enclave on the outskirts of Ravenna Park.

o Landmarks

• **Bettie Page Mural** • 700 NE 59th St
Giant Bettie seduces commuters from the side of a house.
• **Green Lake Park** • 7201 E Green Lake Dr N
206-684-4075
A water-wood oasis of calm, even in spite of crowds.

Coffee

• **72nd Street Cafe** • 308 NE 72nd St
206-523-5623
Very locally-focused and laid back folks. Enjoy Green Lake no matter how crappy the weather is.
• **Bus Stop Espresso** • 800 NE 65th St
206-528-5997
Not quite near enough to your bus stop.
• **Cafe Javasti** • 8410 5th Ave NE
206-985-9903
It's all about the crepes.
• **Café Lulu** • 6417 Latona Ave NE
206-465-4800
Open until early afternoon.
• **Cafe Momo** • 7119 Woodlawn Ave NE
206-985-6900
Vaguely French home of the iSalad and a to-die-for tofu sandwich.
• **Cafe Racer** • 5828 Roosevelt Way NE
206-523-5282
The heart of the community and just the coolest people ever.
• **Forza Coffee Company** • 6900 E Green Lake Way N
206-453-4279
Forza is a franchise. This is one of the better ones because they were smart enough to add beer and live music.
• **Peet's Coffee & Tea** • 6850 E Green Lake Way N
206-267-1440
Bay Area interlopers.
• **Revolutions Espresso** • 7012 Woodlawn Ave NE
206-527-1908
Also bakery.

• **Wayward Coffeehouse** • 6417 Roosevelt Way NE
206-525-5191
Vegetarian/vegan-focused joint. Not a bad way to go wayward.
• **Zoka Coffee Roaster & Tea Company** •
2200 N 56th St
206-545-4277
One of the Seattle originals.

Nightlife

• **Atlantic Crossing** • 6508 Roosevelt Way NE
206-729-6266
No need to cross the pond for that Euro pub feeling!
• **Burgundian** • 2253 N 56th St
206-420-8943
Craft beer and all-day breakfast for the barflies who get a late start.
• **Die Bierstube** • 6106 Roosevelt Way NE
206-527-7019
German beers the size of a German head.
• **Elysian Tangletown** • 2106 N 55th St
206-547-5929
Elysian micros in a cozy neighborhood pub.
• **Little Red Hen** • 7115 Woodlawn Ave NE
206-522-1168
Serious honky-tonk for urban cowboys. Slummers get bounced.
• **Mojito** • 7545 Lake City Way NE
206-525-3162
Mojitos are just the Tip of the Plantain.
• **Mutiny Hall** • 1205 NE 65th St
206-524-5020
Their insanely long, rare beer list will keep you plenty subdued.
• **Pies and Pints** • 1215 NE 65th St
206-524-7082
Great concept. Poor execution.
• **Toronado** • 1205 NE 65th St
206-525-0654
So many local brews and spirits on tap, it'll make your head spin.

33 34
29 30 31 32 27
23
24 25 26

🍴 Restaurants

- **Bengal Tiger** • 6510 Roosevelt Way NE
  206-985-0041 • $$
  This Indian food is grrrrreat!
- **Cafe Momo** • 7119 Woodlawn Ave NE
  206-985-6900 • $
  Vaguely French home of the iSalad and a to-die-for tofu sandwich.
- **Cafe Racer** • 5828 Roosevelt Way NE
  206-523-5282 • $
  The heart of the community and just the coolest people ever.
- **Cake Envy** • 7900 East Green Lake Dr N
  206-453-3337 • $
  The cupcake will not die. This one stays up till midnight on weekends.
- **Casa Patron** • 805 NE 65th St
  206-923-7680 • $$
  Sounds like a good place to get shit-faced, but families eat here too.
- **COA Mexican Eatery & Tequileria** •
  7919 Roosevelt Way NE
  206-522-6179 • $$
  A perfectly serviceable place to eat Mexican food and drink tequila.
- **Diggity Dog Hotdog & Sausage Co.** •
  5421 Meridian Ave N
  206-633-1966 • $
  You'll diggity these hot dogs.
- **Duke's Chowder House** • 7850 Green Lake Dr N
  206-522-4908 • $$
  For all you chowda' heads.
- **Eva** • 2227 N 56th St
  206-633-3538 • $$$
  An elegant meal (ties, high heels, expense accounts not necessary).

- **Flying Squirrel Pizza Co** • 8310 5th Ave NE
  206-524-6345 • $$
  Imaginative pies made from local organic ingredients. So very Seatown.
- **Jodee's Desserts** • 7214 Woodlawn Ave NE
  206-525-2900 • $
  Fairy godmother to sweet-toothed people with dietary restrictions.
- **Kisaku** • 2101 N 55th St
  206-545-9050 • $$
  For people who value "authenticity" in their sushi.
- **Krittika's Noodles & Thai Cuisine** •
  6411 Latona Ave NE
  206-985-1182 • $$
  Touch-and-go Thai—some people scarf it up, others barf it up. You decide.
- **Latona Pub** • 6423 Latona Ave NE
  206-525-2238 • $$
  Refuel after a loop around Greenlake with a superb beef pot pie.
- **mkt.** • 2108 N 55th St
  206-812-1580 • $$$$
  Pretentious name. Friendly food.
- **Mighty-O Donuts** • 2110 N 55th St
  206-547-5431 • $
  Spoiler alert: That damn fine donut you're enjoying is vegan!
- **Mutiny Hall** • 1205 NE 65th St
  206-524-5020 • $$
  Their insanely long, rare beer list will keep you plenty subdued.
- **Nell's Restaurant** • 6804 E Green Lake Way N
  206-524-4044 • $$$
  Subtle, lovely dishes showcasing tip-top local ingredients.

Green Lake / Roosevelt

Before enjoying a lap or three around the lake, the avid cyclist should check out **Gregg's Cycle** for expert service and superior selection. By contrast, Roosevelt offers a less athletic and more hippie vibe for those of the mellower persuasion. Establishments like **East West Bookshop**, Whole Foods, and **Sunlight Café,** Seattle's oldest vegetarian restaurant, define the neighborhood's shopping district. **Nell's** is one of Seattle's best secrets: pitch-perfect Euro/New American dishes that are elegant but not ostentatious.

- **Pies and Pints** • 1215 NE 65th St
  206-524-7082 • $
  Buttery, flaky, savory pies and, um…pints.
- **Salvatore Ristorante** • 6100 Roosevelt Way NE
  206-527-9301 • $$$
  Straightforward and spensy Italian.
- **Savatdee Thai** • 5801 Roosevelt Way NE
  206-331-9666 • $$
  Another Thai place? Luckily, it's really good.
- **Spud Fish & Chips** • 6860 E Green Lake Way N
  206-524-0565 • $
  This place has been around for 75 years for a good reason.
- **Sunlight Café** • 6403 Roosevelt Way NE
  206-522-9060 • $
  Super-crunchy vegetarian place—aptly named, too.
- **Sushi Tokyo** • 6311 Roosevelt Way NE
  206-526-2935 • $$
  Sushi + teriyaki = yum.
- **Tacos Guaymas** • 6808 East Green Lake Way N
  206-729-6563 • $$
  Delicious tacos of all kinds including braaaaiiiins for your zombie friends.
- **Taste of India** • 5517 Roosevelt Way NE
  206-528-1575 • $$
  A decidedly better buffet, with above-average Indian standards.
- **Toronado** • 1205 NE 65th St
  206-525-0654 • $$$
  One of the more affordable "farm-to-table" establishments.
- **Wayward Vegan Café** • 801 NE 65th St
  206-524-0204 • $$
  Vegan comfort food with a punk vibe.

🛒 Shopping

- **Derby Salon** • 6315 Roosevelt Way NE
  206-526-1470
  Great haircuts you won't need a derby to cover up.
- **East West Bookshop** • 6500 Roosevelt Way NE
  206-523-3726
  When you feel like some new-age reading, or learning how to meditate.
- **The Fish Store** • 6109 Roosevelt Way NE
  206-522-5259
  Specialized equipment for the aquarium enthusiast.
- **Gregg's Cycle** • 7007 Woodlawn Ave NE
  206-523-1822
  Voted best bike shop in Seattle.
- **Ma Mo Jewelry Design** • 6317 Roosevelt Way NE
  206-525-4653
  Custom jewelry and services.
- **Trading Musician** • 5908 Roosevelt Way NE
  206-522-6707
  Good prices on great gear for musicians of all kinds.
- **Zenith Supplies** • 6300 Roosevelt Way NE
  206-525-7997
  Hippie emporium. In bulk!
- **zoëyogurt** • 6900 East Green Lake Way N
  206-829-8270
  Post Green Lake jog, replenish your calories with self-serve froyo.

Map 31

Map 32 • **Ravenna**

Map 32

Ravenna is a residential wasteland that lies just north of the U District. It is populated largely by grad students and young families. However, the densely green surroundings and the amazing woodland bubble of Ravenna Park lend a refreshing, non-suburban ambiance to the area.

○ Landmarks
• **Wedgwood Rock** • 28th Ave NE & NE 72nd St
It's a bad sign when a neighborhood's major landmark is a rock.

☕ Coffee
• **Cowen Park Grocery** • 1217 NE Ravenna Blvd
206-525-1117
Cafe attached to lovely Mom & Pop grocery with friendly baristas, Le Fournil pastries and Manny's on tap.
• **Diva Espresso** • 8014 Lake City Way NE
206-525-5920
Local chain with unpredictable service. I guess it's kind of like ordering coffee from a diva.
• **Espresso Express** • 6500 15th Ave NE
206-524-6326
Also food.
• **Herkimer Coffee** • 5611 University Way NE
206-525-5070
Roasting great coffee.
• **Muddy Waters Coffee Company** • 2258 NE 65th St
206-729-7587
Some places just get grandfathered in.
• **Rooster's** • 7809 Lake City Way NE
206-632-6351
Open early. Cock a doodle doo.

🍸 Nightlife
• **Knarr Shipwreck Lounge** •
5633 University Way NE
206-525-3323
Play pool and shuffleboard with grizzled Seattleites.
• **The Pub at Third Place** • 6504 20th Ave NE
206-523-0217
Board games and wood decor make you feel comfortably snowed in.
• **Ravenna Alehouse** • 2258 NE 65th St
206-729-9083
A decent neighborhood pub.

Map 32

33 34

29 30 31 32
23   27
24 25 26

Ravenna

Restaurants

- **Bagel Oasis** • 2112 NE 65th St
206-526-0525 • $
Boiled bagels! Just like Bubby used to make.
- **Cafe Kopi** • 8056 Lake City Way NE
206-523-6197 • $
Cuteing up Lake City with pastries and yummy rice bowls.
- **Chiang's Gourmet** • 7845 Lake City Way NE
206-527-8888 • $$
You don't have to be Chinese to eat here, but it sure helps.
- **Frank's Oyster House & Champagne Parlor** •
2616 NE 55th St
206-525-0220 • $$
Funky Montana meets the 80's decor.
- **Gaudi** • 3410 NE 55th St
206-527-3400 • $$$
Just like Spain (except the early closing time).
- **Harissa Mediterranean Cuisine** •
2255 NE 65th St
206-588-0650 • $$
Lebanese cuisine, cocktails, and belly dancing.
- **Heidelberg Haus** • 2122 NE 65th St
206-466-5369 • $$$
The uber German experience.
- **Kidd Valley** • 5502 25th Ave NE
206-522-0890 • $
Hey, at least they have veggie burgers.
- **Mamma Melina** • 5101 25th Ave NE
206-632-2271 • $$
An Italian experience that will get you laid.
- **Mars** • 5247 University Way NE
206-632-5132 • $
There's nothing alien about this cozy late-night bistro.

- **Mr. Villa Mexican Restaurant** •
8064 Lake City Way NE
206-517-5660 • $$
As friendly and authentico as they come.
- **Pair** • 5501 30th Ave NE
206-526-7655 • $$$
Small, seasonal plates—you guessed it—"paired" with wine. NFT approved.
- **Persepolis Grill** • 5517 University Way NE
206-524-3434 • $
Soups, stews and BBQ at ancient Persian prices.
- **Pizza Pi Vegan Pizzeria** • 5500 University Way NE
206-343-1415 • $
Who says vegans have to compromise? All vegan, all the time.
- **Queen Mary Tea Room** • 2912 NE 55th St
206-527-2770 • $$$
Snack on proper British crumpets and tea. Don't forget to raise your pinky.
- **Tempero do Brasil** • 5628 University Way NE
206-523-6229 • $$$
A thrilling mix of cuisines is the remedy for "what-to-try-next" syndrome.
- **Vios Café** • 6504 20th Ave NE
206-525-5701 • $
Beautiful Greek dishes. Wines for the adults, play area for the kiddies.
- **Wayward Vegan Café** • 5253 University Way NE
206-524-0204 • $$
Vegan comfort food with a punk vibe.
- **Zeek's Pizza** • 2108 NE 65th St
206-285-8646 • $$
Pizzas with pizzazz, like the Thai version with peanut sauce.
- **Zouave Restaurant** • 2615 NE 65th St
206-525-7747 • $$
Small but eclectic menu in an adorable hole-in-the-wall bistro.

Ravenna

Entertainment-wise, Ravenna isn't quite a destination. But if you live there and feel 'hoodbound, there are some options: board games and wood decor at **The Pub at Third Place** will make you feel snowed in at a ski lodge, **Ravenna Alehouse** is a decent enough neighborhood pub, and **Knarr** is a comfortable dive. The restaurant scene is looking good with the excellent **Pair** leading the way, along with **Gaudi**.

Shopping

- **Cowen Park Grocery** • 1217 NE Ravenna Blvd
  206-525-1117
  Your friendly neighborhood mini mart. Fresh Korean tacos spring-summer!
- **Planet Happy** • 2914 NE 55th St
  206-729-0154
  See a baby hedgehog who lives in an old converted TV while you buy toys.
- **Ravenna Third Place Books** • 6504 20th Ave NE
  206-525-2347
  Revitalized neighborhood bookstore; bar downstairs.

- **Recess** • 5235 University Wy NE
  206-729-5099
  Designer casual hoodies, hats and sneakers for the urban man.
- **Rising Sun Farms & Produce** • 6329 15th Ave NE
  206-524-9741
  So cheap and delicious, you'll feel like you're scamming them.
- **Spotted Owl Berger Variety Shop** •
  5502 University Way NE
  206-632-1611
  Creative and original glasswear for, you know, your "coffee table."
- **Vegan Haven** • 5270 University Way NE
  206-523-9060
  Ethically-minded consumers shop at the only 100% vegan store in WA.

Map 32

Map 33 • **Northwest Seattle**

Map 33

Like its NE counterpart, NW Seattle contains a blight (Aurora), a hidden corner of wanna-be elitists (Broadview), and a few funky neighborhoods that defy sensibilities of affordability. It isn't as dull as NE, but that's not saying much. It's slightly more developed and neighborhoody than the other side of I-5, but still nothing to get excited about.

○ Landmarks

- **Aurora Rents Elephant** • 8808 Aurora Ave N
  The fate of this elephant is still unknown, so see it while you can.
- **Golden Gardens Park** • 8498 Seaview Pl NW
  206-684-4075
  Puget Sound at its finest and then some.
- **Granite Curling Club** • 1440 N 128th St
  206-362-2446
  Only dedicated curling rink on the West Coast. Need we say more?

☕ Coffee

- **Blue Saucer** • 9127 Roosevelt Way NE
  206-453-4955
  Seven Coffee Roasters brew and plenty of GF options make it a fine on-the-way stop.
- **Diva Espresso** • 14419 Greenwood Ave N
  206-417-1639
  Local chain with unpredictable service. I guess it's kind of like ordering coffee from a diva.
- **Gourmet Latté** • 8762 Holman Rd NW
  206-782-1535
  The most gourmet coffee available at this particular PetCo.
- **Holy Grounds Coffee** • 9000 Holman Rd NW
  206-783-1797
  Brewing Caffé Vita beans.
- **Sip & Ship** • 7511 Greenwood Ave N
  206-783-4299
  Like a home office with an espresso bar.

🍸 Nightlife

- **Baranof** • 8549 Greenwood Ave N
  206-782-9260
  Classic dive bar with low hipster encroachment, sloppy burgers and daily karaoke.
- **Crosswalk** • 8556 Greenwood Ave N
  206-789-9691
  For serious drinkers only.
- **The House Sports Pub** • 8551 Greenwood Ave N
  206-403-1464
  For health-conscious sports enthusiasts who crave a brew and a salad.
- **Gainsbourg** • 8550 Greenwood Ave N
  206-783-4004
  Sip on absinthe and keep an eye out for Bob in the Black Lodge by the bathrooms.
- **Naked City Brewery & Taphouse** •
  8564 Greenwood Ave N
  206-838-6299
  Balls-out beer selection and a killer food menu to boot.
- **The Ould Triangle** • 9736 Greenwood Ave N
  206-706-7798
  A solid Irish dive complete with heavy pours and Dropkick Murphys.
- **Rickshaw** • 322 N 105th St
  206-789-0120
  '70s karaoke paradise.

Map 33

33 | 34
28 | 29 | 30 | 31 | 32
23
24 | 25 | 26

Northwest Seattle

🍴 Restaurants

- **Ampersand Pantry & Cafe** • 424 N 85th St
206-257-5671 • $
Adorable gourmet foodstuffs shop with a dine-in option and the occasional wine tasting.
- **Baranof** • 8549 Greenwood Ave N
206-782-9260 • $
Classic dive bar with low hipster encroachment, sloppy burgers and daily karaoke.
- **Bick's Broadview Grill** • 10555 Greenwood Ave N
206-367-8481 • $$$
Fusion that's in your face.
- **Blue Saucer** • 9127 Roosevelt Way NE
206-453-4955 • $
Seven Coffee Roasters brew and plenty of GF options make it a fine on-the-way stop.
- **Burgermaster** • 9820 Aurora Ave N
206-522-2044 • $
Drive up, park, and let the old-school car-side service do all the work.
- **Burrito Loco** • 9211 Holman Rd NW
206-783-0719 • $$
The burritos here are loco good.
- **Dick's Drive-In** • 9208 Holman Rd NW
206-783-5233 • $
A local obsession, specializing in cheap burgers and shakes. Perfect at 1 am.
- **El Camion** • 11728 Aurora Ave N
206-367-2777 • $
Amazing truck tacos and tamales you can trust.
- **Fu Shen Chinese Seafood Restaurant** •
9019 Aurora Ave N
206-624-3888 • $$
Worth braving the dodgyness of Aurora for.
- **Kidd Valley** • 14303 Aurora Ave N
206-364-8493 • $
Hey, at least they have veggie burgers.
- **Lucy Ethiopian Restaurant and Lounge** •
10000 Aurora Ave N
206-402-3058 • $
Lucy's finally got her own club.
- **Mr. & Mrs. Wok** • 10000 Holman Rd NW
206-789-0558 • $
A marriage of deliciousness.
- **Patty's Eggnest** • 9749 Holman Rd NW
206-297-1545 • $
Fat omelets and fresh-squeezed OJ make this the best breakfast in town.
- **Saffron Grill** • 2132 N Northgate Wy
206-417-0707 • $$
Another offering from the Cedars empire dishing up bottomless chai.
- **Taqueria la Pasadita #2** • 2143 N Northgate Way
$
Calling these tacos some of Seattle's best is a serious claim. We're serious.
- **Wood Shop BBQ** • 10740 1st Ave NW
206-618-8510 • $$
Order the ribs if they're not sold out.

NW has a few pockets of commercial activity that contain life, most notably along 85th and north on Greenwood. The farther north you go, the more suburban the setting. Sticking to Aurora, you'll find an abundant selection of $2 beers, pull tabs, used cars and meth heads, with the occasional hooker waiting to reveal her "hidden neighborhood treasure."

Shopping

- **Ampersand Pantry & Cafe** • 424 N 85th St
  206-257-5671
  Not your mother's pantry (Unless your mother is a gourmet foodie and wino).
- **Childish Things** • 10002 Holman Rd NW
  206-789-1498
  Sell-me-downs and vintage maternity wear.
- **Lenny's Produce** •
  10410 Greenwood Ave N
  206-781-0619
  Cheaper cilantro, you'll never find.
- **Ocean Greens** •
  9724 Aurora Ave N
  206-453-4145
  Knowledgeable staff but you need an ocean of money to afford their goods.
- **Swansons Nursery** • 9701 15th Ave NW
  206-782-2543
  You don't have to live in Wenatchee to grow your own produce!
- **Value Village** • 8532 15th Ave NW
  206-783-4648
  Enormous second-hand store that sells everything from furniture to clothes.

Map 34 · **Northeast Seattle**

Map 34

Like its NW counterpart, NE Seattle is a smattering of obscure neighborhoods and a horrid blight (Lake City Way). The neighborhood's defining monstrosity, **Northgate Mall**--the nation's first--should probably be avoided unless you're nostalgic for Forever 21. On the upside, the residential areas are quaint and hide a few gems. The libraries are good, the parks clean, and it's...um, a nice place to raise kids? If it's any consolation, it gets worse in Shoreline.

Coffee

- **Bark! Espresso** • 11335 Roosevelt Way NE
206-364-0185
Great for those who don't enjoy leaving your dog tied up outside while they drink their coffee.
- **Bean City Coffee Company** •
12547 Lake City Way NE
206-650-5598
The best quick-stop in the area, (unless you're one of those bikini espresso creeps).
- **Cloud City Coffee** • 8801 Roosevelt Way NE
206-527-5552
Great coffee and quiche. Better still, Darth Vader is nowhere in sight.
- **Kaffeeklatsch** • 12513 Lake City Way NE
206-462-1059
Bakery and coffee the German Hausfrau way.
- **Spotted Pony Espresso** • 12539 33rd Ave NE
206-457-4187
A little taste of Vashon in NE Seattle.
- **Treehouse Coffee Company** • 12303 15th Ave NE
206-365-3224
For those who prefer their treehouses heated, coffee-equipped and on the ground.

Nightlife

- **El Norte Lounge** • 13717 Lake City Way NE
206-954-1349
Mr. Villa's equally Mexican lounge.
- **Fiddler's Inn** • 9219 35th Ave NE
206-525-0752
When Wedgwoodies can find a babysitter.

Restaurants

- **Dick's Drive-In** • 12325 30th Ave NE
206-363-7777 • $
A local obsession, specializing in cheap burgers and shakes. Perfect at 1 am.
- **Enat Ethiopian** • 11546 15th Ave NE
206-362-4901 • $
Best Ethiopian restaurant in Seattle.
- **Five Guys** •
311 NE 103rd St
206-729-5028 • $
Chain burgers & fries that are actually good.

- **Jebena Cafe** • 1510 NE 117th St
206-365-0757 • $$
They're practically giving away their enormous platters of deliciousness.
- **Judy Fu's Snappy Dragon** •
8917 Roosevelt Way NE
206-528-5575 • $
Sopping-greasy Chinese—and still, mysteriously, a Seattle favorite.
- **Kaffeeklatsch** • 12513 Lake City Way NE
206-462-1059 • $
Bakery and coffee the German Hausfrau way.
- **Patty's Eggnest** • 1000 NE Northgate Way
206-364-3463 • $
Fat omelets and fresh-squeezed OJ make this the best breakfast in town.
- **Tengu Sushi** • 301 NE 103rd St
206-525-9999 • $$
Three words: Conveyor belt sushi!
- **Toyoda Sushi** • 12543 Lake City Way NE
206-367-7972 • $$$
Trend seekers go elsewhere: the sushi here is simple, fast, affordable.
- **Tub's Gourmet Subs** • 11064 Lake City Way NE
206-361-1621 • $
It ain't no Subway. Five stars for the "Hawaiian."

Shopping

- **Fred Meyer** • 13000 Lake City Way NE
206-440-2400
Just like Target but with groceries too!
- **Grass** • 14343 15th Ave NE
206-367-1483
Keeping things pricey while the market is sparse.
- **Math 'n' Stuff** • 8926 Roosevelt Wy NE
206-522-8891
Brains get a workout at (unaccountably) an actual math store.
- **Northgate Mall** • 401 NE Northgate Way
206-362-4778
Large indoor shopping mall. Ugh.
- **Party @ Display & Costume** •
11201 Roosevelt Way NE
206-362-4810
Go here if you are throwing a party or need a costume.
- **Silver Platters** • 9560 1st Ave NE
206-524-3472
No, it wasn't named after The Brady Bunch's band.

Map 35 • **Alki / West Seattle / North Admiral**

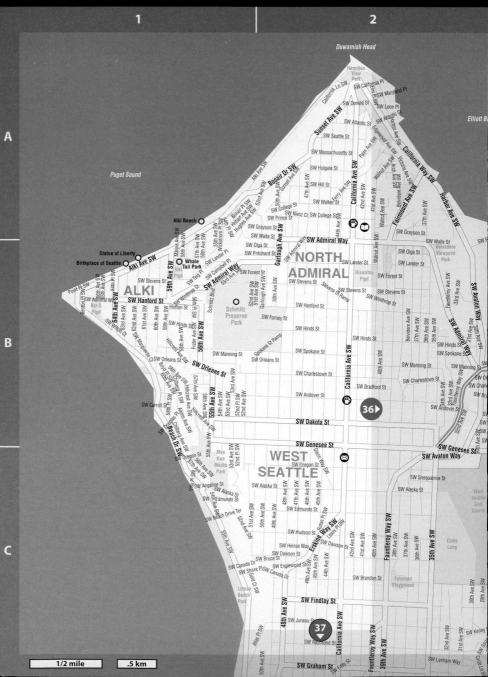

Duwamish Head

Hamilton View Park

California Ln SW
SW California Pl
55th Pl SW Maryland Pl
SW Donald St
SW Leon Pl
SW Atlantic St
SW Atlantic St

Elliott B

Sunset Ave SW

SW Seattle St

Puget Sound

SW Massachusetts St

SW Holgate St

California Way SW

Bonair Dr SW

Alki Ave SW

50th Ave SW Sunset Ave SW

SW Hill St

47th Ave SW

42nd Ave SW

Walnut Ave SW

California Ave SW

Harbor Ave SW

SW Walker St

52nd Ave SW

Perry Ave SW

Bonair Pl SW
Hobart Ave SW
Hughes Ave SW

SW College St
SW Prince St
SW Niesz Ct

45th Ave SW
44th Ave SW

Fairmount Ave SW

SW College St

37th Ave SW

Belvidere

Alki Beach

SW Grayson St

SW Grayson St

Walnut Ave SW

SW Waite St

Belvedere

SW Waite St

Marine Ave SW
56th Ave SW

57th Ave SW

55th Ave SW
56th Ave SW

SW Olga St

SW Admiral Way

SW Olga St

Viewpoint Park

Lander Ave SW

SW Pritchard St

SW Lander St

SW Lander St

Statue of Liberty

Alki P SW
Wickstrom Pl SW

SW Campbell Pl

NORTH

Birthplace of Seattle

Whale Tail Park

SW Admiral Way

53rd Ave SW

SW Forest St

50th Ave SW

ADMIRAL

Hiawatha Plgd

SW Forest St

Alki Ave SW

Alki Plgd

SW Stevens St

50th Ave SW

Garlough Ave SW

SW Stevens St

Stevens St Ramp

SW Stevens St

Fauntleroy Ave SW

ALKI

59th Ave SW

SW Fing Pl

Schmitz Blvd

SW Stevens St

SW Winthrop St

SW Avalon Way

SW Hanford St

SW Winthrop Pl SW

MS SW

Horton St

52nd Ave SW
51st Ave SW

SW Hanford St

Belvidere Ave SW

37th Ave SW
36th Ave SW

64th Ave SW

63rd Ave SW

60th Ave SW

Frater Ave SW

SW Forney St

SW Hinds St

SW Hinds Ave SW

SW Hinds St

SW Admiral Way SW

SW Margarine Ct

56th Ave SW

SW Hinds St

SW Hinds St

40th Ave SW

SW Spokane St

SW Manning St

SW Manning St

54th Ave SW

53rd Ave SW

Fauntleroy Way SW

Spokane St Ramp

SW Orleans St

SW Spokane St

SW Charlestown St

SW Charlestown St

32nd Ave SW

SW Orleans St

SW Orleans St

57th Ave SW

SW Bradford St

California Ave SW

SW Andover St

SW Carroll St

55th Ave SW

54th Ave SW

53rd Ave SW

52nd Pl SW
52nd Ave SW

SW Andover St

36▶

Beach Dr SW

SW Dakota St

SW Dakota St

SW Genesee St

SW Genesee St

Mee Kwa Mooks Park

53rd Ave SW
52nd Ave SW

SW Oregon St

Glenn Way SW

WEST

SW Avalon Way

SW Oregon St

SEATTLE

SW Snoqualmie St

West Seattle Golf Course

SW Angeline St

SW Alaska St

48th Ave SW
47th Ave SW
46th Ave SW
45th Ave SW

SW Alaska St

SW Alaska St

SW Edmunds St

SW Edmunds St

Camp Long

51st Ave SW

50th Ave SW

49th Ave SW

SW Beach Drive Ter

52nd Ave SW

SW Hudson St

Erskine Way SW

42nd Ave SW

40th Ave SW

38th Ave SW

37th Ave SW

35th Ave SW

SW Heinze Way

SW Dawson St

SW Dawson St

Fauntleroy Way SW

Lewis Pl SW

SW Bruce St

45th Ave SW

Fairmont Playground

SW Canada Dr

SW Englewood Ave SW

SW Brandon St

30th Ave SW

29th Ave SW

SW Shore Pl SW Canada Dr

44th Ave SW

Lomar Beach Park

SW Dodd Ct SW

SW Findlay St

48th Ave SW

California Ave SW

32nd Ave SW

31st Ave SW

SW Juneau St

SW Kenny

37▼

SW Graham St

50th Ave SW

Atlas Pl SW

California Ave SW

38th Ave SW

Fauntleroy Way SW

35th Ave SW

SW Eddy St

SW Lanham Way

SW Raymond St

1/2 mile .5 km

Map 35

Many Seattleites believe West Seattle is on the other side of the world. The monstrous West Seattle Freeway Bridge connects this area with the rest of the city. The California Avenue and Alaska Way intersection--known as The Junction--feels like a small, hip town of its own, littered with fabulous restaurants, shops, and historical landmarks. Similarly, west-facing Alki Avenue feels like a California beach town--with little sunshine, snow-capped mountains, and ferry boats.

o Landmarks

- **Alki Beach Park** • Alki Ave SW & Bonair Dr SW
  206-684-4075
  The closest Seattle gets to SoCal for two months a year.
- **Birthplace of Seattle Monument** •
  Alki Ave SW & 62nd Ave SW
  Includes a piece of Plymouth Rock transported on the first cross-country road trip to Seattle.

- **Schmitz Preserve Park** •
  5551 SW Admiral Way
  206-684-4075
  Old-growth forest paths wind along a creek.
- **Statue of Liberty** • Alki Ave SW & 61st Ave SW
  In honor of the little New York that Alki never became.
- **Whale Tail Park** • SW Lander St & 58th Ave SW
  Families come from all over Seattle to this little gem of a park. Close to the beach too!

Map 35

Alki / West Seattle / North Admiral

Coffee

- **Alki Juice & Java** • 1619 Harbor Ave SW
206-938-0153
Delicious organic smoothies and coffee. Why not get both enjoy the view?
- **Alki Mail and Dispatch** • 4701 SW Admiral Way
206-932-2556
Come for the fair trade espresso, stay for the notary.
- **C&P Coffee Company** • 5612 California Ave SW
206-933-3125
Lighthouse Roasters and wine tastings.
- **Cafe Osita** • 7349 35th Ave SW
206-932-4299
Coffee and Mike's Famous Chowdah. It's not as weird as it sounds.
- **Caffè Fiorè** • 2206 California Ave SW
206-588-0708
Makes the bold claim of being Seattle's first organic coffee.
- **Coffee to a Tea with Sugar** •
4541 California Ave SW
206-937-1495
Brewing Vashon Coffee Company beans.
- **Cupcake Royale/Verite Coffee** •
4556 California Ave SW
206-883-7656
Cupcakes and coffee go well together.

- **Easy Street Records & Cafe** •
4559 California Ave SW
206-938-3279
Jacked up record shopping is a Seattle tradition.
- **Freshy's** • 2735 California Ave SW
206-937-4316
Plus beer, wine, food and arcade games.
- **Hotwire Online Coffeehouse** •
4410 California Ave SW
206-935-1510
Small-batch roaster.
- **Pearl's Tea & Coffee** • 4800 Delridge Way SW
206-937-6036
THE place for boba and crepes in West Seattle.
- **Portside Coffee Company** •
6720 W Marginal Way SW
206-762-7509
Coffee's not bad, though the quality matters less when it's served out of a big silver barge.
- **Red Cup Espresso** • 4451 California Ave SW
206-913-0230
Some of the best chai around and a convenient drive-thru.
- **Uptown Espresso** • 4301 SW Edmunds St
206-935-3753
Self-proclaimed "Home of the Velvet Foam", but the coffee underneath is just so-so.

Park free in lots around The Junction and start roaming. Get caffeinated before the in-store appearance at **Easy Street Records**. Stock up on potato guns, slingshots and other wholesome toys for the child in your life at **Max and Quinn's Atomic Boy's Shop-O-Rama**. Head downhill and west to **Alki Beach** for a Guinness at **The Celtic Swell** and explore what's referred to as the birthplace of Seattle.

Nightlife

- **Bamboo Bar & Grill** • 2806 Alki Ave SW
  206-937-3023
  The location and hours ('til 2 am) are the best thing they've got going.
- **Bang Bar Thai Restaurant & Lounge** •
  4750 California Ave SW
  206-935-8888
  A little bit of Belltown in West Seattle.
- **The Benbow Room** • 4210 SW Admiral Way
  206-922-3313
  A secret pirate ship bar inside a family restaurant.
- **The Celtic Swell** • 2722 Alki Ave SW
  206-932-7935
  Children and fiddles welcome, just like Ye Olde Country.

- **Elliott Bay Brewery Pub** •
  4720 California Ave SW
  206-932-8695
  Top-notch beers and organic local beef.
- **The Matador** • 4546 California Ave SW
  206-932-9988
  Loud. Dark. Fifty kinds of tequila.
- **OutWest Bar** • 5401 California Ave SW
  206-937-1540
  A cozy little bar for the gays who have gone west.
- **Poggie Tavern** • 4717 California Ave SW
  206-937-2165
  Not for the timid drinker.
- **West 5 Lounge & Restaurant** •
  4539 California Ave SW
  206-935-1966
  Hip yet homey, but always crowded.
- **Yen Wor Village** • 2300 California Ave SW
  206-932-1455
  Known round the hood as the Young Whore. Karaoke seven nights a week.

🍴 Restaurants

- **Angelina's Trattoria** • 2311 California Ave SW
206-932-4550 • $$
Affordable, cozy, and consistently delicious Italian food.
- **Bakery Nouveau** • 4737 California Ave SW
206-923-0534 • $
World Cup-winning baker crafts inexplicably perfect croissants.
- **Cactus** • 2820 Alki Ave SW
206-933-6000 • $$
Pretend you're in SoCal, straight chillin' with a margarita by the beach.
- **Christo's on Alki** • 2508 Alki Ave SW
206-923-2200 • $$
Family friendly with Greek gusto.
- **Circa** • 2605 California Ave SW
206-923-1102 • $$
Exquisite food makes you forget the uncomfortable booths.
- **Coastline** • 4444 California Ave SW
206-743-8027 • $$
Quality burgers and beers served fast food style.
- **Duke's Chowder House** • 2516 Alki Ave SW
206-937-6100 • $$
The chowder truly is what it's cracked up to be.
- **Easy Street Records & Cafe** •
4559 California Ave SW
206-938-3279 • $
Coffee, breakfast, and music. This place rocks.
- **El Chupacabra** • 2620 Alki Ave SW
206-933-7344 • $$
Frighteningly delicious Mexican munchies and margaritas.
- **Elliott Bay Brewery Pub** • 4720 California Ave SW
206-932-8695 • $$
Ice cream floats made with stout. C'mon, you know you wanna try it.
- **Heartland Cafe** • 4210 SW Admiral Way
206-922-3313 • $$
A little midwestern hospitality, doncha know.
- **Jak's Grill** • 4548 California Ave SW
206-937-7809 • $$$$
Both the food and atmosphere are upbeat.
- **La Rustica** • 4100 Beach Dr SW
206-932-3020 • $$$$$
Escape the beach buzz. Meat, seafood, and pasta in a seemingly remote setting.
- **Lee's Asian Restaurant** • 4510 California Ave SW
206-932-8209 • $$
The Seven-Flavor Beef will haunt your dreams.
- **Ma'ono Fried Chicken & Whisky** •
4437 California Ave SW
206-935-1075 • $$
They sell other dishes, but the star attractions are in the name.
- **Mashiko** • 4725 California Ave SW
206-935-4339 • $$
Sit back and let the chef choose for you. Good luck
- **Mission Tapas and Bar** • 2325 California Ave SW
206-937-8220 • $$$
Expensive and inviting atmosphere. Appetizers outdo the entrees.
- **Pagliacci Pizza** • 4449 California Ave SW
206-726-1717 • $$
Local favorite pizza chain makes crispy-chewy delights with seasonal ingredients.
- **Pailin Thai** • 2223 California Ave SW
206-937-8807 • $$
Gigantic fish tank and fresh food makes for peaceful dining.
- **Pegasus Pizza & Pasta** • 2770 Alki Ave SW
206-932-4849 • $$
Starved? Generous salads and loaded pizzas will do the trick.
- **Pepperdock's Restaurant** • 2618 Alki Ave SW
206-935-1000 • $
Tasty, cheap beach food.
- **Pho Than Brothers'** • 4822 California Ave SW
206-937-6264 • $
Cheap, fast, and filling, with a free cream puff to boot.
- **Pizzeria 22** • 4213 SW College St
206-687-7701 • $
Actual Neapolitan-style pizza forged in fire.
- **Shadowland** • 4458 California Ave SW
206-420-3817 • $$
Hearty.

Get the chef specials at **Mashiko**. Hit **Lee's Asian Restaurant** for its encyclopedic Asian cuisine; their Seven-Flavor Beef will haunt your dreams. Meanwhile, there is homemade ice cream to be had at the historic **Husky Deli**. If you get a jonesing for lubrication be fish and chips, **Spud** on Alki is classic. Dig on swine at **The Swinery**. And local chains **Pagliacci** and **Than Brothers'** serve up competent 'za and pho, respectively.

- **Shoofly Pie Company** • 4444 California Ave SW
  206-938-0680 • $
  Tons of sweet and several savory pies to please your pie hole.
- **Spud Fish & Chips** • 2666 Alki Ave SW
  206-938-0606 • $
  This place has been around for 75 years for a good reason.
- **Sunfish** • 2800 Alki Ave SW
  206-938-4112 • $$
  The best grilled halibut kabobs—batter not included.
- **The Swinery** • 3207 California Ave SW
  206-932-4211 • $$
  For those that dig on swine.
- **Tacos Guaymas** • 4719 California Ave SW
  206-935-8970 • $$
  Delicious tacos of all kinds including braaaaiiiins for your zombie friends.
- **Talarico's** • 4718 California Ave SW
  206-937-3463 • $
  Huge slices of pizza, but we miss the old New Luck Toy.
- **Top Pot Doughnuts** • 2758 Alki Avenue SW
  206-466-6839 • $
  Top Pot is tops!
- **Zatz A Better Bagel** • 2348 California Ave SW
  206-933-8244 • $
  Super fresh.

🛍 Shopping

- **Bin 41** • 4707 California Ave SW
  206-937-0411
  Great selection including many NW wines. Good tastings too.
- **Capers** • 4525 California Ave SW
  206-932-0371
  Classy, overpriced house wares that you really can't live without.
- **Click! Design That Fits** • 2210 California Ave SW
  206-328-9252
  Drool over cement-in-silver jewelry.
- **Coastal Surf Boutique** • 2532 Alki Ave SW
  206-933-5605
  Costly surf, brand names. Offers bike rental in summer.

- **Curious Kidstuff** •
  4740 California Ave SW
  206-937-8788
  Let your kids run wild while you buy them super-cool toys.
- **Easy Street Records & Cafe** •
  4559 California Ave SW
  206-938-3279
  You can't go to W. Seattle without stopping here for music.
- **Husky Deli** • 4721 California Ave SW
  206-937-2810
  Old-fashioned deli counter and homemade ice cream.
- **Max and Quinn's Atomic Boys Shop-O-Rama** •
  4311 SW Admiral Way
  206-938-3255
  The Archie McPhee's of West Seattle.
- **Metropolitan Market** • 2320 42nd Ave SW
  206-937-0551
  Fine grocery shopping.
- **Northwest Art & Frame** • 4733 California Ave SW
  206-937-5507
  Find an equal amount of useless gifts and art necessities.
- **PCC Natural Markets** • 2749 California Ave SW
  206-937-8481
  Organic to the core.
- **Pegasus Book Exchange** • 4553 California Ave SW
  206-937-5410
  Family-owned used bookstore.
- **Seattle Fish Company** • 4435 California Ave SW
  206-938-7576
  Support the independents who don't sell farm-raised fish.
- **Small Clothes** • 3215 California Ave SW
  206-932-2222
  Upscale second-hand for the toddler set.
- **The Swinery** • 3207 California Ave SW
  206-932-4211
  For those that dig on swine.
- **West Seattle Farmers Market** •
  44th Ave SW & SW Alaska St
  May thru December.
- **Zamboanga** • 4531 California Ave SW
  206-933-6399
  Eclectic trinkets and flowy clothes.

Map 36 · **North Delridge**

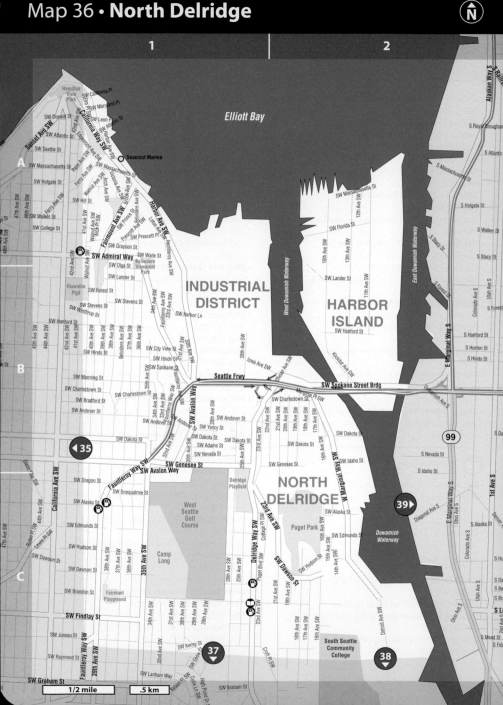

Map 36

The charm of this part of town is that they seem to have one foot in the 1950s while the other foot steps bravely into the 21st century. A large elderly population thrives amongst a strong influx of young families seeking kid-friendly goods and services. Snap the ideal panoramic photograph of Seattle's skyline from Harbor Avenue or up steep Admiral Way. There's really nothing pretentious in this neck of the woods. A coffee stop at **Java Bean** in Luna Park is worth the detour.

○ Landmarks

- **Seacrest Park** • 1660 Harbor Ave SW
  206-684-4075
  Scuba divers galore. Elliott Bay Water Taxi to
  downtown leaves from here.

🖥 Coffee

- **Diva Espresso** • 4480 Fauntleroy Way SW
  206-937-5225
  Local chain with unpredictable service. I guess it's
  kind of like ordering coffee from a diva.
- **Java Bean** • 2920 SW Avalon Way
  206-938-5665
  Since 1989: organic, shade grown, fair trade.
- **Uptown Espresso** • 3845 Delridge Way SW
  206-933-9497
  Self-proclaimed "Home of the Velvet Foam," but the
  coffee underneath is just so-so.

🍸 Nightlife

- **The Bridge** • 4439 35th Ave SW
  206-402-4606
  Attempts to bridge the gap between West Seattle
  and the rest of the world.
- **Skylark** • 3803 Delridge Way SW
  206-935-2111
  Real Seattle rock-n-roll happens here. No cover.
- **West Seattle Bowl** • 4505 39th Ave SW
  206-932-3731
  A dying breed.

🍴 Restaurants

- **Beloved Mexico** • 4721 Fauntleroy Way SW
  206-478-0496 • $
  You'll be-like this healthy-ish taco truck. "Love" is a
  little strong.
- **Buddha Ruksa** • 3520 SW Genesee St
  206-937-7676 • $$
  Enlightenment attained.
- **Chaco Canyon Organic Café** • 3770 SW Alaska St
  206-937-8732 • $$
  A voyage into the Raw Food Universe.
- **Chelan Cafe** • 3527 Chelan Ave SW
  206-932-7383 • $
  Solid blue collar greasy spoon.
- **Luna Park Cafe** • 2918 SW Avalon Way
  206-935-7250 • $
  Plenty of fun for the kids; mimosas and piles of
  eggs for the adults.
- **Marination Ma Kai** • 1660 Harbor Ave SW
  206-328-8226 • $
  Grown-up shave ice and korean tacos with a water
  view that can't be beat.
- **Pho Aroma** • 5605 Delridge Way SW
  206-932-4343 • $
  Way better than the Tacoma Aroma.
- **Salty's on Alki Beach** • 1936 Harbor Ave SW
  206-937-1600 • $$$$
  The brunch is a must at least once in your lifetime.

Map 37 • **Fauntleroy / Arbor Heights**

Fauntleroy Way, the street from which this area gets its name, is basically the "Gateway to Vashon," with its direct route to the ferry terminal through quaint, garden-lush, old neighborhoods bordering **Lincoln Park**. Arbor Heights and communities east of Fauntleroy, including White Center, reflect populations struggling to keep afloat as well as young families who can't afford to live closer to the water or in one of Seattle's pricier, more central neighborhoods.

o Landmarks

- **Lincoln Park** • 8011 Fauntleroy Way SW
206-684-4075
Bluff trails and a shoreline walk to salt-water filled Colman Public pool. Fun for the whole family.

Coffee

- **Bird On A Wire Espresso** • 3509 SW Henderson St
206-932-1143
Also beer, wine and small plates.
- **Café Rozella** • 9434 Delridge Way SW
206-762-7223
Plus food.
- **Caffe Ladro** • 7011 California Ave SW
206-938-8021
Strong coffee for strong coffee drinkers.

Nightlife

- **Beveridge Place Pub** • 6413 California Ave SW
206-932-9906
Grab a happy hour deal or sip a $75 brew.
- **Company Bar** • 9608 16th Ave SW
206-257-1162
White collar themed joint serves food and drink with soul.
- **Feedback Lounge** • 6451 California Ave SW
206-453-3259
A place for alcoholics who like music.
- **Roxbury Lanes** • 2823 SW Roxbury St
206-935-7400
Keeping bowling weird and sketchy.
- **Tug Inn** • 2216 SW Orchard St
206-768-8852
Mini pitchers, shag carpeting, duct taped furniture—dive in.

Map 37

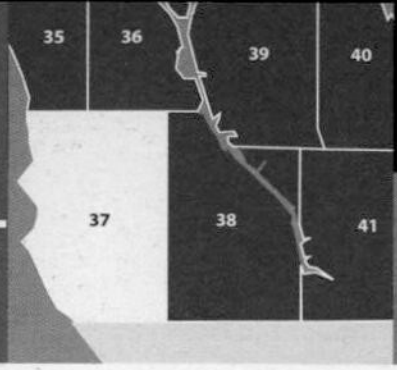

Map 37

Fauntleroy / Arbor Heights

🍴Restaurants

- **3.14 Bakery** • 9602 16th Ave SW
206-420-4784 • $
You don't have to be a math wiz to guess their specialty.
- **88 Restaurant** • 9418 Delridge Way SW
206-768-9767 • $
Your standard, ol' reliable pho/banh mi purveyor.
- **Café Rozella** • 9434 Delridge Way SW
206-762-7223 • $$
Plus coffee.
- **Eats Market Café** • 2600 SW Barton St
206-933-1200 • $$
A dual-purpose after-work pub and post-hangover breakfast spot.
- **Endolyne Joe's** • 9261 45th Ave SW
206-937-5637 • $$
American classics that are updated every season.
- **Locöl Barley & Vine** • 7902 35th Ave SW
206-708-7725 • $$
Comfort yourself with "a trio of beans" and a glass of wine.

- **Meander's Kitchen** • 9809 16th Ave SW
206-491-8571 • $
Otherwise ordinary diner wins with bourbon-battered challah French toast.
- **Proletariat Pizza** • 9622 16th Ave SW
206-432-9765 • $
Common pizza for the common people.
- **Salvadorean Bakery** • 1719 SW Roxbury St
206-762-4064 • $
Specialties from El Salvador: Stay for the sopa de pollo and the pupusas.
- **Tacos Guaymas** • 1622 SW Roxbury St
206-767-4026 • $$
Delicious tacos of all kinds including braaaaiiiins for your zombie friends.
- **Uncle Mike's BBQ** • 9640 16th Ave SW
206-588-2713 • $
A decent BBQ place with real vegetarian options.
- **West Seattle Fish House** • 9005 35th Ave SW
206-457-8643 • $
It's a fish house in West Seattle. A damn good one, too.
- **Zippy's Giant Burgers** • 1513 SW Holden St
206-763-1347 • $
How a quarter-pounder should be—chargrilled and served with a smile.

Map 37

Not much nightlife around these parts, but when you're done shopping at Westwood Town Center, Mother Nature can show you a spectacular time at **Lincoln Park**. A labyrinth of easy trails lead to a saltwater community pool and wild beaches. Just up from the Fauntleroy Ferry Terminal at the park's south entrance, **Endolyne Joe's** offers a divine, ever-changing menu. **Salvadorean Bakery** is beyond delicious and **88 Restaurant** offers fat bahn mi and fragrant pho. If you really need a beer, dive right in with the colorful locals at **The Tug Inn**.

Shopping

- **Full Tilt Ice Cream** • 9629 16th Ave SW
  206-767-4811
  Ice cream in an arcade. It don't get no icier.

- **Sea Mart** • 1513 SW
  Holden St
  206-766-9669
  Wide variety of international beers + lottery tickets.
- **West Seattle Thriftway** • 4201 SW Morgan St
  206-937-0245
  Locally owned and operated grocery store!

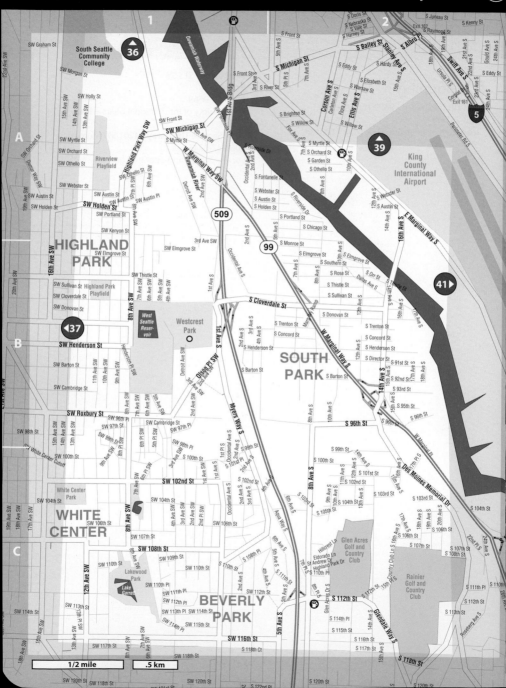

Map 38

Where can you find two spacious, members-only country clubs poised over an industrial waterway area rivaling the worst of North Jersey and a town hub thick with ethnic markets and seedy tattoo parlors? Step right up folks--it's all here! Yup, life in White Center (a.k.a Rat City for reasons best left to urban legend) means never having to leave the 'hood for fun.

○ Landmarks
- **Westcrest Park** • 9000 8th Ave SW
  206-684-4075
  Four-acre dog park has trails, balls, water dishes, and an obstacle course!

🖳 Coffee
- **Caffè Delia** • 9622 16th Ave SW
  206-457-8860
  The darling of White Center, serving Velton's coffee and Macrina pastries out of Proletariat Pizza.
- **Dubsea Coffee** • 9910 8th Ave SW
  206-708-6806
  The Bohemian coffee house is alive and well.
- **Hecka Good Cafe** • 10801 Myers Way S
  206-453-5682
  Not bad. Not bad at all.
- **Java Express** • 11600 Des Moines Memorial Dr
  206-248-7933
  On way to or coming from SeaTac.

🍸 Nightlife
- **Loretta's Northwesterner** • 8617 14th Ave S
  206-327-9649
  Wood paneling and classic beer signs from the 9 LB Hammer folks.

🍴 Restaurants
- **Muy Macho** • 8515 14th Ave S
  206-763-3484 • $
  Good and cheap. Brain and tripe.

🛍 Shopping
- **Pacific Industrial Supply Co.** • 1231 S Director St
  206-682-2100
  Industrial hardware junkie? Get your fix here.

Map 39 · **SoDo / Beacon Hill / Georgetown**

Map 39

This part of town is kind of like the one on the '90s sitcom, *Roseanne*; an industrial community that loves their burgers, BBQ, and Mexican food. Townies gather in dive bars after work for beer and conversation. They are so proudly blue-collar that their park houses beloved Sea-Town landmark, **Hat n' Boots**. This precious sculpture was rescued from an old Texico station and stands proudly next to a children's play structure. Ain't that America.

○ Landmarks

- **Hat 'n' Boots** · 6430 Corson Ave S
  Former roadside attraction now safely ensconced in Oxbow Park.
- **SoDo Freewall** · 2250 Occidental Ave S
  Graffiti on a wall.
- **Starbucks Headquarters** · 2401 Utah Ave S
  Still waiting for that giant mermaid to jump out and go Godzilla on downtown.

Coffee

- **All City Coffee** · 1205 S Vale St
  206-767-7146
  Where Georgetown caffeinates.
- **The Daily Coffee & Tea** · 5400 E Marginal Way S
  206-486-6088
  A nice little coffee oasis in a vast industrial dessert.
- **Espresso by Design** · 511 S Mead St
  206-768-1061
  Plus food.
- **The Station** · 2533 16th Ave S
  206-453-4892
  A nice Light Rail stop. Fill up on coffee before standing in the TSA line.
- **Victrola Coffee** · 3215 Beacon Ave S
  206-860-7767
  From a time before coffee was good.

Nightlife

- **9lb. Hammer** · 6009 Airport Way S
  206-762-3373
  More fun than you can shake a hammer at. Plus free peanuts!
- **Aston Manor** · 2946 1st Ave S
  206-382-7866
  Just the place for folks who long for the exclusivity and superficiality of Vegas clubs.
- **Bogart's Airport Way** · 3924 Airport Way S
  206-622-1119
  Guitar Hero Tuesdays and karaoke with trannies.
- **Brass Tacks** · 6031 Airport Way S
  206-397-3821
  Perpetuating the bacchanalian celebration of meat and alcohol.

- **Georgetown Liquor Company** ·
  5501 Airport Way S
  206-763-6764
  Atari 2600 and beer. Can life get any better?
- **Hooverville Bar** · 1721 1st Ave S
  206-264-2428
  A bar for recovering corporate junkies.
- **Jules Maes Saloon** · 5919 Airport Way S
  206-957-7766
  Century-old tavern where punk meets country.
- **Marco Polo Bar & Grill** · 5613 4th Ave S
  206-762-3964
  Blue collar dive bar with all the fixins. You'll be happy you found it.
- **The Mix** · 6006 12th Ave S
  206-767-0280
  Another Georgetown gem from the overachiever of neighborhoods.
- **The Oak** · 3019 Beacon Ave S
  206-535-7070
  The folks from Redwood present a family-friendly pub for grownup hipsters.
- **Showbox SoDo** · 1700 1st Ave S
  206-628-3151
  Where the Showbox is concerned, bigger is NOT better.
- **Siren Tavern** · 3403 4th Ave S
  206-223-9167
  Both firemen and longshoremen answer the call of the Siren.
- **Studio Seven** · 110 S Horton St
  206-286-1312
  Jam to live music with grandma and your teenager.

Restaurants

- **American Pie** · 5633 Airport Way S
  206-708-7813 · $
  Sweet and savory pies and empanadas good for eating or boning.
- **Bar del Corso** · 3057 Beacon Ave S
  206-395-2069 · $$
  Wood-fired pizza and wine to share with your (adult) family.

Map 39

SoDo / Beacon Hill / Georgetown

- **Brass Tacks** · 6031 Airport Way S
206-397-3821 · $$
Perpetuating the bacchanalian celebration of meat and alcohol.
- **Bread and Circuses** · 4700 Ohio Ave S
206-374-3081 · $
A delicious food freak show.
- **By's Drive-In** · 2901 4th Ave S
206-622-9901 · $
It's no Dick's, but it's better than the chains.
- **Calozzi's Cheesesteaks** · 7016 E Marginal Way S
206-762-1777 · $$
Tough-to-please Chicago ex-pats say these are ALMOST as good as the real thing.
- **Caravan Crêpes** ·
$
Crepes. But, like, REALLY good ones.
- **Dahlak Eritrean Cuisine** · 2007 S State St
206-860-0400 · $$
Complex and layered dishes that outshine most. Superfun with friends.
- **Denny's** · 2762 4th Ave S
206-623-8375 · $
Putting moons over Seattle's hammies once again.
- **El Sabroso** · 2524 16th Ave S
206-551-1432 · $
Best damn tortas in town.
- **The Essential Baking Company** · 5601 1st Ave S
206-876-3746 · $
Essentially delicious.
- **Ezell's Express** ·
$
Oprah's favorite chicken joint goes mobile.
- **Fonda La Catrina** · 5905 Airport Way S
206-767-2787 · $$
Enjoy their small but solid menu in an adorable Dia de los Muertos shrine.
- **Gastropod** · 3201 1st Ave S
206-403-1228 · $$
The fancy pants snack bar inside Epic Ales' tasting room.
- **Georgetown Liquor Company** ·
5501 Airport Way S
206-763-6764 · $
Veggie sandwiches that Yoda would approve of.
- **Hudson** · 5000 E Marginal Way S
206-767-4777 · $$
Food good enough to die for, luckily located next to a mortuary.

- **Katsu Burger** · 6538 4th Ave S
206-762-0752 · $$
Exactly what it sounds like, but way better than you might imagine.
- **Matt's Famous Chili Dogs** · 6615 E Marginal Way S
206-768-0418 · $
Midwestern folks affirm this is a true Chicago dog.
- **The Oak** · 3019 Beacon Ave S
206-535-7070 · $$
The folks from Redwood present a family-friendly pub for grownup hipsters.
- **Papa Bois** · 2401 Utah Ave S
425-341-3657 · $$
The sandwiches that Caribbean/Asian Fusion dreams are made of.
- **Pecos Pit BBQ** · 2260 1st Ave S
206-623-0629 · $
Spicy sandwiches for hardworkin' tongues.
- **Philly Boys Cheesesteaks** · 3201 4th Ave S
206-414-7707 · $
Settles the cheese steak authenticity debate by having all the options.
- **Pho Cyclo** · 2414 1st Ave S
206-382-9256 · $
The fragrant pho ga really is chicken soup for the soul.
- **Pig Iron Bar-B-Q** · 5602 1st Ave S
206-768-1009 · $$
Southern-style eats and a tattooed ambiance.
- **The Sammich Truck** · 6100 4th Ave S
206-992-6255 · $
Simple American classics.
- **Slim's Last Chance** · 5606 1st Ave S
206-762-7900 · $$
Rockabilly chili.
- **Smarty Pants** · 6017 Airport Way S
206-762-4777 · $$
Covering all the bases from knockout veg grub to roasted pork. Smart!
- **SODO Deli** · 3228 1st Ave S
206-467-0306 · $
The food is Sodo-licious.
- **The Square Knot Diner** · 6015 Airport Way S
206-915-5244 · $
There's nothing square about this ice-cream laden 24-hour diner.

SoDo is great for pork lovers (**Pecos Pit BBQ**), those who worship at the temple of the mermaid (**Starbucks' corporate headquarters** is located here), and hardware store junkies. Georgetown is for the urban cowboy/girl. It contains a **9lb. Hammer** (a biker/punk hangout), a **Stellar** pizza joint, and a **Liquor Company**.

- **The Station** · 2533 16th Ave S
  206-453-4892 · $
  A nice Light Rail stop. Fill up on coffee before standing in the TSA line.
- **Stellar Pizza, Ale & Cocktails** · 5513 Airport Way S
  206-763-1660 · $
  Stellar. Really.
- **Viengthong** · 2820 Martin Luther King Jr Way S
  206 725 3884 · $
  Quality Thai-Laotian dishes that tend toward fire-engine spiciness.
- **Willie's Taste of Soul BBQ** · 3427 Rainier Ave S
  206-722-3229 · $
  Soul-satisfying baby backs and some insanely buttery yams.

🛍 Shopping

- **A Dog's Dream Natural Pet Supply** ·
  5913 Airport Way S
  206-763-1546
  It's a good thing dogs don't have credit cards.
- **Borracchini's Bakery** · 2307 Rainier Ave S
  206-325-1550
  An adored local bakery with an emphasis on affordable.
- **Cannabis City** · 2733 4th Ave S
  206-682-1332
  Some of the cheapest grams in town.
- **Counterbalance Brewing Company** ·
  503 S Michigan St
  206-453-3615
  10 rotating, seasonal taps, lovingly curated from former coffee guys.
- **Daniel Smith** · 4150 1st Ave S
  206-223-9599
  Mega mart art supplies. Make an artist happy.
- **Earthwise Architectural Salvage** · 3447 4th Ave S
  206-624-4510
  "Junk can be beautiful."
- **Epic Ales** · 3201 1st Ave S
  206-351-3637
  Seasonal microbrewery with a gourmet snack bar in their tasting room. Epic, indeed.
- **Esquin Wine Merchants** · 2700 4th Ave S
  206-682-7374
  Guess what they sell?

- **Ganja Goddess** · 3207 1st Ave S
  206-682-7220
  Boutique weed for the high-rolling stoner.
- **Georgetown Music Store** · 6111 13th Ave S
  206-767-2718
  Supplying the next generation of G-town artists with axes.
- **Georgetown Records / Fantagraphics** ·
  1201 S Vale St
  206-762-5638
  Cool record store that now shares a space with the Fantagraphics flagship store.
- **Ghostfish Brewing Company** · 2942 1st Ave S
  206-397-3898
  Gluten free beer that doesn't taste like a compromise.
- **Goodwill Outlet** · 1765 6th Ave S
  206-957-5516
  Paw thru bins of cast offs from the unwashed masses.
- **Grocery Outlet** · 1702 4th Ave S
  206-812-6622
  Why is the food so cheap? Don't ask, just buy.
- **JC Marble & Granite** · 2920 1st Ave S
  206-388-0909
  Stone good enough for Jesus Christ's tomb.
- **Maruta Shoten** · 1024 S Bailey St
  206-767-5002
  Ultra-authentic japanese grocery; like a tiny Uwajimaya without the foreign influence.
- **Northwest Shower Door** · 3223 1st Ave S
  206-264-1010
  Elegant doors for clean people.
- **Seattle Cannabis Co.** · 3230 1st Ave S
  206-294-5839
  Over 30 unique strains for around $14 a gram.
- **Seattle Pottery Supply** · 35 S Hanford St
  206-587-0570
  When you want to recreate that scene from *Ghost*.
- **Second Use** · 3223 6th Ave S
  206-763-6929
  A (living) museum of old appliances.
- **Silver Platters** · 2930 1st Ave S
  206-283-3472
  No, it wasn't named after The Brady Bunch's band.
- **Visions Espresso Service** · 2737 1st Ave S
  206-623-6709
  The Wizard of Oz would be jealous of their coffee machine collection.

Map 40 • **Mount Baker / Seward Park / Columbia City**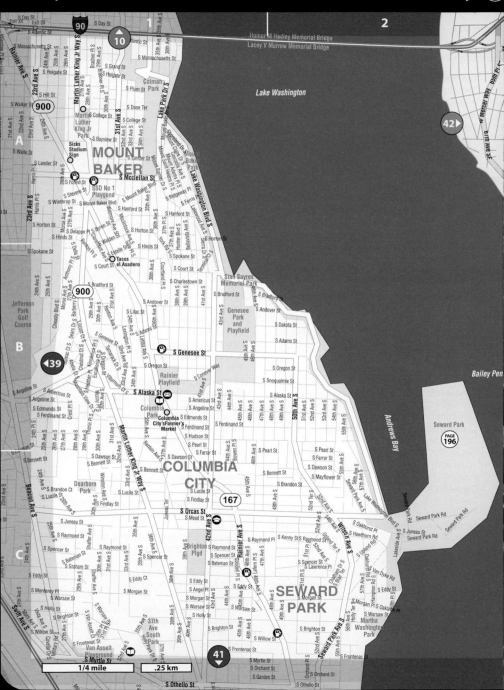

Map 40

Are your surroundings feeling a little homogeneous? Head south to the increasingly desirable Mount Baker, Seward Park, and Columbia City 'hoods. Orthodox Jews mingle with Vietnamese Presbyterians. Folks fishing from lake piers make way for Mount Baker's rowing crews. Potters, joggers, and picnickers frequent Seward Park. Warning: Seattle's answer to NASCAR, the Seafair Hydroplane and Blue Angel extravaganza takes over in early August. Locals exit (or turn their yards into parking lots) while 300,000+ party hearty.

○ Landmarks

- **Columbia City Farmers Market** •
  4801 Rainier Ave S
  Foodie heaven every Wednesday from May to October.
- **Martin Luther King Jr. Memorial Park** •
  2200 Martin Luther King Jr Way S
  206-684-4075
  A mountain of inspiration; words are inadequate.
- **Seward Park** • 5900 Lake Washington Blvd S
  206-684-4396
  Gigantic 300-acre thumb of lakefront on scenic Lake Washington.
- **Sicks Stadium Sign on Lowe's Hardware in Rainier Valley** • 2700 Rainier Ave S
  Once, men hit homers and grounded out here. Now they buy drill bits and caulk.
- **Tacos El Asadero** • 3517 Rainier Ave S
  206-722-9977
  The famous Taco Bus!

🖳 Coffee

- **Café Hope** • 3639 Martin Luther King Jr Way S
  206-805-8894
  All proceeds go to the Asian Counseling and Referral Service so your fix aids the greater good.
- **Caffe Vita** • 5028 Wilson Ave S
  206-721-0111
  The best of the local chains.
- **Empire Espresso** • 3829 S Edmunds St
  206-659-0588
  In case beer isn't enough to get you jacked up for the footie match.

🍸 Nightlife

- **AMF Imperial Lanes** • 2101 22nd Ave S
  206-325-2525
  Good clean fun. Which is rare for a bowing alley.
- **Billiard Hoang** • 3220 S Hudson St
  206-723-2054
  A couple reqular tables, some of those weird pocketless ones and banh mi (!).
- **Lottie's Lounge** • 4900 Rainier Ave S
  206-725-0519
  Comfortable neighborhood joint with live music and full menu.
- **Rainier Billiards** • 5041 Rainier Ave S
  206-722-6508
  The World Pool-Billiard Association ain't sanctioning tournaments here any time soon, but it'll do.

Map 40

Mount Baker / Seward Park / Columbia City

🍴Restaurants

- **Bananas Grill** • 4556 Martin Luther King Jr Way S
  206-420-4839 • $
  Not your average gyrocery. There's always money in the banana grill.
- **Bent Burgers** • 5100 S Dawson St
  206-760-0291 • $
  Not as "bent" as they'd have you believe. But they'll do.
- **Big Chickie** • 5520 Rainier Ave S
  206-946-1519 • $$$
  Brave the line and take home big piles of poultry pleasure.
- **Cafe Ibex** • 3218 Martin Luther King Jr Way S
  206-721-7537 • $
  Decent Ethiopian open late.
- **Columbia City Ale House** • 4914 Rainier Ave S
  206-723-5123 • $$
  Not a chicken wing in sight: just catfish sandwiches, gumbo, fish tacos. Poor you.
- **Columbia City Bakery** • 4865 Rainier Ave S
  206-723-6023 • $
  Bread to make your grandmamma proud. Fabulous baguettes.
- **Tacos El Asadero** • 3517 Rainier Ave S
  206-722-9977 • $
  Mexi cola and carne asada for less than a latte.
- **Emerald City Fish and Chips** • 3756 Rainier Ave S
  206-760-3474 • $
  Local boys bring New Orleans flavor to their meticulous fish & chips experience.
- **Flying Squirrel Pizza Co** • 4920 S Genesee St
  206-721-7620 • $$
  Imaginative pizzas made from local organic ingredients. So very Seatown.
- **Geraldine's Counter** • 4872 Rainier Ave S
  206-723-2080 • $$
  Diner fare that's far better than it needs to be.
- **Grilled Cheese Experience** • 5718 Rainier Ave S
  206-661-5225 • $$
  An experience you won't soon forget. Because cheese overdoses cause nightmares.
- **Island Soul** • 4869 Rainier Ave S
  206-329-1202 • $$
  Steel drums fuel the Caribbean favorites and rum cocktails.
- **Jones Barbeque** • 4417 Fauntleroy Way SW
  206-257-4946 • $
  The tenderest, juiciest dead cows one could imagine.
- **Jus Bar** • 4908 Rainier Ave S
  206-420-2535 • $
  They have pretty silly names, but these juices are serious business.
- **La Medusa** • 4857 Rainier Ave S
  206-723-2192 • $$$
  Sicilian food for the soul meets the neighborhood farmer's market.
- **La Teranga** • 4903 Rainier Ave S
  206-725-1188 • $$
  Tiny portal to a Senegalese kitchen of delights.
- **Mioposto** • 3601 S McClellan St
  206-760-3400 • $$
  A splendid park view and light, family-friendly fare from the Chow Foods crew.
- **Spice Room** • 4909 Rainier Ave S
  206-725-7090 • $$
  Thai-rific.
- **St. Dames** • 4525 Martin Luther King Jr Way S
  206-725-8879 • $$
  Vegetarian comfort food that's actually comforting.
- **Tutta Bella Neopolitan Pizzeria** •
  4918 Rainier Ave S
  206-721-3501 • $
  Their pizza has been certified by the Italian government. 'Nuff said.
- **Wabi-Sabi** • 4909 Rainier Ave S
  206-721-0212 • $$
  Solid sushi and pleasant ambiance.

Map 40

Columbia City is a tiny triangular hub on Rainier Avenue between Orcas and Alaska, which during the boom exploded with condos and adorable eateries. Our favorite cafe is **La Medusa**, where they serve edible miracles. It's **Columbia City Bakery** for artisanal fare, **Tutta Bella** for family dining, **Full Tilt** for dessert, and **Lottie's Lounge** for Beer-O'Clock.

Shopping

- **Andaluz** • 4908 Rainier Ave S
  206-760-1900
  Gifts for girlie girls.
- **Bike Works!** • 3709 S Ferdinand St
  206-725-9408
  Non-profit bike shop that teaches maintainance to kids.
- **Bob's Quality Meats** • 4861 Rainier Ave S
  206-725-1221
  Seattle needs more old-school butchers like Bob.

- **Full Tilt Ice Cream** • 5041 Rainier Ave S
  206-226-2740
  Ice cream, beer, and pinball. Sweet.
- **PCC Natural Markets** • 5041 Wilson Ave S
  206-723-2720
  Organic to the core.
- **Vientian Asian Grocery** •
  6059 Martin Luther King Jr Way S
  206 723-3160
  This tiny Lao grocery and cafe packs a big punch.

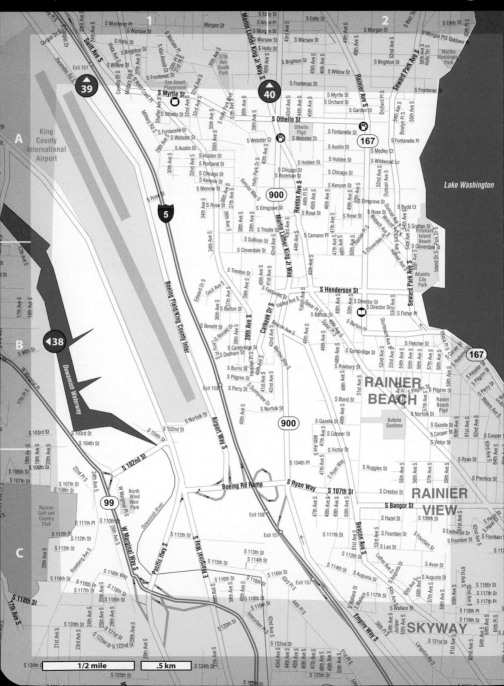

Map 41 • **Rainier Beach / Rainier View / Skyway**

Map 41

You know real estate prices are insane when few can afford homes even in this predominantly low – to middle-income area. The exception is the recession-proof string of waterfront homeowners bordering Lake Washington. Kubota Gardens and the **Rainier Beach Library** are lovely and the public boat launch is handy.

Coffee

• **Jet Fuel Espresso** •
11234 Tukwila International Blvd
206-764-4944
Drive thru.

Shopping

• **Van Asselt Beauty Salon** • 7136 Beacon Ave S
206-725-2058
They are committed to you looking fabulous.

Restaurants

• **Cafe Vignole** • 9252 57th Ave S
206-721-2267 • $$$
Y'all ready to mangia?
• **Hong Kong Seafood Restaurant** •
9400 Rainier Ave S
206-723-1718 • $$
Great Cantonese dim sum and noodles.
• **King Donut** • 9232 Rainier Ave S
206-721-3103 • $
Terrific trifecta of donuts, teriyaki, and laundromat.
We kid you not.
• **Maya's Mexican Restaurant** • 9447 Rainier Ave S
206-725-5510 • $
Seafood is the speciality; wash it down with a
fresh-queezed 'rita.
• **Nate's Wings and Waffles** • 9261 57th Ave S
206-722-9464 • $
Veg friendly Nate slings everyone's favorite sweet/
savory power couple.
• **Pho Van** • 9150 Rainier Ave S
206-725-2989 • $$
Vietnamese soup. The perfect hangover cure!
• **Sunset Cafe** • 8115 Rainier Ave S
206-722-0342 • $$
Where else can you get Ethiopian food OR chicken
and waffles? I love America!
• **Tammy's Bakery** •
7101 Martin Luther King Jr Way S
206-760-1172 • $
Vietnamese baked goods and sandwiches (banh
mi).
• **Taqueria Costa Alegre Taco Bus** •
9000 Rainier Ave S
206-725-0300 • $
Board the awesome taco bus. Literally.

Map 42 • **Mercer Island**

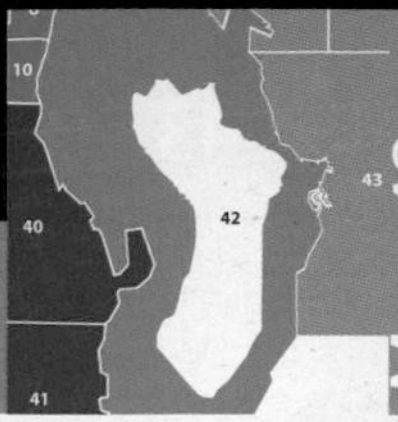

Map 42

Once a mild-mannered dairy farm community, they soon turned that milk into gold and now Mercer Island is home to Seattle's rich and/or famous. This is the 'hood where Paul Allen sleeps, dreaming up new ways to show off his money. Regular folks are welcome too, as long as they know their place and enter around back.

Coffee

- **The J Cafe** • 3801 East Mercer Way
  206-232-7115
  The place for nosh inside the Stroum Jewish Community Center.

Restaurants

- **Bennett's** • 7650 SE 27th St
  206-232-2759 • $$
  Deli by day, fine dining by night.
- **Phobulous** • 3033 78th Ave SE
  206-232-0828 • $
  Pho and bubble tea on Mercer Island.
- **Pon Proem** • 3039 78th Ave SE
  206-236-8424 • $$
  They don't mess around with the chilies here.
- **Roanoke Inn** • 1825 72nd Ave SE
  206-232-0800 • $$
  Nuzzle up to the cozy fire in the company of millionaires.
- **Roberto's** • 7605 SE 27th St
  206-232-7383 • $
  A pizza place with salads that are actually tasty.
- **Seven Star** • 2775 78th Ave SE
  206-230-8665 • $
  More like two stars, but who's counting?

Shopping

- **Island Books** • 3014 78th Ave SE
  206-232-6920
  Neighborhood independent bookstore, still kicking.

Map 43 • Bellevue (Southwest)

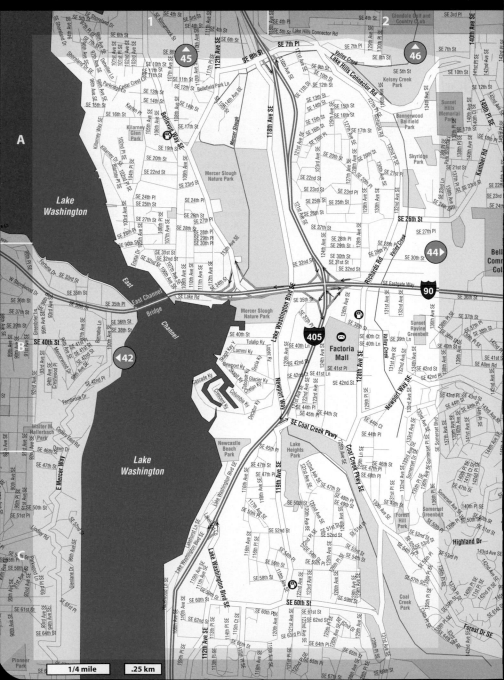

Map 43

Bellevue is home to a ton of smart teenagers—several high schools rank among the finest in the nation and it's safe to say that these Bellevue braniacs will probably be your boss one day. When not studying, you can find them hanging out at the food court in the Factoria Mall.

Restaurants

- **Shanghai Café** • 12708 SE 38th St
  425-603-1689 • $$
  Homemade noodles keep 'em coming back.
- **Square Lotus** • 3540 Factoria Blvd SE
  425-679-0680 • $$
  Family-owned Vietnamese with substantial vegetarian menu.
- **Top Gun Seafood** • 12450 SE 38th St
  425-641-3386 • $$
  Take a ride into the dim-sum zone.

Map 44 • **Bellevue (South)**

Map 44

As the third largest institution of higher education in Washington, Bellevue Community College sends more transfer students to four-year universities than any other community college in the state. At first glance the region appears to be quiet residential suburbs, but the proximity of I-90 and I-405 can make this area hell during rush hour.

Coffee

- **148th Ave Coffee Shop** •
  2649 Landerholm Circle SE
  Spacious non-chain option.
- **BigFoot Java** • 5157 Lakemont Blvd SE
  425-391-1976
  Decent joe courtesy your favorite blurry hirsute pal.

- **Cafe Bella** • 106 148th Ave NE
  425-747-2781
  Roadside coffee with a nice personality.
- **Megan's Coffee Corner** • 15100 SE 38th St
  425-747-4410
  Beloved Bellevue coffee shack.
- **Sawdust Coffee Company** • 4055 Factoria Blvd SE
  425-643-2518
  They're selling themselves short. Their coffee is way better than sawdust.

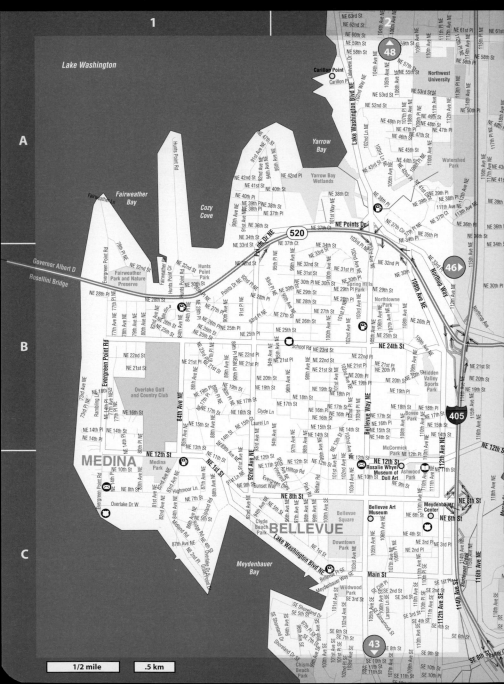

Map 45 • **Bellevue (West) / Medina**

Map 45

As business continues to boom, construction cranes have become a permanent fixture amid shiny skyscrapers in downtown Bellevue. Bellevue Way becomes "Snowflake Lane" during the holiday season with nightly parades and Christmas lights on display. Upscale and strictly residential Medina is known for its homes right on Lake Washington's shoreline.

○ Landmarks

- **Bellevue Art Museum** • 510 Bellevue Way NE
  425-519-0770
  Across the street from Bellevue Square, exhibits arts and crafts from local artists.
- **Carillon Point** • 4100 Carillon Point
  425-822-1700
  Marina waterfront with carillons that ring every 30 minutes.
- **Meydenbauer Center** • 11100 NE 6th St
  425-637-1020
  Convention center featuring cultural, theater, and musical events.

Coffee

- **Café Cesura** • 1015 108th Ave NE
  425-633-2362
  For those who like coffee, but think they should be paying more for it.
- **T'Latte** • 37 103rd Ave NE
  425-709-6868
  Bubble tea.

Nightlife

- **Black Bottle Postern** • 919 Bellevue Way NE
  425-223-5143
  This Belltown favorite brings the noise to Bellevue.
- **Lucky Strike Lanes** • 700 Bellevue Way NE
  425-453-5137
  Bowling gone upscale, with creative televisions and plasma cocktails.
- **Parlor Billiards & Spirits** • 700 Bellevue Way NE
  425-289-7000
  Upscale pool hall.

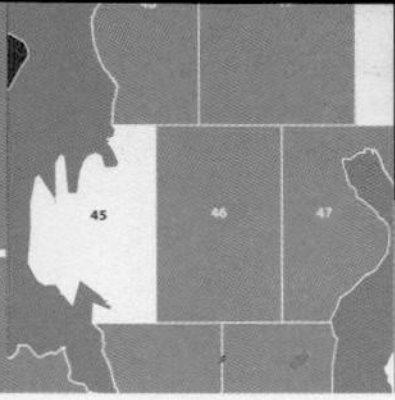

Map 45

Bellevue (West) / Medina

🍴Restaurants

- **99 Park** • 99 102nd Ave NE
  425-999-3991 • $$$
  Best thing to happen to middle-aged Bellevue since the SUV.
- **Bamboo Garden** • 202 106th Ave NE
  425-688-7991 • $
  Cheap, spicy Sichuan in a strip mall (adjacent to an adult entertainment store).
- **Bis on Main** • 10213 Main St
  425-455-2033 • $$$$
  Perfect for wining and dining—as long as you got the dough.
- **Cheesecake Factory** • 401 Bellevue Sq
  425-450-6000 • $$$
  Overpriced food straight from the assembly line.
- **Daniel's Broiler** • 10500 NE 8th St
  425-462-4662 • $$$$$
  Fancy folk (or those whose parents are paying) head here for decent steak.
- **Din Tai Fung** • 700 Bellevue Wy NE
  425-698-1095 • $$
  Seattle outpost of major dumpling multi-national.
- **Facing East Taiwanese Restaurant** •
  1075 Bellevue Way NE
  425-688-2986 • $
  Bet you never thought you'd the words oysters and pancakes together.
- **Ginza** • 103 102nd Ave SE
  425-709-7072 • $$$
  Specializing in Japanese barbecue—rare find (not literally).
- **John Howie Steak** • 11111 NE 8th St
  425-440-0880 • $$$$$$
  Highest-end steakhouse, no corners cut, priced accordingly.
- **Koral Bar & Kitchen** • 900 Bellevue Way NE
  425-623-1125 • $$
  A consolation for finding yourself at the Bellevue Hyatt Regency.
- **Mediterranean Kitchen** • 103 Bellevue Way NE
  425-462-9422 • $$$
  Garlicky Greek goodness.
- **The Melting Pot** • 302 108th Ave NE
  425-646-2744 • $$$$
  Gimmicky and retro, perhaps, but dipping things in cheese can never be bad.
- **Pagliacci Pizza** • 563 Bellevue Sq
  425-726-1717 • $$
  Local favorite pizza chain makes crispy-chewy delights with seasonal ingredients.
- **Pasta & Co.** • 10218 NE 8th St
  425-453-8760 • $$
  One-stop gourmet chain has fresh bread, wine, and risotto cakes to go.
- **PF Chang's China Bistro** • 525 Bellevue Way SE
  425-637-3582 • $$$
  Shamelessly Americanized Chinese food.
- **PinkaBella Cupcakes** • 320 Bellevue Sq
  425-453-2253 • $$
  Keeping the overpriced sugar bomb dream alive.
- **Pogacha** • 119 106th Ave NE
  425-455-5670 • $$$
  Translation: yummy Croatian pizza.
- **Ruth's Chris Steak House** • 565 Bellevue Sq
  425-451-1550 • $$$$$
  Ubiquitous chain dishes out gargantuan portions of meat.
- **Seastar Restaurant and Raw Bar** •
  205 108th Ave NE
  425-456-0010 • $$$
  Known for the seafood and oysters.
- **Tap House Grill** • 550 106th Ave NE
  425-467-1730 • $$$
  160 beers on tap. We repeat: 160 beers. On tap.

Expect crowds and long waits at every nice restaurant within walking distance of Bellevue Square (or "Belle Square" if you're nasty). Skip the lines at **Lincoln Square Cinemas** by scoring tickets from kiosks sprinkled around Belle Square. If you've got the dough, the membership-only Bellevue Club is recognized for its vast athletic facilities, including an Olympic-size swimming pool and indoor track. **Carillon Point** is a perfect place to stroll and watch the sunset after dinner.

Shopping

- **Bellevue Square** • NE 8th St & Bellevue Way NE
  425-646-3660
  Bellevue behemouth.
- **Element** • 575 Bellevue Way NE
  425-453-3448
  Looking cool in Bellevue can be hard to pull off.
- **Fireworks** • 196 Bellevue Sq
  425-688-0933
  Colorful gifts and home décor handmade by local artists.
- **Green Theory** • 10697 Main St
  425-502-7033
  Their theory is people will pay a ton of money for legal weed.
- **Lincoln Square** • NE 8th St & Bellevue Way NE
  425-646-3660
  Just what Bellevue needed—an expansion of Bellevue Square.
- **Made In Washington** • 190 Bellevue Sq
  425-454-6907
  If you must give Northwest smoked salmon as a gift.
- **Oil & Vinegar** • 2086 Bellevue Sq
  425-454-8497
  Olive oil on tap. Not to mention pestos, dips, mustards, sun-dried tomatoes…
- **Rudy's Barbershop** • 5 Bellevue Way NE
  206-467-1462
  Absolute best cheap haircut!
- **Sephora** • 141 Bellevue Sq
  425-467-1337
  All the make-up you can dream-up in one store.
- **University Book Store** • 990 102nd Ave NE
  425-462-4500
  UW text books and Husky gear.

Map 46 · **Bellevue (Central)**

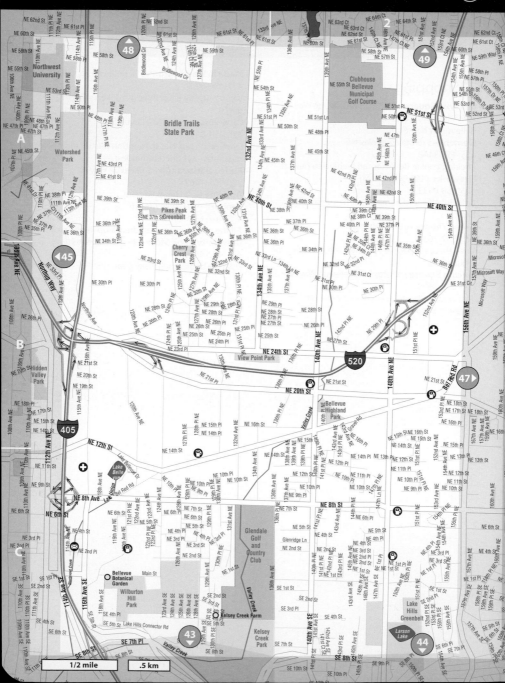

Map 46

The latest census reported Bellevue to have the highest percentage of non-white residents in the state, with the Chinese and Indian populations having increased twofold since 2000. Despite the materialistic air of the "SoCal of Puget Sound," Bellevue ranks consistently high in *Money's* "Best Places to Live." Have you noticed how much Western Washingtonians love their magazine list rankings?

○ Landmarks
- **Bellevue Botanical Garden** • 12001 Main St
  425-452-2750
  Free guided tours on weekends through their 36 acres of gardens and woodlands.
- **Kelsey Creek Farm** • 410 130th Ave SE
  425-452-7688
  Ponies and farm animals for the kids.

Coffee
- **Bellisimo Espresso** • 11909 NE 8th St
  425-451-7795
  Walk-up stand.
- **Boba Express** • 15600 NE 8th St
  425-641-1165
  Food court bubble tea and coffee. It is what it is.
- **Jitters Coffee** • 2200 148th Ave NE
  425-644-4645
  Go-to for Microsofties.

Nightlife
- **Skate King** • 2301 140th Ave NE
  425-641-2047
  Bounce. Roll. Skate.

Restaurants
- **Bai Tong Thai Restaurant** • 14804 NE 24th St
  425-747-8424 • $$$
  Thai with stylish decor and prices to match.
- **Blue Ginger Korean Grill and Sushi** •
  14045 NE 20th St
  425-746-1222 • $$
  BBQ up some Korean beef at your table.
- **Boba Express** • 15600 NE 8th St
  425-641-1165 • $
  Food court bubble tea and coffee.
- **Can-Am Pizza** • 15400 NE 20th St
  425-747-7777 • $
  Indian food on a pizza. Good news: Butter. Bad news: Bellevue.
- **Dixie's BBQ** • 11522 Northup Way
  425-828-2460 • $$
  Louisiana-style brisket slopped into styrofoam—it's so right.

- **I Love Sushi** • 11818 NE 8th St
  425-454-5706 • $$$
  We love I Love Sushi.
- **Malay Satay Hut** • 15230 NE 24th St
  425-564-0888 • $$
  Three cuisines unite under one roof, with delicious results.
- **Noble Court** • 1644 140th Ave NE
  425-641-6011 • $$
  Freakin' huge Hong Kong-style treats and dim sum. Gets packed.
- **Pho Hoa** • 15169 NE 24th St
  425-641-7898 • $
  Pho for an MSG fix.
- **Regent Bakery & Cafe** • 15159 NE 24th St
  425-378-1498 • $
  Family run Chinese bakery well known for their massive selection of cakes.
- **Saigon City** • 15045 Bel Red Rd
  425-401-0823 • $
  Mediocre pho, but cute menu adorned with family photos.
- **Seoul Hot Pot** • 2560 152nd Ave NE
  425-885-3355 • $$
  Korean convenient to Microsoft campus.
- **Szechuan Chef** • 15015 Main St
  425-746-9008 • $$
  Spicy red Szechuan hotpots with floating peppercorns are the trend.
- **Thai Kitchen** • 14115 NE 20th St
  425-641-9166 • $
  Curries and peppers will have you oohing and aahing in satisfaction.
- **Tosoni's** • 14320 NE 20th St
  425-644-1668 • $$$$$
  Loyal regulars hope the secret doesn't get out. Oops.

Shopping
- **BelMar** • 614 116th Ave NE
  425-453-5749
  If you want to get stoned in Bellevue (and who wouldn't) you may as well come here.
- **The Novel Tree** • 1817 130th Ave NE
  425-867-2700
  You can't do better than these guys for getting baked on the East Side.
- **Uwajimaya** • 699 120th Ave NE
  425-747-9012
  Awesome Asian superstore.

Map 47 • **Bellevue (East) / Redmond**

Ⓝ

REDMOND

BELLEVUE

Marymoor Park

Lake Sammamish

Microsoft Corporate Headquarters

Cascade View Park

Westside Park

Bridle Crest Trail Park

Kennebec Ave

Brae Burn Golf and Country Club

Tam O Shanter Park

Tam O Shanter Golf and Country Club

Current Corp Limit

Ivanhoe Park

Crossroads Park Golf Course

Ivanhoe Battlefields

Crossroads

Crossroads Park

Hillaire Park

Suffich Greenbelt

Microsoft Way

NE Bellevue Redmond Rd

W Bellevue Redmond Rd

W Lake Sammamish Pkwy NE

E Lake Sammamish Pkwy NE

Sammamish River

Marymoor Park Rd

Redmond Fall City Rd

Evans Creek

Bel Red Rd

Northup Way

NE 24th St

NE 8th St

Lake Hills Blvd

NE 40th St

NE 51st St

Rosemont Blvd

Mallard Ln

520

202

49

46

44

1

2

A

B

C

N

1/4 mile   **.25 km**

Map 47

Trees and scattered parks with numerous sports camps surround the quiet residential areas, keeping the moms and soccer vans busy. An ideal location for picnics and water sports, Idylwood Beach Park on Lake Sammamish is a popular hangout for teenagers eager (and longing) for the sun and warm weather. Rural farmland less than sixty years ago, Redmond is now a pricey city and home to a certain gazillion-dollar behemoth that goes by the unaccountably modest moniker of **Microsoft**.

○ Landmarks
- **Microsoft Corporate Headquarters** •
  1 Microsoft Way
  425-882-8080
  Tiny software company named after that famous street in Redmond, Microsoft Way.

🍴 Restaurants
- **Firenze Ristorante Italiano** • 15600 NE 8th St
  425-957-1077 • $$$
  A go-to date place; the simplest dishes are the bestest.
- **New York Cupcakes** • 15600 NE 8th St
  425-283-5445 • $
  Mmmmm…Buttercream.

🛍 Shopping
- **Crossroads** • 15600 NE 8th St
  425-644-1111
  Less than glitzy shopping mall.

Map 48 · **Kirkland**

Map 48

With a landscape view of the Seattle skyline, apartments and condos here will eat your paycheck like it's a steak dinner. A waterfront and a quiet, romantic lifestyle attracts retirees. Kirkland's pedestrian-friendly (translation: major traffic), village-like character is maintained by the assortment of little consignment boutiques, art galleries, coffee shops, and restaurants. The home of the original headquarters of Costco (hence the Kirkland Signature brand), Kirkland also hosts of the Junior League Softball World Series.

o Landmarks

- **Kirkland Marina** • 25 Lake Shore Plaza
  Dig your toes into the sandy beach.
- **Kirkland Performance Center** • 350 Kirkland Ave
  425-893-9900
  400-seat theater hosting an array of performances.

Coffee

- **Artesano Espresso** • 1431 Market St
  Solid drive-thru coffee.
- **Caffe Ladro** • 104 Central Way
  425-827-5838
  Strong coffee for strong coffee drinkers.
- **Gourmet Latté** • 13270 100th Ave NE
  425-248-0663
  Gourmet is a relative term, but the coffee at this unassuming roadside shack is A-OK.
- **The Green Beanery** • 13039 NE 70th Pl
  425-893-9760
  A particularly eco-mindful coffee stand serving organic fair-trade, naturally.
- **Kitanda Açaí and Espresso** • 12700 NE 124th St
  425-820-4381
  The Brazilian coffee and pastries that you didn't know your life was missing.
- **Mercurys Coffee Co.** • 8506 122nd Ave NE
  425-406-8059
  Organic fair trade coffee that's good enough to forgive a missing apostrophe.
- **Rococo Coffee Roasting** • 136 Park Ln
  425-803-9081
  Their house-roasted coffee is good enough to make you forget you're in Kirkland.
- **St. James Espresso** • 355 Kirkland Ave
  425-896-8272
  Brewing Caffe D'arte beans.
- **Urban Coffee Lounge** • 9744 NE 119th Way
  425-820-7788
  Trying to approximate an actual urban coffee shop in Kirkland.
- **Zoka Coffee Roaster & Tea Company** •
  129 Central Way
  425-284-1830
  A true Seattle original. But in Kirkland.

Map 48

48   49

45   46   47

Kirkland

Nightlife

- **TechCity Bowl** • 13033 NE 70th Pl
  425-827-0785
  32 lanes and a booming sound system.
- **Tiki Joe's Wet Bar** • 106 Kirkland Ave
  425-827-8300
  Cheap specials and rowdy karaoke for you and the frat boys.

Restaurants

- **Anthony's** • 135 Lake St S
  425-822-0225 • $$$$
  Pacific Northwest fare with expansive view of Lake Washington.
- **Cactus** • 121 Park Ln
  425-893-9799 • $$$
  Outstanding mojitos and Mexican.
- **Café Juanita** • 9702 NE 120th Pl
  425-823-1505 • $$$$$
  Serenity exemplified, and stellar Italian. A must.
- **Hanuman Thai Cafe** • 115 Central Way
  425-605-2181 • $
  Too satisfying for words. You'll actually think you're in Thailand.
- **Izumi** • 12539 116th Ave NE
  425-821-1959 • $$$
  An affordable Eastside alternative to Seattle's uberspendy sushi spots.
- **Lynn's Bistro** • 214 Central Way
  425-889-2808 • $$$$
  Bistro fare with an Asian flair.
- **The Original Pancake House** •
  130 Park Place Center
  425-827-7575 • $$
  Homemade batter! A dozen types of flapjacks! It's breakfast heaven.
- **Padria Mediterranean Cafe** • 9708 NE 119th Way
  425-814-1693 • $
  A challenge for the fast food generation…real food.

Your Sunday plans: grab a newspaper and a latte at **Caffe Ladro**, take a walk with your dog and feed the ducks at Marina Park, satisfy your stomach with a juicy burger at **The Slip**, catch a musical performance at the **Kirkland Performance Center**, then grab dinner at one of the many Thai restaurants. For the most authentic Japanese food on this side of the lake, it has to be **Izumi**, while **Anthony's** dishes out great seafood. If you must make a fool of yourself, there's karaoke at **Pegasus Pizza** and the "classy" **Tiki Joe's Wet Bar**

- **Pegasus Pizza & Pasta** • 12669 NE 85th St
  425-822-7400 • $$
  Starved? Generous salads and loaded pizzas will do the trick.
- **Purple Café & Wine Bar** • 323 Park Place Center
  425-828-3772 • $$
  Tome-like wine list can be intimidating; food is upscale café fare.
- **Ristorante Paradiso** • 120 Park Ln
  425-889-8601 • $$$
  A little bit of Sardinia on the Eastside.
- **Santorini Greek Grill** • 106 Central Way
  425-822-0555 • $$
  Eastside local favorite is closer than a Greek island getaway.
- **Sarducci's Sub** • 955 6th St S
  425-827-8253 • $
  They claim to be the best in town. And it's no BS.
- **Shamiana** • 10724 NE 68th St
  425-827-4902 • $$$
  Generous buffet.
- **The Slip** • 80 Kirkland Ave
  425-739-0033 • $$
  Burgers so juicy they…slip.
- **Thai Kitchen** • 11701 124th Ave NE
  425-820-5630 • $
  Curries and peppers will have you oohing and aahing in spicy satisfaction.
- **Wing Dome** • 232 Central Way
  425-822-9464 • $
  Flamin' baskets of flavored chicken wings.

Shopping

- **Champagne Taste** • 147 Park Ln
  425-828-4502
  Designer gown consignment store.
- **Parkplace Books** • 348 Central Way
  425-828-6546
  Independent bookstore for the 'burbs, since 1986.
- **PCC Natural Markets** • 10718 NE 68th St
  425-828-4622
  Organic to the core.
- **Simplicity Décor** • 126 Park Ln
  425-803-0386
  Classy, simple Thai-style furniture.
- **Tim's Seafood** • 224 Park Ln
  425-827-0195
  Fresh, seasonal seafood for sale. They pack and ship for you.

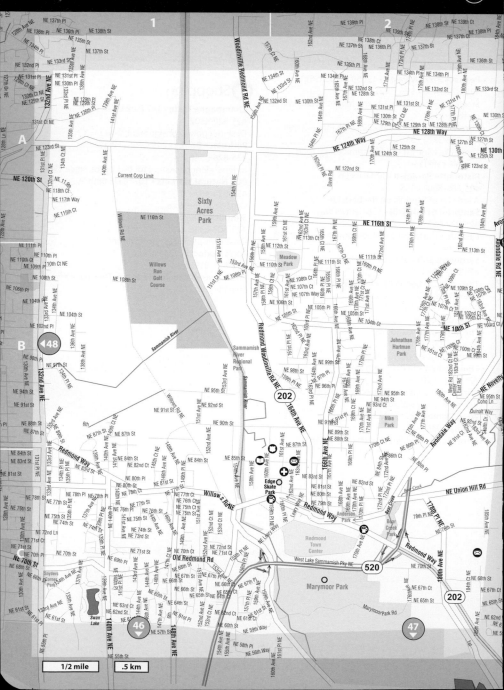

Map 49 · Redmond

Map 49

Easily accessible to and from the surrounding Eastside cities and Seattle, Redmond claims the title "Bicycle capital of the Northwest"—the eleven-mile Sammamish River Trail takes cyclists to the Burke Gilman Trail ending in Seattle. With what seems like hundreds of Starbucks (and counting) within a five-mile radius, the daily mocha will prevent you from dwelling on the drizzle. Picnic or catch a summer concert at **Marymoor Park**.

○ Landmarks

- **Edge Skate Park** • NE 83rd St & 161st Ave NE
  Skateboard park and graffiti wall sponsored by the city. Cool.
- **Marymoor Park** •
  6046 W Lake Sammamish Pkwy NE
  206-205-3661
  640 acres for picnics, summer concerts, and chasing dogs.

Coffee

- **Cascade Grind** • 8005 161st Ave NE
  206-881-2500
  Recognizing that you can get good coffee from attractive people who keep their clothes on.
- **Jitters Coffee** • 15010 NE 20th Pl
  425-747-8030
  Go-to for Microsofties.
- **Kitanda Açaí and Espresso** • 16349 NE 74th St
  206-556-7999
  The Brazilian coffee and pastries that you didn't know your life was missing.
- **Mercurys Coffee Co.** • 17980 Redmond Way
  425-881-0959
  Organic fair trade coffee that's good enough to forgive a missing apostrophe.
- **Peet's Coffee & Tea** • 17887 Redmond Way
  425-968-6125
  Bay Area interlopers.
- **Tapioca Express** • 15230 NE 24th St
  206-643-9406
  Espresso and bubble tea the Taiwanese way.
- **Victor's Celtic Coffee & Roasters** • 7993 Gilman St
  425-881-6451
  Own roasters plus wholesale.

Nightlife

- **Celtic Bayou** • 7281 W Lake Sammamish Pkwy NE
  425-869-5933
  Irish/Cajun hybrid in case you need to fill that void.
- **The Matador** • 7824 Leary Way NE
  425-883-2855
  One of the few bar scenes in Redmond. Buffalo wings and stuff.

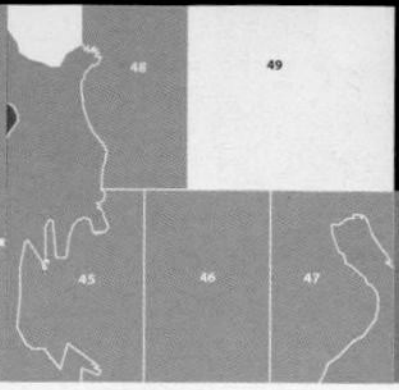

Map 49

48 49

45 46 47

Redmond

Restaurants

- **Family Pancake House** • 17621 Redmond Way
  425-883-0922 • $
  Chocolate chip pancakes that melt in your mouth.
- **Frankie's Pizza and Pasta** • 16630 Redmond Way
  425-883-8407 • $$
  Local favorite serving gourmet pizza and the usual Italian fare.
- **Marinepolis Sushi Land** • 8910 161st Ave NE
  425-284-2587 • $$
  Fun, cheap sushi.
- **Matt's Rotisserie & Oyster Lounge** •
  16651 NE 74th St
  425-376-0909 • $$
  Almost upscale, but tempered by kids and baseball caps.
- **Nara Japanese Restaurant** • 16564 Cleveland St
  425-885-0703 • $$
  Head for the sushi bar.
- **Ooba Tooba** • 15802 NE 83rd St
  425-702-1694 • $
  Flavorful, fresh Mexican.

- **Pomegranate Bistro** • 18005 NE 68th St
  425-556-5972 • $$
  Cute and tasty.
- **Sages Restaurant** • 15916 NE 83rd St
  425-881-5004 • $$$
  Intimate, rustic, mouthwatering Italian with candles and white tablecloths.
- **Spicy Talk Bistro** • 16650 Redmond Wy
  425-558-7858 • $$
  Authentic Szechuan in Redmond.
- **The Stone House** • 16244 Cleveland St
  425-558-5625 • $$$$
  Inventive cuisine in a charming setting.
- **Stone Korean Restaurant** • 16857 Redmond Wy
  425-497-0515 • $$$
  Especially the Korean fried chicken.
- **Thai Ginger** • 16480 NE 74th St
  425-558-4044 • $$$
  Try their trout salad.
- **Three Lions Pub** • 8115 161st Ave NE
  425-284-3399 • $$
  British cuisine? Yes, it's not always an oxymoron.
- **Yummy Teriyaki** • 17218 Redmond Way
  425-861-1010 • $
  Big portions of just that.

For most, the phrase, "Redmond Nightlife," is an oxymoron. Don't count on much being open after 10 p.m. With the exception of a few movie theaters and a few restaurants with decent happy hours, people head for downtown Seattle to get their kicks. Organic grocery chains **Whole Foods** and **PCC** are decent shopping options. But you can simultaneously support local farmers and save some coin at the **Redmond Saturday Market**.

Shopping

- **Bergman Luggage** • 16516 NE 74th St
  425-883-8400
  Serious stuff for serious travelers.
- **Half Price Books** • 7805 Leary Way NE
  425-702-2499
  New and used books at discounted prices.
- **PCC Natural Markets** • 11435 Avondale Rd NE
  425-285-1400
  Organic to the core.

- **Redmond Saturday Market** • 7730 Leary Way NE
  425-556-0636
  Eastside's oldest market—go early for the best pick in local fruits and vegetables.
- **Redmond Town Center** • 7525 166th Ave NE
  425-867-0808
  A mall. Outdoors.
- **REI** • 7500 166th Ave NE
  425-882-1158
  Heaven for wealthy weekend warriors.
- **Snapdoodle Toys** • 15752 Redmond Way
  425-869-9713
  Toys galore.

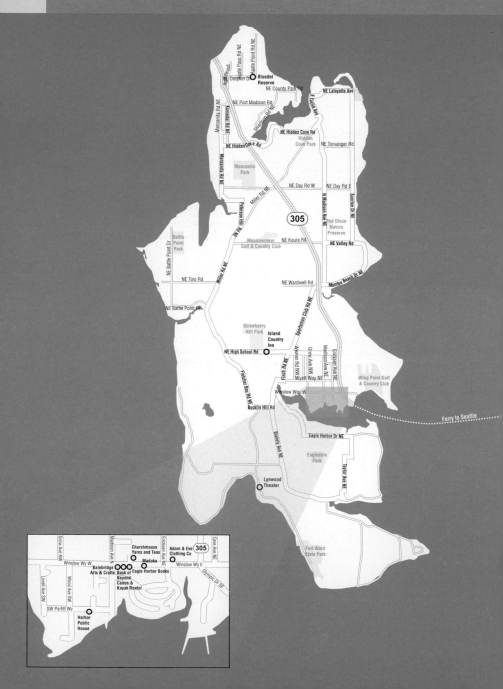

Overview

Over the centuries, Bainbridge has seen a little of everything—Native American battlefields, logging camps, strawberry farms, artist colonies, and more. Fort Ward and Battlepoint Park were two important military outposts. Battlepoint was the first place to receive the signal that Pearl Harbor had been bombed. No longer a sleepy little bohemian enclave, Bainbridge Island's recent growth has been tremendous, with condos sprouting like fungus and a highly affluent population flocking to live in them. Today, it's an upscale bedroom community, with the majority of its working citizens commuting across the Puget Sound to Seattle.

Attractions

In addition to a nice main street, where an excellent Fourth of July parade happens every year, Bainbridge enjoys a lively arts scene. The Island Theater produces free play readings every two months and Bainbridge Arts and Crafts (bacart.org) features local artists in their gift shop (no crocheted toilet paper covers here!). Bainbridge Performing Arts (www.bainbridgeperformingarts.org) hosts theater, dance, and musical performances with 100 percent less Guffmanesque amateurism than most communities its size. The Lynwood Theatre (206-842-3080), with its tudor facade and Art Deco style marquee, is Bainbridge's arty movie house and has been continuously running since 1936. The strawberry farms are still around and deliver delectable fruit in the state, which can be sampled at the festival held every July. Stars are hard to come by on the mainland but Bainbridge can bring the skies back to you. Battle Point has an observatory tower that is open to the public (bpastro.org).

The Bloedel Reserve (www.bloedelreserve.org) is an immaculately kept wildlife and garden sanctuary. The waterfront park behind the main street offers tennis courts, a playground, and a dock for the nautical minded. Canoes and kayaks can be rented seasonally from Back of Beyond Canoe and Kayak Rentals (tothebackofbeyond.com).

Shopping

Not exactly bargain territory, Bainbridge shops are upscale but casual. For the sewing crowd, Churchmouse Yarns and Teas (118 Madrone Ln; www.churchmouseyarns.com) carries the finest yarns available, and Esther's Fabrics (181 Winslow Wy E; www.esthersfabrics.com) stocks cloth that is expensive and worth every cent. With peaceful surroundings, frequent readings, and a fine selection, Eagle Harbor Books (157 Winslow Wy E; www.eagleharborbooks.com) is everything a bookstore should be.

Restaurants

Oddly enough for an island, there aren't many restaurants with a water view. Worth noting, however, is the Harbour Public House (231 Parfitt Wy SW; www.harbourpub.com) with exceptional pub grub and a bar stocked with choice Washington State wines and beers. Cafe Nola (101 Winslow Wy E; www.cafenola.com) is a European style cafe with an excellent, reasonably priced menu. For a casual breakfast or lunch, try Streamliner Diner (397 Winslow Wy E; streamlinerdiner.com), or check out Pegasus Coffee (131 Parfitt Wy; www.pegasuscoffeehouse.com) for great java in a rustic, ivy-covered brick structure.

Lodgings

The Island's two hotels, Best Western and Island Country Inn, which can be found next to the Safeway strip mall, both provide reasonably priced lodging. A better choice is selecting from one of the many bed-and-breakfast establishments on the Island, where all the amenities of home make an extended visit to Bainbridge a lot more inviting; the Bainbridge Island Lodging Association is a good place to start (www.bainbridgelodging.com).

How to Get There

Ferry
Washington State Ferries leave from Coleman Dock at Pier 52 on Alaskan Way every 50 minutes or so, but make sure to double check the schedule (www.wsdot.wa.gov/ferries). One-way fare is $8 for adults, $4 for youth ages 6-18 (children under 6 ride free). Cars are $13.65 or $17.30 depending on length of vehicle; each passenger is additional. Kitsap Transit buses meet the boats during commuter hours (www.kitsaptransit.org).

Driving
Driving to Bainbridge Island from Seattle without using the ferry is inconvenient, but not impossible. Take I-5 through Tacoma, then follow Highway 16 north through Bremerton. From there take Highway 3 to 305 and cross the Agate Pass Bridge. Depending on traffic, the whole trip takes about an hour and forty-five minutes and is recommended only for those desperate to get to or from the airport when the ferries aren't running.

General Information

NFT Map: 4
Address: 1635 11th Ave Seattle, WA 98102
Phone: 206-684-4075
Cal Anderson Park Alliance:
www.calandersonpark.org or @CalAndersonPark
Hours: 4 am–11:30 pm

Overview

The 7.37 acre Cal Anderson Park, named after Washington's first openly gay state legislator, is located in the heart of Capitol Hill and includes the Lincoln Reservoir and the Bobby Morris Playfield. Formerly Lincoln Park, Cal Anderson has had numerous, and regrettably appropriate, nicknames over the years such as "Hobo Park" and "Heroin Park." However, in 2005, Cal Anderson was the recipient of a major overhaul that transformed the strung-out little duckling into a beautiful countercultural swan.

Many doubted the renovations would do any good, but the success was undeniable when the park reopened. The makeover included lush, manicured grass, new paths and benches, a wading pool, a reflecting pool, a fountain, a giant chess board, and a small playground. Most impressively, not a hint remains of its former desolate state. Cal Anderson is now a joyful, welcoming place where people from all walks of life come to relax and partake in their favorite outdoor activities, from dog walking to sunbathing, Live Action Role Playing to chillin' with their didgeridoo. It is a glimpse into a utopian society wherein hipsters, yuppies, and punks can all come together on a warm summer day and play kickball.

Attractions

Between the wading pool, the reflecting pool, the fountain, and the reservoir, water features abound. And luckily, Cal Anderson is a park for the people, so none of these enticing fixtures are off limits. Adults climb to the top of the volcano-esque fountain. Kids splash each other in the reflecting pool or play on the jungle gym. It's also one of the best places to people-watch in Capitol Hill. Where else can you see a goth couple read under matching black parasols whilst a group of hippies fly their homemade kites several yards away? The Shelterhouse, a 900-square-foot venue accommodating up to 45 people, has reasonable rates for small gatherings (206-684-7254).

Sports

Bobby Morris Playfield is mostly used for soccer, baseball, tennis, and the occasional kickball practice. The Underdog Sports League (www. underdogseattle.com) also uses it for their amateur league games which include a dodgeball division. In other parts of the park, the word "sports" is used a bit more loosely. There are always joggers, skaters, and cyclists, but you can also find such alternative sports as lawn bowling, urban golf, Frisbee golf, kung fu, tai chi, and hula hooping. Capitol Hillites are nothing if not creative about their means for exercise.

General Information

NFT Map: 3
Address: 700 Seneca St Seattle, WA 98101
Freeway Park Association:
freewayparkassociation.org
Hours: 6 am–10:00 pm daily

Overview

The 5.2 acre Freeway Park, the first park to be built over a freeway, links First Hill and downtown between 6th and 9th Avenues in a series of boxy concrete plazas surrounded by lush vegetation. The park's fountains, when they are on, are visually stunning: geometric waterfalls, almost like a pixelated form of nature. The park makes for a great spot to escape downtown during lunch, and the various trails and paths that wind through it pad out a longer visit.

The idea to cover the freeway dated back to the 1960s, when the Seattle portion of Interstate 5 was completed. The park is the work of landscape architect Lawrence Halprin, who also designed the similarly sprawling FDR Memorial in Washington DC. When Freeway Park opened in 1976 it was deemed a triumph of urban landscaping, deftly combining city and nature in a kind of urban topography.

The evocative design also created many maze-like and shadowy areas that seemed to call out to criminals, "Come! Do your evil deeds here!" Which they did. An endless stream of seedy and downright scary events went down in Freeway's dark nooks and zigzagging pathways, culminating in the violent murder of a deaf and mute woman in 2002, which finally got people talking about redesigning the park. The Freeway Park Association sprung up to lead the cause, advocating for better lighting, increased security, and the removal of particularly obscuring trees and shrubbery. In addition, regular programming has increased usership. Crime rates, in turn, went down. The renovations also created more sun-filled spots, nice when the weather gets good. The summer months (July-August) usher in some fun Freeway events, like free lunchtime music concerts, public theater performances, and "intergenerational" activities that are geared toward children and seniors.

How to Get There

Tons of Metro buses will take you almost directly to the park; routes 16, 255, and 358 are a few from downtown. Somewhat ironically, given the park's name, driving is best avoided; there is no designated parking lot for the park; try your luck on the street or pay for a parking garage.

General Information

NFT Map: 25
Address: 2101 N Northlake Wy, Seattle, WA 98103
Hours: 6 am-10:00 pm daily

Overview

If ever you feel disenchanted with Seattle, head directly to Gas Works Park and stand at the top of the kite-flying hill. Even on a dreary day, the vista of water, sky, and rusted metal is dramatic, and the juxtaposition of natural beauty and industrial rust is lyrical in ways only Sir Mix-a-Lot can touch. The 19.1 acre park juts out into the north shore of Lake Union, creating a panoramic view of the downtown skyline framed by the hills of Queen Anne and Eastlake. On the water, seaplanes launch at regular intervals over a serene flotilla of kayaks, sailboats, and yachts. On a quiet afternoon, the proclamations of those dreadful Ride the Ducks tour guides are clearly audible from shore, but at least they don't wave at you from that distance.

The city first cleared this land in 1906 for use by the Seattle Gas Light Company. The Lake Station Plant, as it was then known, converted coal into methane gas until 1956, when natural gas became available via interstate pipeline. The City of Seattle purchased the gas works six years later and opened the public park in 1975. The gargantuan ruins of the plant have been left standing, now fenced off and scrubbed of decades of graffiti. Exhauster-compressor machinery has been converted into a children's play area. The former boiler house now houses picnic tables, barbecue grills, and a concession stand that operates sporadically during the summer months.

For some Seattle residents, the large quantities of benzene and other goodies left behind by the gasification plant raise the question, "Will picnicking at Gas Works shave precious years off of my life?" According to the Washington State Department of Ecology, no. The site underwent a massive, $3 million cleanup project in 2001 to remove contaminants from the soil, and chemical levels remain under constant observation. Nevertheless, visitors are still advised not to eat the dirt. Swimming, wading, and fishing are prohibited.

Sports

Conveniently located along the Burke-Gilman Trail, Gas Works Park receives its share of bicycle traffic, though trails within the park are relatively few. The park's abundance of concrete and freestanding metal is a draw for skateboarders. Yoga and tai chi classes are also known to congregate on the lawns. However, the most numerous enthusiasts at the park seem to be the kite flyers that flock to the landscaped hill, faces tilted to the sky, fists holding tight to the strings of their kites.

Festivals & Events

Gas Works Park leads Seattle in events for naked people. The annual Solstice Parade, featuring the famous (and fabulous) naked cyclists, pedals its way from Fremont to Gas Works where the pageant continues into the evening. The park has also served as the starting point of Seattle's World Naked Bike Ride, an event that protests oil dependency and suggests better living through nudity.

The Independence Day festivities at Gas Works are an all-day affair, complete with food vendors, a beer garden, and loud music. Though the fireworks over Lake Union are spectacular, sitting in the squalor beneath a giant inflatable Statue of Liberty head is likely to make you feel like a huddled mass.

How to Get There

Driving
From I-5, take the 45th Street exit and go west on NE 45th Street. Turn left on Meridian Avenue N and continue to the end of the street. Turn right on N Northlake Way and turn into the parking lot.

Public Transportation
Take Metro bus 26 and get off at 35th and Wallingford. It's only a two block walk south until you're relaxing and flying your kite at Gas Works.

General Information

NFT Map: 33
Address: 8498 Seaview Pl NW, Seattle, WA 98117
Hours: 4 am–11:30 pm

Overview

Originally designed as a destination at the end of an electric car line for folks to escape hectic city life, Golden Gardens is just that, minus the electric car line. Hidden from (or hiding) the city behind immense bluffs, Golden Gardens is Puget Sound at its finest and then some—romantic vistas of the Olympics, tranquil waters, barking sea lions locked in a floating cage, an occasional thundering train, and heaps of hippies drumming randomly around bonfires. On any given day you'll find a black-tie wedding, a Mexican barbecue, Chinese karaoke, beach volleyball, the ubiquitous drum circle, a pick-up soccer game, and young lovers smooching in the tall grass.

The park is divided by train tracks into lower and upper sections. The lower section features sandy beaches, picnic areas, fire pits, restored wetlands, a renovated bathhouse (available for events), beached logs, and lots and lots of bonfires. The upper portion is a maze of trails zigzagging up the bluffs, a 2.2 acre off-leash dog area, and tons of blackberry bushes.

The park has overcome "problems" of the past—namely, excessive drinking, loud music, and out-of-control bonfires. The city took efforts to get things under control (you'd think that people would know not to burn things like futons and wooden crates, but alas the police had to intervene to reinforce that rule). Now sentries are present on the summer weekends to make sure you're burning firewood and that you don't have any alcohol (try keeping a straight face when you say "no," and they'll try to believe you). Also long gone are the days when you could cavort with friends around a toasty fire late into the evening. Park officials promptly come by at 10:30 pm and without saying a word, douse all bonfires with a large bucket of water. At 11:30 pm the park closes and the gates are locked.

How to Get There

Driving
Take Market Street through Ballard and beyond the locks, where it turns into Shilshole Avenue. Another mile past the marina sits the entrance to the park; a public boat launch is at the south end (next to Coney's, a burger/shake/fish joint), and the first of several parking lots. The road turns right and winds up the bluffs to 85th Street. There is parking at the south end of the park, in the middle of the park, and just across under the railroad tracks.

Public Transportation
Transfer from major north-south routes to the 48 bus, which travels along NW 85th from the U District via Green Lake.

Bike
Golden Gardens should be the natural end of the Burke-Gilman Trail, though planners haven't yet put those pieces together.

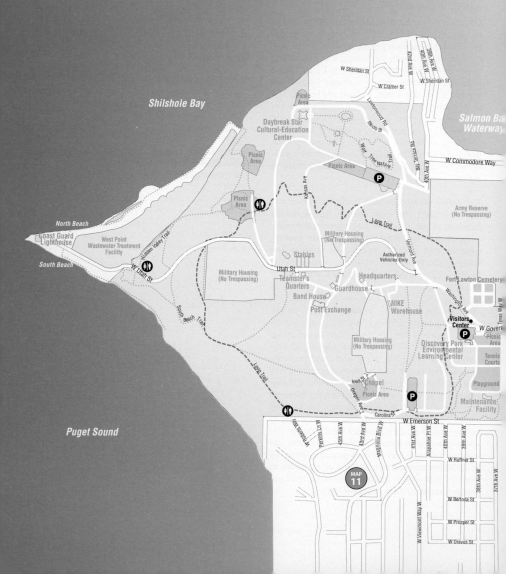

Shilshole Bay

Salmon Bay Waterway

W Sheridan St
W Cramer St
W Sheridan St

42nd Ave W
40th Ave W
38th Ave W

Daybreak Star Cultural-Education Center

Picnic Area

Picnic Area

Picnic Area

Picnic Area

Wolf Tree Nature Trail

Lawtonwood Rd

Illinois St

Kansas Ave

Texas Way Trail

W Commodore Way

Army Reserve (No Trespassing)

Loop Trail

North Beach

Coast Guard Lighthouse

West Point Wastewater Treatment Facility

South Beach

Hidden Valley Trail

W Utah St

Military Housing (No Trespassing)

Stables

Military Housing (No Trespassing)

Utah St

Teamster's Quarters

Band House

Post Exchange

Guardhouse

Headquarters

Authorized Vehicles Only

Vermont Ave

40th Ave W

Fort Lawton Cemetery

Washington Ave

NIKE Warehouse

Visitors Center

Military Housing (No Trespassing)

South Beach Trail

Loop Trail

Chapel

Iowa St

Oregon Ave

Picnic Area

Carolina St

W Govern

W Emerson St

Texas Way W

Discovery Park Environmental Learning Center

Picnic Area

Tennis Courts

Playground

Maintenance Facility

Puget Sound

W Viewmont Way W

Perkins Ln W

45th Ave W

43rd Ave W

W Bliss Pl W

Arapahoe Pl W

41st Ave W

40th Ave W

39th Ave W

38th Ave W

37th Ave W

MAP 11

W Ruffner St

W Bertona St

W Prosper St

W Dravus St

General Information

NFT Map: 11
Address: 3801 Discovery Park Blvd,
Seattle, WA 98199
Phone: 206-386-4236
Hours: 4 am–11:30 pm

Overview

Discovery Park is by far Seattle's largest park, covering 534 acres. Located on the Magnolia bluffs, the park occupies most of the former Fort Lawton military base. Discovery offers the most extensive hiking trails within the city, just under 12 miles worth of trails, making it the perfect destination for those times when you've just had enough of the city, but don't want to go too far away.

You will find that Discovery has an amazing amount of natural diversity. On a single trail you will encounter meadows, sea cliffs (don't get too close!), forested areas, thickets, streams, and even an active sand dune. There is a short hike down to two miles of protected tidal beaches with tree houses along the way for scenic views of the Puget Sound and a resting place for the brutal hike back. All of the trails are well marked, but be sure to remember which parking lot you left your car in, because it's easy to get lost. You can print out a map of the trails from the Discovery Park website.

The views you'll find at Discovery are phenomenal. You can see Puget Sound spread out before you, framed by the majestic Olympic Mountains. On a clear day, there is also the opportunity to gaze upon Mt Rainier, which Seattleites never get sick of seeing. Stroll by the Coast Guard Lighthouse or look for the enormous West Point Treatment Facility located just next to Discovery Park.

Park History

Discovery's history is an interesting one. The city of Seattle originally donated this land to the Federal Government to use as a military base. In 1938 the US Army offered to give all of Fort Lawton back to Seattle for the bargain price of one dollar. The city actually refused this sweet deal because they weren't sure they could afford the upkeep. Then in 1964, the US Secretary of Defense decided that 85% of Fort Lawton was to be surplus and Seattle would have to cough up 50% of fair market value (whoops). Luckily, in 1965, legislation was passed that said Seattle could have it for free because it was given as a donation in the first place (phew). Then the United Indians of All Tribes jumped into the mix in 1970, claiming that all lands might be declared surplus, so they were allowed to lease 17 acres. You can now find the Daybreak Star Cultural-Education Center on those 17 acres.

How to Get There

Driving
Discovery is huge, and if you stray from the main path, it is easy to get lost in the maze of homes surrounding the park. When all else fails, just keep heading west. However, if you follow these directions, you can't miss it.

From I-5 take the 45th Street exit and head west. 45th Street becomes 46th Street then turns into Market Street. From Market, turn left onto 15th Avenue NW and take the first right after the bridge onto Emerson Street. Turn right onto West Gilman, which becomes West Government Way. Follow that until you come to the east entrance of the park. Go straight and you will find the Visitor Center to your left. Once you get to the east entrance of the park from West Government Way, you can go straight to find several parking lots or turn left and head towards the south parking lot.

Public Transportation
If you don't mind a long bus ride, the 33 and 24 will take you to Discovery Park. The 33 lets you off at the North Parking Lot while the 24 stops at the South Parking Lot.

General Information

NFT Map: 30 & 31
Address: 7201 E Green Lake Dr N, Seattle, WA 98103
Hours: Open 24 hours a day

Overview

For over a century, Seattleites have enjoyed the cool tranquility of Green Lake Park, a popular destination for joggers, dog walkers, bikers, roller skaters, and what have you. This is one of Seattle's loveliest parks, which guarantees crowds on pleasant weekends, but the calming vibe of the water and the woods tends to ease everyone's need for personal space. A paved 2.8-mile trail circles the lake, providing two separate tracks for those on foot and those on wheels, and another unpaved trail for joggers meanders a bit longer at 3.2 miles. A stroll around Green Lake is a painless way to grab some exercise in the city without an overdose of auto exhaust or having to dodge panhandlers.

As for wildlife, waterfowl abound, from ducks to Canadian Geese to majestic herons, and they're not only unafraid of the constant human traffic, they're nearly confrontational about it. Don't feed these birds, no matter how adorable they seem—it's not allowed. New visitors to Green Lake will remark on the robust rabbit population, the result of certain short-sighted folks letting their domesticated pet bunnies free in the foliage by the water. Many generations hence, great fat rabbits infest the area, breeding and burrowing and wreaking havoc on native plant life. As with the waterfowl, do not feed these cuddly-yet-feral beasts.

Activities

The lake's moniker stems from its susceptibility to algae blooms, a picturesque affliction that the city has fought often during the park's history, leading to a number of beach closures throughout the years. While some brazen water-worshipers insist that Green Lake is the best swimming hole in Seattle, the city's official website warns of the possibility of contracting swimmer's itch. Consider dipping instead into the chlorinated safety of Evans Pool, a large indoor swimming facility on the lakeshore, or take the kids to the outdoor wading pool, which writhes every summer with the kinetic energy of splashing toddlers.

Green Lake's Small Craft Center offers classes for young and old alike in the arts of kayaking, canoeing, sweep rowing, and sculling (don't forget to pass your "float test" first—it's required). For private paddleboat rentals, the Green Lake Boat Rental company is at your service, and there's no nicer way to share the lake with someone special. Three annual rowing regattas invade the lake each year for exhibition-style water sports, sponsored by the local Rowing Advisory Council.

Or you could ignore the water altogether. Work out on one of the park's tennis courts, try a few holes of mild golfing at the Green Lake Pitch & Putt, or just laze beneath a shady pine and take in some people-watching. The park draws groups of tai chi and martial arts devotees, novice tightrope walkers, and even medieval faire types practicing their swordplay in full costume. Meanwhile, the strains of bagpipes and plaintive guitar strummers float among the Frisbee tossers and sunbathers. Indeed, the whole thing is rather idyllic, an open space Xanax of sorts.

How to Get There

Driving
If coming by Aurora Avenue, take the Green Lake Way exit and follow it until you're circling the lake. If coming by I-5 southbound, take exit 171 toward NE 71st Street/NE 65th Street, merge onto 6th Avenue NE, turn right on NE 71st Street and follow it to East Green Lake Drive N. If coming by I-5 northbound, take exit 170 toward NE 65th Street, merge onto NE Ravenna Boulevard and follow it to E Green Lake Drive N.

Public Transportation
The 48 rolls past Green Lake frequently during the day, serving the University District, Montlake, Greenwood, and Loyal Heights among other neighborhoods. The 16 stops along the east side of the lake and will cart you up from downtown or down from the Northgate Mall. The 26 is slightly less frequent and a longer ride, starting off downtown, threading up through Fremont and Wallingford until reaching the end of the line on Green Lake Way.

Pontiac Bay

NE 77th St

NE 75th St

**Main
Entrance**

NE 74th St

MAP
27

National Oceanic &
Atmospheric
Administration

The Brig

Dog Run

Magnuson
Park
Fields

Tennis Courts

Playground

Magnuson
Community
Center

Sand Point
Fields

Sand Point Way NE

NE 65th St

NE 64th St

65th Ave NE

nd Point Way NE

E Windermere Rd

NE 61st St

Boat
Launch

Lake Washington

General Information

NFT Map: 27
Address: 7400 Sand Point Wy NE, Seattle, WA 98115
Phone: 206-684-4946
Hours: 4 am-11:30 pm

Overview

There are parks, and then there are parks. With 350 acres on the shores of Lake Washington, Warren G. Magnuson Park, Seattle's second-largest park, is a recreational wonderland. It wasn't always so. The park was purchased by the government at the turn of the century and given to the federal government to turn into a naval base. Over the years, parts of the park were relinquished to the public and became Warren G. Magnuson Park, so named for the community-friendly senator who advocated for public use of the land, in lieu of a noisy airfield. The Navy continued to use part of the park all the way until 1990, when it was officially closed for military purposes and handed over to the city.

The park is crammed full of things to do. The historic Art Deco and Colonial Revival buildings are now home to a variety of nonprofit community groups, ranging from sailing enthusiasts to an organization dedicated to protecting bats (nocturnal, not wooden). There's a boat launch, playground, basketball courts, tennis courts, picnic facilities, trails, windsurfing areas, and a huge off-leash dog park. Then there's the public art. And the community garden. And the butterfly garden. And, well, a million other things. The south end of the park was transformed in the mid-2000s by a major wetlands restoration project; the park is home to dozens of species of birds and is a great spot for birdwatching. The 20,000-square-foot Junior League of Seattle Children's Playground is the largest in Seattle. If you've exhausted all the possibilities of the park's resident features, there are a multitude of events throughout the year, like the Puget Sound Mycological Society's Wild Mushroom Show in the fall (www.psms.org).

Magnuson Community Center
7110 62nd Ave NE, 206-684-7026
The Community Center has always been a recreational hub and meeting ground, even during its military years, during which there was a library, swimming pool, and a bowling alley, all integral to Navy training exercises. Nowadays, one may find amenities no less entertaining, such as a 560-seat auditorium, gymnasium, racquetball court, and meeting room. Still, bringing back the bowling alley would be pretty cool.

The Brig
6344 NE 74th St
The Brig is another community center that's had a colorful past, from its original purpose as a jail for holding military prisoners and somewhat more recently as a set for several episodes of the X-Files. It's adjacent to the community garden and features large, wood-floored activity spaces and meeting rooms.

Warren G. Magnuson Off-Leash Dog Area
The largest off-leash area in Seattle, this dog heaven stretches out over nine acres and includes several varied environments such as dirt hills, flat gravel for fetch, tall brush, and a mud pit. The highlight is the accessible shoreline on Lake Washington—dogs go crazy for it, and Magnuson boasts the only dog park with water access within city limits. To get to the shore, there's a winding fenced-in trail so you can get some walking in while Rover is permitted to roam and sniff off-leash alongside. Small and shy dogs will appreciate their own separate and spacious pen. As always, be sure your pooch is properly vaccinated and that you clean up after him. The Magnuson Off Leash Group (molg.org) helps maintain the site.

Magnuson Community Garden
This former parking lot has been converted into a thriving garden with the purpose of serving the community of Seattle. There's the outdoor amphitheater, which hosts various performances and events during the year, a garden tailored to gardeners with disabilities, and orchards and P-patches growing food for local food banks. It's a nice little oasis that just warms your heart.

NOAA Art Walk and Sound Garden
www.wrc.noaa.gov, 206-526-6163
Right in the park's backyard is a bunch of outdoor art installations made by some well-known artists (at least in the outdoor art installation crowd). The National Oceanic and Atmospheric Administration (NOAA) campus is located at the northern end of the Sand Point Peninsula. Though it's not technically included in the park, its close proximity invites a lot of park visitors to come check out the half-mile trail that passes by six outdoor artworks. The most popular is the Sound Garden (from which a certain 1990s grunge powerhouse got its name). Per its self-descriptive title, the installation is composed of pipes that generate different tones that vary with the changing wind. The site is only open Monday-Friday 9 am to 5 pm; stop at the security gate for access.

Sail Sand Point
7777 62nd Ave NE #107, 206-525-8782; www.sailsandpoint.org
Sail Sand Point is Seattle's new community sailing center. It's located on the north shore of the park on Lake Washington. There are programs and classes for both youth and adults.

How to Get There

Driving
From I-5 you can exit at either NE 45th Street (Exit 169) or NE 65th Street (Exit 171). From the NE 45th Street exit, go east on 45th, past the UW campus, and down the 45th Street ramp. Continue east past University Village Shopping Center. Bear left and continue about 2 miles. From the I-5 NE 65th Street exit, head east approximately four miles on 65th (stay on the arterial!) until you have crossed Sand Point Way NE into the NE 65th Street entrance. Parking is free and ample. There are two lots—one on 65th and a larger lot on 77th.

Public Transportation
Metro bus routes 30 and 75 serve the park along Sand Point Way NE. Connections are in the University District (Route 30) and Northgate (Route 75).

Bike
The Burke-Gilman Trail is approximately 1/4 mile west of Warren G. Magnuson Park. With a traffic signal and crosswalks, the NE 65th Street crossing is the safest point to enter the park. Once on the east side of Sand Point Way NE bicyclists can continue either east along NE 65th Street, or north along 62nd Avenue NE. Note that bicycle riding is limited to paved surfaces within Warren G. Magnuson Park. There are no designated bike trails in the park.

Overview

Plopped between Puget Sound and Lake Washington, Lake Union is the baby bear of the Seattle waterways. On the east, it has a watery arm that stretches to Lake Washington—Portage Bay—and another to the west that connects it to Puget Sound.

Lake Union itself is riddled with marinas and a vibrant, eclectic houseboat community (eclectic in this instance means high-end homes as well as scows). The area around the lake was fairly neglected and somewhat industrial until the 2000s. It's got a rapidly growing biotechnology corridor along the east side; the south side underwent rapid development—condos, coffee shops, spas, and tons of upside for developers. The north side has **Gas Works Park**, the site of an old gas manufacturing plant that features a playground, trails, and stellar views of the Seattle skyline and Lake Union. The Seattle Streetcar connects South Lake Union to downtown (www.seattlestreetcar.org). And then there's **Lake Union Park**, whose 12 acres reconnect the lake to the surrounding booming neighborhood. The **Museum of History and Industry** (www.mohai.org) chronicles the growth of Seattle using interactive and hands-on exhibits.

As you'd expect for a lake, most of the attractions have at least something to do with water. At the south end of Lake Union, located at Valley Street and Fairview Avenue North, is **The Center for Wooden Boats** (www.cwb.org). There is a small museum, of sorts, and you can rent both sailboats and rowboats. Moving up the west side of the lake, on aptly named Westlake Avenue N, catch a scenic tour of Seattle in a seaplane for about $100 with Kenmore Air. (866-435-9524 or www.kenmoreair.com) It's also possible to fly to Vancouver, Victoria, or the San Juan Islands from here. Unless you're in the market for a yacht, there's not much shopping around the lake. One notable exception is the flagship store of **REI** (222 Yale Ave N, www.rei.com), which satisfies all your outdoor needs (and which in Seattle, can be considerable).

What Lake Union does have plenty of, other than water, is restaurants. There's **Daniel's Broiler**, a steak house with a view (809 Fairview N, 206-621-8262). Nearby is **Chandler's Crabhouse** (901 Fairview N, 206-223-2722), which relies heavily on fresh fish dishes. While we're on fresh fish, there's **I Love Sushi** (1001 Fairview N, 206-625-9604). Try to overlook the silly name; it's a great sushi place with more spectacular views. For great happy hour hooch and hot, handmade soft pretzels with dipping sauces perfect for soaking up the drink, head to the **Brave Horse Tavern** (310 Terry Ave N, 206-971-0717), owned by superstar chef and restaurateur Tom Douglas. If you want to spend big money (and here you actually do get what you pay for), try **Canlis** (2576 Aurora Ave N, 206-283-3313). It features the absolute best of Northwest cuisine.

How to Get There

Driving
Lake Union is immediately off I-5 at exit 167. Turn right off the exit onto Fairview Avenue N, then left on Valley Street. Lake Union is bound by Valley Street on the south, Westlake Avenue N on the west, N Northlake Way on the north, and on the east is Eastlake and Fairview Avenue N. You can pretty much circumnavigate it in roughly 20 minutes. On a good traffic day. With no construction anywhere. This, of course, never happens.

Public Transportation
The South Lake Union Streetcar stops at Lake Union Park and Fairview & Campus Drive. Metro bus routes 70, 71, 72, and 73 will all deliver you to the south end of the lake, and continue up the east side of the lake. The 40 runs up the west side toward Ballard.

General Information

NFT Map: 1
Address: 2901 Western Ave, Seattle WA, 98121
Phone: 206-654-3100
Website: www.seattleartmuseum.org/visit/
olympic-sculpture-park
Hours: Daily, 30 minutes before sunrise to
30 minutes after sunset

Overview

Seattle Art Museum's magnificent 8.5-acre waterfront sculpture park opened in 2007 in a former industrial parcel, a rare spot of open space in the downtown area. The world-class collection—free admission 365 days a year—includes a massive piece by Richard Serra, *Wake*, as well as pieces by Claes Oldenburg, Alexander Calder, and Louise Bourgeois. There's also a *Vivarium* by Mark Dion featuring a nurse log and its attendant nurslings—all told, some phenomenal works. (If you like a little controversy with your art, check out *Father and Son*. A popular target for those whose mantra is "Think of the children!", it depicts a man and a boy, both nude, facing each other with arms outstretched as water from a fountain rises and falls around them.)

Art is only part of the attraction. As well as monumental sculpture, the park has meadows, forests, and stunning views. The other reason to visit the park is the setting. Walking on the z-path from the Pavilion, as you come through a recreated Northwest native trees forest, the view is, well, OK, breathtaking...an unobstructed view of the Olympics and Puget Sound. Seattle's chronic rainfall can't mess with that. Even if you hate museums, maybe especially if you hate museums, this place will afford you an entirely different experience of art—art like it's s'posed to be.

How to Get There

Driving
The park occupies 8.5 acres between Western Avenue and Elliott Avenue at Eagle and Broad Streets. Take exit 167 at Mercer Street, turn right on Fairview, left on Valley. Valley becomes Broad Street. (The Space Needle should appear on your right.) Turn right on Western Avenue. There is parking under the Pavilion at the park.

Public Transportation
Metro routes 1, 2, 8, 13, and RapidRide D head north from downtown stop close to Olympic Sculpture Park.

General Information

NFT Map: 3
Location: 1st Ave and Pike St
Phone: 206-682-7453
Website: www.pikeplacemarket.org or @pike_place
Hours: 9 am-6 pm daily (5 pm Sun); fish and produce
open 7 am; closed Thanksgiving and Christmas

Overview

While it doesn't share the Space Needle's phallic elegance, Pike Place Market matches the monument's importance as a symbol of Seattle. The oldest farmers market in the country has experienced myriad changes over its past century of operation, but still exists primarily for the purpose of bringing farmers and consumers together without the sticky fingers of the middleman. Early on a weekday morning is the best time to hit the Market if sustenance-shopping is the goal. Perusing the bounty of ripe fruit, crisp root vegetables, and tender greens while contending with the bovine rush of tourists isn't always an attractive option for the average city dweller. But sometimes the Pike Place Market is worth a little hassle—supporting local farmers is easy when the produce is this fresh and priced better than the average supermarket.

A project funded by a $75 million property tax levy to renovate Pike Place's aging innards was completed in 2012. More recently, the mixed-use MarketFront project reclaims the parcel formerly used as the Municipal Market Building, which was demolished in 1974 after a fire. The project, undertaken in concert with the demolition of the Alaskan Way Viaduct, will add low-income housing, space for social services, more retail and parking (replacing parking lost with the elimination of the viaduct).

Fresh Fish

A Seattle-centric trope as strong as coffee, rain, and dot-coms, the flashy flying fish of the imaginatively-named **Pike Place Fish Market** pack in gawking yokels from around the world every day with their zany antics. A crew of handsome (but smelly) fishmongers engage their shoppers in boisterous banter and throw fish corpses to each other (and potential buyers) all day long, usually with uncanny accuracy. Other fishmongers at the market feel obliged to compete with such flamboyance, so you'll find most white-smocked fin-handlers at **Pure Food Fish** and **City Fish** to be fairly gregarious, handing out samples, and gladhanding their prey. For a no-nonsense retail experience, **Jack's Fish Spot** isn't trying to impress anybody; they're good for fresh flounder, live crabs, or a quick snack of fried salmon at Pike Place Market without all the jive.

Fresh Meat

The old-school butcher shop is quickly disappearing in Seattle (and everywhere else for that matter). Even at Pike Place there used to be dozens of great little meat markets back in the day. Luckily, there are still a few high quality shops left. **Don & Joe's** prides itself on good quality and personal service. Don't see it? They'll order it for you. For your next Oktoberfest party, head to **Bavarian Meats** for all kinds of brats and wursts. And for the best sausage in Seattle, **Uli's Famous Sausage** will hook you up.

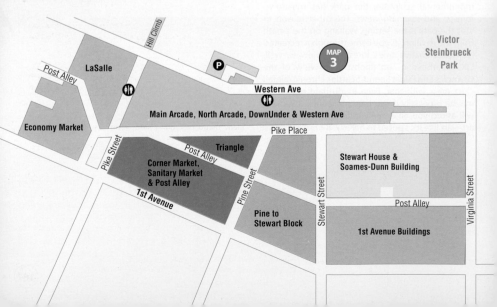

Specialty Shops

The lower levels and hidden corners of the market hold plenty of weird little shops that vary from straight-up tourist fleecing joints to truly eccentric stands that couldn't exist anywhere else. Choose **Market Magic** when shopping for the professional magician, clown, or ventriloquist in your life—card tricks, collapsible canes, juggling clubs, and vintage magic ephemera. The **Polish Pottery Place** sells very pretty, traditionally patterned tableware and kitchenware, sourced from an artisan pottery collective in Poland. A handful of shops offer upscale kitchen equipment, including national chain **Sur La Table**, and there's a plethora of unique boutiques dedicated to eclectic fashions for all.

One could spend hours sifting through the vintage posters, advertisements, and postcards available at **Old Seattle Paperworks**. Readers can peruse used books at **Lamplight Books** or **BLMF Literary Saloon**, grab specialty magazines at **First and Pike News**, or study rabble-rousing political screeds from **Left Bank Books**. Imported art, clothing, and products from Africa, Mexico, China, and other exotic climes can also be had. And if you just happen to need a haircut, head straight to Sergio's Barber Shop in the Stewart House.

Restaurants & Bars

Pike Place is an eating and drinking wonderland. Hungry shoppers can grab a quick snack of French pastries from **Le Panier**, Italian gelato at **Bottega Italiana**, Russian fare at **Piroshky-Piroshky**, piping hot dunkers at **The Daily Dozen**, free cheese samples at **Beecher's**, Greek food from **Mr. D's**, and almost anything else you can think of. If you have more time, grab a seat at **Matt's in the Market** or **Le Pichet**. Gluttons for punishment are welcome to visit the "first" **Starbucks** store—actually the beast was born on Western Avenue in 1971 and didn't relocate to the market until 1976, but no matter.

Say, who needs a drink? **Lowell's** is a homely three-floor operation that still looks as scruffy as it probably did when it opened in 1957. But the food is cheap and plentiful, and you'll get a fine eyeful of the Puget Sound. The **Athenian** is the requisite old-school hang-out complete with great views and colorful locals. Head there for the latest Market gossip. If the **Alibi Room** is too cool for school, head to **Zig Zag** for a classic drink or to **Copacabana** for a Bolivian beer on the deck to check out the real scenery at the market—the people.

Arts & Crafts

Buskers can apply for a performer's badge, which allows them to entertain the shopping throng for up to an hour at a time at one of twelve designated points. A variety of music flows forth as a result, from ham-fingered folk strummers to electrifying doo-wop vocalists. Remember the Spoonman of Soundgarden fame? He's there too. It's not just music—puppeteers, dancers, and sleight-of-hand artists pass the hat at Pike Place Market, as well as the "cat guy" who wears modified cat suits and brings his feline pets along as visual aids as he solicits funds for a local animal shelter.

Most of the art hawked on the upper level of the market falls into the tie-dyed, air-brushed, pastel-colored variety, of interest only to those who feel compelled to buy something to commemorate their dream vacation in Seattle. Want a generic pink or teal souvenir t-shirt festooned with a cartoon salmon or the Space Needle? You got it, along with wind chimes, dream catchers, belt buckles, incense burners, and "specialty pipes." But if you look hard and long enough, you'll find some good and interesting art hidden amongst the kitsch. Plenty of Mother Nature's art is on hand too, in the form of gorgeous fresh floral bouquets available for very reasonable prices every few steps, so take your time when picking out that perfect arrangement.

How to Get There

Driving
Parking at Pike Place Market can be a pain. People expect to drive right down the ever packed Pike Place and find a spot right next to Rachel the Pig. It's not gonna happen. And if it does, you'll probably get a ticket. Try your luck on the metered spots downtown or head to the main parking garage at 1531 Western Avenue for the best deals.

From I-5 northbound, take exit #165, turn left on Madison Street and follow to Western Avenue. Turn right on Western, follow for five blocks to the parking garage

From I-5 southbound, take exit #166 toward Stewart Street, follow to 1st Avenue and turn right. After two blocks turn left onto Lenora Street, then left onto Western Avenue, follow three blocks to the parking garage.

Public Transportation
Many metro bus routes stop along First Avenue or Pine Street, including RapidRide routes C, D, and E. The Westlake Sound Transit Link Light Rail station is located only four blocks away from the Market.

General Information

San Juan Islands Visitors Bureau: www.visitsanjuans.com
or @visitSJIslands
Washington State Ferries: www.wsdot.wa.gov/ferries
or @wsferries

Overview

Only 80 miles northwest of Seattle, the San Juan Islands provide an idyllic weekend escape from the city and a memorable excursion into pristine wilderness. Situated in the San Juan Channel between the Strait of Juan de Fuca and the Georgia Strait, there are more than 400 islands in the archipelago (and more than 700 at low tide); of those, 172 have been named, and most are uninhabited. The main four are San Juan Island, Orcas Island, Lopez Island, and Shaw Island. If your mind immediately conjured images of *Free Willy* when you heard "Orcas Island," you're on the right track: killer whales are common in these parts, and whale watching is a big business.

Coast Salish tribes originally inhabited these islands, taking advantage of the plentiful aquaculture. The Spanish landed in this area in the late-1700s, lending Spanish place names, like "San Juan," for one. And the islands' proximity to British Columbia (Victoria, B.C. is actually south of most of the islands) is a reminder of the decades-long boundary dispute between the United States and United Kingdom, originally set off by a pig digging up a farmer's potatoes (no, seriously), that began in 1859 and basically lasted until 1874, when both nations' troops eventually exited the island.

Lopez Island

City slickers might find themselves questioning whether they've got long lost relatives here, as nearly every person who passes waves at visitors. It's a bit like the *Twilight Zone* until one realizes that inhabitants of this small, exceedingly friendly island are just genuinely nice.

Lopez Village

This street is the meeting place for island folk, filled with cafes, antique shops, a bookstore, and small grocery store. Take a stroll along the nearby hiking trail on a weekend morning, and don't miss the summer farmers market.

Shark Reef Recreation Area

A popular hiking spot noted for its beautiful bluff, Shark Reef will delight any nature enthusiast.

Orcas Island

The largest of the islands, Orcas Island maintains a tranquil balance of creature comforts and natural outdoor adventures.

Eastsound

The epitome of quaint, Eastsound is a place to lose yourself in the many restaurants, spa services, and bookstores bordering the water. Stock up on essentials at the natural food store or the larger supermarket, or catch a performance at Orcas Center (917 Mt. Baker Rd, Eastsound, 360-376-2281; www.orcascenter. org). Don't miss the Orcas Island Historical Museum (181 N Beach Rd, Eastsound, 360-376-4849; www.orcasmuseums.org) for a recreated glimpse into the island's past.

Olga

Catkin Cafe (11 Point Lawrence Rd, Olga, 360-376-3242, www. catkincafe.com) is a homey place with good food and a local art gallery. The last commercial business in the bend in the road which is the tiny town of Olga, the cafe is located within an old strawberry packing plant. It's definitely worth the drive and the perfect place for a quiet lunch or brunch away from the more populous Eastsound and Orcas Village. Be cautious when driving its winding roads, since many deer graze close to the roadsides.

Orcas Village

This tourist trap is the central hub of activity as passengers load and depart the ferries at the harbor. The elegant Orcas Hotel (360-376-4300; www.orcashotel.com), overlooking the waterfront, is a nice place for a relaxing beverage on the wrap-around porch while waiting for the ferry.

Cascade Lake

Family fun abounds at this wilderness lake, located between Eastsound and Olga. Swimming, paddle boats, a nature trail, and a wooded picnic area are just some of the ways to enjoy this day use area situated at the base of Mt. Moran.

Moran State Park/Mt. Constitution

Moran State Park is a nature lover's dream, with camping and 30 miles of hiking trails. Those who challenge themselves to climb from base to summit of Mt. Constitution, the highest point in the San Juan Islands, should come well-equipped with a compass, plenty of water, good hiking shoes, and a cell phone for emergencies. Look across to distant Vancouver, BC from atop the stone observation tower at the peak of the mountain.

San Juan Island

San Juan Island is the most commercial and the second-largest of all the islands. It was originally inhabited by Native Americans before sailors arrived in the 1850s and transformed the area into a busy seaport by the end of the century.

Friday Harbor

The only incorporated town in the islands, Friday Harbor has something for everyone, especially the shopping-inclined. Enjoy the Whale Museum (62 First St, Friday Harbor, 360-378-4710, whalemuseum.org) for an education about the area's native underwater inhabitants. Or, spend an afternoon browsing the local art galleries, cafes, and a multitude of specialty shops.

Roche Harbor

This resort and marina on the northwest tip of the island provides a quiet retreat from the bustling tourism of Friday Harbor. Explore the nearby English Camp on West Valley Road, part of the San Juan Island National Historical Park (www.nps. gov/sajh).

Shaw Island

If Shaw Island had a motto, it would be, fittingly, "Not For Tourists." The least-welcoming of the four ferry-accessible islands, its residents prefer their remote isolation and have chosen to avoid the commercialism of their island sisters. Expect to find a primitive campsite and not much else.

Island Activities

There's a plethora of things to do and see in the San Juans, and more businesses that provide sightseeing excursions, vehicle rentals, and adventure packages than there's room to print.

Bicycling is a great way to get around. On San Juan Island, Island Bicycles (380 Argyle Ave, 360-378-4941; www.islandbicycles.com) is located just a few blocks from the ferry in Friday Harbor. On Orcas Island, Wildlife Cycles in Eastsound (350 North Beach Rd, 360-376-4708; www.wildlifecycles.com) outfits both cyclists who want to explore the shoreline, orchards and valleys and those who wish to conquer the 2400-foot-high Mt. Constitution. And if you're on Lopez Island, Lopez Bicycle Works (2847 Fisherman Bay Rd, 360-468-2847; www.lopezbicycleworks.com) is offers standard and tandem bikes, and invites walk-ins.

San Juan Island County Parks (www.co.san-juan.wa.us/parks) operates 18 parks and facilities, including camping at sites on San Juan, Lopez and Shaw Islands. During summer reservations are strongly recommended. Moran State Park offers more than 150 spaces spread across five sites in the park, including along the waterfront.

Perhaps the best way to explore the shoreline is in a kayak, and, indeed, kayaking is quite popular on the islands. Lopez Island Sea Kayak (2845 Fisherman Bay Rd, 360-468-2847; www. lopezkayaks.com) is a nice spot along the water for rentals. On San Juan Island, Outdoor Odysseys (86 Cedar St, 800-647-4621; www.outdoorodysseys.com) is based in Friday Harbor and offers kayak tours and whale watching, assuming you feel comfortable hobnobbing with killer whales while bobbing around in a kayak. And Orcas Outdoors (360 376 4611, www.orcasoutdoors.com) organizes overnight tours by kayak around the San Juan Islands.

Ferries

The islands are only accessible by air and water. By far the most popular way to travel to there, for those without private planes and boats, is via the Washington State Ferry system. Plan to arrive in Anacortes extra early in the summer, at least two hours before your scheduled ferry departs. Bring books, playing cards, or other amusements, as a minimum of three-hour-long waits are not unusual during the busy season.

Two ways to avoid the long lines is to walk on or bring a bike rather than a car onto the ferry; there are peak and off-season parking rates if you choose to leave your car behind. Ferries from Anacortes travel to the four largest and most populated islands: Lopez, Orcas, San Juan, and Shaw.

Fares vary depending on the island destinations. During the peak season, be prepared to pay an average of $30-40 per vehicle and driver, and an additional $13 or so per passenger. Discounted rates are available for seniors and children. Bicycle surcharge rates are only $4 during the peak season.

The Anacortes Ferry Terminal in Anacortes is about two hours north of Seattle. Take I-5 North for approximately 85 miles to SR 20. Take exit 230, turn left at the light and follow the signs into downtown Anacortes. Turn left on 12th Street and follow the signs to the terminal.

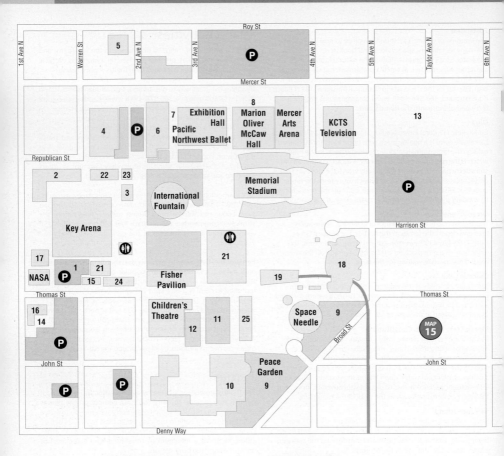

1 South Court Secured Parking
2 KEXP
3 Northwest Craft Center
4 Seattle Repertory Theater
5 Cornish Scene Shop
6 Cornish Playhouse
7 Founder's Court
8 SIFF Film Center
9 Sculpture Garden
10 Pacific Science Center / IMAX
11 Mural Amphitheater
12 Children's Garden
13 Bill & Melinda Gates Foundation

14 Pottery Northwest
15 Blue Spruce
16 Park Place
17 Key Arena Box Office
18 Experience Music Project / Sci-Fi Museum
19 Seattle Center Monorail
20 Armory / The Children's Museum
21 Seattle Center Pavilion
22 The VERA Project
23 SIFF Center
24 Skatepark
25 Chihuly Garden & Glass

General Information

NFT Map: 15
Address: 305 Harrison St, Seattle, WA 98109
Phone: 206-684-7200
Website: www.seattlecenter.com or @seattlecenter

Overview

The site of the 1962 World's Fair, Seattle Center offers 74 acres of cultural resources and entertainment amenities between Belltown to the south and Queen Anne to the north. The Space Needle, Seattle's most famous landmark, sits in Seattle Center, and the Monorail, that quirky two-stop relic of public transportation, travels between downtown and the Seattle Center. Both the Space Needle and the Monorail were built for the Fair, as was the International Fountain in the center of the campus.

While Seattle Center may be the focal point of tourism it also serves as a destination for locals. Sure, out-of-towners flock to the Space Needle, Monorail, and EMP (or board those damned Ducks across the street), but Seattleites attend concerts or sporting events at the Key Arena, see plays at one of several theaters on the campus, and hang out at festivals like Bumbershoot, Folklife, or BeerFest. Each year on New Year's Eve, the Space Needle is lit up by an impressive fireworks display. And then there's the 10,000-square-foot skatepark next to Key Arena.

Seattle Center is also a destination to get your learn on. The Children's Museum and the Pacific Science Center have interactive exhibits year-round. The IMAX Theater provides the typical educational fare as well as some new releases in 3D. And of course, each weekend you can rock out to your favorite psychedelic band at the Laser Dome.

There have been a few news-making events at Seattle Center. After his suicide in 1994, Nirvana fans came out in droves for a candlelight vigil memorializing Kurt Cobain. It has also been the site of several protests. And in 2006, the annual Gay Pride Parade was moved from Broadway in Capitol Hill to the Seattle Center.

Space Needle

When it comes to landmarks, the 520-foot-high Space Needle (400 Broad St; www.spaceneedle.com) may be overrated and overexposed, and sure, there's something hokey about eating on a moving platform, but there's also something brilliant and grand about a totem to the space age. And while so much stuff from the 1960s gets demolished with barely a second thought, it's nice that this big hulking time capsule fills up the skyline. Besides, just think of the title sequences we'd be missing out on were it not to exist.

Experience Music Project

Perhaps no one but architect Frank Gehry and owner Paul Allen thinks it actually looks like a smashed guitar— the phrase "psychedelic clown poop" comes to mind— but if you're a music fan, the EMP (325 5th Avenue N; www.emplive.org or @EMPmuseum) is a treat. That is, if you're really into Jimi Hendrix and looking at famous sweaters. Where EMP surpasses being merely a big Hard Rock Cafe is in its fascinating interactive installations. And it's not all rock music: exhibits run the gamut of popular culture, making the museum of interest to more than just superfans.

Monorail

Like the Space Needle, the Monorail (www. seattlemonorail.com) is a novelty that was built for the World's Fair. It runs about a mile from the Seattle Center to Westlake Center Mall. One-way fare for adults is $2.25 and $1 for children 5-12. 65+ are $1 and kids 4 and under are free. If you think this seems steep for a two-minute trip, then you should take the bus. Even if no Seattle resident has ever used the Monorail as public transportation it did not prevent a serious initiative in the late 1990s/early 2000s to create an entire system of monorails across the city. That failed, in part, when people realized that then there'd be these blasted monorails all over the city. Thus, the light rail.

Children's Museum

Located on the first floor of the Center House, the Children's Museum (305 Harrison St, 206-441-1768; www.thechildrensmuseum.org or @tcmseattle) features several child-sized environments designed for education, including a mountain forest, a global village, a mini-Seattle neighborhood, and Cog City. They also offer the typical gambit of youth programs and workshops. Admission is $8.25 for adults and children and $7.25 for grandparents. Children under 1 are free.

Cornish Playhouse

Housed in a World's Fair-era building, the Cornish Playhouse (201 Mercer St; www.cornish.edu/playhouse) has a 476-seat main theater and a separate black-box theater. The space was formerly the Intiman Theatre, which won a Tony Award in 2006 for outstanding regional theater. Unfortunately, it wasn't enough to keep them in the black as debts mounted, and the theater was forced to fire its entire staff and abruptly cancel a portion of its 2011 season. Subsequently, the space formerly occupied by Intiman was taken over by Cornish College and renamed The Cornish Playhouse. Since its precipitous fall, the Intiman has been reconceived as a yearly summer festival in its former home at the Seattle Center (www.intiman.org).

Seattle Children's Theatre

Comprised of the Charlotte Martin Theatre and the Eve Alvord Theatre, the Seattle Children's Theatre (201 Thomas St, 206-441-3322; www.sct.org or @SCTdotORG) offers a season of family-oriented plays as well as classes, workshops, and even birthday parties.

Seattle Repertory Theatre

The Seattle Rep (155 Mercer St, 206-443-2222; www. seattlerep.org or @seattlerep) includes the Bagley Wright Theatre, the Leo Kreielsheimer Theatre, and the PONCHO Forum. Major company performing classic and contemporary plays with a commitment to original works.

Seattle Center Armory

Predating the World's Fair, the Armory dates to 1939 and is home to the Children's Museum, administrative offices, and an above-average food court showcasing some of the best in Seattle cuisine. The surprisingly cheap, freshly fired mini pizzas at MOD are worth the line and the vegan burgers at Plum would make even the most staunch carnivore reconsider their dietary stance. The upscale comfort food at Skillet is a fine lunch option. The food court is also a good alternative to expensive fair food during the big events.

McCaw Hall

McCaw Hall (321 Mercer St; www.mccawhall.com) is to home to the Pacific Northwest Ballet (www.pnb.org or @PNBallet) and the Seattle Opera (www.seattleopera. org or @SeattleOpera). A lecture hall and an array of meeting rooms are available for rent for your next grandiose function.

Key Arena

Since its ugly divorce with the SuperSonics in 2007, Key Arena (www.keyarena.com or @KeyArenaSeattle) has had a hard time picking up the pieces, though it still hosts concerts and is the home court for the WNBA Seattle Storm basketball team and the home rink of the Rat City Rollergirls.

Pacific Science Center/IMAX

The Pacific Science Center (200 2nd Ave N, 206-443-2001; www.pacificsciencecenter.org or @PacSci) houses a very good collection of science-related entertainment. From the dinosaur exhibit to the Butterfly House, the Insect Playground to the interactive Science Playground, adults and children alike owe it to themselves to explore the grounds at least once. Don't miss the Planetarium. In addition to the usual documentaries and nature films at the IMAX, they also present the odd theatrical release in giant wrap-around screen splendor, and, occasionally 3D. And, of course, there's always Laser Floyd.

SIFF Film Center

The SIFF Film Center (206-324-9996; www.siff.net or @SIFFnews) is a 95-seat theater with seats from the balcony of the Cinerama Theatre. Their flagship event, the Seattle International Film Festival, take place in June.

Chihuly Garden and Glass

Dale Chihuly's glassblowing empire arrived at Seattle Center after the endearingly rickety Fun Forest amusement park finally closed in 2011. Chihuly Garden and Glass (www.chihulygardenandglass.com) features Chihuly works in several settings: traditional galleries, a greenhouse-esque "glasshouse," and a garden. Over the course of his decades-long career the Tacoma native has achieved widespread popular and critical praise, and the long-term exhibition at the Seattle Center is a must-see for fans of Chihuly.

Art & Fountains

As you stroll through the Seattle Center, you will notice a multitude of abstract sculptures and unusual fountains. Many of them, such as the whale-esque *Neototem* series, and the can't-miss-because-it's-a-giant-ball-in-the-center-of-the-grounds *International Fountain*, double as jungle gyms for the kids. The *Olympic Iliad*, a series of orange tubes intertwined, sits on the lawn of the Pacific Science Center. *Grass Blades*, a row of 30-foot steel reeds, divide the walkway and parking lot outside of the EMP. And the vortex-y *Encircled Stream* fountain swirls between the Cornish Playhouse and McCaw Hall.

How to Get There

Driving
From I-5, take the Mercer Street/Seattle Center Exit #167. At the first light, turn right onto Fairview and follow the flow of traffic to the left, turning onto Broad Street. Take a right onto Fifth Avenue and a left onto Roy Street. From there you can find on-street parking, or use one of the lots or garages.

Public Transportation
Many buses serve the Seattle Center area. For the west side of the campus, use routes 1, 2, 8 and RapidRide D. For the east side of the campus, use routes 3 and 4. Then of course there's the Monorail. Not the worst idea in the world, mind you.

General Information

NFT Map 3
Address: 1000 Fourth Ave, Seattle, WA 98104
Phone: 206-386-4636
Website: www.spl.org or @SPLBuzz
Hours: Mon–Thurs: 10 am–8 pm, Fri–Sat: 10 am–6 pm, Sun: 12 pm–6 pm

Overview

The Rem Koolhaas-designed Seattle Central Library opened in 2004 to much fanfare, and helped to rescue the city from its growing reputation as an architectural vacuum. The stunning, avant-garde glass and steel structure is actually the third incarnation of the Central Library, with over 160,000 more square feet of program space than its dingy 1960s predecessor. The new building's diamond-grid "glass skin" makes the most of Seattle's scarcest resource—sunlight—filling the library's vast open spaces with light and framing 360-degree views of the surrounding buildings. The interior combines striking, modern decor with more serene touches. Polished steel surfaces abut scrap wood floors; fluorescent yellow escalators lead to grass-patterned carpeting. Particularly eccentric are the blood red hallways of the Meeting Level on the fourth floor. The place is downright trippy. But unlike other starchitectural landmarks around town (sorry EMP), this gem actually lives up to the hype.

True to Seattle ideals, the building is energy efficient, earthquake safe, and unbelievably high-tech, with self-checkout terminals, an automated book-sorting system, and wireless communication devices for staff members. The library's nonfiction stacks are housed in an innovative "books spiral," which, much like the Guggenheim Museum in New York, allows uninterrupted progress through the collection. Other highlights include the 400-seat Betty Jane Narver Reading Room featuring views of Elliott Bay, a wall of audio booths for language study, several video art installations, and the 275-seat Microsoft Auditorium where free author events are a regular occurrence.

Internet

The Central Library, housing nearly 400 public computers, was designed with access to technology in mind. A valid library card or a temporary guest pass is required for internet use on a library PC. Free WiFi access is available throughout the building. Most seating in reading rooms and in the stacks is equipped with electrical outlets for laptops.

For the Kids

Kid-sized bookshelves and a toddler play area can be found in the cheerfully rubberized Faye G. Allen Children's Center on Level 1. The Anne Marie Gault Story Hour Room hosts children's activities almost every day of the week. On Level 3, recognizable by its colorful flooring, is the Starbucks Teen Center, complete with young adult books and graphic novels, a special teen reference desk, and computers and workstations exclusively for teen use.

Food and Gifts

The FriendShop on Level 3 near the Fifth Avenue entrance sells an assortment of trendy gift items and is one of the better places to buy a greeting card downtown. You can purchase espresso, pastries and sandwiches at the adjacent coffee cart. You must consume snacks in the cafe area, but feel free to roam the stacks with your lidded latte.

How to Get There

Driving
From the north take I-5 exit 165B at Union Street. Follow Union three blocks west to Fifth Avenue, then turn left and go south three blocks to Spring Street. From the south, take I-5 exit 165 at Seneca Street. Follow Seneca one block west. Turn left on Fifth Avenue and go south one block to Spring Street. From the east, drive to the end of I-90 and take the ramp toward northbound I-5. Take the second exit at Madison Street. Turn left on Madison Street and go west two blocks to Fifth Avenue.

Underground parking is accessible on Spring Street between Fourth and Fifth Avenues. Weekday rates are pricey but weekend rates are relatively reasonable. Bike racks are located at all major entrances and inside the parking garage.

Public Transportation
Most downtown buses stop within walking distance of the Central Library. The closest Sound Transit Light Rail stop is University Street Station.

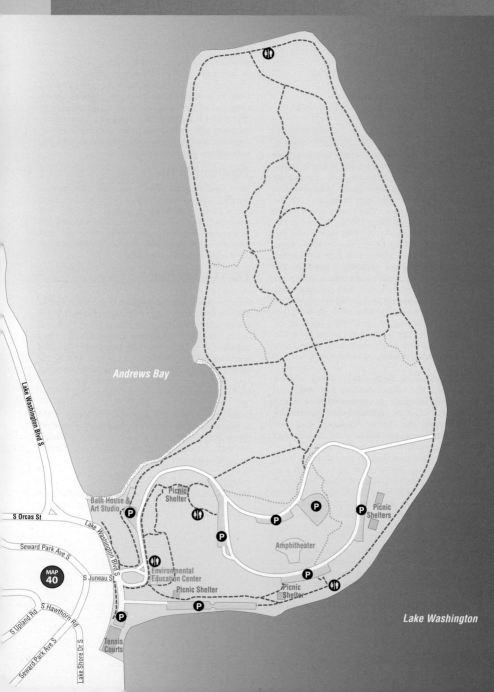

General Information

NFT Map: 40
Address: 5900 Lake Washington Blvd S,
Seattle, WA 98118
Phone: 206-684-4396
Friends of Seward Park: www.sewardpark.org
Seward Park Audubon Center:
sewardpark.audubon.org or @sewardaudubon
Seward Park Clay Studio: sewardparkart.org
Park Hours: 6 am–10 pm

Overview

Seward Park was purchased by the city in 1910 for $322,020, or less than a tiny home in south Seattle's nearby neighborhoods. It is a gigantic 300-acre thumb of land jutting into the (relatively) fresh water of Lake Washington, and much of the acreage encompasses old-growth forest—one of the last remaining within Seattle city limits. Thanks to the ongoing work of Friends of Seward Park and city staff weeding out invasive non-indigenous plants, the park retains much of its splendid original habitat and native flora and fauna. On a clear day, walking around the peninsula's 2.4-mile lakefront loop allows views of Mount Rainier to the south, the Cascade Mountain range to the east, Mount Baker to the north, and a glimpse of the Olympic Mountain range to the west. You won't find a better walking trail in Seattle for a 360-degree vista of the glories of the Pacific Northwest. Located amid the ethnically and income-diverse neighborhoods of Mount Baker, Leschi, Seward Park, and Rainier Beach, the park hosts many community events, from running and bicycle races to charity pet walks—check the park calendar for the schedule of evening hayrides, concerts in the spacious outdoor amphitheater, and the listing of classes offered by park naturalists.

Activities

This 300-acre park packs a wallop. Stay all day and you'll see the sun rise over Mount Rainier and set over downtown Seattle's Columbia Tower. In between, fish off the dock, swim in the lake, study lichens and mushrooms, add diving ducks to your life list of birds, use the Art Studio to fire your pottery, overhear a half dozen different languages, and glaze over watching a tai chi class on the beach. Your Aunt Mildred can focus her binoculars on the bald eagle nests in the old-growth forest, while your nephews play tennis on the waterfront courts. After catching his day's quota of fish, Dad can relax with a cool one in the picnic shelters overlooking the lake and he'll enjoy the same views as Lake Washington's multi-millionaire waterfront homeowners. There is anchorage for your uncle's yacht in protected Andrews Bay; in the summer he can row ashore to buy a hot dog and a sno-cone from the park's snack truck. If your family includes canine members, they are welcome, but keep them on a leash—if your rambunctious Airedale runs off you can (and will) be ticketed by park rangers intent on keeping the grebes, herons, and cormorants in the lake and the dogs out. There are hiking trails through the woods, grassy playfields for Frisbee tossing, and a small but well-used playground for the kids. Best of all, you can paddle off from the whole fam-damily in your kayak without anyone knowing you've slipped away.

Seward Park Environmental & Audubon Center

After years of planning, fundraising, and community input, the Seward Park Environmental & Audubon Center opened its doors in 2008. The multi-million dollar project, a joint venture of Audubon Washington and Seattle Parks & Recreation, included the renovation of the old Tudor-style brick building at the entrance to the park. The building was transformed into an environmental education center complete with an extensive library, a laboratory, and a gift shop.

How to Get There

Car, bike, bus, boat, or kayak will all get you there from here. Parking lots are plentiful and usually only crowded on summer weekends and sunny days.

Driving south along Lake Washington Boulevard is scenic—if the route is open. From May to September, the stretch of road along the lakeshore from Mount Baker to Seward Park is closed on various Sundays for bicycle use. When the road is open to car traffic, you may be tempted to cut in front of the hordes of cyclists, but bear in mind that bicycles have the right of way. If you can't beat 'em, hop on an expensive Klein racing bike or a beat up Schwinn, and join 'em. Metro Bus Route 50 stops at Seward Park Avenue S and S Juneau Street.

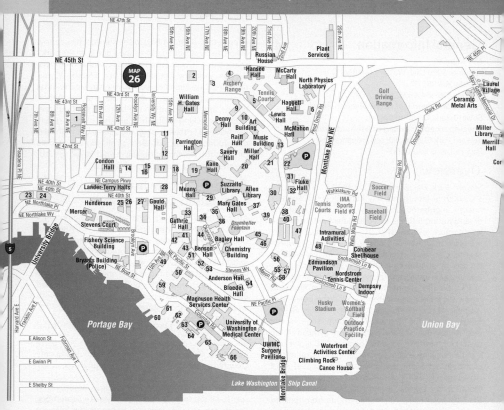

1. UWMC Roosevelt
2. Burke Memorial Museum
3. Theodor Jacobsen Observatory
4. Hughes Penthouse Theatre
5. Hutchinson Hall
6. Cyclotron Shop
7. NorthWest Horticultural Society Hall
8. Issacson Hall
9. Balmer Hall
10. Mackenzie Hall
11. Eagleson Hall
12. Social Work/Speech and
    Hearing Sciences Building
13. Clark Hall
14. Brooklyn Building
15. Playhouse Theater
16. Staff HR Center
17. Schmitz Hall
18. Henry Art Gallery
19. Odegaard Undergrad Library
20. Smith & Gowen Halls
21. Thomson Hall/Communications Building
22. Padelford Hall
23. Research & Technology Building

24. Publications Services Building
25. Child Care Center
26. Ethnic Cultural Center
27. Instructional Center/Theater
28. Commodore-Duchess Apartments
29. Gerberding Hall
30. Student Union Building (HUB)
31. Hall Health Center
32. The University of Washington Club
33. Architecture Hall
34. Cunningham Hall
35. Johnson Hall
36. Atmospheric Sciences-Geophysics
37. Sieg Hall
38. Engineering Library
39. Kirsten Aeronautical Lab
40. Loew Hall
41. Physics/Astronomy Building
42. Physics/Astronomy Tower
43. Physics/Astronomy Auditorium
44. Chemistry Library Building
45. Electrical Engineering Building
46. Paul G. Allen Center for Computer Science
    & Engineering

47. Power Plant
48. Graves Hall
49. W.H. Foege Bioengineering
    & Genome Sciences Buildi
50. Hitchcock Hall
51. Kincaid Hall
52. Botany Greenhouse
53. Plant Lab
54. Winkenwerder Forest Lab
55. Roberts Hall
56. More Hall
57. Wilcox Hall
58. Wilson Ceramic Lab
59. Ocean Sciences Building
60. Marine Sciences Building
61. Oceanography Teaching
62. Harris Hydraulics Lab
63. South Campus Center
64. Oceanography Building
65. Fisheries Center
66. Experimental Education Un

General Information

NFT Map: 26
Address: 1410 NE Campus Parkway, Seattle, WA 98195
Phone: 206-543-2100
Website: www.washington.edu or @UW
Enrollment: 45,213 (2015)
Budget: $6.9 billion (FY15)
Endowment: $2.8 billion (2014)

Overview

Founded November 4, 1861, the University of Washington, or UW (pronounced U-Dub) is the oldest university on the west coast and the largest in the Pacific Northwest. There are three campuses—Tacoma, Bothell, and Seattle—Seattle being the main one and largest of the three. It is a public research school of over 45,000 students with many of its programs ranked in the top ten in the country. It doesn't hurt that UW gets a great deal of funding from—yeah, those guys again—Microsoft masterminds Paul Allen and Bill Gates. It also boasts one of the most beautiful campuses in the country, with dramatic views of Mt. Rainier. It's well worth a stroll, even if you're not the studious type.

The 700-plus-acre Seattle campus is home to over 200 buildings and contains a courtyard full of cherry trees that are in the shape of a W when viewed from the sky. Unfortunately, they always seem to be in bloom when school is out of session for spring break. Although UW is best known for its medical programs, including its highly-ranked medical and nursing schools, the clinical psychology, statistics, social work, and library and information sciences programs are also well regarded.

Tuition

Undergraduate tuition and fees for the University of Washington are north of $12,000 for residents and $33,000 for non-residents. On campus room and board is about $11,000.

Sports

Students and Seattle citizens are extremely proud of their Huskies (www.gohuskies.com) and flock to the football games at Husky Stadium. You'll find die-hard fans tailgating on their boats on Lake Washington during games, even in miserable weather. The Huskies participate in the NCAA Division I-A and the Pac-12. The Huskies fortunes in the competitive Pac-12 come and go, but the women's volleyball team and men's soccer teams had some recent successes. The football team won a national championship in 1991 and finished #3 in 2000. The men's basketball team made it to the Sweet 16 in 2010. That aside, rowing is where the Huskies really shine: UW crews have won 30 national titles and more than 15 Olympic gold medals. The Marching Band of UW is also well known, using a traditional high step, one of very few marching bands left to use this strategy of hyping up the already excited crowds. And UW can claim at least partial credit for popularizing "The Wave" during the 1981 football season.

Culture on Campus

The University of Washington's Seattle campus has no shortage of culture. If you're into museums, try the Burke (www.burkemuseum.org or @burkemuseum), which is the state museum of natural and cultural history. There is also the Henry Art Gallery (henryart.org or @henryartgallery), the first public art museum in the state of Washington, which features contemporary art (including the trippy *Skyspace* by James Turrell). Meany Hall is the place for performing arts and is home to the performances of UW's School of Drama, often ranked as one of the top theater programs in the country. They put on at least seven shows per year, but you can also catch performances from the Schools of Dance and Music, and Digital Arts and Experimental Media Program (DXARTS). If you're more into the outdoors, head over to the Botanic Gardens, otherwise known as the arboretum. You will run out of time and energy before you run out of land to explore. The university also runs the Rainy Dawg Radio (rainydawg.org or @RainyDawgRadio), a student-run internet radio station and UWTV (www.uwtv.org or @UWTV) which is broadcast state-wide and is available to cable television viewers.

Departments

Visitors & Information Center: 206-543-9198
Undergraduate Admissions and Campus Tours: 206-543-9686
Graduate School: 206-543-5929
UW Medical Center: 206-598-3300
University Bookstore: 206-634-3400
University Libraries: 206-543-0242
Husky Ticket Office: 206-543-2200
Registrar: 206-543-5378

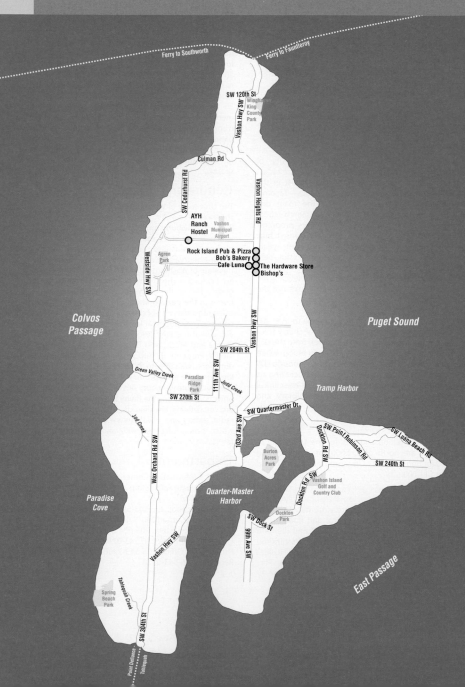

Ferry to Southworth

Ferry to Fauntleroy

SW 120th St

Wingham King County Park

Vashon Hwy SW

Culman Rd

SW Cedarhurst Rd

Vashon Heights Rd

AYH Ranch Hostel

Vashon Municipal Airport

Westside Hwy SW

Agren Park

Rock Island Pub & Pizza
Bob's Bakery
Cafe Luna
The Hardware Store
Bishop's

Colvos Passage

Puget Sound

Vashon Hwy SW

SW 204th St

Green Valley Creek

Paradise Ridge Park

111th Ave SW

Judd Creek

Tramp Harbor

SW 220th St

SW Quartermaster Dr

103rd Ave SW

Joe Creek

SW Point Robinson Rd

Dockton Rd SW

SW Luana Beach Rd

Wax Orchard Rd SW

Burton Acres Park

SW 240th St

Paradise Cove

Quarter-Master Harbor

Vashon Island Golf and Country Club

Dockton Rd SW

Dockton Park

SW Dock St

99th Ave SW

Spring Beach Park

Tahlequah Creek

Vashon Hwy SW

SW 304th St

East Passage

Point Defiance
Tahlequah

Overview

Vashon Island plays the role of that forgotten, oddball, isolated community populated with eccentric characters and legendary landmarks only locals can appreciate (a bike in a tree, a strawberry festival without strawberries, and so on). Vashon is less a destination than Bainbridge or the San Juans. In fact, with no hotels, only a couple dozen B &Bs or guest houses, and virtually no camping allowed anywhere on the island, Vashon doesn't exactly encourage tourism.

Roughly the same size as Seattle, but with only about 10,000 inhabitants, Vashon is rural and decentralized—perfect for the organic farmers and lovable lefties who call it home (these guys make Seattle look like a Young Republican convention). Vashon is great for a short visit, especially if you have friends on the island.

Lacking any stoplights, "Downtown Vashon" at Vashon Highway and Bank Road lies two miles from the ferry. There you'll find independent cafes, bookshops, art galleries, and restaurants. Red Bicycle Bistro is the center of nightlife (and that's not a snotty "the," but a singular "the" as in the only place). The locals go to Thriftway to hobnob and gossip. The Hardware Store was just that for over 100 years until 2005, when it was turned into a happening eatery.

The rural, getaway nature of Vashon has attracted a flock of artists and galleries. A few of them have banded together for the First Friday Gallery Cruise. Also, twice a year (May, December) over 40 artists open their studios to the public (vashonislandartstudiotour.com). The famed Vashon Island Strawberry Festival happens every July. It's much like small town fairs all over the country—elephant ears, nauseating rides, creepy carnies—but oddly, no strawberries. A highlight for car enthusiasts is the classic car parade which attracts gear heads from all over the state to show off their retro beauties that spend the rest of the year hiding under tarps.

As for landmarks, nothing beats the bicycle-eating tree near the intersection of Vashon Highway and SW 204th Street. The rusty old bicycle was abandoned in the 1950s and the tree began growing around it, in effect "eating" the bike.

Where to Eat and Drink

The Hardware Store, 17601 Vashon Hwy SW, 206-463-1800. Serving lunch and dinner, plus breakfast on Sundays, the menu features straightforward cafe fare that includes buttermilk fried chicken and a nice selection of salads. Don't miss the bar area, a perfect perch for watching the ferry traffic stream into town while you sip some good vino from their wine list.

Rock Island Pub & Pizza, 17322 Vashon Hwy SW, 206-463-6813. A good range of pies and pastas. Take it outside to the patio with a pitcher of beer on a nice day or sidle up to the stone fireplace in the winter.

Cafe Luna, 9924 SW Bank Rd, 206-463-0777. Serves up the best mocha on the island and offers a range of teas, baked goods, and grilled paninis.

Red Bicycle Bistro & Sushi, 17618 Vashon Hwy SW, 206-463-5959. The local restaurant/bar that frequently has live music on the weekends.

How to Get There

By car, take I-5 south to the West Seattle Bridge, keep to your left toward Alaska Junction to Fauntleroy and follow the signs to the ferry.

Ferries leave from the Fauntleroy terminal in West Seattle seven days a week. On weekdays, you can take a passenger-only ferry from Pier 50 in Seattle. The RapidRide C line will take you directly to the Fauntleroy ferry terminal from downtown. To get to Fauntleroy by car, take I-5 to exit 163 to the West Seattle bridge to Fauntleroy Way SW. Follow Fauntleroy Way SW to the end, and look for signs for the ferry.

Where to Stay

The Vashon Island Chamber of Commerce (www.vashonchamber.com) has an extensive list of B &Bs and guest houses on the island. AYH Ranch Hostel (www.vashonhostel.com), although no longer affiliated with AYH and no longer a hostel, is still a good budget option and allows camping on its grounds, the only such facility on the island (reservation required).

General Information

NFT Map: 17 & 20
Address 1247 15th Ave E, Seattle, WA 98112
Volunteer Park Conservatory:
www.volunteerparkconservatory.org
Asian Art Museum:
www.seattleartmuseum.org/visit/asian-art-museum
Hours: 6 am–10 pm daily

Overview

Volunteer Park, so named in 1901 to honor Spanish-American War recruits, is yet another jewel in Seattle's crown of gorgeous public spaces. The 48.3-acre park features a museum, a conservatory, many fine public art pieces, and a reputation for public sex. That said, Volunteer Park suffers not a whit from purported nocturnal dalliances—it's still a peaceful place to stroll away from the city with assorted trails and paths that allow one to gently meander or stretch the legs in a vigorous jog. A children's wading pool draws countless tykes all summer long, a quartet of tennis courts welcomes the net set, and the bandstand provides a stage for regular outdoor music performances.

Volunteer Park has long been a popular destination for lovers of art and botany. Abstract sculptures and statues honoring local pioneers, military heroes, and public servants distinguish the grounds. The park is also home to the Seattle Asian Art Museum, an extensive collection of historical and modern art with ever-changing exhibits. The nearby Volunteer Park Conservatory has been here since 1912, featuring five different habitats for a wild assortment of exotic plants from around the world.

The water tower on the south side of Volunteer Park is a popular landmark for those planning to meet up for a little Frisbee golf or friendly dogwalking. If you can handle 106 steps, you can visit the tower's observation deck, which automatically puts you at the highest point of Capitol Hill and affords a beautiful view. While there, take the time to peruse the historical exhibit that celebrates the Olmsted brothers, early-20th-century pioneers in establishing the park system in Seattle, including Volunteer Park.

Volunteer Park borders the Lake View Cemetery, a historical spot filled with graves of the many founding fathers and mothers of Seattle. Those who know names like Denny, Mercer, and Yesler only from street signs will come face to face with the resting places of the fabled men themselves. Lake View also boasts the graves of the mighty Bruce Lee and his son Brandon, both charismatic martial arts action heroes who died under mysterious circumstances. Sorry Mr. Mercer, but being in the eternal presence of Kato and the Crow is a bigger thrill, even if you did clear the trees to make way for the University of Washington.

How to Get There

Driving
From I-5 northbound, take exit 166 and turn right on E Olive Way, following until it merges with E John Street. Turn left on 15th Avenue E, then enter Volunteer Park after 3/4 mile.

From I-5 southbound, take exit 168A and turn left on E Roanoke Street. Turn right at 10th Avenue E, turn left onto E Boston Street until it becomes 15th Avenue E. Volunteer Park will be on the left.

Public Transportation
The 10 bus hits Volunteer Park frequently (every 10-20 minutes) with service from downtown.

General Information

NFT Map: 22 & 19
Address: 2300 Arboretum Dr E, Seattle, WA 98122
Phone: 206-543-8800
Website: depts.washington.edu/wpa
or @uwbotanicgarden
Arboretum Foundation: www.arboretumfoundation.org
or @ArboretumFound

Overview

The Washington Park Arboretum is 230 acres of sprawling beauty that contains more than 5,000 different plant species. You will find a large collection of mountain ash and maple as well as an abundance of wildlife. The Arboretum is huge. It is difficult to see it all in one day, but definitely fun to try. There are many meandering trails with few hills, so it's perfect for jogging (just look out for people taking pictures!). You will find a strange combination of the beauty and serenity in the view in front of you and the constant din of traffic from the nearby freeway. However, once you push that out of your head, it is a wonderful place to get away from it all. And speaking of traffic, it can be pretty bad surrounding the park, so give yourself extra time to navigate it. Once there, take a stroll to Foster Island, where the floating bridges provide extra fun when boats go by and create a wake. Here especially, keep your eye out for birds and turtles. But don't go too quickly! The fragile earth under your feet wishes you to walk, not run. If you really love the plants and desperately want to take them home with you, seedlings are available for purchase at the Arboretum Shop.

Japanese Gardens

Address: 1075 Lake Washington Blvd E, Seattle, WA 98122
Phone: 206-684-4725
Website: www.seattlejapanesegarden.org
Hours: Apr-Sept: Daily, 10 am-7 pm (shoulder seasons generally until 5 pm and closed Mon)
Admission: $6; youths 6-17, seniors 65+, college students with ID, and disabled $4; children 0-5 free.

This 3.5-acre, formal garden was dreamed up by world-renowned Japanese garden designer Juki Iiada in 1960. He oversaw all construction of this garden, which includes a koi pond and a traditional tea house. The Garden is exceptionally beautiful and unique as it incorporates both plants traditionally found in a Japanese garden and plants native to the Northwest. It can be a welcome sanctuary from busy city life and well worth the admission fee. Try to catch a tea ceremony, which is periodically offered in the tea house.

Guided Tours

To better appreciate the diversity of the different plant species at the arboretum, take a free guided tour on Sundays, January through November. Guides expertly highlight the plant collections, different seasonal displays of beauty, and the history of the arboretum in 60-90 minutes. Tours start at the Graham Visitor Center (2300 Arboretum Drive E); check schedule online. Free self guided tours and maps are also available online, as are downloadable audio guides.

Boating

The arboretum now includes three public, non-motorized boat-launching sites and is a part of the Lakes to Locks Water Trail which starts in Lake Sammamish and ends at Puget Sound. Since it used to be illegal to land your boat at a public park, it's a welcome addition. If you don't own a boat or kayak, you can rent one from the Washington Activities Center (206-543-9433) just across the lake from the park. Once you're on the water, paddle around the water lilies and under the famous "ramp to nowhere" as you head over to Foster Island to explore its watery corridors. You will be treated to excellent bird watching, and the chance to see otters, turtles, or perhaps even a beaver dam. Once again, you'll come face to face with a thriving eco-system next to a busy freeway, giving you renewed hope for the future of planet Earth.

How to Get There

Driving
From Downtown: Go east on Madison Street to Lake Washington Boulevard E then turn left into the arboretum.

From I-5: Take exit 168 onto highway 520. Take the first exit to Lake Washington Boulevard E and follow it into the arboretum.

Public Transportation
Bus routes 43 and 48 run near the arboretum (McGraw Street stop). Route 11 is another option; stop at Lake Washington Boulevard East and walk north.

Deception Pass
State Park

Ala
Spit

Skagiit
Bay

Ault Field Rd
20

Oak Harbor

Fort Nugent Rd

Crescent
Harbor

West Beach Rd

Ebey's
Landing

Penn Cove
Coupeville

Fort Ebey
State Park

Engle Rd

20

Wannamaker Rd

Port Townsend - Keystone Ferry

525

Admiralty
Bay

Greenbank
Farm

Greenbank

S Smuggler's Cove Rd

Saratoga Rd

SE Harbor Rd

Langley

Double Bluff
Beach

Cultus Bay Rd

525

Clinton

Clinton - Mukilteo Ferry

Useless
Bay

General Information

Whidbey and Camano Islands Tourism:
www.whidbeycamanoislands.com
or @GoWhidbeyCamano

Overview

One of Seattle's biggest perks is its proximity to an endless variety of retreats and getaways. Just miles from the hustle and bustle lay idyllic islands that can wipe away any memory of hellish downtown traffic. One of the prettiest and closest of these is Whidbey Island, known for its scenic shores, quaint island communities, and increasingly precious real estate.

As with most of the territory in North America, Whidbey was once occupied by several local Native American tribes until those pesky Europeans came over. A guy named Joseph Whidbey came along and circumnavigated the whole island, which apparently was impressive enough for it to be named after him. Full colonization of the island took its sweet time, though. The first permanent arrival was murdered and beheaded by some unhappy natives, and understandably there was a bit of healthy skepticism on the part of would-be immigrants. Nowadays Whidbey is a thriving agricultural community as well as home to a naval station, a healthy tourism industry, and the most visited state park in Washington. Despite all that Whidbey's got goin' on, it remains an extremely laid-back kind of place.

Activities

Though the island's one-time marketing campaign featuring the joyously ambiguous phrase "Do Nothing Here" might imply a lazy sort of attitude on the part of Whidbey residents, that's certainly not the case. If you feel compelled to do more than skipping rocks on the bay or snuggling in your cottage (both more-than-acceptable activities), the island teems with things to do for all tastes and energy levels. There are no fewer than ten public beaches on the island where you can go clamming, watch gray whales in season, or, if you're brave, go swimming. A few favorites include Ala Spit (popular with birdwatchers) and Double Bluff (with an off-leash area for your pup).

Adults can check out the different wineries and pubs, like the Whidbey Island Winery (5237 Langley Rd, Langley; www.whidbeyislandwinery.com), or go treasure-hunting at the scores of antique shops. There are also several farmers markets during the peak of the season where you can buy local loganberries and homemade ice cream. And if you really want to do something instead of nothing, there are sites for almost every type of outdoorsy activity, from hiking to fishing to kayaking. Basically, Whidbey's got it all.

Towns

One of the biggest draws is the quaint postcard towns scattered across the island. Visitors and residents alike enjoy spending an entire day strolling and soaking up the charm. Towards the south and only a few miles from the Clinton ferry dock is Langley, an artists' village with the highest concentration of boutique lodgings in the state. Farther north, historic Coupeville is situated on Penn Cove (home to the famously delectable mussels of the same name) and is the second oldest town in the entire state. It's loved for its charming shops and B &Bs, the Historical Society Museum, and the town ice cream parlor (yum).

Tours

The Whidbey Island Garden Tour (www.wigt.org) is an extremely popular once-yearly event. Tickets are limited, so reserve well in advance in early summer. Also fun, is the annual Whidbey Island Farm Tour, held in September (www.whidbeyfarmtour.com), when you can explore the island's crops and critters for free!

Deception Pass State Park

Deception Pass State Park is a 4,134-acre marine and camping park just north of Oak Harbor with amazing stretches of saltwater shoreline, as well as freshwater shoreline on three lakes. The park is the most popular in the state, and for good reason. There are breath-taking views, rugged cliffs, old-growth forests, and abundant wildlife. The park is open year-round for camping and day use, although select campgrounds are closed during the winter.

How to Get There

Driving
There's only one way to go if you're choosing to drive all the way to Whidbey—the breathtaking entrance to the north end of the island otherwise known as Deception Pass Bridge. Take the Anacortes exit off I-5, just north of Mt. Vernon. There are pull-outs and several points along the way where you can get out and take it all in. Trust us, it's stunning.

Ferry
Ferries are probably the most popular way to get to the island and the easiest from Seattle. The Mukilteo-Clinton ferry departs every 30 minutes from Mukilteo. Take I-5 north from Seattle and follow the Mukilteo/Whidbey Island exit (#189), which will take you straight to the ferry dock. At peak times there can be a significant wait, so check the current wait times before you go (www.wsdot.wa.gov/ferries). The ride takes about 20 minutes and will take you to the town of Clinton on the southern end of the island.

The Pt. Townsend-Keystone ferry also takes about 30 minutes and connects the Olympic Peninsula to Keystone Landing in Ebey's National Historical Reserve on the island. From the Peninsula, head east on Highway 101 and take the SR20 East exit. The highway will turn into Sims Way and then Water Street, which will take you to the ferry dock.

Plane
Seaplanes are a fun and incredibly scenic way to go, departing from Lake Union. If you want to bypass the whole ferry trip (which, on a bad day, can take hours), Kenmore Air (www.kenmoreair.com) features charter flights to Whidbey for up to ten passengers.

Public Transportation
If you're up farther north, the Island Transit system will take you on and off and the island for absolutely nothing. Check out the schedules at www.islandtransit.org.

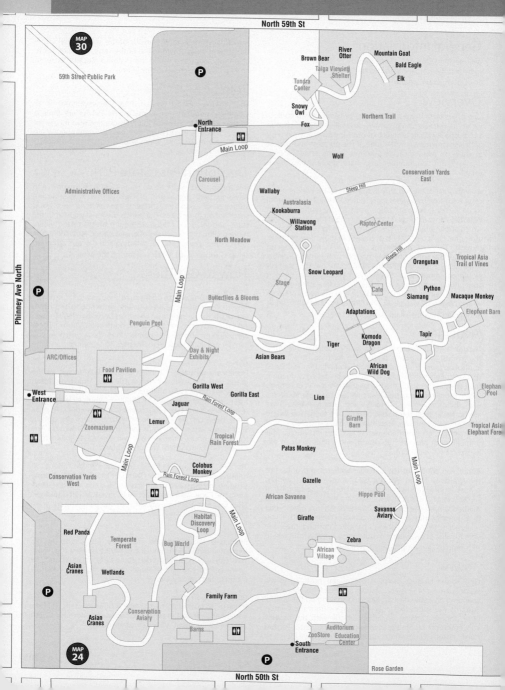

General Information

NFT Map: 24 & 30
Address: 5500 Phinney Ave N, Seattle, WA 98103
Phone: 206-548-2500
Website: www.zoo.org or @woodlandparkzoo
Hours: Open every day of the year, except Dec 25;
May 1–Sep 30: 9:30 am–6 pm,
Oct 1–April 30: 9:30 am–4 pm
Admission: May 1–Sep 30 $19.95 adults, $12.25
kids age 3–12; Oct 1–April 30 $13.75 adults, $9.25
kids (3–12); $2 discount off regular admission
prices for seniors (65+) and disabled; kids 0–2 are
free.

Overview

It may not be the biggest, it may not have the rarest
animals, but what the Woodlawn Park Zoo lacks in
size, it makes up for in style. There is a strong focus
on education and conservation and the exhibits
themselves will not leave you feeling depressed
like some other zoos can. It's easy to tell why this
zoo is world renowned for its animal exhibits and
education programs.

Geared to kids eight and younger, the all-
weather Zoomazium facility is the coolest indoor
playground ever. You will find a stage, a project
place, and an active space where parents let their
kids loose to tire them out before the drive home.
It's a great place for kids to learn as they play. There
is a 20-foot tree to climb, caves to explore, and a
watering hole that reflects an animal face when
you look into it.

The zoo's Jaguar Cove exhibit contains a large
pool and waterfall as jaguars are the only large
cat willing to get their tootsies wet. Even more
impressive, this is the only zoo to boast a cross-
section for underwater viewing of an enormous
hungry jaguar coming right at you.

Other interesting zoo offerings include the fun
summer concert series ZooTunes and the Zoo
Overnight Adventure, where small groups can
reserve overnight accommodations that include
private tours and breakfast (approximately $50 per
person). And even though it's technically located
outside of the zoo, the free Rose Garden offers a
pleasant (quick) stroll through its 2.5-acre garden.
This is a popular and affordable spot for weddings,
especially owing to its 280 varieties of roses and
over 5,000 individual plants, one of only 24 All
American Rose Selections Test Gardens in the US.
You can smell it before you even walk in.

Eating at the Zoo

When you get hungry like the wolf, there are a
couple options: the Rain Forest Food Pavilion has
various light fare and Caffe Vita-roasted coffee
at Zoo Java. The Pacific Blue Chowder House has
heartier fare to take away, and specializes in local
seafood, along with above-average burgers. And
then of course there are the requisite seasonal
kiosks serving up zoo classics like Dippin' Dots and
lemonade.

How to Get There

Driving
From I-5 take the 50th Street exit (#169) west for
1.3 miles to the south gate located on N 50th Street
and Fremont Avenue N. Parking is $5.25 for cars,
but try snagging a free spot on the street first.

Public Transportation
From downtown take the 5 from 3rd Avenue and
Pine Street to the west gate at N 55th Street &
Phinney Avenue N.

Come the weekend, Seattleites don't mess around with their bicycle recreation. This usually means snapping their expensive Trek mountain bike to their Subaru and hitting the nearby off-roading trails. But for a growing number of city slickers, Saturday means grabbing their bike out of their living room and hitting the urban trails. The granddaddy of them all is the The Burke-Gilman Trail, a 27-mile route along a former railway corridor that stretches from Redmond all the way to Ballard. Other car-free escapes include Green Lake Trail, Ship Canal Trail, and Alki Beach Trail in West Seattle. Wherever you ride, you can't miss the hills. But luckily, they work both ways. They can be a pain in the butt to climb (especially early in the morning on your way to a coffee shop), but for those willing to conquer them, you are rewarded with picture perfect views usually reserved for postcards. Unless of course it's raining. Again. The Seattle Department of Transportation has a good bike map (http://www.seattle.gov/transportation/bikemaps.htm); check out the handy interactive feature on the SDOT website.

Bicycle Sundays is becoming an annual tradition when sections of Lake Washington Boulevard are completely shut down to vehicle traffic on select weekends in the spring and summer from Mount Baker Beach to Seward Park. Cruise along this beautiful stretch of Seattle without the stress of a giant SUV racing to cut you off. If only biking in Seattle were like this everyday. Check out the website for more information and specific dates: www.seattle.gov/transportation/bikesatsun.htm

There's still a lot of work to be done to eclipse Northwest rival and biking utopia Portland. If you find yourself frustrated with the Emerald City's progress, sign up for the annual Seattle to Portland Classic. Over 10,000 riders join in this summer tradition (sponsored by the Cascade Bicycle Alliance) for a 200-mile journey by bike to Puddletown. While you're there, cruise around America's most bike-friendly city and hope that Seattle can follow in their impressive bikesteps.

Burke-Gilman Trail

The Burke-Gilman Trail (www.seattle.gov/transportation/BGT.htm) is the crown jewel of Seattle's trail system. Starting from Lake Sammamish on the Eastside (with extensions to Issaquah), the trail runs 25 miles around the north of Lake Washington to the University of Washington. But beware! Even the official bike map warns about neglected stretches along the north Seattle section. From the UW, the BGT traces the ship canal and Lake Union through Wallingford and Fremont to the edge of Ballard, where it mysteriously disintegrates into a gravel-strewn truck route. Commuters from north Seattle can cross the Fremont Bridge onto Dexter, which has protected bike lanes all the way to Denny Way. It's not difficult to cut across to Second Avenue, which features a two-way protected bike lane.

Elliott Bay Trail

Starting from Golden Gardens, a short trail leads you to the Ballard Locks. After walking across the locks, you can either follow the truck lane to the left or go straight uphill on the dead-end street to one hell of a suspension bridge. Take the bridge across some railroad tracks before turning onto a proper bike lane on Government Way/Gilman Avenue. The lane turns into a bike trail that cuts right through the rail yard, with some harrowing and extremely narrow sections, before blossoming into the Elliott Bay Trail. The trail empties into downtown, becoming a designated bike route that leads to the West Seattle Bridge. After the West Seattle Bridge, turn north for the Alki Trail or south toward the Duwamish Trail to South Park. From there, a spotty connection of side roads connects you to W Marginal Way S before smoothing out to the Green River Trail, which takes you all the way to Kent.

Lake Washington Loop

You can also use a combination of the Burke-Gilman to make a less frustrating trip circling Lake Washington. Depart the BGT at Montlake, cross the Montlake Bridge, and wind through the Arboretum (a nice ride, even with all the cars). From there, a route leads to Lake Washington Boulevard, one of Seattle's more pleasant and peaceful rides that continues all the way to Renton. A series of other trails bring you up the east side of the lake. Neither of southeast Seattle's main arteries, Rainier Avenue or Martin Luther King Way, are known for being bike-friendly.

Coming to/from the Eastside, the I-90 Trail makes for an interesting ride alongside eight lanes of traffic. Luckily, the trail has its own tunnel and connects to downtown.

Face it. In a city where it's fashionable to commute to work by kayak, Seattle's traffic problems aren't isolated to the Mercer mess; they spill over into the area's multiple salt and fresh waterways. Everyone and their sister owns some sort of boat in Seattle, and many Seattleites have more boats than kids. After all, you need different kinds of boats for salmon fishing, river kayaking, sculling, cruising the San Juans, racing Vic-Maui, or rounding the buoys on a Wednesday night Duck Dodge. Plus, you gotta have a Zodiac or a dinghy to row into shore when your yacht is anchored out in Andrews Bay during Seafair. And of course it takes a little Boston Whaler to buzz over from Portage Bay on a summer night to have a beer and a bowl of steamed clams in a waterfront joint on Lake Union.

In Elliott Bay, Seattle's main harbor, tugboats, barges, container ships, fishing vessels, ferries, sailboats, powerboats, and cruise ships as big as football fields all vie for the same waterway space. Floating homes with deepwater boat moorage on Lake Union are more highly coveted than a landlubber's three-car garage, and if you have room to tie up your float plane, so much the better. Seattle's boating scene can be as silly as it can be serious—more than one yacht club has a tavern as its clubhouse, but Seattle has produced world class rowers, some of the America Cup's best crews, and Olympic-class kayakers.

Of course, there are rivalries between the "stinkpotters" and vessels powered by sails, oars, or paddles. Hydroplanes? Love 'em or get out of town the first weekend of August, when the gas guzzling, engine whining hydros churn up Lake Washington at Seafair, Seattle's answer to NASCAR, and the lake fills up with log booms of yachts, festooned with bikini-clad women and beer-guzzling men intent on partying hearty. All of this is in stark contrast to Lake Washington's typical bucolic scene of rowers and scullers practicing for the next regatta. Many local universities, private schools, city parks, non-profit rowing clubs, and kayaking organizations teach water skills and advocate to preserve Seattle's precious waterways for future generations.

Like the human body, Seattle is made up primarily of water. So find your boat of choice and get out there. You'll have lots of company.

Small Boats Centers

The Center for Wooden Boats: 1010 Valley St, 206-382-2628, cwb.org
Green Lake Boat Rental: 7351 E Green Lake Dr N, 206-527-0171, www.greenlakeboatrentals.net
Moss Bay Row, Kayak, Sail & Paddle Board Center: 1001 Fairview Ave N, 206-682-2031, www.mossbay.net
Waterfront Activities Center: 3710 Montlake Blvd NE, Behind Husky Stadium at the University of Washington, 206-543-9433, www.washington.edu/ima/wac

Yacht and Cruising Clubs

Corinthian Yacht Club: 7755 Seaview Ave NW, 206-789-1919, www.cycseattle.org
Hidden Harbor Yacht Club: www.hhycseattle.com
Meydenbauer Yacht Club: 9927 Meydenbauer Wy SE, Bellevue, 425-454-8880, www.mbycwa.org
Puget Sound Yacht Club: 2321 North Northlake Wy, 206-634-3733, www.pugetsoundyc.org
Queen City Yacht Club: 2608 Boyer Ave E, 206-709-2000, www.queencity.org
Rainier Yacht Club: 9094 Seward Park Ave S 206-722-9576, www.rainieryachtclub.com
Seattle Yacht Club: 1807 E Hamlin St, 206-325-1000, www.seattleyachtclub.org
Sloop Tavern Yacht Club: 2830 NW Market St, www.styc.org
Tyee Yacht Club: 3229 Fairview Ave E, tyeeyachtclub.org
Washington Yacht Club: University of Washington Husky Union Building, 425-298-5670, www.washingtonyachtclub.org

Rowing Clubs and Centers

Lake Washington Rowing Club: 910 N Northlake Wy, 206-547-1583, lakewashingtonrowing.com
Green Lake Crew: 5900 W Greenlake Wy N, 206-684-4074, www.greenlakecrew.org
Green Lake Small Craft Center: 5900 W Greenlake Wy N 206-684-4074
Lake Union Crew: 2520 Westlake Ave N, 206-860-4199, lakeunioncrew.com
Mount Baker Rowing and Sailing Center: 3800 Lake Washington Blvd S, 206-386-1913, mbrsc.com
Pocock Rowing Center: 3320 Fuhrman Ave E, 206-328-0778, www.pocockfoundation.org

Kayaking Clubs and Centers

Kayak Academy: 11801 188th Ave SE, Issaquah, 206-527-1825, www.kayakacademy.com
Mountaineers Club: 206-521-6000, www.mountaineers.org
Northwest Outdoor Center: 2100 Westlake Ave N, 206-281-9694, www.nwoc.com
Seattle Canoe and Kayak Club: 5900 W Greenlake Wy N, 206-684-4074, www.seattlecanoekayak.club
University of Sea Kayaking: 425-741-0960, www.useakayak.org
Washington Water Trails Association: 206-545-9161, wwta.org

Bowling alleys have not quite gone the way of the drive-in theater yet, but sophisticated, urbane Seattle seems to have little use for them. Over the years bowling spots have declined in the heart of the city, leaving downtown-bound hipsters dry, but on Capitol Hill the **Garage (Map 4)** filled the gap in 2003 by adding fourteen swanky lanes for metrosexual pin pals. By contrast, **Imperial Lanes (Map 40)** is old-school bowling at its finest. The popular **Underdog Sports League** (www.underdogseattle.com) holds team competitions here while locals hang out at the no-frills bar. Aside from that, Seattle bowlers are forced to seek their sport in outlying townships and unfashionable parts of the city proper.

ACME Bowl houses the newest, shiniest lanes in the greater Seattle area, adjacent to the Southcenter Mall in Tukwila and decked out in a sleek faux-retro fashion. This is the bowling alley for people who are afraid to go to bowling alleys. It's an open, well-lit place that serves gourmet pizzas and portobello mushroom sandwiches directly to your lane. Private bowling with cool blue neon lighting and projection screens is available, the perfect spot for bachelorette parties or an ironic evening out with co-workers.

For those after a more traditional bowling experience, South Seattle can satisfy. **Skyway Park Bowl** tore out their indoor miniature golf course to expand its casino, but retained its warmth and old-school appeal. **Roxbury Lanes (Map 37)** advertises "saloon and casino" in the same breath as "family-friendly" and that's about the size of it—expect exuberant children on the lanes and enthusiastic drinkers in the bar.

West Seattle Bowl (Map 36) strikes a nice compromise between the sterility of ACME and the earthier tones of the older bowling alleys, with a Chinese restaurant on site, comfy booths on the lanes, and a video bowling game if you really are that lazy. And to the north, **Lynnwood Bowl & Skate** brings pins and wheels together for all-ages action, or check out **Spin Alley** in Shoreline, which opened in 1997 as a smoke-free bowling emporium (a fine sentiment rendered moot by Initiative 901, which banned smoking in public places statewide eight years later). For information on tournaments and other bowling-related news, check out the **Greater Seattle USBC Association** (www.seattlebowling.org).

Bowling

Bowling	Address		Phone	Map
Garage Billiards & Bowl	1130 Broadway	Seattle	206-322-2296	4
West Seattle Bowl	4505 39th Ave SW	Seattle	206-932-3731	36
Magic Lanes	10612 15th SW	Seattle	206-244-5060	37
Roxbury	2823 Roxbury St	Seattle	206-935-7400	37
Imperial Lanes	2101 22nd Ave S	Seattle	206-325-2525	40
AMF Sun Villa Lanes	3080 148th SE	Bellevue	425-455-8155	44
Lucky Strike Lanes	700 Bellevue Wy NE	Bellevue	425-453-5137	45
TechCity Bowl	13033 NE 70th Pl	Kirkland	425-827-0785	48
ACME Bowling	100 Andover Park W	Tukwila	206-340-2263	n/a
Adventure Bowling Center	3740 Railroad Ave SE	Snoqualmie	425-888-1377	n/a
Brunswick Majestic Lanes	1222 164th SW	Lynnwood	425-743-4422	n/a
Chalet Bowl	3806 N 26th St	Tacoma	253-752-5200	n/a
Daffodil Entertainment Center	1624 E Main	Puyallup	253-845-9166	n/a
Evergreen Lanes	5111 Claremont Wy	Everett	425-259-7206	n/a
Glacier Lanes	9630 Evergreen Wy	Everett	425-353-8292	n/a
Hi-Line Lanes	15733 Ambaum Blvd SW	Burien	206-244-2272	n/a
Kenmore 50 Lanes & Casino	7638 NE Bothell Wy	Bothell	425-486-5555	n/a
Kent Bowl	1234 Central N	Kent	253-852-3550	n/a
Lynnwood Bowl and Skate	6210 200th St SW	Lynwood	425-778-3133	n/a
Pacific Lanes	7015 S D St	Tacoma	253-474-0594	n/a
Paradise Bowl	12505 Pacific Ave S	Tacoma	253-537-6012	n/a
Rocket Alley Bar and Grill	420 N Olympic Ave	Arlington	360-435-8600	n/a
Secoma Lanes	34500 Pacific Hwy S	Federal Way	253-927-0611	n/a
Skyway Park Bowl Casino	11819 Renton Ave S	Seattle	206-772-1200	n/a
Spin Alley Bowling Center	1430 NW Richmond Beach Rd	Shoreline	206-533-2345	n/a
Strawberry Lanes	1067 Columbia Ave	Marysville	360-659-7641	n/a
Tower Inn & Lanes	6323 6th Ave	Tacoma	253-564-8853	n/a
Twin City Lanes	27120 92nd Ave NW	Stanwood	360-629-3001	n/a

Golf

Golf	Address	Phone	Map	Fees		Par, Holes
Interbay Golf Center	2501 15th Ave W	206-285-2200	12	Mon-Fri $13, Sat-Sun $15		Par-28, 9 holes
Green Lake Pitch & Putt	5701 E Green Lake Way N	206-632-2280	30	$7–9		
Battle Creek Golf Course	6006 Meridian Ave N	360-659-7931	31	Mon-Fri $25, Sat–Sun $32		Par-73, 18 holes
Jackson Park Golf Course	1000 NE 135 St	206-363-4747	34	Mon-Fri $28, Sat–Sun $33		Par-71, 18 holes
Jefferson Park Golf Course	4101 Beacon Ave S	206-762-4513	34	Mon-Fri $28, Sat–Sun $33		Par-70, 18 holes
West Seattle Golf Course	4470 35th Ave SW	206-935-5187	36	Mon-Fri $28, Sat–Sun $33		Par-72, 18 holes
Bellevue Municipal Golf Course	5500 140th Ave NE	425-452-7250	46	Mon-Thurs $27, Fri–Sun $31		Par-71,18 holes
Foster Golf Links	13500 Interurban Ave S	206-242-4221	n/a	Mon-Fri $21, Sat–Sun $23		Par-69, 18 holes

Tennis

Tennis	Address	Phone	Map	
Bobby Morris Playfield	1635 11th Ave	206-684-4075	4	2 courts, Lighted
Garfield Playfield	23rd Ave & E Cherry St	206-684-4075	5	3 courts, Lighted
Madrona Playfield	3211 E Spring St	206-684-4075	6	2 courts, Lighted
I-90 Lid/Sam Smith	1400 Martin Luther King Jr Wy S	206-684-4075	10	2 courts
Leschi Park	201 Lakeside Ave S	206-684-4075	10	1 court
Discovery Park	3801 W Government Wy	206-386-4236	11	2 courts
Magnolia Park	1461 Magnolia Blvd W	206-684-4075	11	2 courts
Magnolia Playfield	2518 34th Ave W	206-684-4075	11	4 courts
David Rodgers Park	2800 1st Ave W	206-684-4075	13	3 courts, Backboard
Kinnear Park	899 W Olympic Pl	206-684-4075	14	1 court
Miller Playfield	400 19th Ave E	206-684-4075	18	2 courts, Lighted
Volunteer Park	1247 15th Ave E	206-684-4075	18	4 court, Lighted, Backboard
Rogers Playground	Eastlake Ave E & E Roanoke St	206-684-4075	20	3 courts
Madison Park	4201 E Madison St	206-684-4075	22	2 courts, Lighted
Gilman Playground	923 NW 54th St	206-684-4075	24	2 courts
Woodland Park (Lower)	5851 West Green Lake Wy N	206-684-4075	24	10 courts
Woodland Park (Upper)	Midvale Ave N & N 50th St	206-684-4075	24	4 courts
Wallingford Playfield	4219 Wallingford Ave N	206-684-4075	25	2 courts
University Playground	9th Ave NE & NE 50th St	206-684-4075	26	2 courts, Backboard
Bryant Playground	4103 NE 65th St	206-684-4075	27	2 courts
Laurelhurst Playfield	4544 NE 41st St	206-684-4075	27	4 courts, Lighted, Backboard
Magnuson Park	6500 Sand Point Wy NE	206-684-4075	27	6 courts
Froula Playground	7200 12th Ave NE	206-684-4075	31	2 courts
Green Lake Park	7201 E Green Lake Dr N	206-684-4075	31	5 courts
Cowen Park	5849 15th Ave NE	206-684-4075	32	3 courts
Ravenna Park	5520 Ravenna Ave NE	206-684-4075	32	2 courts, Backboard
Ravenna-Eckstein	6535 Ravenna Ave NE	206-684-4075	32	1 court
Bitter Lake Playfield	13030 N Park Ave N	206-684-4075	33	4 courts, Lighted
Soundview Playfield	1590 NW 90th St	206-684-4075	33	2 courts
Meadowbrook Playfield	10533 35th Ave NE	206-684-4075	34	6 courts, Lighted
Victory Heights Playground	1737 NE 106th St	206-684-4075	34	1 court
Alki Playground	5817 SW Lander St	206-684-4075	35	1 court, Lighted
Hiawatha Playfield	2700 California Ave SW	206-684-4075	35	3 courts, Lighted, Backboard
Delridge Playfield	4458 Delridge Wy SW	206-684-4075	36	2 courts
Jefferson Park	4165 16th Ave SW	206-684-4075	36	2 courts, Lighted
High Point Playfield	6920 34th Ave SW	206-684-4075	37	2 courts
Lowman Beach Park	7017 Beach Dr SW	206-684-4075	37	1 court
Solstice Park	8603 Fauntleroy Wy SW	206-684-4075	37	6 courts, Lighted, Backboard
Highland Park Playground	1100 SW Cloverdale St	206-684-4075	38	1 court
Riverview Playfield	7226 12th Ave SW	206-684-4075	38	2 courts
South Park Playground	738 S Sullivan St	206-684-4075	38	2 courts
Beacon Hill Playground	1902 13th Ave S	206-684-4075	39	2 courts, Backboard
Cleveland Playfield	5512 13th Ave S	206-684-4075	39	2 courts
Georgetown Playfield	750 S Homer St	206-684-4075	39	1 court
Amy Yee Tennis Center	2000 Martin Luther King Jr Wy S	206-684-4764	40	4 courts
Beer Shiva Park	55th Ave S	206-684-4075	40	1 court
Brighton Playfield	6000 39th Ave S	206-684-4075	40	2 courts
Dearborn Park	2919 S Brandon St	206-684-4075	40	2 courts
Mount Baker Park	2521 Lake Park Dr S	206-684-4075	40	2 courts, Lighted
Rainier Playfield	3700 S Alaska St	206-684-4075	40	4 courts, Lighted
Seward Park	5902 Lake Washington Blvd S	206-684-4075	40	1 court
Hutchinson Playground	S Norfolk St & 59th Ave S	206-684-4075	41	2 courts
Rainier Beach Playfield	8802 Rainier Ave S	206-684-4075	41	4 courts, Lighted
Homestead Park	82nd Ave SE & SE 40th St	206-236-3545	42	4 courts
Luther Burbank Park	2040 84th Ave SE	206-236-3545	42	3 courts
Park on the Lid	I-90 & W Mercer Wy	206-236-3545	42	4 courts
Robinswood Tennis Center	2400 151st Pl SE	425-452-7690	44	6 indoor, 2 outdoor
Everest Park	500 8th Ave S	425-587-3347	48	1 outdoor
Heritage Park	111 Waverly Wy	425-587-3342	48	2 outdoor
Juanita Beach Park	9703 NE Juanita Dr	425-587-3340	48	2 outdoor
Peter Kirk Park	202 3rd St	425-587-3342	48	2 outdoor
Grass Lawn Park	7031 148th Ave NE	425-556-2311	49	2 outdoor

Overview

The Northwest is famous for its mountainous terrain, so finding a trail to hike in these parts is not difficult. But if you don't have a car, or don't feel like venturing outside of King Country, there are plenty of urban hikes to keep your Nalgene bottle dust-free. In the Seattle area or outside it, the Washington Trails Association (www.wta.org) is a great resource to get you started.

The Burke-Gilman is the most popular urban trail. Parks like Carkeek, Lincoln, and Magnuson have trails along the waterfront as well as beautiful vistas that will make you forget you're a stone's throw from civilization. If it's communing with nature you're after, visit the Arboretum or the Schmitz Park Reserve. If you crave a real endorphin-kicker, you still need only drive a few minutes east to the switchbacks of Tiger Mountain. Since none of the parks are very expansive, it's difficult to lose your way. But if you're the type to get lost in your own museum, never fear. All of these parks have kiosks with trail maps.

If most of your friends consider lifting pint glasses exercise, you can meet other hiking enthusiasts by means of the Seattle Mountaineers (www.mountaineers.org). They offer regularly scheduled hikes as well as other outdoor activities.

Carkeek Park

950 NW Carkeek Park Rd, 6 miles, Easy, (Map 29-30)
Carkeek is most famous for the salmon preserve in Pipers Creek. In the late fall, you can follow the Piper's Creek trail to catch a glimpse of the fish-filled waters. Year-round, North Bluff Trail provides fantastic views of the Olympic Mountains and Puget Sound. The Wetland Trail leads you down to the beach.

Mt. Si

North Bend, 4 miles, Moderate-Difficult
Another great day hike just a short drive out of the city, Mt. Si, rewards your workout with amazing views of the Snoqualmie Valley and Puget Sound. Everyone in Seattle seems to know about this hike, which is reflected in the lack of parking spaces on a sunny Saturday. The trail gains 3,100 feet over the four miles and will really get the heart rate up. If you get a late start and are looking for a shorter walk, you'll come to the first vista about one mile in. This also serves as a good place to turn around.

Burke-Gilman Trail

60th Place NE and Bothell Wy to 8th NW, 14 miles, Easy-Moderate, (Map 23-27, 34)
This multi-purpose trail covers over 14 miles from 11th Ave NW to Tracy Owen Station in Kenmore, then picks up again between the Hiram M. Chittenden Locks and Golden Gardens Park. It allows bikers and joggers as well as hikers, so it can sometimes be a bit too crowded for a contemplative, woodsy walk. But it is the longest urban trail around, so no matter what neighborhood you live in, there is most likely an access point near you. Among the many entrances to the trail are Ballard, Fremont, Sand Point, and Matthews Beach Park. The trail also runs through the University of Washington campus. Planning is ongoing to complete the "missing link" through Ballard; stay tuned.

Lincoln Park

8011 Fauntleroy Wy SW, 5 miles, Easy-Moderate (Map 37)
If you're after a mostly water vista for your hike, Lincoln Park is the place for you. The 100-foot high Bluff Loop trail provides a stunning view of Puget Sound. The South Beach trail borders Fauntleroy Cove. Those trails are fantastic in the warm weather, but the wind can make them unpleasant during the off-season. The North Beach Trail is slightly more shielded by trees, so it is ideal for a hike on those blustery winter days. In the summer, you can conclude your hike by taking a dip in the heated saltwater Colman Pool.

Schmitz Park Preserve

5551 SW Admiral Wy, 2 miles, Easy (Map 35)
One of the few urban areas to boast old-growth forest, the Schmitz Park Preserve is a great place to stroll in quiet contemplation amidst the majesty of nature. Despite its size—a mere 53 acres—it isn't difficult to feel secluded as you stroll along the often-empty figure 8 trail that curves through the area. Be on the lookout for foxes, bats, and coyotes.

Seward Park

5900 Lake Washington Blvd, 3 miles, Easy (Map 40)
Like Schmitz Park, Seward Park possesses the splendor of old-growth forest: 250 acres of impressively ancient Douglas Firs and Western Red Cedars. The perimeter path, popular with joggers and bikers, runs along the beach and presents views of the Seattle skyline, Lake Washington, Mercer Island, and Mount Rainier. The interior path, which breaks off into several shorter trails, runs through the thick of the forest. Despite being surrounded by urban sprawl, the area is often dead quiet, particularly in the winter.

Discovery Park

3801 W Government Wy, 7 Miles,
Easy-Moderate (Map 11)
The city's largest public park was built on an old Army base. This urban oasis is a veritable checklist of habitats including forest, meadow, saltwater beach, and sand dunes. Aptly named, Discovery Park is a versatile dominion in which you can take a quick 30-minute jaunt or play "Blair Witch" and get lost in the wilderness. The grounds are rife with fruit during blackberry season, providing a delectable mid-hike snack. The main trail is the 3-mile Loop Trail, which meanders through many of the aforementioned habitats and past the abandoned army barracks. Several steep trails will take you down to the beach and to the West Point lighthouse, which was built in 1881. Off of West Point, you can sometimes spot sea lions, seals, orcas, or porpoises. While the water is never quite warm enough to swim in, people often sunbathe on the beaches during those scorching 75-degree summer days. Some of the less-modest park visitors have deemed the beach clothing-optional. The South Bluff Trail will lead you to spectacular views of Mount Rainier and the city skyline. For a short but interesting jaunt, the half-mile Wolf Tree nature trail brings you through the dwellings of coyotes, river otters, muskrats, and bobcats. Additionally, more than 270 species of birds dwell within the park.

Washington Park Arboretum

2300 Arboretum Dr E, 4 miles, Easy (Map 22)
Stroll through the 250 acres of one of the Northwest's largest collections of plants and trees, with thousands upon thousands of species. The Arboretum Waterfront Trail starts at the parking lot and leads to Marsh and Foster Islands. In the warm seasons, this trail is ideal for bird watching. From Foster Island, you can hike to the north tip and enjoy a stunning view across Union Bay. Azalea Way is an easy-going 3/4-mile walk through the—you guessed it—azaleas. To get there from downtown Seattle, drive east on Madison Street to Lake Washington Boulevard and turn left into the Arboretum.

Sand Point Magnuson Park

7400 Sandpoint Wy NE, 4 miles, Easy (Map 27)
Magnuson Park is a 350-acre area located in the middle of a former Navy facility. Parts of it are paved and crowded, but you can also find secluded grass and wetland habitats to wander through. The trailhead to the Cross-Park Trail, located next to the playground, will take you through the grasslands. Promontory Point meanders through a restored wildlife habitat. You can find that trail at the south end of the park.

Tiger Mountain

Issaquah (Moderate)
If the above-mentioned urban hikes aren't extreme enough for your lifestyle, but you still don't want to travel far from the city, Tiger Mountain affords the perfect temporary wilderness retreat. It's also a good alternative for hardcore hikers who can't get their cars over the snowy passes in the wintertime. The West Tiger 3 provides a 2,000-foot elevation stretched over five miles. Its switchback-heavy path will definitely make you feel worthy of your fleece. For a less-strenuous wander through the woods, try the Around The Lake Tradition Trail. The Tradition Plateau and Bus Trail are moderate hikes. Look for the skeleton of an abandoned Greyhound bus that gives the latter trail its name. To get there, take exit 20 off I-90 East and follow the signs.

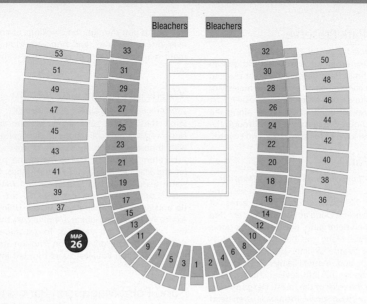

General Information

NFT Map: 26
Address: 3800 Montlake Blvd NE, Seattle, WA 98195
Tickets: 206-543-2210
Website: www.huskystadium.com

Overview

Husky Stadium, home to the University of Washington Huskies, is recognized as one of the nation's most scenic football stadiums. From the upper deck on the stadium's north side, fans have views of downtown Seattle, the Olympic Mountains, and Mt. Rainier (when it's clear, that is). Built in 1920, the stadium seats just over 70,000 fans—more than 70 percent between the end zones—and ranks among the nation's loudest venues. Game days have turned into ten-hour events, thanks to the pre – and post-game tailgating, which takes place in automobiles, RVs, and boats that dock in special moorings. A $280 million renovation, completed in 2012, updated the facility without sacrificing the stadium's distinctive look and feel, preserving the unique Husky Stadium experience for future generations.

1991 saw the peak of Husky football glory with its second National Championship (the other was way back in 1960). In 2001 the Huskies won the Rose Bowl, and things were looking good for the future. Tickets were almost impossible to come by, and Husky pride was near an all time high. But in the coming years, former head coach Rick Neuheisel became embroiled in a seemingly harmless NCAA betting scandal that took down the athletic director and signaled a downward spiral in the team's fortunes. Despite a few coaching changes, the Huskies have been floundering near the bottom of the conference ever since. A word of advice:

Unless you are on foot, bike or Segway, get a copy of the Husky schedule and avoid the U-District at all costs during game times lest it quadruple your travel time.

How to Get Tickets

Individual game tickets can be purchased from the Huskies' website, by calling 206-543-2200, or in person at the ticket office (3910 Montlake Blvd, Graves Building 101). The office is open Monday through Friday from 8:30 am-5 pm.

How to Get There

Driving
From I-5 north or south, take the Highway 520 exit toward Bellevue-Kirkland, then exit on Montlake Boulevard. Turn left and cross the bridge. Husky Stadium is on the right. From Highway 405 north or south, take Highway 520 exit toward Seattle and cross the Evergreen Point Floating Bridge heading west. Exit on Montlake Boulevard. Turn left and cross the bridge. Husky Stadium is on the right.

Parking in adjoining neighborhoods is prohibited. Public parking lots on the east side of the UW campus generally fill 30-60 minutes before kick-off. Parking is on a first-come, first-served basis. Remote Park & Ride lots across the region with special bus service is available; check website for details.

Public Transportation
Metro routes 43, 44, 48, 65, 75, and 271 serve the stadium. In addition, special Husky bus service (routes 715 and 725) is available on game days. Sound Transit's University of Washington light rail station is located right next to the stadium.

General Information

NFT Map: 15

Address: 305 Harrison St, Seattle, WA 98109

Seattle Storm: storm.wnba.com or @seattlestorm

Rat City Rollergirls: ratcityrollergirls.com or @RCRG

Arena Website: www.keyarena.com
or @KeyArenaSeattle

Overview

Located in Seattle Center under the Space Needle, KeyArena dates to 1962 when the facility was used as the Washington State Pavilion during the World's Fair. After the Fair it was adapted for use as an arena, hosting major events like concerts by the Beatles in 1964 and Elvis Presley in 1970 (as well as Led Zeppelin, Kiss, and hometown pride Jimi Hendrix). In 1967 the SuperSonics began playing at KeyArena. In 1995 the arena received a $75-million renovation that left the exterior as is, while dropping the playing court 22 feet underground to provide 3,000 additional seats. A 15-year naming rights deal with a certain bank of the same name provided TV announcers endless pun opportunities such as "the Key to tonight's game" and "the defense is really Keyed in right now."

The Sonics won a championship in 1979 (Dennis Johnson! Jack Sikma!) and enjoyed much success in the 1990s (Gary Payton! Shawn Kemp!) before going on an extended dry spell lingering well into the new millennium. The team, as teams often do, looked to the city for public funds to update the "aging" facility, and when those negotiations foundered, the franchise was sold and moved to Oklahoma City in 2007, just when the team started to get really, really good (Kevin Durant!).

Since then the 17,000-seat stadium has been taken over by the ladies. The two-time world champion (2004 and 2010) Seattle Storm of the WNBA and the bad-ass babes of the Rat City Rollergirls (throw on your Sockit Wenches or Grave Danger team jersey and get ready for some hair pulling and spectacular wipeouts) both call KeyArena home. The Storm play from late May into September while the Rat City Roller Girls roller derby season runs February to October. It also hosts circuses, ice skating exhibitions, professional wrestling, NCAA basketball and any musical acts who don't have the fan base for the much large CenturyLink Events Center.

How to Get Tickets

If you want to save on service charge fees, you can buy individual tickets in person at the Key Arena box office (Mon-Sat, 10 am-6 pm) located near the team shop at West Plaza off 1st Ave. You can also get tickets by calling 1-800-745-3000 or by buying them online via Ticketmaster.com. If you're feeling brave, scalpers are known to wander the grounds of Seattle Center looking to unload tickets before a game.

How to Get There

Driving

From the north or south on I-5, take the Mercer Street exit and follow the signs to Seattle Center. Key Arena is on the northwest corner of the Seattle Center grounds, with street access along First Avenue North and cross streets Thomas and Republican. Public lot, meter, and street parking are available along First Avenue and Fifth Avenue North, Mercer Street, and throughout the lower Queen Anne neighborhood.

Public Transportation

Fifteen Seattle Metro buses serve KeyArena from throughout the Puget Sound region. By Ferry, boats arrive hourly at Colman Dock on the waterfront. Key Arena is about 1 1/2 miles north of the ferry terminal, best reached by Seattle Metro buses. And yes, let it be known that the Monorail does run between Seattle Center and downtown.

With more than 67,000 seats and a sloping roof design that covers 70 percent of the seating area, the CLink is both comfortable and loud. Fans enjoy wide seats that, in the front rows, are only 40-50 feet from the playing field. If you're up for it, grab a aluminum bleacher seat in the Hawk's Nest on the north side of the field and bond with the die-hards. This joyful atmosphere has provided the Seahawks with one of the NFL's top home field advantages, and helped the franchise become a perennial playoff contender. The CLink also hosts the other kind of football, Seattle's well-adored MLS soccer team, the Sounders. But good luck getting a ticket. They sold 22,000 season tickets the first year. Attendance continues to soar, with nearly every game selling out. Between the Sounders and the Timbers, their insanely popular rivals to the south, footie seems to be the perfect sport for cloud-covered cities.

How to Get Tickets

Tickets sell out fast, so buy them early from the Seahawks website, by calling 888-635-4295, or in person at the CenturyLink box office when they go on sale. Tickets are required for children ages 2 and up. For Sounders games, get tickets thru Ticketmaster or at the stadium box office (weeks in advance if you actually want to get in).

How to Get There

Driving
From the north and south, exit I-5 at James Street, Fourth Avenue or Airport Way. From the east, exit I-90 where it ends at Fourth Avenue and turn right. Then turn right at Royal Brougham Way.

For Sunday afternoon games, street parking can be had for free if you get there at least three hours early to snag a space. It can be found in Pioneer Square, SoDo, and the International District. Three parking lots near the stadium open three hours prior to game time, however many of these spaces are sold in advance so be aware of limited status. Private lots are available on First and Fourth Avenues surrounding the stadium.

Public Transportation
Seattle Metro buses swing through downtown close to the stadium, and more than a dozen regular routes stop within three blocks of the stadium. That said, keep in mind the traffic associated with large events, and plan accordingly. Both Sound Transit and Metro run special shuttle/express routes, as well. To skip surface streets, the light rail has two stops close to the stadium at, er, Stadium and International District/Chinatown. For Seahawks games, Sound Transit (www.soundtransit. org) runs special trains on Sundays from Tacoma and Everett to King Street Station when the Seahawks are playing (Amtrak Cascade service also is quite convenient). If traveling by ferry, boats arrive hourly at Colman Dock on the waterfront, just a 10-minute walk from the stadium. Walk east on Occidental Avenue and turn right.

General Information

NFT Map: 7

Address: 800 Occidental Ave S Seattle, WA 98134

CenturyLink Field Box Office: 206-381-7848

CenturyLink Field Lost & Found: 206-381-7544

Seattle Seahawks: www.seahawks.com or @Seahawks

Seattle Sounders: www.soundersfc.com
or @SoundersFC

CenturyLink Field: www.centurylinkfield.com
or @CenturyLink_Fld

Overview

After years of sweating inside the dark and dingy (but beloved) Kingdome, the Seattle Seahawks finally moved to a place where they could play football as it was meant to be played: outside in the elements. At the start of the 2002 season, Seattle's favorite underdogs abandoned the Kingdome for the newfangled Seahawks Stadium, as it was then called. Thanks to corporate interest, the stadium was soon re-named, Qwest Field. In 2011, CenturyLink bought Qwest and changed the stadium's name again. Suddenly, we were asked to start calling it, "CenturyLink Field." Not ones to fall in line easily, Seattleites immediately dubbed it "the CLink." And that's how it shall be known until the next corporate merger.

General Information

NFT Map: 7

Address: 1250 First Ave S, Seattle, WA 98134

Seattle Mariners: www.mariners.com
or @Mariners

Overview

Mariners fans like to revel in the glory days of 1995, when the team played in the Kingdome and almost (yeah, almost) made it to the World Series. But baseball purists point to the opening of Safeco Field on July 16, 1999, as the real crowning achievement for the Mariners. Finally, Seattle fans had a real ballpark with real grass, real sky, and real natural light. Since then, Safeco Field has become the city's summer cathedral, a gathering place for families, friends, couples, and singles to watch baseball, nosh on fancy baseball fare, and socialize in the ballpark's many congregation areas—all of which offer unobstructed views of the field. And in case the rain clouds come rushing in, a mechanical roof can cover the ballpark in just 12 minutes to keep the faithful dry. More than 3 million people jammed into Safeco annually during the early 2000s, especially during the Mariners' record-setting 116-win season in 2001. But thanks to the traitor trifecta (Ken Griffey, Jr., Randy Johnson, and Alex "Pay-Rod" Rodriguez) and clueless ownership, a million or so have been whittled from that attendance figure. The M's were smart enough to sign Ichiro Suzuki in 2001 and fans flocked to right field to watch him work his magic until 2012 when he was taken away by those damn Yankees. The crowd is one of the most polite in baseball which makes for a fun-for-the-whole-family type of environment. If you like your games a little rowdier, head for the beer garden in center field. They have a bunch of micro brews on tap to ensure an eventful and entertaining evening, even if the Mariners' bullpen gives up the lead in the eighth inning again. Accompany your overpriced beer (last call is at the first pitch of 8th inning) with a basket of their inexplicably delicious nachos. Damn, those things are tasty.

How to Get Tickets

Individual game tickets can be purchased from the Mariners website, in person at Mariners Team Stores at Safeco Field and downtown Seattle, or the Safeco Field Box Office, open on non-game days from 10 am-6 pm and on game days from 10 am until the end of the game. You can also try your luck with a variety of scalpers that troll Occidental Avenue before the games. Bargains can be had, but beware of scams. Tickets are required for children older than two.

How to Get There

Driving

Seattle is notorious for its freeway traffic, so travel with care and patience on the way to weeknight games. From the south, exit I-5 at Spokane Street and turn right on First Avenue. From the north, exit I-5 at James Street, and turn left on First Avenue. From the east, exit I-90 where it ends at Fourth Avenue and turn right. Then turn right at Royal Brougham Way. Street parking can be found in Pioneer Square, SoDo, and the International District. The Mariners operate a parking garage across Edgar Martinez Way. In addition, dozens of parking lots within ten blocks of Safeco Field provide game day parking for anywhere from $10 to $40, depending on convenience and location.

Public Transportation

The light rail stops close to the stadium at the self-evidently titled Stadium stop. In addition, any bus that goes downtown will get you close, since Safeco is only a 10-minute walk from downtown. Ferryboats arrive hourly at Colman Dock on the waterfront, just a 10-15 minute walk from the ballpark—walk two blocks east to First Avenue and turn right.

General Information

Directions and hours for beaches, pools, and parks: www.seattle.gov

Overview

Since there are only 1-2 months out of the year when the water in Seattle becomes warm enough to swim in without the threat of hypothermia, there are not a great deal of favorable options for swimming. Even when it's been hot for a while, the water rarely heats up enough to entice most people, particularly in the open water areas. Still, on any given sunny day, many Seattleites adorn their ashen bodies with bathing suits and take to the beaches and pools. Options may be slightly deficient, but they are numerous nonetheless.

Beaches

The water in Lake Washington remains frigid year round, but that can feel pretty good on those rare stiflingly hot summer days. Of course, everyone in town has the same idea, so most of the beaches get crowded fast. **Magnuson Park (Map 27)** and **Madison Park (Map 22)** are by far the most popular, followed by **Madrona (Map 6)** and **Mount Baker (Map 40) Parks**. They are more for waders and sunbathers. **Matthews Beach Park (Map 34)**, **Seward Park (Map 40)**, and **Prichard Island Beach (Map 41)** tend to be less crowded and a bit more pleasant overall. All of the beach parks have rafts, diving boards, picnic areas, and lifeguards on duty. If you are looking for open water swimming, you can find it off the beaten path at Matthews and Seward. Matthews Beach is a welcome end to a hike along the Burke-Gilman Trail.

Golden Gardens (Map 33), which overlooks the Puget Sound, is by far the most beautiful swimming location. Unfortunately, the water is almost always unbearably cold, but the nice sandy beach is good for sunbathing, strolling, and BBQs.

The water in Green Lake is notoriously filthy (swimmer's itch, anyone?), but that doesn't appear to deter people on a hot day. There are two beaches on Green Lake, **East Beach (Map 31)** and **West Beach (Map 30)**. They both have rafts, diving boards, and lifeguards.

Pools

If you want to swim in clean water that isn't just warmed by the urine of children, Coleman and Mounger pools are another option. They both heat their water to 85 degrees. **Coleman (Map 37)** is an Olympic-sized pool which overlooks the beach and is filled with saltwater. It also boasts a giant tube slide. **Mounger (Map 11)** has a large pool with a corkscrew slide and a smaller pool for wading and children's swimming lessons. Both of these outdoor pools are only open during the summer.

If you are dying for a dip in the off-season, you can always pay a visit to one of Seattle's warm-water indoor pools which offer lap swimming and water aerobics. There are nominal admission fees.

Wading Pools & Water Features

If you just want to cool off your feet, there are numerous shallow wading pools in parks and playfields around the city. They are, of course, usually crawling with children. Wading pools are drained in the off-season.

For that invigorating, running-through-the-sprinklers sensation, check out the water features at **Judkins Park (Map 9)** and **Pratt Park (Map 9)**. **The International Fountain (Map 15)** (the giant, water-spewing ball) in Seattle Center is usually full of tourists, but if you find yourself sweltering at the Bite, Folklife, or Bumbershoot, it can be welcome refreshment. It's also great fun to play in the volcano fountain at **Cal Anderson Park (Map 3)**.

Beaches	Address	Phone	Map
Madrona Park Beach	853 Lake Washington Blvd	206-684-4075	6
Madison Park Beach	E Madison St & E Howe St	206-684-4075	22
Warren G Magnuson Park Beach	7400 Sand Point Wy NE	206-684-4075	27
Green Lake Park West Beach	7312 West Green Lake Dr N	206-684-4075	30
Green Lake Park East Beach	7201 East Green Lake Dr N	206-684-4075	31
Golden Gardens Park	8498 Seaview Pl NW	206-684-4075	33
Matthews Beach Park	49th Ave NE & NE 93rd St	206-684-4075	34
Mount Baker Park Beach	2521 Lake Park Dr S	206-684-4075	40
Seward Park Beach	5898 Lake Washington Blvd S	206-684-4075	40
Prichard Island Beach	8400 55th Ave S	206-684-4075	41
Calkins Landing	SE 28th St & 60th Ave SE	206-236-3545	42
Clarke Beach	7700 E Mercer Wy	206-236-3546	42
Groveland Beach	80th Ave SE & SE 58th St	206-236-3547	42
Luther Burbank Park	2040 84th Ave SE	206-236-3548	42
Enatai Beach Park	3519 108th Ave SE	425-452-6914	43
Newcastle Beach Park	4400 Lake Washington Blvd SE	425-452-6914	43
Chesterfield Beach Park	2501 100th Ave SE	425-452-4445	45
Chism Beach Park	1175 96th Ave SE	425-452-6914	45
Clyde Beach Park	2 92nd Ave NE	425-452-6914	45
Medina Beach Park	501 Evergreen Pt Rd	425-233-6400	45
Meydenbauer Beach Park	419 98th Ave NE	425-452-6914	45

Pools	Address	Phone	Map	Type
Medgar Evers Pool	500 23rd Ave	206-684-4766	5	Indoor
Mounger Pool	2535 32nd Ave W	206-684-4708	11	Outdoor
Queen Anne Pool	1920 1st Ave W	206-386-4282	13	Indoor
Ballard Pool	1471 NW 67th St	206-684-4094	29	Indoor
Evans Pool	7201 E Green Lake Dr N	206-684-4961	31	Indoor
Madison Pool	13401 Meridian Ave N	206-684-4979	33	Indoor
Meadowbrook Pool	10515 35th Ave NE	206-684-4989	34	Indoor
Coleman Pool	8603 Fauntleroy Wy SW	206-684-7494	37	Outdoor
Southwest Pool	2801 SW Thistle St	206-684-7440	37	Indoor
Rainier Beach Pool	8825 Rainier Ave S	206-386-1944	41	Indoor
Bellevue Aquatic Center	601 143rd Ave NE	425-452-4444	46	Indoor
Redmond Pool	17535 NE 104 St	425-233-3031	49	Indoor

Wading and Sprinklers	Address	Phone	Map	Type
Cal Anderson Park	1635 11th Ave	206-684-4075	3	Wading
Judkins Park	2150 S Norman St	206-684-7796	9	Wading, Sprinkler
Pratt Park	1800 S Mainv St	206-684-7796	9	Sprinkler
Peppi's Playground	3233 E Spruce St	206-684-7796	10	Wading
Powell Barnett Park	352 Martin Luther King Jr Wy	206-684-7796	10	Wading
E Queen Anne Playfield	160 Howe St	206-684-7796	13	Wading
International Fountain	305 Harrison St	206-684-7200	15	Sprinkler
Miller Playfield	330 19th Ave E	206-684-7796	18	Wading
Volunteer Park	1247 15th Ave E	206-684-7796	18	Wading
Ballard Commons Park	5701 22nd Ave NW	206-684-7796	23	Sprinkler
Gilman Playground	923 NW 54th St	206-684-7796	23	Wading
Wallingford Playfield	4219 Wallingford Ave N	206-684-7796	25	Wading
View Ridge Playfield	4408 NE 70th St	206-684-7796	27	Wading
Warren G Magnuson Park	7400 Sand Pointt Wy NE	206-684-7796	27	Wading
Green Lake Park	N 73rd St & W Green Lake Dr N	206-684-7796	31	Wading
Dahl Playfield	7700 25th Ave NE	206-684-7796	32	Wading
Ravenna Park	5520 Ravenna Ave NE	206-684-7796	32	Wading
Bitter Lake	13035 Linden Ave N	206-684-7796	33	Wading
Sandel Playground	9053 1st Ave NW	206-684-7796	33	Wading
Soundview Playfield	1590 NW 90 St	206-684-7796	33	Wading
Northacres Park	12800 1st Ave NE	206-684-7796	34	Wading
Hiawatha Playfield	2700 California Ave SW	206-684-7796	35	Wading
Delridge Playfield	4501 Delridge Wy SW	206-684-7796	36	Wading
EC Hughes Playground	2805 SW Holden St	206-684-7796	37	Wading
Lincoln Park	8011 Fauntleroy Wy SW	206-684-7796	37	Wading
Highland Park Playfield	1100 SW Cloverdale St	206-684-7796	38	Wading
South Park Playground	8319 8th Ave S	206-684-7796	38	Wading
Beacon Hill Playfield	1820 13th Ave S	206-684-7796	39	Wading
Georgetown Playfield	750 S Homer St	206-684-7796	39	Wading
Van Asselt Playground	2820 S Myrtle St	206-684-7796	41	Wading

General Information

Reservations and Customer Service:
1-800-USA-RAIL (872-7245)
Website: www.amtrak.com or @Amtrak
King Street Station Address: 303 S Jackson St 98104
Hours: 6 am–11 pm daily

Overview

Some travelers hate to fly. Others just hate the airlines. And don't even mention Greyhound. When the fear and anger become too profound, there's always Amtrak. Amtrak is hardly a perfect substitute—because of geographic and commercial concerns, train routes can't match the flexibility of flying, and the bureaucracy can get just as snarled and inefficient as any airline. However, there's a sweet Zen to the experience of sitting still for hours as the train chugs towards its destination, with nothing to do but read or stare out the windows as America flies by.

Located in Pioneer Square on the cusp of the International District, King Street Station services Seattle Amtrak traffic. It's a handsome rust brick building complete with a clock tower; it was the city's tallest structure when erected in 1906. Clueless mid-century renovations dulled the station's luster, and travelers dwindled over the years, leading to a certain defeated quality in the air as one waits for a train. A renovation project, completed in 2013, restored King Street Station's original stateliness while implementing a seismic upgrade that added more than 1400 tons of steel to the structure (accounting for more than 40% of the $55 million budget).

Fares

Amtrak prices tend to fluctuate wildly, so like airlines, it's best to book your trip early. Bargain hunters with sufficient lead time can find promotional discounts. Last minute types may find themselves paying near airline prices for a trip that takes ten times as long. Student and senior discounts are available, so consider lying about your age. Amtrak coach seats are very comfortable, and many passengers elect to sleep sitting up (or hunched over) on red-eye trips. But it's a rare voyager who can take that kind of punishment more than one night in a row, so contemplate a sleeping car for marathon train sessions. It's not cheap—a private car can easily double the price of a ticket, and they're hardly deluxe accommodations (imagine a closet with bunk beds). But lying prone behind a locked door is a dream shared by every coach passenger after the first 24 hours of travel.

Service

Amtrak doesn't own the tracks their trains roll on, giving freight trains the right of way. This can occasionally lead to frustrating delays. If you need to get there fast, it is advisable to find alternate means. Rail travel is as much about the journey as the destination. Speaking of which, alcohol is available in the lounge and cafe cars at airport bar prices. Luckily, they don't have that blasted three-ounce rule, so sneaking your own adult beverages on board is a piece of delicious cake. Cafe cars feature snacks and light fare and long-distance trains include a full-service dining car that serves hot meals. Which is to say, it's not a bad idea to carry a stash of food along, adjusting quantities to suit the length of the trip.

Going to Portland

Stumptown is a fun place to visit, and the Amtrak Cascades takes you there in style. The Spanish-designed Talgo trains provide comfy seats with big windows for great views of Puget Sound. They thankfully discourage the use of cell phones on board, and they even offer a free film (just make sure to bring your own headphones). And once you dig into some Ivar's clam chowder and sip on a Black Butte Porter in the dining car, you'll never take Greyhound to Portland again.

Going to Vancouver, BC

The Amtrak Cascades departs Seattle every morning for a four-hour trip to Vancouver. As Vancouver, British Columbia is located in the sovereign nation of Canada, you should make sure to bring your passport and remember that all Amtrak trains are subject to random searches by border officials. It's a beautiful journey up along the coast, but pesky freight train traffic will inevitably cause delays. For a fun Friday night getaway, Amtrak also offers a very un-Greyhound like bus from King Street Station for a good price.

Going to Los Angeles

The Coast Starlight leaves Seattle every morning headed south and makes Los Angeles in about 36 hours. Popular stops along the way include Portland, OR (although take the Cascades if you can) and Emeryville, CA (about 23 hours of travel, and only an hour's bus ride from San Francisco).

Going to Chicago

The Empire Builder leaves Seattle daily and reaches the Windy City in a mere 46 hours. That's a long ride with two guaranteed nights sleeping upright in coach and not bathing, but such asceticism can sometimes lead to spiritual fulfillment. So think of it as time to get to know yourself. Among the cities the Empire Builder services are Whitefish, MT, Fargo, ND, Minneapolis, MN, and Milwaukee, WI. Plus, there's no better way to appreciate the scenery of the heartland than through the window of a train.

General Information

Address: 503 S Royal Brougham Wy, Seattle, WA 98134
Main Phone/Customer Service: 206-624-0618
Baggage/Package Express: 206-624-1825
Website: www.greyhound.com or @GreyhoundBus
Hours: 6:30 am–11:45 pm daily

Overview

Nothing epitomizes a "long day's journey into night" like traveling on a bus full of folks bridging the many miles between Los Angeles and Vancouver. Sure, Amtrak is cleaner, faster, and more scenic, but there's nothing like the open highway and ten-minute breaks at the Flying J. Suffice it to say, it's dirt cheap, especially considering perennially eye-gouging gas prices.

Station

Seattle's Greyhound station is a diminutive facility in SoDo, just steps from the Stadium light rail station. For years, Seattle's Greyhound station. The facility is nice and clean but rather spare; round up your victuals in advance. (For years the station had been located on Stewart Street at 8th Avenue in one of the last truly sketchy parts of downtown; that site fell to the gentrigods in 2013 and is now set to make way for some massive hotel/condo towers.)

Tickets

Tickets may be purchased in person at the terminal, online at www.greyhound.com, or over the phone at 1-800-231-2222. The first option is the least convenient due to the long and disorderly lines at the Seattle station; advance reservations are not necessary.

Fares

Greyhound offers special web-only fares, advance purchase savings, and friends and family buy-one-get-get-up-to-two-cheaper discounts; check with them for details before you pay full fare. Discounted fares are also available for students, seniors, children, and military personnel.

Baggage

First bag is free and the second bag is $15. One carry-on bag up to 25 pounds is allowed on the bus, provided it fits in overhead bin or under the seat. An additional fee will be charged for baggage over the 50 pound weight limit, or parcels whose total dimensions exceed 62 inches.

Other Services

Greyhound Package Express (shipgreyhound.com or 800-739-5020) is available for fast shipping on oversized or overweight items, or as a shipping alternative to USPS, FedEx, and UPS. They offer door-to-door and online service.

General Information

Cascade Bicycle Club: www.cascade.org
or @CascadeBicycle
Bicycle Alliance of Washington: wabikes.org
or @WAbikes
City of Seattle Bicycle Program:
www.seattle.gov/transportation/bikeprogram.htm
Seattle Bike Blog: www.seattlebikeblog.com
or @seabikeblog

Commuting

Environmentally conscious Seattle is finally starting to bloom as a true bike-friendly city. A massive transportation levy approved by voters in 2006 helped build dozens of miles of dedicated bike lanes, signed routes, and bicycle parking spaces. To plan your route from the comfort of your own living room on the nearest bike trails and on-street lanes, check out the city's bike map, available online via the Seattle Department of Transportation website: www.seattle.gov/transportation

But before you hop on your brand new Schwinn and take off down Capitol Hill, just remember it's not a biking paradise just yet. Trails can end abruptly in the middle of nowhere, paths and routes can be poorly marked, and many major arteries have no bike lanes. Plus, you'll have to come back up that hill after a long day at the office. And it will probably be raining, so pack a breathable coat and waterproof pants if you want to look respectable at your next destination.

Drivers are aware and cautious for the most part, but most of the infrastructure is still set up for cars. Case in point: sometimes the light won't change until a vehicle rolls up. Look for a t-shaped symbol on the ground to plant your front wheel. Hopefully, this will change the light and get you moving again. Other cyclist-friendly features include green bike boxes, so bikes can pull up ahead of vehicles, and bike dots on the pavement with arrows to show the path of a bike route without having to look up. Plus, there's even serious talk of bike share launching in the next few years. Watch your back, Portland…

Safety and the Law

Part of biking is riding responsibly, so to that end, obey traffic laws. And by "obey traffic laws," we don't mean running red lights, riding against traffic and generally giving non-bicyclists any reason to carp. Ride defensively: avoid blind spots, pass on the left, keep three feet away from parked cars (even the word "dooring" sounds violent), and use hand signals (yes, even if they seem lame). Unlike other cities, in Seattle bicyclists are permitted use the sidewalk, but bikes must yield the right-of-way to pedestrians. Helmets are required in Seattle. Cyclists may ride two abreast on streets but not more than that. Reflectors and lights at night are mandatory. A single arrow on the road indicates a dedicated bike lane, while the double chevron "sharrow" is used to indicate a shared lane. When a portion of a bike lane is painted green, it means that cars are permitted to cross into the lane.

Bikes on Mass Transit

If you really don't want to bike back up the hill, had a few too many at happy hour with your coworkers, or are just feeling plain lazy, you're in luck. Metro and Sound Transit both have bike racks on the front of buses to make it a breeze to get around town with your two wheels in tow. Just alert the driver first, then place your bike in one of the two racks. The rails are even easier to use. Bicycles are allowed on Sounder commuter lines, Link light rail, and the Seattle Streetcar. Just look for the doors marked with a bike symbol and make sure to always have your bike securely in hand while in motion, so it doesn't smack a fellow passenger in the leg. Light rail stations even offer bike lockers for rent at a rate of $50/month.

A Few Bike Shops

Bike Works, 3709 S Ferdinand St, 206-725-9408, www.bikeworks.org

Coastal Surf Boutique, 2532 Alki Ave SW, 206-933-5605, www.coastalseattle.com

Electric Vehicles Northwest, 4810 17th Ave NW, 206-547-4621, www.electricvehiclesnw.com

Gregg's: 7007 Woodlawn Ave NE, 206-523-1822, www.greggscycles.com

Montlake Bicycle Shop: 2223 24th Ave E, 206-329-7333, www.montlakebike.com

Recycled Cycles: 1007 NE Boat St, 206-547-4491, www.recycledcycles.com

REI: 7500 166th Ave NE, 425-882-1158, www.rei.com

Taxis

For its size, Seattle has much fewer taxis than some might expect. It seems that most of the residents here simply prefer hoofing, biking, or busing it around town (if they're not cruising in their hybrids). Thus, hailing a cab can be a bit dicey, and it's dang near impossible to find one outside downtown. Your best bet is to call ahead. Normally, you won't be kept waiting much longer than 10-15 minutes. If you're cabbing it home after a night at the bars, try to leave before last call or you'll be waiting at least an hour for a ride home. For ease of travel, use designated taxi stands, which are located around town. If cabs are cruising at all, hotels are a good place to spot one. The standard drop rate is $2.60 plus $2.70 per mile. A $.50 per minute charge is assessed for stopped or slow traffic. On top of that, a 10-15% tip is expected. If you don't happen to have wads of cash on you to pay for all that, most cabs do come equipped with credit card devices, although some drivers get pretty surly if you use plastic for a short trip.

Should you be heading to Sea-Tac, the Central Link light rail (www.soundtransit.org) will take you there for not much more than a cab's standard drop rate. But should you be toting an obscene amount of baggage or are extremely averse to the idea of traffic-free public transit, taxis will chauffeur you gladly for a flat rate of $40 from downtown. Coming back to Seattle from the airport is a whole 'nother ballgame, as there is no flat rate from Sea-Tac. There appears to be no satisfying explanation for this. Just take the light rail.

Yellow Cab: 206-622-6500;
www.seattleyellowcab.com or @SEAYellowCab

Farwest Taxi: 206-622-1717;
www.farwesttaxi.net

Orange Cab: 206-522-8800;
www.orangecab.net

Car Service

After years of unreliable service from our local cab companies (i.e., showing up late or not at all and getting lost with the meter running) San Francisco-based car services arrived on the scene to make everything better. You can do it all from your smartphone, from ordering a car to paying for it and you can rate your drivers, too (cab dispatchers balk at customer service complaints). Best of all, you can track your car via GPS so you know exactly where it is and when it will arrive. Uber (www.uber.com) is the classy one, Lyft, with their giant pink car mustaches and fist-bump greetings, (www.lyft.com) is the fun one, and Side Car (www.side.cr) is the thrifty one.

General Information

Seattle is a walkable city with fairly adequate public transportation, so it's feasible for denizens to live comfortably without owning a car. In fact, the freedom that comes with removing that albatross from around the neck can be quite exhilarating. Farewell to high insurance and fuel costs, the travails of big city parking, and the constant threat of mechanical breakdown—hello to the smug satisfaction of reducing one's ecological impact on the tender earth. Still, schlepping laundry, groceries, and children around the city on the bus isn't always ideal, and sooner or later, a private conveyance becomes temporarily necessary. Thus, car sharing.

Zipcar

Website: www.zipcar.com or @Zipcar
Phone: 866-4ZIPCAR (866-494-7227)

Zipcar provides customers with access to a fleet of autos parked in dozens of convenient parking spots throughout the area. For an annual subscription fee, users can reserve a vehicle up to fifteen minutes in advance (via website or Zipcar app) and drive for $8-$8.50 an hour (depending on the plan and day of week). A membership card and a PIN unlocks the car, which is programmed to start only for the particular subscriber holding the reservation. Frequent drivers can choose various monthly packages that include pre-paid road time and reduced hourly rates. Zipcar covers gas, insurance and maintenance costs, and well over 100 cars, trucks, SUVs and hybrids are available— even a few sporty convertibles for a spontaneous joy ride.

Zipcar took over Flex Car, a Seattle-based company with a similar business plan, which was partly funded by the King County government. Flex Car suffered some growing pains which caused grief to its customers in the early days. Of course there were customer complaints about Zipcar at first as well. How many Seattleites does it take to change a light bulb? Five: One to change it and four to complain about how the old one was better. Nonetheless, most citizens of the Emerald City agree that car sharing is an excellent idea in light of current affairs.

Car2go

Website: seattle.car2go.com or @car2goSeattle
Phone: 877-488-4224

Car2go, from Germany by way of Austin is a cross between ZipCar and bike share. The super-tiny green Smart Fortwo cars are parked in any City of Seattle metered or time-limited on-street parking space in the "Home Area." Users pick up and return cars to any spot within this area—now expanded to include all of the City of Seattle. Note that certain destinations in the home area are designated as stopover only, meaning you may not leave the car there and you are on the hook for parking fees: Magnuson Park, Discovery Park, University of Washington, Broadmoor Golf Club/Washington Park Arboretum, Greenlake/Woodland Park, and Seward Park. It costs $35 to register with car2go, but unlike Zipcar, there are no monthly fees or charges. Trips are 41 cents a minute up to $14.99 per hour and $84.99 per day. Charges are billed to your credit card. Cars include parking, fuel, insurance, GPS, and roadside assistance.

General Information

City of Seattle Department of Transportation (DOT):
www.seattle.gov/transportation or @seattledot
Traffic Cameras: www.seattle.gov/trafficcams
WSDOT Seattle Area Traffic: www.wsdot.com/traffic/seattle
Washington State Department of Licensing:
www.dol.wa.gov

Orientation

The bad news is, Seattle is not an easy city to drive in without getting lost or frustrated. There are tons of one-way streets, dead ends, windy roads, and many bridges. Sometimes a street will disappear for a while, then reappear blocks later. And then there's the fact that Seattle drivers seem to be among the worst in the country. And oh by the way, traffic, especially on I-5, is absolutely horrendous, with no cure on the horizon, all due to the fact that Seattle keeps growing at a furious pace and is split between large bodies of water and I-5, making it nearly impossible to get from point A to point B via a straight line. The good news is, once you do figure out how to get around, there are many alternative routes to take to avoid traffic. Just get out there, strap on your seatbelt, and force yourself to learn the roads. Once you get a route down, try changing it up. Sometimes it can be as simple as going one street over to avoid traffic.

Generally, only streets that run more or less east-west are called "streets." Only streets that run for the most part north-south are called "avenues." However, roads, boulevards, and ways can go any direction they please. In other words, good luck. Also, Seattle is full of bold cyclists, but if you just keep reminding yourself that they mean one less car on the road, you'll find your patience for them will increase.

Bridges

Seattle is surrounded by water, so get used to dealing with lots of bridges. Drawbridges are enemy number one for the hurried driver. There is no way to know when a bridge is going to go up, unless you are in a really big hurry. Then it's guaranteed. Drawbridge hijinks include the Ballard, University District, and Montlake bridges. And that's when someone hasn't decided to make stopping traffic their final act, by leaping off of it. The other drawbridges you will have to deal with are the Ballard, University District, and Montlake Bridges. If you get stuck when a bridge is going up, all you can do is turn off your engine (idling cars are bad for the environment) and wait it out. Another notable bridge that serves I-90 and connects Seattle to Mercer Island is the Lacey V. Murrow Memorial Bridge—the second longest floating bridge in the world. If you're keen to experience the longest floating bridge in the world, you're in luck—the Evergreen Point Floating Bridge (also known as Bridge 520) is just a few miles north. Both of these get you to I-405, and one is usually busier than the other, so be sure to check traffic status on the WSDOT (Washington State Department of Transit) website before you make your choice. Either way, you will be treated to a beautiful view on your way across. Also important to water-body navigation are the West Seattle Bridge and the George Washington Memorial Bridge (also known as the Aurora Bridge).

Dealing with Highway 99

Highway 99, the original superhighway of Seattle, runs parallel to I-5. It can be a useful route when I-5 is congested (which is almost always). However, it can be difficult to navigate. You may find yourself heading north on the stretch from Greenlake Avenue N to Denny and you need to be going south or vice versa. Well, that's too bad. Sometimes you just have to stick it out until you find an exit or risk turning off into the black hole that is Queen Anne Hill. Also, the Alaskan Way Viaduct Replacement Program (the viaduct, part of Highway 99, has been torn down and is being replaced by an underground car tunnel) is kind of underway and may or may not be finished before men's professional basketball returns to the Emerald City. Until then, check WSDOT for traffic closures and updates on Seattle's version of the Big Dig.

Major Expressways

I-5, Seattle's main freeway, running north/south, is almost always congested. From I-5 you can access either I-90 or SR520 running east/west parallel to each other. One is often busier than the other, so pay attention to traffic reports. Running parallel to I-5 is Highway 99, which will go no farther than five miles west of it, and I-405 running on the other side of Lake Washington. I-5 has expressways in the center of the freeway that anyone can access, but be careful because exits are limited and you may end up going farther than you would have liked. The city provides real-time traffic and traffic cameras via the web.

DMVs

Visits to the Seattle DMV are relatively painless, especially if you go on a weekday morning. If you must go on a Saturday, be prepared to wait. Save time and stress by going online (www.dol.wa.gov) for useful pre-visit utilities (renewals can often be done online as well). There are two official state DMV offices in the Seattle area. The full-service location is in West Seattle (8830 25th Ave SW, Seattle, WA 98106; 206-764-4144) and is open on Saturdays. A limited service office (without testing services) is located downtown (205 Spring St, Seattle, WA 98104; 206-464-6845). Private subagents handle vehicle licensing registration renewals; the WSDOT website has a full list of vendors.

General Information

City of Seattle Parking Information:
www.seattle.gov/transportation/parking

Parking Meters

Seattle has computerized meters throughout the city that accept credit cards. Pick the amount of time you want, slide your credit card, and a sticker will be printed for you to place on the inside of the window closest to the sidewalk. Seattle has also implemented performance-based parking, which raises or lowers rates based on availability and time of day in an effort to reduce congestion and lower emissions. As part of the city's Nightlife Initiative, stickers are available at night for the following morning in the event you need to find alternative arrangements to get home (or end up in a different home, we suppose). The ePark program offers real-time parking information at participating garages; look for the mobile app.

Residential Parking Zone Program

Many high-traffic Seattle neighborhoods, especially near commercial strips or hospitals and universities, participate in a permit program meant to discourage long-term parking by non-residents. Look for the green and white signs which limit you to two-hour parking except by permit. Generally, permits cost $65 and are good for two years. Permits can only be issued to residents who live on a block with signs installed or within the boundaries of the RPZ. In order to apply, you must have proof of residency and current Washington State vehicle registration. One permit is issued per vehicle per household (up to four vehicles) and one guest permit. Temporary permits may be issued for up to sixty days for construction, out of state, new, and student vehicles. You may obtain a new permit by mail or in person. Renewals are handled online.

Curbs

It is important to understand Seattle's curb color system. After searching for a parking spot on Capitol Hill for two hours, you finally find the perfect one right in front of your apartment. Too good to be true, right?

Well, it probably is. If the curb is painted white, it is either a three-minute loading zone or police and fire department parking. If the curb is yellow, it is a thirty-minute loading zone. Red means no parking anytime and they mean it. You will get towed so fast it'll make your head spin. Alternating yellow and red makes it a bus zone, so don't even think about parking there.

Parking Tickets and Impound

Parking tickets issued by the Seattle Police Department are handled by the Seattle Municipal Court. You can pay them online (convenience fee applies) or at neighborhood service centers (handy drop boxes available). If you fail to pay your ticket within 15 days, the fine will automatically double. Unpaid parking tickets will result in a hold on your vehicle registration tabs. To contest a parking ticket, you can request a hearing before a Municipal Court Magistrate to gently explain why they should shove their fines where the sun doesn't shine.

If your car gets towed, call the SPD Automobile Records Unit at 206-684-5444 or visit seattleimpound.com. Towed cars are taken to one of three impound lots in Seattle. In order to get your vehicle free, you will be required to pay the fine to the impound lot immediately, and the registered owner must be present with appropriate documentation. Impounded vehicles are subject to an impound fee and a charge for every 12 hours of storage.

Extra Parking Tips

Seattleites enjoy parking facing the opposite direction of a street, and even though the police tolerate this quirk, know that it's not strictly legal. Also illegal is parking a car in the same spot for more than 72 hours. Failure to move your car around the block for no good reason will result in a ticket or towing. In addition, do not let your car bumper hang even a millimeter over the driveway (including your own) into the sidewalk. If a traffic cop is bored, they will slap you with a not insignificant fine with no apologies.

General Information

Mailing Address: Metro Transit Division,
201 S Jackson St, Seattle, WA 98104

Website: metro.kingcounty.gov or @kcmetrobus

Customer Service (includes Lost and Found):
206-553-3000

Overview

Many city dwellers who lack wheels for ideological or financial reasons find getting around Seattle on Metro buses a necessity. Service is extensive, reaching throughout the city, but the quality and comfort of the ride varies from one line to the next. Buses between Capitol Hill and the University District run reliably every ten minutes or so for most of the day. You can also count on regular bus service connecting downtown with the northern hoods like Wedgwood and Ravenna. The express buses that rocket passengers to outlying suburbs are always on time. However, like any modern urban transit system, the city faces unique geographical challenges (in this case hills, water, and bridges) that can lead to trouble. Some Metro routes are chronically late, crowded with standing passengers, or peppered with anti-social types, and woe be to the rider who depends on such a bus to get to work every day. Check Metro's website for alternate (if inconvenient) itineraries, and take advantage of Metro's various apps and trip planners.

Riders pay upon boarding the bus. On RapidRide lines with stations that have ORCA readers (and on Sound Transit Light Rail and Sounder), riders may enter through any door (RapidRide is Seattle's bus rapid transit: pay before boarding, dedicated lanes, and the like). The standard adult fare is $2.50 off peak, but during peak hours (weekdays 6 to 9 am and 3 to 6 pm) it's $2.75 for one zone and $3.25 for two zones. It's exact change only and drivers and riders alike are impatient to people fiddling in their pockets, so make sure you have your money and pass ready when you step on board. The price rises depending on how far out of the city limits the ride takes you. Discounts for students, seniors, and the disabled cut the cost, and buses are fully equipped to handle those with mobility challenges. Transfers allow re-boarding for up to two hours on Metro lines.

To make it easier for regular riders, the ORCA (One Regional Card for All) is a single card for Seattle's various transit options. You can buy and add value to your ORCA at many locations downtown including the Metro office and kiosks located in the bus tunnel. You can also do it online or create an "e-purse," which will automatically refund your ORCA from your credit card or bank whenever the balance dips below the lowest possible fare. Cards cost $5. See the ORCA website (www.orcacard.com) for more details about how to receive and add value to a card of your very own.

Bicyclists can stash their machines on racks attached to the front of the bus; review the procedure online before holding up everyone though. Bike lockers are available at many park & ride locations around the area; check website for details. In addition, bicycles (and bicyclists) are allowed to ride for free on out-of-service buses going over the SR-520 Evergreen Point Floating Bridge; a nice little perk.

Anyone who isn't convinced that Seattle is a colorful town of eccentrics and madmen needs to ride the bus. This could be true about many American cities, but Seattle's lost souls take to public transportation in a major way. A Seattle transplant will have a "Bus Nut" story within a week of moving here. This is not to dissuade the timid rider, but one should always expect the unexpected when facing so much humanity within an enclosed space. Oh, and a charming custom in Seattle is the bus rider's habit of thanking the driver as he/she disembarks. Most Metro drivers deserve this simple courtesy. It must be a stressful, monotonous task battling traffic to haul sullen strangers to their jobs every day. So don't forget to give your driver a verbal tip for a job well done.

Seattle Streetcar

Streetcars—seeming relics of the alleged golden age of public transportation and sometime allegorical beacon of desire—have made a comeback in Seattle. Seattle Streetcar (www.seattlestreetcar.org or @TheStreetcar) is owned by the city but is operated under contract by Metro. The first route, the South Lake Union Line, opened in 2007 and comprises eleven stops scattered along a 2.6-mile loop around the Denny Triangle and South Lake Union neighborhoods. Its pretty purple streetcars cruise by every fifteen minutes. Apocryphally, the streetcar was originally named the South Lake Union Trolley until officials realized the unfortunate acronym. Indeed, the S.L.U.T. T-shirts were cool, but that was never really the name; everyone knows "trolleys" are for children and rubber-tired art tours. The First Hill Streetcar, opened in 2015, travels between Pioneer Square and the intersection of Broadway and Denny Way via Jackson, 14th Ave S, Yesler, and Broadway. A Broadway Extension to Roy Street is scheduled to open in 2017, and a Center City Connector to link the South Lake Union and First Hill lines downtown is being hashed out. Full fares are $2.25 and ORCA and bus transfers (from ORCA) are accepted. Purchase tickets from machines located at the stations. Bicyclists can store their wheels in the open center section of the streetcars.

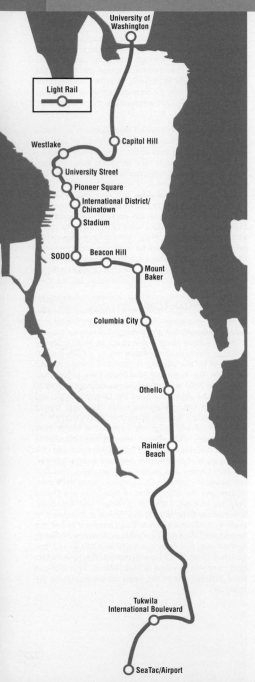

University of Washington

Light Rail

Westlake

Capitol Hill

University Street

Pioneer Square

International District/ Chinatown

Stadium

SODO

Beacon Hill

Mount Baker

Columbia City

Othello

Rainier Beach

Tukwila International Boulevard

SeaTac/Airport

General Information

Sound Transit Address: 401 S Jackson St, Seattle, WA 98104

Phone: 888-889-6368

Website: www.soundtransit.org or @SoundTransit

Email: main@soundtransit.org

Sound Transit Overview

Sound Transit was created by the Washington State Legislature to build a mass transit system that connects King, Pierce, and Snohomish Counties. The organization has the Central Puget Sound region covered with a broad range of bus, light rail, and commuter rail services.

In addition to operating Link light rail, Sound Transit operates express buses and commuter rail, called Sounder, around the region, connecting major employment centers such as Everett, Bellevue, and Renton. Though many of the buses operate on weekends, Sounder is strictly a weekday affair. If you're lucky enough to live near one of the stations in Everett or Edmonds, commuting into Seattle via the cushy, wifi-equipped Sounder as it winds its way along Puget Sound's breathtaking shoreline, is one of the nicest ways to start your day. Sounder and Express Bus stations outside of Seattle city limits often do have free parking, though the lots are often full by 8 am.

Light Rail History

Seattle's Link Light Rail—which opened in 2009—was a long time in the making.

Underground transit had been proposed in Seattle as far back as 1912, but wasn't until 1968 that the idea really took off. These were the heady, messy days of "urban renewal" in America's cities, and Seattle had been on the list for a federally-financed rapid transit system like the one being built in Washington DC. Senator Warren G. Magnuson secured a $900M earmark (an eye-popping $6 billion in 2013 dollars) to pay for the majority of the system, which would have consisted of two lines crossing the city in an X shape. Seattle voters, however, earning their reputation for fickleness, said "thanks, but no thanks" and didn't give the ballot measure the 60% supermajority it needed to pass. The money instead went to finance Atlanta's MARTA.

In the 1990s, talk of rail transit heated up again, with basically the same X-shaped system that had been outlined in 1968. Not coincidentally, this is around the time of Cameron Crowe's 1992 film *Singles*, in which the main character tries unsuccessfully to convince the city of the value of building a "super train." (He does, however, succeed in finding love, so there's that.) After failing on the first three votes, the Central Puget Sound Regional Transportation Authority (now known as "Sound Transit") was approved in November of 1996, just two days before the release of the documentary *Hype!* chronicling the rise and fall of Seattle's grunge scene.

The plan was for a 21-mile line connecting Sea-Tac airport and Northgate Mall, roughly along the I-5 corridor. Sound Transit ran into trouble, though, when the costs spiraled and years of delays mounted. Frustrated, Seattle voters approved a monorail along the western half of the city. After buying up land and spending hundreds of millions of taxpayer dollars, the monorail plan, too, went over budget and was eventually killed by another popular vote.

Sound Transit survived, however, thanks to support from the local political establishment. A shortened, 14-mile line between Downtown Seattle and Tukwila, known as Central Link, finally opened in 2009. A short extension to Sea-Tac Airport followed in 2010, along with the University Link (2016). Extensions are being built to Capitol Hill and UW (opening in 2016), Northgate (2021), and finally Bellevue, Redmond, and Lynwood (2023).

Light Rail Operating Hours

Central Link operates from 5 pm to 1 am Monday through Saturday, and 6 am to midnight on Sunday. On average, it carries more than 30,000 passengers each weekday. Trains operate every 7.5 minutes during rush hour and every 10-15 minutes in the evenings.

Light Rail Fares

Fares on the system are distance-based, ranging from $2.25 to $3 for adults depending on how far you're traveling. You pay your fare using the ORCA card system (though built by Sound Transit, Link is operated by Metro). You can buy tickets from a machine at any station.

When it comes time to board, however, Seattle's true nature shines. Since we're such nice, honest folk, Link stations don't have the turnstiles or gates you might find in a crowded East Coast subway station. No sir. Like the Europeans, whose traditions of soccer and espresso we so adore, Link uses "proof-of-payment," which means you tap your card on a mechanical reader when you get on, and again when you get off. It's all very civilized. Of course, that doesn't mean you can ride for free. As in Europe, fare enforcement officers board the trains from time to time to ensure that riders have paid. Civilized as it might be, proof-of-payment is a bit confusing in action, especially in the downtown bus tunnel. If you're riding Link, you should tap your ORCA on one of the yellow card readers when you get on and when you get off (because the fares are based on distance traveled). If you're riding a bus, however, you tap your card once you get on the bus.

The Sounder

Everett Station

Edmonds Station

FARE ZONE

King St Station

FARE ZONE

Tukwila Station

Kent Station

Auburn Station

FARE ZONE

Tacoma Dome Station

Puyallup Station

Summer Station

Light Rail Stations & Destinations

Downtown, the stations can be a bit hard to find. Look for the blue Sound Transit "T" to enter the bus tunnel, which is shared by buses and Link (at least for the next few years). One entrance to Westlake Station, for example, is inside the downtown Nordstrom, while an entrance at University Street is tucked into Benaroya Hall.

The SeaTac/Airport station is accessible via a five-minute walk from the terminal. Follow the signs for Link, which will take you through the parking garage and to the Link station on the other side.

While many tourists use Link from the Airport to downtown, locals know there are many interesting destinations along the route, including Pioneer Square, the sports stadia, the International District, Beacon Hill and the Rainier Valley. Some of the best Vietnamese food and some of the freshest, cheapest produce in the city can be found along the route. And there are great views of the city to be had from the elevated portions.

Light Rail Parking

Unlike the 1960s-era systems in DC, Atlanta, and San Francisco, Link stations aren't surrounded by oceans of parking. Only Tukwila station, outside of the Seattle limits, has free parking (and it's almost always full). Paid parking is available near several Rainier Valley stations including Mt. Baker. If you're not within walking distance of a station, your best bet is to get there via bus, bicycle, or a car share service like Car2Go.

Bicycles

Taking the bike to the train is encouraged. There are bike lockers at several of the stations and bike areas inside the train cars. Keep in mind you might find yourself in a passive-aggressive Seattle-style standoff with a tourist using the bike storage area for his or her giant wheeled luggage. Proceed with caution.

ST Express

The Sound Transit Regional Bus line connects Seattle, Bellevue, Everett, and Tacoma with the largest urban centers in the region. Transit centers, park-and-ride lots, and HOV access projects throughout the region have improved transit service for all bus riders and provide some help to the daily commute. The line connects more than 60,000 people each weekday throughout the three counties.

Fares: Adults ages 19-64 pay $2.50 for one zone and $3.50 across multiple zones. Youths ages 6-18 pay $1.25 and $2.50. Senior citizens and the disabled pay $0.75 and $1.50. Children under 6 ride free with a paying passenger.

The Sounder

Sounder commuter trains run 75 miles every weekday (Monday to Friday only) between Everett and Tacoma. The Sounder North train connects Everett with Seattle (with stops in Edmonds and Mukilteo). The Sounder South train runs from Tacoma to Puyallup, Sumner, Auburn, Kent, Tukwila, and downtown Seattle. The Sounder also runs special trains for Seahawks home games and for select Mariners and Sounders FC games. Check with Sound Transit for more details.

Fares: Ranges from $2.75 to $5.25, depending on how far you travel.

Tacoma Link Light Rail

The Tacoma Link light rail line began operating in August 2003 and quickly became a major factor in the renaissance of downtown Tacoma. The 1.6-mile route connects downtown Tacoma with the Tacoma Dome Station, where connections can be made to ST Express regional bus and Sounder commuter rail.

Fares: At the outset, the cost of collecting fares outweighed the income derived from fares, meaning that the Tacoma Link light rail was free. Although it took ten years to get to the point where it literally paid to collect fares, expect a $1.50 fare to be implemented on the line in late 2016.

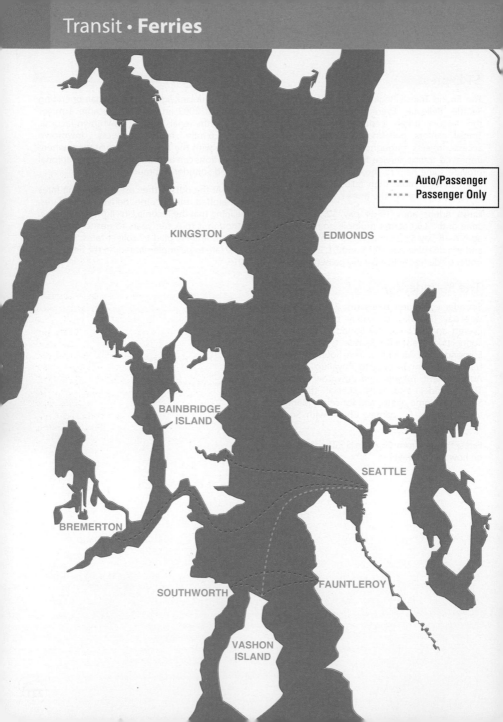

KINGSTON

EDMONDS

BAINBRIDGE
ISLAND

SEATTLE

BREMERTON

SOUTHWORTH

FAUNTLEROY

VASHON
ISLAND

---- Auto/Passenger
---- Passenger Only

General Information

Website: www.wsdot.wa.gov/ferries or @wsferries

Overview

The largest ferry system in the country, Washington State Ferries can actually make commuting pleasurable—once you're on the boat. The ferry system encompasses a total of ten routes and twenty terminals, so be sure you know where you want to go. The boats running to Bainbridge, Bremerton, and a passenger-only boat to Vashon Island are located at Colman Dock at Alaskan Way and Marian Street. The most popular route, from Seattle to Bainbridge, sails 15 times a day between roughly 5/6 am to 12 midnight/1 am. Check the website for exact schedules, and note that there is a slight variation at the end of the day on weekends and holidays. The ferries run in all weather, but the Port Townsend and Vashon runs are occasionally limited by extreme low tides. The website will have current information as well as real-time webcams on the docks. Bikes and motorcycles load through the auto gates and are given preference over cars at loading time. Colman Dock has recently added several food and coffee vendors as well as a small wine bar. (Commuter Comforts is the best of the lot.) There is food, beer, and wine available on the boats (hooray!) until about 8 pm, but don't get too excited since the food is abysmal and everything is overpriced. Once you're actually on the boat, settle in and enjoy the ride. There's an open deck upstairs for viewing. The scenery on a good day is awe-inspiring—the Cascades to the east, Mt. Rainier to the south, the Olympic mountain range to the west, and Puget Sound is, obviously, everywhere. It's a good guess that there are frequent proposals (of one kind or another) on the ferries.

Parking

Parking? Oh please. Your choices are to drive your car on (expensive and time-consuming—during peak hours, you can sometimes wait through several boat departures), or find a parking spot near the terminal. There are a number of them sprinkled on Western Avenue between Yesler Way and Spring Street. There are also buses that stop in front of Coleman Dock. Check Metro's website (metro.kingcounty.gov) for details.

Fares

Fares can vary depending on where and when you'll be going, so make sure to check the website before heading out. Of course, bringing a car always drives up the price and in the peak season (May 1 to the second Saturday in October) you'll have to pay more. Thankfully, the ferry system accepts all major credit cards, so you won't have to abandon your car and make a run for an ATM. Round trip fare for passengers from Seattle to Bainbridge/Bremerton and from Edmonds to Kingston is $8 for adults and $4 for children, seniors, and disabled. Car and driver is $17.30 (peak). Fauntleroy to Vashon is $5.20 for adults and $2.60 for children, seniors, and disabled. Car and driver is $22.05. When possible, leave the car at home and pay an extra buck to bring your bicycle aboard. Your wallet and body will thank you. Finally, for those who ride the boats often, commuter books are available and will save you a bunch of dough.

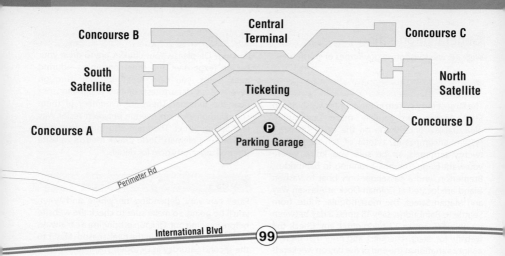

Concourse B

Central Terminal

Concourse C

South Satellite

Ticketing

North Satellite

Concourse A

Parking Garage

Concourse D

Perimeter Rd

International Blvd   99

General Information

Address: 17801 International Blvd, Seattle, WA 98158
Airport Code: SEA
Phone: 206-787-5388 or 800-544-1965
Websites: www.portseattle.org/Sea-Tac
or @SeaTacAirport
Ground Transportation: 206-787-5906
Airport Police: 206-787-3490
Lost & Found: 206-787-5312
Customer Service: 800-508-1705

Overview

Prior to 1944, Boeing Field was Seattle's main passenger airport. When the military took it over for use in World War II, we needed a new commercial airport. Thus, Sea-Tac International Airport was born.

Though one of the country's busiest airports, serving nearly 40 million passengers each year, Sea-Tac isn't a terribly harrowing travel experience. Indeed, Sea-Tac is well run and organized, consisting of a main terminal with four concourses and two satellite terminals connected to the main terminal via an underground tram. Trains run every 5-10 minutes, so it never takes long to get from one terminal to another.

As with most airports these days, it is advisable to either check in online or at a self check-in station. However, our TSA agents seem to have a handle on security checks, as the line moves fairly quickly most of the time. Of course, in terms of airport travel, it is always advisable not to tempt fate.

If you find yourself with some time, you can grab a bite to eat in the food court or take your chances with the inevitable Starbucks or gift shops in your terminal. For a decent sit-down meal, Anthony's in the Central Terminal is your best bet for quality. Beecher's Handmade Cheese, in Concourse C, serves up great Mac and Cheese and Caffe Vita coffee and espresso. For a cocktail, glass wine, or pint of microbrew, there are several choices, none of which particularly stand out from the other.

How to Get There—Driving

From the north or south, take I-5 to Exit 154 B and drive west on State Route 518 to the Sea-Tac Airport Exit. Heading east, take I-405, which turns into State Route 518, to the Sea-Tac Airport Exit. Signs are clearly marked from that point on.

Parking

With cost-effective alternatives available, choosing to drive to Sea-Tac is akin to burning money, but there are many options for those willing to lighten their wallet. The top four floors of the garage offer hourly parking ($4 for the first and up to $35 a day). Long-term parking is also available for $28 a day with a weekly rate of $130. Pay with credit or debit cards at exit lanes or bring your ticket with you to pay in advance in pay stations. If you've managed to bribe a friend into picking you up, he or she can wait for you in the Cell Phone Waiting Lot. To get there, take the 170th/Air Cargo exit from the Airport Expressway. Turn right and take an immediate left into the clearly marked lot. To get to Baggage Claim from the lot, take a right out of the lot and then an immediate left at the To Terminal sign. Follow the signs to Arrivals.

How to Get There—Mass Transit

Take the Light Rail straight to the airport from downtown in about 35 minutes; it's cheap, clean, and easy. The station is connected to the fourth floor of the parking garage, about a five-minute walk to the terminals. The 560 Sound Transit Express Bus serves Burien and West Seattle the 574 travels to Lakewood. Metro also has route 180 to service Auburn, Kent, and Burien.

How to Get There—Shuttle

For shared rides, Shuttle Express (shuttleexpress.com or 425-981-7000) serves areas within a 30-mile radius. Pick-up and drop-off is on the third floor of the Airport Garage. The check-in for scheduled Airporter services is on the Baggage Claim level. Airporter Shuttle (www.airporter.com or 866-235-5247) serves Western Washington. Capital Aeroporter (www.capair.com or 800-962-3579) serves the Greater South Puget Sound Area including Seattle, Olympia, and Tacoma.

Car Rentals

Sea-Tac has a single car rental location (3150 S 160th St, SeaTac) from which all car rental companies do business. A 24-hour, free shuttle takes customers to the location. Exit the baggage claim area at either the north or south end for the designated pick-up area.

Alamo: 800-462-5266 or www.alamo.com

Avis: 800-331-1212 or www.avis.com

Budget: 800-527-7000 or www.budget.com

Dollar Car Rental: 206-433-5825 or www.dollar.com

Enterprise: 206-246-1953 or www.enterprise.com

EZ Rent-A-Car: 206-444-4974 or www.e-zrentacar.com

Firefly Car Rental: 888-296-9135 or www.fireflycarrental.com

Fox Rent A Car: 800-225-4369 or www.foxrentacar.com

Hertz: 800-654-3131 or www.hertz.com

National: 800-328-4567 or www.nationalcar.com

Payless: 800-PAYLESS or www.paylesscar.com

Sixt Rent A Car: 888-749-8227 or www.sixt.com

Thrifty: 877-283-0898 or www.thrifty.com

Airline/Terminal

Air Canada & Air Canada Jazz/Concourse A

Alaska Airlines/Concourse C, Concourse D, North Satellite

American Airlines/Concourse D

AMC (Air Mobility Command)/South Satellite

All Nippon Airways/South Satellite

Asiana Airlines/South Satellite

British Airways/South Satellite

Condor/South Satellite

Delta & Delta Connection/South Satellite

Emirates/South Satellite

EVA Air/South Satellite

Frontier Airlines/Concourse B

Hainan Airlines/South Satellite

Hawaiian Airlines/South Satellite

Icelandair/South Satellite

JetBlue Airways/Concourse D

Korean Air/South Satellite

Lufthansa Airlines/South Satellite

Southwest Airlines/Concourse B

Sun Country Airlines/Concourse A

United & United Express/Concourse A

US Airways/Concourse A

Virgin America/Concourse B

January

Martin Luther King Jr. Day: March and rally to commemorate MLK, Jr. and advance what he fought for; www.mlkseattle.org.
Children's Film Festival Seattle: Films for kids and their families from all over the world; childrensfilmfestivalseattle.nwfilmforum.org.

February

Mardis Gras: Head to Pioneer Square, if that's your scene.
Seattle Asian American Film Festival: Specialty showcase for Asian-American filmmakers nationwide; seattleaaff.org.
Northwest Flower & Garden Show: Annual flora fest bringing together green thumbs of all abilities since 1989; www.gardenshow.com.

March

Seattle Moisture Festival: A twisted cabaret with the scope of vaudeville; www.moisturefestival.com.
The Seattle Center Irish Festival: Celebrating true Irish heritage; irishclub.org.

April

Seattle Cherry Blossom & Japanese Cultural Festival: Martial arts, kites, and tea at Seattle Center; www.cherryblossomfest.org.
Seattle Restaurant Week: Spring edition of twice yearly event featuring reduced-price three-course prix fixe menus at restaurants across the city; www.seattlerestaurantweek.com.
Seattle Erotic Art Festival: Promotes freedom of sexuality, speech, and creativity; www.seattleerotic.org.
Emerald City Comicon: Geek out at the largest gathering of comic book and pop culture fans in the Pacific NW; www.emeraldcitycomicon.com.

May

Ballard Jazz Festival: Multi-day, multi-venue festival featuring internationally renowned jazz musicians and a Swedish pancake jazz brunch; ballardjazzfestival.com.
U District Street Fair: First of the big summer festivals, crowded with art and dripping with funnel cake grease; udistrictstreetfair.org.
Northwest Folklife Festival: Keeping traditional art and music alive; www.nwfolklife.org.
Seattle International Film Festival: Massive month-long film fest; www.siff.net.
Seattle Beer Week: A celebration of all things beer at tastings and events across the city; www.seattlebeerweek.com.

June

Fremont Solstice Parade: The wildest art-solstice party in the city, with lots of naked people, for better or worse; www.fremontfair.com.
Seattle Pride: Series of events supporting LGBT community around anniversary of Stonewall riots; www.seattlepride.org.
Juneteenth: A celebration of freedom from slavery in Pratt Park; scacc2108.org.
Ballard Locks Summer Concerts and Events: Picnic every Saturday and Sunday at this free event, June through Labor Day. Just don't eat the migrating salmon.

July

Seafair: A month-long celebration of the water, with loud fighter jets, noisy hydroplanes, and a milk carton derby; www.seafair.com.
Seafair Summer Fourth: Fireworks over Lake Union; www.seafair.com.
Wooden Boat Festival: Take a boat ride on Lake Union; www.cwb.org.
Bite of Seattle: A showcase for local culinary excellence; www.biteofseattle.com.
Capitol Hill Block Party: Who's who of Cap Hill rock culture—get on the guest list; www.capitolhillblockparty.com.
Ballard Seafood Fest: Weekend-long celebration of music, craftiness, seafood, and of course Ballard; www.seafoodfest.org.
International District Dragon Fest: Here there be food and dragons at this Pan-Asian American party around the ID; www.cidbia.org.
Seattle International Beerfest: Three-day keg party at Seattle Center; www.seattlebeerfest.com.

August

Sunset Supper: Sip, taste, and sample at Pike Place Market for a good cause; www.pikeplacemarketfoundation.org.
Hempfest: The protestival that evolved into a weekend of networking opportunities; www.hempfest.org.
Arab Festival: Celebrating Arab culture with food, panels, music, dances, and demos; arabcenterwa.org.
Central Area Festival & Parade: Fostering community pride and cultural diversity in the Central Area; www.cacf.com.

September

Bumbershoot: The granddaddy of all Seattle festivals, with big stars and long lines; www.bumbershoot.org.
Washington State Fair: Head south and Do the Puyallup—livestock, rides, rodeos; www.thefair.com.
Fremont Oktoberfest: Squeeze two weeks of beer into one bleary-eyed weekend; www.fremontoktoberfest.com.

October

St. Demetrios Greek Festival: Going strong since 1960. Eat, drink, and summon your inner Zorba in Montlake; www.seattlegreekfestival.com.
Earshot Jazz Festival: Bringing top jazzers to the Emerald City since 1989; www.earshot.org.
Seattle Restaurant Week: Fall edition of twice yearly event featuring reduced-price three-course prix fixe menus at restaurants across the city; www.seattlerestaurantweek.com.
Turkfest: Indulge your senses with a strong dose of Turksih culture; www.turkfest.org.

November

Seattle Marathon: Begins and ends at Seattle Center, via I-90, Seward Park, Lake Washington Blvd, and South Lake Union; www.seattlemarathon.org.

December

Christmas Ship Festival: Big boats in bright lights, and vice-versa.
Pacific Northwest Ballet's Nutcracker: Tchaikovsky's score with fun and inventive sets and costumes—the Maurice Sendak collaboration is a classic; www.pnb.org
ACT A Christmas Carol: Bah humbug to you if you don't go see this classic Seattle holiday show at least once; www.acttheatre.org

General Information

Off-Leash Areas: www.seattle.gov/parks/offleash.asp

Overview

Seattleites aren't just tree-huggers; they're dog lovers, too. With the gorgeous backdrop that is the Emerald City, Seattle's dog parks are a far cry from most of the drab, chain-link gravel pits you'll find in other large cities. The 14 dog areas in Seattle are usually well maintained, spacious, and just as much fun for man as it is for his best friend. Of course, there are a few obvious rules to follow. Keep your dog on a leash outside of the off-leash area (duh), make sure he or she has had all of the proper shots and licensing, and please, for heaven's sake, scoop the dang poop. The Citizens for Off-Leash Areas (COLA) is a community of dog owners committed to everything dog-park, so check out their site (www.coladog.org or @ seattlecola) for all you need to know. If you're not a good little doggie owner, beware—you could be slapped with a stiff fine. Now, that's ruff! (Ahem.)

Off-Leash Areas

Genesee Park (Map 40)
4316 S Genesee St
Genesee Park and Playfield is a broad, rough meadow stretching for about five blocks north from Genesee Street to Stan Sayres Memorial Park on Lake Washington Boulevard. There is a separate fully-fenced off-leash area, complete with a doggie drinking fountain (aw!). It's gravelly and not all that interesting, but is flat and open—perfect for playing fetch.

Golden Gardens (Map 33)
8498 Seaview Pl NW
This waterfront park is huge, running alongside Puget Sound. There are hiking trails for a nice little walk, restored wetlands, sandy beaches, fishing, boating, picnic tables—you name it, Golden's got it. The icing on the cake is the stunning view of the Olympics along the rugged coastline. Uphill to the east is a moderately-sized off-leash area for your doggie. Just be sure to bring your galoshes if there's a hint of rain, as it can get extremely mucky.

I-5 Colonnade (Map 20)
Beneath I-5, south of E Howe St b/w Lakeview Blvd & Franklin Ave E
This is a weird, creepy park underneath roaring I-5 on Capitol Hill. It's a huge, maze-like gravel pit with lots of chain-link fence, no open areas, and concrete blocks everywhere, their function mysterious. Not the best for fancy-free frolicking with your dog, but if you're just taking Fido out to do his business, it works. There is however a cool mountain bike course under construction and an art installation by John Roloff.

Magnuson Park (Map 27)
7400 Sand Point Wy NE
The absolute creme de la creme of dog parks in Seattle. The park itself is 40 acres, with a whopping nine of them dedicated to an off-leash pooch area. It's a veritable Disneyland for dogs, with several different scenic areas (dirt hills, grassy brush, mud pit), an exclusive shy/older dog pen, and a flat gravel area for fetch. The highlight is a long winding trail leading down to the shores of Lake Washington—Magnuson is the only dog park within city limits with water access. It's also a great park for socializing with other owners.

Northacres Park (Map 34)
12718 1st Ave NE
Tucked away next to some athletic fields, this park is small but lots of fun. It's an intimate maze-like affair with lots of short trails through dense, well-kept foliage. Small open areas spring up along the way with benches for a quick rest while your dog bounds through the brush.

Blue Dog Pond (Map 9)
Martin Luther King Jr Wy S & S Massachusetts

Dr. Jose Rizal Park (Map 8)
1008 12th Ave S

Denny Park (Map 2)
100 Dexter Ave N

Kinnear Park (Map 14)
899 W Olympic Pl

Magnolia Manor Park (Map 11)
3500 28th Ave W

Plymouth Pillars Park (Map 3)
Boren Ave b/w Pike St & Pine St

Regrade Park (Map 1)
2251 3rd Ave

Westcrest Park (Map 38)
8806 8th Ave SW

Woodland Park (Map 31)
W Greenlake Wy N

Best Rainy Day Activities

Here are a several places to help you and your kids battle cabin fever and keep your sanity during those long, rainy months of winter.

International District: Yes, honey, those ducks are for eating.

Waterfront/Piers: Fish n' chips! Seagulls! An arcade! Pirates!

Pacific Science Center: Giant insects.

Seattle Central Library: Holy cow, this place is huge!!!

Ballard Library: The roof is alive and growing!

Experience Music Project: Mommy, what's that man doing to his guitar?

Burke Museum: Dinosaurs!

Museum of History and Industry (MOHAI): Learn about Seattle from its humble beginnings to its dotcom boasting present-day. Speculate about its future in the excellent Compass Cafe.

Seattle Center: A big, urban park with museums, food courts, and a huge fountain.

PlayDate SEA: This 8,500 square foot indoor playground is custom made for free-range children and the coffee-addicted parents who love them.

Seattle Children's Museum: Kid-centered museum.

Seattle Aquarium: Pretty fish.

Woodlawn Park Zoo: Yes, it's mostly outside, but those animals sure are cool.

The Best of the Best

Rock on, Dude

The Vera Project is a long-time all-ages music venue and teen-centered non-profit at the Seattle Center. Kids rock out to Seattle bands big and small while parents go to the opera. They also have volunteer projects for kids and host a variety of classes including breakdancing and punk rock.

Feed the Seagulls

Take your kids to Ivar's on the pier, munch on fish and chips while watching the ferries come and go, then fend off the seagulls with those crusty, hard leftover bits at the bottom.

Ice Cream Cruise

Yeah, kids like ice cream. But what's better than ice cream? Ice cream on a boat! Sip on a classic root beer float and enjoy the scenery. Departs hourly 11 am to 5 pm, every Sunday from South Lake Union Park next to MOHAI (www.seattleferryservice.com).

Learn to Build a Bike

Through Bike Works' Earn-a-Bike program kids can learn how to fix and build a bike in an eight-week afterschool program. After earning enough hours, youths are eligible to pick out and fix up their own bike.

Give Them Gas

The giant iron wrought structures of Gasworks Park make this a great kid-friendly destination. Fly a kite at the top of the hill, watch the seaplanes land on Lake Union, or look for unrefined oil ooze out of the ground (and if you find some, please contact the authorities).

Ferries

Did you see that? Was that a Whale? They say 90 orcas (once known by the killer nickname, killer whales) live in Puget Sound, so if you take a ferry ride you should see one, right? Wait! What's that? Is that a whale? Maybe it's a shark? Or a sturgeon? Can you see sturgeons from the ferries? Ride the ferries and find out.

Culture: Seattle Style

Quirky Fremont is a kid-like, permanently silly place. Start the tour off at 36th and Fremont Place at the Lenin Statue, and ponder the future of communism in Seattle. Head across the street towards the water a block to The Rocket, which traveled to the moon thirty-five times before retiring in 1986. From there, take a left to the other end of the block and you'll be standing at the actual Center of the Universe. Pretty cool, huh? But don't stand too long or you'll cause an imbalance. Next, cross the street and head downhill until you see those people Waiting for the Interurban. They've been waiting so long, they've turned to stone. Head under the Aurora Bridge to find the infamous Fremont Troll. This troll wandered the thick forests of north Seattle, mercilessly devouring all those who dared to cross the water, until a group of kids turned him to stone in a grueling 22-day battle in 1950. Unfortunately, the troll destroyed their VW Bug in the process.

Let's Go Sledding

It rarely snows in Seattle—bummer, eh? But when it does, boy is it fun. The entire city shuts down with the thought of three inches of snow businesses cut their hours, downtown office workers play hooky, buses take alternate routes, and best of all, schools close. Actually, that's second best. The best part about snow in Seattle is that all these huge hills turn into giant, car-less sledding runs. Grab a cardboard box, wrap yourself in cellophane, and hit the slopes! Be sure to supervise the kids and have hot chocolate ready upon the return to home. If you don't want to wait for Mother Nature to get freaky, hop on I-90 to the reliably snowy Summit at Snoqualmie, where they rent tubes every winter.

Shopping Essentials

Magic Mouse Toys (Map 7) aims for humans of all ages to discover or rediscover or continue to discover their love of toys—from Lego to die-cast cars to Playmobil to classics like puzzles and kites. Meanwhile, **Archie McPhee (Map 24)** sells all the greatest pleasures in life—rubber lizards, fake spider-in-ice, and boxing nun puppets; perfect for kids from two to 52. On a more educational tip, **Top Ten Toys (Map 3, 30)** takes the guesswork out of whether you might be perpetuating gender-normative roles when buying toys for your or someone else's little one; here the entire store is the fibrous middle section of a big-box toy store—as such, it will restore your faith in the next generation. Similarly, **Math N Stuff (Map 34)** has proved to the world that there is in fact a market for a store devoted to math. Deciding between that and a Chains"R"Us, is clearly a no-brainer. You can't get within two time zones of Sea-Tac without feeling the vortex tug of **The Elliott Bay Book Company (Map 4)**, and true to form, it not only has a brilliant kids section but also offers children's storytime every Saturday. **Schmancy (Map 3)** is a super quirky "toy shop," more for the childish adult or the mature-minded child, but why not? **Blue Highway Games (Map 13)** is old school in a 20-sided die kind of way, and cool in a way that gives those who know what that means a safe space to indulge their many sides; think RPGs, board games, brainteasers, card games, jigsaw puzzles, and in-store game nights. And then there's **Greenwood Space Travel Supply Co. (Map 30)**, the perfect place for budding astronauts and freeze-dried dessert aficionados; proceeds help support the Greater Seattle Bureau of Fearless Ideas (fearlessideas.org), an organization devoted to fostering the written word as a vital tool of communication for young people.

Emergency Rooms

	Address	Phone	Map
Children's Hospital and Regional Medical Center	4800 Sand Point Wy NE	206-987-2000	27
Evergreen Hospital Medical Center	12040 NE 128th St	425-899-1000	48
Evergreen Urgent Care	8301 161st Ave NE	425-883-3333	49
Harborview Medical Center	325 9th Ave	206-731-3000	8
Northwest Hospital and Medical Center	1550 N 115th St	206-364-0500	33
Overlake Hospital	1035 116th Ave NE	425-688-5325	46
Swedish Medical Center / Ballard	5300 Tallman Ave NW	206-782-2700	23
Swedish Medical Center – First Hill	747 Broadway	206-386-6000	4
Swedish Medical Center – Providence	500 17th Ave	206-320-2000	5
University of Washington Medical Center	1959 NE Pacific St	206-598-3300	26
Virginia Mason Medical Center	1100 9th Ave	206-223-6600	4

Other Hospitals

City of Hope	1309 114th Ave SE	425-646-9530	43
Fairfax Psychiatric Hospital	10200 NE 132nd St	425-821-2000	48
Group Health Capitol Hill Campus	201 16th Ave E	206-326-3000	18
Kindred Hospital	10631 8th Ave NE	206-364-2050	34
The Polyclinic First Hill	1145 Broadway	206-329-1760	4

Sometimes you need a hotel room that's a step up from Aurora Avenue. Maybe you'd like to offer your visiting Aunt Mildred something more comfy than your futon. Maybe it's late and your condo on the Eastside seems intolerably far away. Maybe there are things you need to do in this hotel that you can't do at home. Whatever your business, here are the options.

Obscenely Expensive

Ranking as the only AAA five-diamond hotel in the Pacific Northwest, the **Fairmont Olympic (Map 3)** is in a class by itself, though it's not cheap. The terrifying grandeur of the lobby is worth a peek, even if you have neither means nor motive to stay there. Or, for an Italianate flair, try the **Sorrento Hotel (Map 4)**, a bit more out of the way on First Hill. **The Edgewater (Map 1)** is a sort of posh Chelsea Hotel steeping with rock history involving the Beatles, Led Zeppelin, and fish. **Hotel Max (Map 2)** doubles as an art gallery. **The Arctic Club (Map 3)** was a private retreat for those who struck it rich in Alaska's Gold Rush. In 2008, Doubletree bought it but it retains the vintage hotel vibe. **Hotel 1000 (Map 3)** is perhaps so called because rooms go for around a grand (but at least they throw in free champagne at check-in). Kimpton Hotels are quirky and fun, great for treating yourself without feeling like a sell-out. In descending rate order: **Hotel Monaco (Map 3)**, **The Alexis Hotel (Map 3)** and **Hotel Vintage Park (Map 3)**. **The Inn at the Market (Map 3)** is an extremely popular boutique hotel located right in tourist central. And if you're staying in Kirkland but want to feel like you're somewhere better, try **The Heathman (Map 48)**.

Indulgent, but Not Ostentatious

Downtown Seattle is glutted with boutique hotels who make their names on style and service. **The Inn at El Gaucho (Map 1)** evokes a retro, boys' club glamour. Take a voyage of discovery to the **Mayflower Park Hotel (Map 3)**, a vintage boutique with a cool bar to match. If you like a more hands-on accommodation, **Pensione Nichols (Map 3)** provides the tenuous experience that's synonymous with B &Bs.

Avoid the Indignities of Motel 6

A fine choice north of Lake Union is the **Watertown Hotel (Map 26)** in the U District. In addition to providing a nice clean place at a reasonable price, they sweeten the deal with free lobby cupcakes. If a glamorous hotel experience just isn't in the cards, your first choice should be Belltown's **Ace Hotel (Map 1)**. Though the cheapest rates require a shared bathroom, that bathroom is the height of modern design. The **Moore Hotel (Map 3)** offers immaculate, no-frills accommodation in a great location for downtown entertainment. The **University Inn (Map 26)** provides a budget experience that is perfectly adequate. The B &B experience at **9 Cranes Inn (Map 30)** is rather reasonable and they don't slack in either B department. **The College Inn (Map 26)** flirts with hostel territory, but if you don't mind sharing a bathroom, you can have your very own bed and wash basin for far less than what you'd pay at some conventional hotels. The **Georgetown Inn (Map 39)** is a decent option within walking distance one of Seattle's hippest strips. Both the **Gaslight Inn (Map 4)** and **11th Avenue Inn (Map 17)** offer an economical and exceedingly pleasant way to experience Capitol Hill. Lest we leave out our backpacking friends, the best bunks are at the friendly and inauspicious **Green Tortoise Hostel (Map 3)**.

Map 1 • Belltown

	Address	Phone	Price
Ace Hotel	2423 1st Ave	206-448-4721	$$
The Edgewater Hotel	2411 Alaskan Way	206-728-7000	$$$
Inn At El Gaucho	2505 1st Ave	206-728-1133	$$

Map 2 • South Lake Union

Hotel Max	620 Stewart St	206-728-6299	$$$

Map 3 • Downtown

Doubletree Arctic Club Hotel	700 3rd Ave	206-340-0340	$$$$
Fairmont Olympic Hotel	411 University St	206-621-1700	$$$$
Green Tortoise Hostel	105 Pike St	206-340-1222	$
Hotel 1000	1000 1st Ave	206-957-1000	$$$$$$
Hotel Monaco	1101 4th Ave	206-621-1770	$$$$
Inn at the Market	86 Pine St	206-443-3600	$$
Mayflower Park Hotel	405 Olive Way	206-623-8700	$$
Moore Hotel	1926 2nd Ave	206-448-4851	$
Pensione Nichols	1923 1st Ave	206-441-7125	$$

Map 4 • First Hill / Pike / Pine

Gaslight Inn	1727 15th Ave	206-325-3654	$$
Sorrento Hotel	900 Madison St	206-622-6400	$$$

Map 17 • Capitol Hill (West)

11th Ave Inn	121 11th Ave E	206-720-7161	$$

Map 26 • U District

The Alexis Hotel	1007 1st Ave	206-624-4844	$$$$
College Inn	4000 University Way NE	206-633-4441	$
Hotel Vintage Park	1100 5th Ave	206-624-8000	$$$
University Inn	4140 Roosevelt Way NE	206-632-5055	$$
Watertown Hotel	4242 Roosevelt Way NE	206-826-4242	$$

Map 30 • Greenwood / Phinney Ridge

9 Cranes Inn	5717 Palatine Ave N	206-855-5222	$$

Map 39 • SoDo / Beacon Hill / Georgetown

Georgetown Inn	6100 Corson Ave S	206-762-2233	$$

Map 48 • Kirkland

The Heathman Hotel	220 Kirkland Ave	425-284-5800	$$$

Seattle is a city of few monuments and has little in the way of epic architecture (the **Central Library (Map 3)** notwithstanding). When other American cities were stockpiling marble and granite, Seattle was still a muddy outpost with wooden sidewalks. Today, post-boom, there remains an unfinished feeling to the landscape. Our most iconic landmark, The **Space Needle (Map 15)**, is largely ignored and sometimes reviled by Seattleites. Same goes for that useless hunk-o-metal better known as the **Monorail (Map 15)**. On the other hand, Seattle possesses no shortage of humorous, weird, usually misguided displays of civic pride and identity.

Historic Seattle

An obvious place to start is the 100-plus-year-old **Pike Place Market (Map 3)**. Beset though it is by tourists determined to see airborne fish, the market still has a lot to offer local residents. **Smith Tower (Map 7)** was the tallest building west of the Mississippi for nearly 50 years. Both the **Paramount Theatre (Map 3)** and **5th Avenue Theatre (Map 3)** take visitors back to vaudeville days. The **Seattle Asian Art Museum (Map 17)** is a 1933 Art Deco wonder in the middle of Volunteer Park. To go back even further, the **Birthplace of Seattle Monument (Map 35)**, an obelisk on Alki Point, marks the arrival of the first white folk in 1851.

Open Spaces

Though there have been a few missteps in the parks department—consider the scary, concrete wonderland of **Freeway Park (Map 3)**—the out-of-doors is what Seattle does best. From the untouched to the intricately landscaped, you are never far away from a patch of green in the Emerald City. For complete respite from the urban din, **Discovery Park (Map 11)** is the largest, and perhaps wildest, park within city limits. If it's botany you're after, **Washington Arboretum (Map 22)** on Union Bay contains an herbarium, horticulture center, the **Japanese Garden (Map 19)**, and it's accessible by kayak. The gardens at **Woodland Park (Map 30)** and the **Hiram M. Chittenden Locks (Map 28)** (a.k.a. the Ballard Locks) are gorgeous in season. Both **Gas Works Park (Map 24)** and **Kerry Park (Map 14)** afford postcard-worthy views of the skyline. Finally, **Volunteer Park (Map 18)** on the Hill is Seattle's ultimate urban oasis.

Public Art

Despite Seattle's reputation for lefty-leaning political attitudes, the existence of a mammoth statue of **Vladimir Lenin (Map 24)** in the heart of the Fremont neighborhood strikes most spectators as puzzling. Built in Slovakia and transported to the Emerald City after the fall of communism, this handsome piece now stands among Mexican restaurants, fashionable clothing boutiques, and other bastions of capitalism. Other public sculptures make for easier contextualization, such as Pioneer Square's life-size bronze **Fallen Firefighters' Memorial (Map 7)**, Fremont's six cast-aluminum **Waiting for the Interurban (Map 24)**, and the **Jimi Hendrix Statue (Map 4)** on Capitol Hill. The alluring **Bettie Page Mural (Map 31)** makes commuting interesting for those stuck on I-5, while the **Martin Luther King Jr. Mural (Map 5)** inspires contemplation and reflection each time you stroll by.

Lowbrow Landmarks

With esoterica such as the mammoth, hippy-hating **Fremont Troll (Map 24)**, Seattle's oddball landmarks expose the real character of the city. Not even Wikipedia can explain the existence of Post Alley's **Gum Wall (Map 3)** or the **Wall of Death (Map 26)**, a sculpture that pays homage to, of all things, a motorcycle stunt. The pink pachyderms of the **Elephant Carwash (Map 2)** offer a comment on the historic value of neon. The **Spooky Coke Machine (Map 17)** is a thirst-quenching mystery. Georgetown's **Hat 'n' Boots (Map 39)** is pure Americana—a roadside wonder built for a gas station now ensconced in a local park. As funky bars go, none is so well-steeped in grime and history as the **Blue Moon Tavern (Map 25)**, a former haunt of beat poets and other counterculture figures.

Shortly after Stonewall's major breakthrough in 1969, Seattle's queer culture began to rally for its rights. Students of the University of Washington united to claim their existence and formed organizations. Political activists set up shop in Pioneer Square to protest discrimination. In 1973, the Seattle City Council passed the Fair Employment Practice Ordinance which protected gays and lesbians in the workforce. Eventually, 1977 gave birth to Gay Pride Week which paraded the streets of downtown and traveled up Capitol Hill's slope, where LGBT culture currently reigns. Throughout years of struggles and victories, the women and men of sexual diversities built a strong community for one another. And to this day their efforts thrive in every proud, queer Seattleite.

Seattle's rainy streets are willing and able to compassionately support you in many ways. Local newspapers and guides post listings of entertainment, organized groups, health centers, and gay-friendly synagogues. Community publications are distributed to coffee bars, restaurants, clubs, bookstores, and well, just about anywhere dry. Flip through pages and pages of gay adventures for any night or day (both if you get lucky). You can find dykes to dance with and cowboys to ride. Whatever floats your boat, plenty of information can easily be found.

For the most part you can feel safe to publicly express gay affection. Not too many straight citizens express hatred when men grasp hands and women passionately embrace. Also, if your gaydar is finely tuned (or you're just obvious), then it's almost certain to acknowledge family anywhere in the city. Even though the rainy city is a bit introverted, Seattle queers are not too shy to engage in friendly chats. Yes indeed, it's a quaint little home for any ol' chap or dyke. In fact, many queer southerners venture north to saddle up here.

Publications/Media

Greater Seattle Business Association (GSBA): Publishes annual guide & directory Directory of businesses and community organizations that are owned or operated by and/or are allies of the LGBT community (www.thegsba.org or @GSBA)

Seattle Gay News: Local comprehensive LBGT-focused publication (206-324-4297, www.sgn.org or @SeattleGayNews)

Arts and Culture

Rainbow City Performing Arts: 866-841-9139; www.rainbowcityband.com

Seattle Men's Chorus/Seattle Women's Chorus: 319 12th Ave; 206-323-0750; www.flyinghouse.org or @SMC_Chorus or @SWC_Chorus

Sports and Recreation

Different Spokes Bicycling Club: www.differentspokes.org

Emerald City Softball Association: emeraldcitysoftball.org or @SeattleSoftball

Orca Swim Team: www.orcaswimteam.org

Seattle Frontrunners: www.seattlefrontrunners.org

Seattle Tennis Alliance: www.seattletennisalliance.org

Team Seattle Gay Sports Network: www.teamseattle.org

Social Groups/Organizations

BiNet Seattle: www.binetseattle.org

Border Riders Motorcycle Club:
www.borderriders.com

Gay Fathers' Association of Seattle:
www.gfas.org

Mature Friends: www.maturefriends.org

Northwest Bears: www.nwbears.com

Puddletown Squares: puddletownsquares.org

Seattle Men in Leather:
www.seattlemeninleather.org

Seattle Prime Timers:
www.seattleprimetimers.org

**Trikone-Northwest: South Asian Queer
Community**: www.trikonenw.org

Political Groups/Activism

Equal Rights Washington: 206-324-2570;
www.equalrightswashington.org

Greater Seattle Business Association (GBSA):
206-363-9188, www.thegsba.org or @GSBA

Pride Foundation: 206-323-3318;
www.pridefoundation.org

Seattle Out and Proud (Seattle Pride):
206-322-9561; www.seattlepride.org
or @SeattleOutProud

Religious/ Spiritual Services

All Pilgrims Christian Church: 500 Broadway E;
206-322-0487; www.allpilgrims.org

Broadview Community United Church of Christ:
325 N 125th St; 206-363-8060;
www.broadviewucc.org

Central Lutheran Church: 1710 11th Ave;
206-322-7500; www.loveiscentral.org

Dharma Buddies/Seattle Gay Buddhist Fellowship:
www.dharmabuddies.org

Dignity/Seattle: 206-659-5519;
www.dignityseattle.org

Welcome Table (Disciples of Christ):
206-725-5067; www.welcometablecc.org

Emerald City Metropolitan Community Church:
206-325-2421; www.mccseattle.org

Plymouth Congregational Church: 1217 6th Ave;
206-622-4865; plymouthchurchseattle.org or @
PlymouthSeattle

Temple De Hirsch Sinai: 1511 E Pike St;
206-323-8486; www.tdhs-nw.org

**University Congregational United Church
of Christ**: 4513 16th Ave NE; 206-524-2322;
www.universityucc.org

University Unitarian Church: 6556 35th Ave NE;
206-525-8400; www.uuchurch.org
or @UUC_Seattle

Wallingford United Methodist Church:
2115 N 42nd St; 206-547-6945;
www.wallingfordumc.org

Health Centers and Support Organizations

Northwest Network: Voice support & advocacy for bisexual, trans, lesbian & gay survivors of abuse & dating violence (206-568-7777 or www.nwnetwork.org)

Seattle Area Support Groups and Community Center (SASG): sasgcc.org

Gay City: Organizes events and activities for LGBTQ community & offers anonymous and confidential HIV/STD testing (206-860-6969 or www.gaycity.org)

Ingersoll Gender Center: Service agency for the Transsexual, Transvestite, & Transgender community offering support groups, referrals to therapists, publications, and trainings (206-329-6651 or ingersollgendercenter.org).

Lifelong AIDS Alliance: Empowering people living with or at risk of HIV/AIDS and/or other chronic conditions to lead healthier lives (206-957-1600 or www.lifelongaidsalliance.org)

PFLAG: Seattle Parents/Families/Friends of Lesbians and Gays (206-325-7724 or www.seattle-pflag.org)

Project Neon: Information group about crystal meth and the gay community (www.projectneon.org)

Seattle Counseling Service: Mental Health counseling for the LGBT community (206-323-1768 or www.seattlecounseling.org)

Youth & Families

Camp Ten Trees: Youth camp for LGBTQ communities and their allies (206-288-9568 or www.camptentrees.org)

Diverse Harmony: Queer-straight alliance youth chorus (206-389-5858 or www.diverseharmony.org)

If you still associate the library with rubber date stamps and dusty card catalogs, you haven't made use of the Seattle Public Library lately. In keeping with our digital culture, the two-million-item catalog and hold system are easily accessed **online** (www.spl.org). From the safety of your home computer you can have books, CDs, and DVDs delivered to your local branch. (Think of it as Netflix for really patient people.) The website also gives library card holders access to a collection of databases including periodical searches, phone and postal directories, and otherwise pricey reference sources such as the Oxford English Dictionary. Patrons can download digital media online and subscribe to library-related podcasts. Many of the 26 branches offer free Wi-Fi, and internet access is available on library PCs with a limit of 90 minutes per patron per day. Audio books and large print editions can be found in most branches, but for a wider selection visit the **Washington Talking Book and Braille Library (Map 2)**.

Libraries	Address	Phone	Map
Washington Talking Book & Braille Library	2021 9th Ave	206-615-0400	2
Central Library	1000 4th Ave	206-386-4636	3
Madrona-Sally Goldmark Branch	1134 33rd Ave	206-684-4705	6
International District / Chinatown Branch	713 8th Ave S	206-386-1300	8
Douglass-Truth Branch	2300 E Yesler Wy	206-684-4704	9
Magnolia Branch	2801 34th Ave W	206-386-4225	11
Queen Anne Branch	400 W Garfield St	206-386-4227	14
Capitol Hill Branch	425 Harvard Ave E	206-684-4715	17
Montlake Branch	2401 24th Ave E	206-684-4720	21
Ballard Branch	5614 22nd Ave NW	206-684-4089	23
Fremont Branch	731 N 35th St	206-684-4084	24
Wallingford Branch	1501 N 45th St	206 684-4088	25
University Branch	5009 Roosevelt Wy NE	206-684-4063	26
Northeast Branch	6801 35th Ave NE	206-684-7539	27
Greenwood Branch	8016 Greenwood Ave N	206-684-4086	30
Green Lake Branch	7364 E Green Lake Dr N	206-684-7547	31
Broadview Branch	12755 Greenwood Ave N	206-684-7519	33
Lake City Branch	12501 28th Ave NE	206-684-7518	34
Northgate Branch	10548 5th Ave NE	206-386-1980	34
West Seattle Branch	2306 42nd Ave SW	206-684-7444	35
Delridge Branch	5423 Delridge Wy SW	206-733-9125	36
High Point Branch	3411 SW Raymond St	206-684-7454	37
Southwest Branch	9010 35th Ave S	206-684-7455	37
Beacon Hill Branch	2821 Beacon Ave S	206-684-4711	39
Columbia Branch	4721 Rainier Ave S	206-386-1908	40
NewHolly Branch	7058 32nd Ave S	206-386-1905	40
Rainier Beach Branch	9125 Rainier Ave S	206-386-1906	41
Mercer Island Library	4400 88th Ave SE	206-236-3537	42
Lake Hills Library	15228 Lake Hills Blvd	425-747-3350	44
Newport Way Library	14250 SE Newport Wy	425-747-2390	44
Belluvue Library	1111 110th Ave NE	425-450-1765	45
Kirkland Library	308 Kirkland Ave	425-822-2459	48
Redmond Library	15990 NE 85th St	425-885-1861	49

General Information • **Media**

Television

4 KOMO (ABC)	www.komonews.com	16 KONG (Independent/NBC)	
5 KING (NBC)	www.king5.com	20 KTBW (TBN)	
7 KIRO (CBS)	www.kirotv.com	22 KZJO (MyNetworkTV)	
9 KCTS (PBS)	kcts9.org	28 KBTC (PBS)	www.kbtc.org
11 KSTW (CW)	cwseattle.cbslocal.com	33 KWPX (Ion)	
13 KCPQ (FOX)	q13fox.com	51 KUNS (Univision)	www.kunstv.com

AM Stations

570 KVI	Talk
630 KCIS	Christian
710 KIRO	Sports (ESPN Radio)
770 KTTH	Talk
820 KGNW	Christian
850 KHHO	Sports
880 KIXI	Oldies
950 KJR	Sports
1000 KOMO	News
1050 KBLE	Catholic (EWTN)
1090 KFNQ	Sports (CBS Sports Radio)
1150 KKNW	Alternative Talk
1210 KMIA S	panish Language
1250 KKDZ	Radio Disney
1300 KKOL	Talk
1360 KKMO	Spanish Language
1380 KRKO	Sports
1420 KRIZ	Urban Adult Contemporary
1460 KKAR	Christian
1490 KBRO	Spanish Language Sports (ESPN Deportes)
1520 KKXA	Country
1540 KXPA	Multicultural
1590 KLFE	Christian
1620 KYIZ	Urban
1680 KNTA	Spanish Language Christian

FM Stations

88.5 KPLU	Public Radio/Jazz
89.5 KNHC S	eattle Public Schools Student-Run Station
89.9 KGRG	Green River Community College
90.3 KEXP	Eclectic Hipster
91.3 KBCS	Bellevue Community College
92.5 KQMV	Top 40
93.3 KUBE	R &B/Hip-Hop
94.1 KMPS C	ountry/Western
94.9 KUOW	UW Public Radio
95.7 KJR	Classic Hits
96.5 KJAQ	Adult Contemporary
97.3 KIRO	News/Talk
98.1 KING	Classical
98.9 KLCK	Adult Contemporary
99.9 KISW	Rock
100.7 KKWF	Country
101.5 KPLZ	Adult Contemporary
102.5 KZOK	Classic Rock
103.7 KHTP	Adult Contemporary
104.5 KLSW	Christian
105.3 KCMS	Christian
106.1 KBKS	Top 40
106.9 KRWM	Adult Contemporary
107.7 KNDD	Alternative

Print Media

Ballard News-Tribune (206-708-1378, www.ballardnewstribune.com): Ballard news.

Capitol Hill Times (206-461-1310, www.capitolhilltimes.com): Capitol Hill and First Hill coverage.

City Arts (206-443-0445, cityartsonline.com): Monthly art news.

City Living Seattle (206-461-1300, citylivingseattle.com): All the news from North Seattle.

Kirkland Reporter (425-822-9166, www.kirklandreporter.com): Kirkland news since 1978 (formerly the Kirkland Courier).

Madison Park Times (206-461-1300, www.madisonparktimes.com): News from Madison Park, Madison Valley, Madrona, and Leschi.

Queen Anne & Magnolia News (206-461-1291, www.queenannenews.com): Queen Anne & Magnolia local news.

Pike Place Market News (206-587-0351, www.pikeplacemarketnews.com): Monthly news and gossip from the market.

Real Change (206-441-3247, realchangenews.org): Raising awareness about local homeless issues.

Seattle Daily Journal of Commerce (206-622-8272, www.djc.com): Daily business news.

Seattle Gay News (206-324-4297, www.sgn.org): Free LGBT weekly.

Seattle Magazine (206-284-1750, www.seattlemag.com): Monthly lifestyle magazine.

Seattle Metropolitan (206-957-2234, www.seattlemet.com): Seattle lifestyle.

Seattle Post-Intelligencer (206-448-8030, www.seattlepi.com): Voice of the Northwest since 1863, online only since 2009.

Seattle Times (206-624-7323, www.seattletimes.com) Seattle's main daily paper.

Seattle Weekly (206-623-0500, www.seattleweekly.com): Free alternative weekly since 1976.

The Stranger (206-323-7101, www.thestranger.com): Seattle's best rag with entertaining political and arts news.

West Seattle Herald (206-708-1378, www.westseattleherald.com): News from West Seattle and White Center.

Police

Police	Address	Phone	Map
West Precinct	810 Virginia St	206-684-8917	2
Seattle Police Headquarters	610 5th Ave	206-625-5011	3
East Precinct	1519 12th Ave	206-684-4300	4
North Precinct	10049 College Wy N	206-684-0850	33
Southwest Precinct	2300 SW Webster St	206-733-9800	37
South Precinct	3001 S Myrtle	206-386-1850	41
Mercer Island Police Dept	9611 SE 36th St	206-275-7610	42
Bellevue Police Dept	450 110th Ave NE	425-452-6917	45
Clyde Hill Police Dept	9605 NE 24th St	425-454-7187	45
Medina Police Dept	501 Evergreen Point Rd	425-233-6420	45
Kirkland Police Dept	123 5th Ave	425-587-3400	48
Redmond Police Dept	8701 160th Ave NE	425-556-2500	49

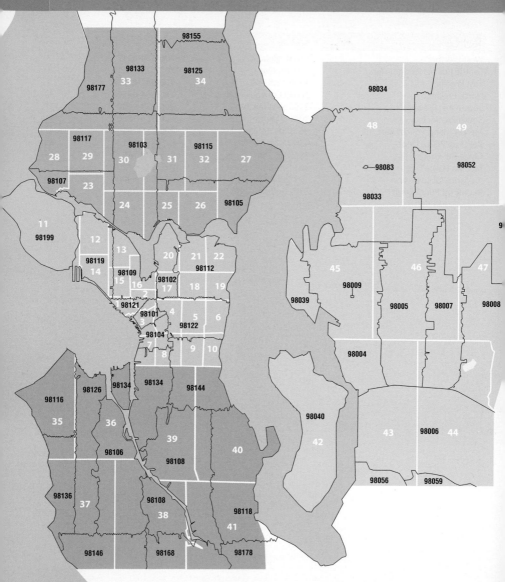

Post Offices

Post Offices	Address	Phone	Map
CPU Harbor Heights 111	2512 5th Ave	206-448-9287	1
Columbia Center	701 5th Ave, Ste 306	206-625-2293	3
Federal	909 1st Ave, Ste 100	206-625-2293	3
Midtown	301 Union St	206-748-5417	3
Seafirst	1001 4th Ave	206-682-3958	3
East Union	1110 23rd Ave	206-328-9712	5
Pioneer Square	91 S Jackson St	206-625-2293	7
International	414 6th Ave S	206-625-2293	8
Magnolia	3211 W Mcgraw St	206-284-5958	11
Queen Anne	415 1st Ave N	206-378-2506	15
Broadway	101 Broadway E	206-324-5474	17
Ballard	5706 17th Ave NW	206-781-4656	23
Wallingford	1329 N 47th St	206-547-1406	24
University	4244 University Wy NE	206-675-8114	26
Wedgwood	7724 35th Ave NE	206-527-8896	27
Greenwood	8306 Greenwood Ave N	206-547-1406	30
Bitter Lake	929 N 145th St	206-364-0663	33
Lake City	3019 NE 127th St	206-364-0608	34
Northgate	11036 8th Ave NE	206-364-0546	34
West Seattle	4412 California Ave SW	206-923-0485	35
Westwood	2721 SW Trenton St	206-938-7769	37
Georgetown	620 S Orcas St	206-764-9565	39
Terminal Finance Station	2420 4th Ave S	206-652-2467	39
Columbia	3727 S Alaska St	206-721-2368	40
Mercer Island	3040 78th Ave SE	206-232-8834	42
CPU Factoria	4020 Factoria Sq Mall SE	425-957-0640	43
Bellevue	1171 Bellevue Wy NE	425-453-5655	45
Medina	816 Evergreen Point Rd	425-656-8111	45
Midlakes	11405 NE 2nd Pl	425-462-7508	46
Crossroads	15731 NE 8th St	425-401-0892	47
CPU Totem Lake	12556 120th Ave NE	425-821-9755	48
Kirkland	721 4th Ave	4255-739-6727	48
Redmond	16135 NE 85th St	425-885-1057	49
Redmond Carrier Annex	7241 185th Ave NE	425-885-0207	49

Useful Contacts

Emergencies: 911
Police Department: 206-625-5011, www.seattle.gov/police
or @SeattlePD
Fire Department: 206-386-1400, www.seattle.gov/fire
or @SeattleFire
King County Elections: 206-296-8683
or www.kingcounty.gov/elections.aspx
King County Medic One: 206-296-8550
Seattle Mayor's Office: 206-684-4000, www.seattle.gov/mayor
or @OfficeofMayor
Animal Control: 206-386-7387 (206-386-PETS)

Websites

www.historylink.org or @HistoryLink: Online home of
Washington state history and more.

www.seattlepi.com or @seattlepi: The great experiment that
seeks to determine whether a print paper can transition to an
online-only format.

seattle.curbed.com or @CurbedSeattle: Seattle nabe and
real estate blog.

seattle.eater.com or @EaterSeattle: In-depth Seattle food
and drink.

www.seattle.gov: Official website of the City of Seattle; good
resource for residents and visitors.

seattle.craigslist.org: Find a job, join a band, buy an armoire,
or fall in love.

www.thestranger.com/blogs/slog: The Slog is Seattle's
sharpest alternative newsweekly's sharpest, most
comprehensive blog.

seattletransitblog.com or @SeaTransitBlog: The deep dive
into transit and land-use issues; for fans only.

www.sevennites.com: Search for happy hours in Seattle and
drink all week.

www.seattlefoodtruck.com or @seattlefoodtrk: Hungry?
Find any of our 100+ food trucks by neighborhood, day or
cuisine.

www.seattlestar.net or @TheSeattleStar: Seattle culture
and politics.

www.threeimaginarygirls.com or @3imaginarygirls:
Seattle's sparkly indie-pop press; local music news, reviews
and commentary.

Essential Seattle Movies

Tugboat Annie (1933)
It Happened At The World's Fair (1967)
Five Easy Pieces (1970)
Cinderella Liberty (1973)
McQ (1974)
WarGames (1983)
Streetwise (1984)
Trouble in Mind (1985)
Say Anything (1989)
My Own Private Idaho (1991)

The Hand That Rocks The Cradle (1992)
Singles (1992)
Sleepless in Seattle (1993)
Hype! (1996)
10 Things I Hate About You (1999)
The Ring (2002)
Police Beat (2005)
Battle in Seattle (2007)
Zoo (2007)
Humpday (2009)
Grassroots (2012)
Safety Not Guaranteed (2012)

We're Number One!!!

When Northgate Mall opened in 1950 it became the first
enclosed mall in the country.

The Washington State Ferry system is the largest in the USA.

The term "skid row" originated in Seattle, derived from the
"skid road" that 19th-century loggers used to transport
lumber through Pioneer Square—the area hit financial ruin
during the Depression and the phrase became shorthand for
any destitute neighborhood.

Bertha Landes became the first female mayor of a large
American city when she won the Seattle mayoral race in 1926.

The first publicized photograph of a flying saucer was taken
by a Lake City man in 1947.

The Wave, that crowd-sourced wacky-armed bit of "Woo!"
during lulls in sporting events, was popularized by a UW
cheerleader during a Husky football game in 1981.

Essential Seattle Songs

"Seattle the Peerless City"—Official Song since 1909
"Seattle Ain't Bullshitting"—Sir Mix-A-Lot
"Posse on Broadway"—Sir Mix-A-Lot
"Seattle"—Public Image, Ltd.
"Seattle"—The Wailers
"Seattle"—Cop Shoot Cop
"Seattle" (from the Screen Gems TV Program Here Come the
Brides)—Bobby Goldsboro, Perry Como, Connie Smith and
others
"Seattle, WA"—Western Keys
"Seattle Hunch"—Jelly Roll Morton
"Seattle Was a Riot"—Anti-Flag
"Seattle Town"—Flatt & Scruggs
"Seattle Sonics Do It"—Luther Rabb
"Chief Seattle"—Gene Parsons
"Seattle Twist"—Rod McKuen
"Flight to Seattle"—DJ Magic Mike
"Seattle Shuffle"—Damo Suzuki's Network
"Seattle to Chicago"—Woody Guthrie
"The Day Seattle Died"—Cold
"Frances Farmer Will Have Her Revenge on Seattle"—Nirvana
"The Last One To Leave Seattle"—Waylon Jennings
"Sub Pop Rock City"—Soundgarden
"Viva! Sea-Tac"—Robyn Hitchcock
"Stranger"—The Presidents of the United States of America
"Nuke Seattle"—Quincy Punx

Essential Seattle Books

Sons of the Profit by William Speidel; entertaining and honest look at Seattle's early history.

Buddy Does Seattle by Peter Bagge; classic slacker comics.

Eccentric Seattle: Pillars and Pariahs Who Made the City Not Such a Boring Place After All by J. Kingston Pierce; the mavericks and misfits who shaped our city.

Never Mind Nirvana: A Novel by Mark Lindquist; former grunge rocker turns lawyer and experiences angst.

Loser: The Real Seattle Music Story by Clark Humphrey; indispensable guide to the city's rich rock and roll heritage.

The Kid: What Happened After My Boyfriend and I Decided to Go Get Pregnant by Dan Savage; openly gay Stranger editor/sex advice columnist adopts a young boy, then writes about it.

J.P. Patches, Northwest Icon by Julius Pierpont Patches and Bryan Johnston; the story behind this beloved local kid's TV star.

Skid Road: An Informal Portrait of Seattle by Murray Morgan; history of Seattle's rough-and-tumble frontier days.

Waxwings: A Novel by Jonathon Raban; British-born UW prof finds his life falling apart in Seattle.

Madison House by Peter Donahue; novel about Seattle at the dawn of the 20th century.

Selling Seattle by James Lyons; academic exploration of Seattle's impact on American culture.

I Sing the Body Electronic: A Year With Microsoft on the Multimedia Frontier by Fred Moody; a freelance writer goes inside the machine and lives to tell the tale.

The World of Chief Seattle: How Can One Sell the Air? by Warren Jefferson; all about the Suquamish tribe and the treaties that changed everything.

Rat City by Curt Colbert; mystery novel set in post-WWII Seattle.

Screaming Life by Charles Peterson; this is what Seattle rock looks like.

21 Dog Years: Doing Time @ Amazon.com by Mike Daisy; hilarious account of Amazon culture during the boom years.

Seattle Timeline

1805: Lewis and Clark explore the Pacific Northwest, including the future state of Washington.
1851: Midwestern settlers led by David and Arthur Denny arrive and begin populating the area that will one day become Seattle.
1869: City of Seattle is incorporated.
1872: Earthquake measuring 7.4 on the Richter scale shakes Seattle.
1878: Seattle's first telephone service established.
1889: Great Seattle Fire destroys downtown.
1890: Bon Marche opens in Seattle as a dry goods store.
1891: Seattle University established.
1893: Transcontinental train line reaches Seattle.
1917: Boeing Airplane Company incorporated, and the Seattle Metropolitans hockey team wins Stanley Cup.
1919: Seattle General Strike begins; the first city-wide strike in the nation.
1928: Inventor/entrepreneur Don Ibsen spends the summer on Lake Washington trying to perfect water skis.
1933: Seattle Art Museum established.
1934: The Muzak corporation established.
1936: University of Washington rowing crew wins Olympic gold.
1938: World's first pressurized airliner, the Boeing Model 307 Stratoliner is launched.
1940: World's first floating bridge opens on Lake Washington.
1942: Jimi Hendrix born in Seattle.
1949: Seattle-Tacoma International Airport established. Also an earthquake measuring 7.1 on the Richter scale shakes Seattle.
1954: Dick's Drive-In serves its first hamburger.
1959: First documented sample of HIV-infected blood collected by University of Washington geneticist Dr. Arno Motulsky while working in the Congo.
1962: Seattle hosts the World's Fair. Science Center, Space Needle, and Monorail are erected for the celebration. Elvis Presley shoots It Happened at the World's Fair on location.
1965: Earthquake measuring 6.5 on the Richter scale shakes Seattle.
1970: Abortion legalized by state voters.

1979: Seattle SuperSonics win NBA Championship.
1980: Mount St. Helens erupts.
1983: Thirteen dead in the Wah Mee massacre in the International District.
1986: Microsoft goes public.
1991: Nirvana releases Nevermind, cementing Seattle's growing reputation as Rock City USA.
1995: Mariners almost make it to the World Series. Amazon.com founded.
1994: Nirvana's Kurt Cobain commits suicide, and major record companies start looking for "the next Seattle."
1998: The US Government sues Microsoft for antitrust violations.
1999: The World Trade Organization holds conferences in Seattle, leading to clashes between protesters and policemen downtown.
2000: Kingdome imploded.
2001: Boeing moves corporate offices to Chicago. Earthquake hits measuring 6.8 on the Richter scale.
2003: Green River Killer pleads guilty to 48 murders.
2004: New Seattle Central Library opens to global fanfare. Storm win WNBA championship. Ichiro sets record for most hits in a season (262).
2005: Citywide monorail plan falls apart (again), and Seattleites resigned to riding the bus for the next 2,000 years.
2007: The ultimate urban bible is published (NFT Seattle).
2008: Ballard's historic Sunset Bowl closes, hipster hearts irreparable.
2009: Light rail link to airport opens. No joke!
2009: Seattle Sounders FC begins play and immediately blows away MLS attendance records.
2010: Lusty Lady closes, changing downtown forever.
2013: Sounders get US Men's Soccer captain Clint Dempsey from Tottenham for MLS record $9 million transfer fee.
2013: Washington becomes the first (or second, if you ask Colorado) state to legalize marijuana for recreational use.
2014: Seahawks crush Peyton Manning and the Broncos on the way to franchise's first Super Bowl.
2015: Seahawks miss out on second straight Super Bowl victory in waning moments of title game thanks to worst offensive play call of all time.

A Contemporary Theatre (ACT) (Map 3) provides some of Seattle's best drama, with two stages to host new plays from nationally recognized playwrights as well as the occasional revival. The Intiman Theatre won a Tony Award in 2006. Unfortunately, it wasn't enough to keep them in the black as they were forced to cancel their 2011 season. Subsequently, the institution has been reconceived as a yearly summer festival and its space has been taken over by Cornish College and renamed **The Cornish Playhouse at Seattle Center (Map 15)**. Another big player in Seattle performance arts is **On the Boards (Map 15)**, a risk-taking organization that specializes in artist development, particularly through their Open Studio program and 12 Minute Max series, which offer brief glimpses of new and in-progress works from up-and-coming performers and writers.

Seattle's live theater scene is also robust enough to support a slew of small stages where aficionados can catch the latest experimental performances, new works from local playwrights, or revivals of much-loved classics. **Theater Schmeater (Map 4)**, **Bathhouse Theatre (Map 31)**, **Eclectic Theater Company (Map 3)**, and others toil tirelessly in often cramped conditions and stumble as often as they soar, but that's how great theater is made. Check out **www.artscrush.org** for the latest theatrical happenings in the Emerald City.

Theaters	Address	Phone	Map
5th Avenue Theatre	1308 5th Ave	206-625-1900	3
ACT Theatre	700 Union St	206-292-7676	3
ArtsWest Theatre	4711 California Ave SW	206-938-0339	35
Bainbridge Performing Arts	200 Madison Ave N	206-842-8569	n/a
Bathhouse Theater	7312 W Green Lake Dr N	206-524-1300	30
Benaroya Hall	200 University St	206-215-4747	3
Capitol Hill Arts	1621 12th Ave	206-388-0569	4
Center House Theatre	305 Harrison St	206-216-0833	15
Historic University Theater	5510 University Wy NE	206-781-3879	32
Intiman Theatre	201 Mercer St	206-269-1900	15
Kirkland Performance Center	350 Kirkland Ave	425-893-9900	48
Langston Hughes Permorning Arts Center	104 17th Ave S	206-684-4657	9
The Little Theatre	608 19th Ave E	206-675-2055	18
Magnuson Community Center Auditorium	7400 Sand Point Wy NE, Bldg 47	n/a	27
Market Theater	1428 Post Aly	206-587-2414	3
McCaw Hall	321 Mercer St	206-733-9725	15
Meany Hall for the Performing Arts	4001 University Wy NE	206-543-4880	26
Meydenbauer Center	11100 NE 6th St	425-637-1020	45
Moore Theatre	1932 2nd Ave	206-682-1414	3
Northwest Puppet Center	9123 15th Ave NE	206-523-2579	34
Odd Duck Studio	1214 10th Ave	206-375-8945	4
On The Boards	100 W Roy ST	206-217-9886	15
Open Circle Theater	429 Boren Ave N	206-382-4250	2
Paramount Theatre	911 Pine St	206-682-1414	3
R.E.D. Performance Loft	89 Yesler Wy	206-331-6673	7
Richard Hugo House	1634 11th Ave	n/a	4
Seattle Children's Theatre at Seattle Center	201 Thomas St	206-441-3322	15
Seattle Repertory Theatre – Bagley Wright Theatre	155 Mercer St	206-443-2222	15
Second Story Repertory	16587 NE 74th St	425-881-6777	49
Spectrum Dance Theater	800 Lake Washington Blvd	206-325-4161	6
Taproot Theatre	204 N 85 St	206-781-9707	30
Teatro Zinzanni	222 Mercer St	206-802-0015	15
Theater Schmeater	1500 Summit Ave	206-324-5801	4

Overview

The city's art gallery epicenter has revolved around the architecturally traditional and not-so-funky Pioneer Square for many years. Perhaps it is the history of the place, the old cobblestones, and faded brick facades that make the neighborhood a natural backdrop for art. But lately the scene has been shifting to new neighborhoods, and Seattle's art scene is now spread out across the city. Make sure to get out and explore beyond Pioneer Square.

Although many neighborhood business associations offer monthly art walks, you'll have vastly differing experiences depending on which locale you choose. Head to Pioneer Square for more traditional art, such as abstract and still life paintings in oils and acrylics, paired with cheap wine and respectful crowds. In the summer months, Occidental Square is abuzz with tents of artists and crafts vendors selling unique jewelry, photography, and smaller works in the street until dark. Wander to Belltown for kitschy, lowbrow art at the nationally esteemed **Roq la Rue (Map 7)**. Ballard has a great art walk the second Saturday of each month. For an alternative to the refined gallery set, check out the personal studios at the **Tashiro-Kaplan Building** (115 Prefontaine Pl S) during public events.

The Georgetown Second Saturday Art Attack showcases the talents of the neighborhood's funky artist community. Most of the art walk takes place along Airport Way South and hits up thirty different galleries, cafes, and shops.

Glass Art

Thanks to the international fame and regional influence of local glass artist/corporation Dale Chihuly, Seattle goes wild for anything fragile and hand-blown. Along with area galleries like **William Traver (Map 3)** and **Foster/White (Map 3, 7)** that carry the famed Chihuly pieces, there are numerous galleries specializing in glass art from less-famous names, such as **Avalon Glassworks (Map 36)** or the **Seattle Glassblowing Studio (Map 1)**. Smaller local boutiques carry knockoffs that only the trained eye might be able to distinguish from so-called "fine art" pieces (or so we assume), proving the popularity of glass art among Seattle's hoi polloi as well as dot-com millionaires and other arbiters of taste.

Off the Beaten Path

The non-profit Jack Straw Productions, founded in 1962, supports local audio arts first and foremost, providing recording studio assistance and performance space for its members. However, with the organization's **New Media Gallery (Map 26)**, the Straw extends the art of noise through combination with various disciplines, creating installations that are as visually arresting as they sound. Locally based alternative comics press Fantagraphics recently opened a flagship store as well at **Georgetown Records (Map 39)**, not only to hawk its wares, but also to host showings of original artwork from renowned cartoonists.

Map 1 • Belltown

	Address	Phone
AT.31 Gallery	109 W Denny Wy	206-283-5253
McLoed Residence	2209 2nd Ave	206-441-3314
Roq La Rue Gallery	2312 2nd Ave	206-374-8977
Seattle Glassblowing Studio	2227 5th Ave	206-448-2181
Suyama Space	2324 2nd Ave	206-256-0809

Map 2 • South Lake Union

Art Not Terminal Gallery	2045 Westlake Ave	206-233-0680
Patricia Cameron Fine Art	234 Dexter Ave N	206-343-9647
Winston Wachter Fine Art	203 Dexter Ave N	206-652-5855
Woodside/Braseth Gallery	2101 9th Ave	206-622-7243

Map 3 • Downtown

Benham Gallery	1216 1st Ave	206-622-2480
Carolyn Staley Fine Japanese Prints	2001 Western Ave	206-621-1888
Facere Jewelry Art Gallery	1420 5th Ave	206-624-6768
Friesen Gallery	1210 2nd Ave	206-628-9501
Gallery Mack	2100 Western Ave	206-448-1616
Jeffrey Moose Gallery	1333 5th Ave	206-467-6951
Kim Drew Studio and Gallery	1311 Post Aly	206-343-4101
The Legacy Ltd	1003 1st Ave	206-624-6350
Lisa Harris Gallery	1922 Pike Pl	206-443-3315
Milagros Mexican Folk Art	1530 Post Aly	206-464-0490
Patricia Rovzar Gallery	118 Central Wy	425-889-4627
Phoenix Rising Gallery	2030 Western Ave	206-728-2332
Vetri International Glass	1404 1st Ave	206-667-9608
William Traver Gallery	110 Union St	206-587-6501

Map 4 • First Hill / Pike / Pine

Bluebottle Art Gallery	415 E Pine St	206-325-1592
Martin-Zambito Fine Art	721 E Pike St	206-726-9509
Photographic Center Northwest	900 12th Ave	206-720-7222
Warren Knapp Gallery	1530 Melrose Ave	206-381-3335

Map 7 • Pioneer Square / SoDo

Artforte Gallery	320 1st Ave S	206-748-0187
Azuma Gallery	530 1st Ave S	206-622-5599
Davidson Contemporary	313 Occidental Ave S	206-624-7684
Flury & Company Gallery	322 1st Ave S	206-587-0260
Foster/White Gallery	220 3rd Ave S	206-622-2833
G Gibson Gallery	300 S Washington St	206-587-4033
Gallery 110	110 S Washington St	206-624-9336
Gallery 4 Culture	101 Prefontaine Pl S	206-296-8674
Glasshouse Studio	311 Occidental Ave S	206-682-9939
Greg Kucera Gallery	212 3rd Ave S	206-624-0770
Grover/Thurston Gallery	309 Occidental Ave S	206-223-0816
Howard House Contemporary Art	604 2nd Ave	206-256-6399
James Harris Gallery	206-587-4033	206-903-6220
Kagedo Japanese Art	520 1st Ave S	206-467-9077
Kibo Galerie	323 Occidental Ave S	206-442-2100
La Familia Gallery	117 Prefontaine Pl S	206-291-4608
Linda Hodges Gallery	316 1st Ave S	206-624-3034
NorthWest Fine Woodworking	101 S Jackson St	206-625-0542
Pacini Lubel Gallery	207 2nd Ave S	206-326-5555
Platform Gallery	114 3rd Ave S	206-323-2808
Punch Gallery	119 Prefontaine Pl S	206-621-1945
Soil Art Gallery	112 3rd Ave S	206-264-8061
Stonington Gallery	119 S Jackson St	206-405-4040
The Underground Gallery	214 1st Ave S, B-12	206-340-9395

Map 8 • International District

Lawrimore Project	831 Airport Wy S	206-501-1231

Map 12 • Queen Anne (North)

Fountainhead Gallery	625 W McGraw St	206-285-4467

Map 15 • Lower Queen Anne / Seattle Center

Pottery Northwest	226 1st Ave N	206-285-4421
Judith Kindler	570 Mercer St	206-283-5253

Map 18 • Capitol Hill (East) / Madison Valley

Lewis/Wara Gallery	1121 15th Ave E	206-405-4355
Miner Gallery	346 15th Ave E	206-568-7604

Map 24 • Fremont

Black Box Gallery	4911 Aurora Ave N	206-883-4903
Edge of Glass Gallery	513 N 36 St	206-632-7807
TimesInfinity Gallery	122 NW 36th St	206-973-4470

Map 26 • U District

Henry Art Gallery	4100 15th Ave NE	206-543-2280
Jack Straw / New Media Gallery	4261 Roosevelt Wy NE	206-634-0919
Kirsten Gallery	5320 Roosevelt Wy NE	206-522-2011

Map 28 • Ballard (West)

Sev Shoon Arts Center	2862 NW Market St	206-782-2415

Map 30 • Greenwood / Phinney Ridge

Francine Seders Gallery	6701 Greenwood Ave N	206-782-0355

Map 34 • Northeast Seattle

Snow Goose Associates	8806 Roosevelt Wy NE	206-523-6223

Map 36 • North Delridge

Avalon Glassworks	2914 SW Avalon Way	206-937-6369

Map 39 • SoDo / Beacon Hill / Georgetown

Georgetown Records / Fantagraphics	1201 S Vale St	206-762-5638
Mix Lounge	6006 12th Ave S	206-767-0280
Western Bridge	3412 4th Ave S	206-838-7444

Map 40 • Columbia City / Mount Baker / Seward Park

Columbia City Gallery	4864 Rainier Ave S	206-760-9843

Map 43 • Bellevue (Southwest)

East Shore Gallery	12700 SE 32nd St	425-747-3780

Map 45 • Bellevue (West) / Medina

Elements Gallery	10500 NE 8th St	425-454-8242
Gunnar Nordstrom Gallery	127 Lake St S	425-827-2822
Ming's Asian Gallery	10217 Main St	425-462-4008

Map 48 • Kirkland

Howard/Mandville Gallery	120 Park Lane	425-889-8212

With literary events cropping up all over Seattle—not just in libraries and bookstores, but in coffee houses, bars, art museums, and rock music venues—it's hardly a shock that each year we rank as highly as we do in CCSU's yearly America's Most Literate Cities study. We love our libraries, devour our newspapers (even online papers!), and keep our bookstores in business. Independent bookstores here, as everywhere, struggle to compete with the big conglomerates. But despite housing Amazon.com headquarters, bookstores in Seattle have maintained a strong presence and a loyal customer base.

Literary Treasures

The Elliott Bay Book Company (Map 4) on Capitol Hill is the favorite son of Puget Sound literati. Established in 1973, the store long ago carved its niche as a cultural gathering place with frequent readings by big-name authors and book groups. It can be argued, however, that the only advantage Elliott Bay really has over the competition (besides all that exposed brick) is killer PR. Ask Seattleites to name the best local bookstore, and you'll rarely hear the same answer twice. Here are some contenders: **Magus Books (Map 26)** in the U-District has a grandpa's attic feel. **Ravenna Third Place Books (Map 32)** offers excellent variety, as does **Twice Sold Tales (Map 4)**, which has several resident cats. **Wessel & Lieberman Booksellers (Map 7)** is ideal for more high-brow browsing, if you will, offering many antiquarian and out-of-print titles as well as prints.

Books by the Mile

If your true desire is to surround yourself with an immense acreage of reading material (no shame in that), **University Bookstore (Map 26)** has an impressive collection of books including substantial technology, health science, and periodical sections (not to mention an art supply store). **Half Price Books (Map 26, 49)** is a regional chain with locations around Puget Sound and an ever-changing stock of used books, plus deals on CDs, DVDs, and magazines. To satiate your inner Comic Book Guy, check out their disorganized comics bin which is peppered with treasures cast off by boneheads who didn't know what they had.

Specialty

Open Books: A Poem Emporium (Map 25) bravely limits its stock to poetry—one of only two such bookstores in the US. **Cinema Books (Map 26)** is devoted solely to the silver screen. Collectors of art and architecture books should see **Peter Miller Books (Map 3)** downtown. **Seattle Mystery Bookshop (Map 3)** is a paradise for readers of whodunits, thrillers, and true crime, but look to **Edge of the Circle Books (Map 4)** for your pagan and occult literature. **Left Bank Books Collective (Map 3)** is the place for all you lefty-commie-pinkos who still care about the world. May our numbers increase.

For travelers, **Wide World Books & Maps (Map 25)** has all manner of portable goodies in addition to an excellent selection of guidebooks and travel writing. **Metsker Maps** of Seattle **(Map 3)** in Pike Place Market also carries a variety of travel and recreational guidebooks, as well as carrying our favorite retail item—maps. Birders and botanists will love **Flora & Fauna Books (Map 12)** in Magnolia near Discovery Park. And for young minds, try **Secret Garden Bookshop (Map 23)** and **Alphabet Soup (Map 24)**.

One of the truer stereotypes about Seattle is our intense love for the brown stuff—and no, we don't mean heroin (although that cruel mistress has certainly claimed plenty of our own). We owe much of Seatown's coffee omnipresence to that little-mermaid-that-could. Starbucks mass-produced our obsession to the whole of the First World. But it doesn't take much effort to find something better. All over the city, independent coffee shops compete for the expendable income of our resident caffeine junkies. Many places even seem justified in charging $4+ for their artwork in mug. Some NFT neighborhood favorites: **Joe Bar (Map 17)** has been a Capitol Hill staple since 1997. That's like 100 years in Seattle restaurant time. **Vivace (Map 2, 17)** uses their old-world coffee knowledge to make a perfecto cappuccino. **Fuel (Map 18, 21, 25)** is one of the more welcoming spots for long-term table residents. (Seattle etiquette dictates that you must order something for every hour that you occupy your seat). **Verite Coffee (Map 4, 6, 23, 35)** diabolically teamed up with Cupcake Royale to ensure you put on that winter weight. **Caffe Vita (Map 4, 7, 15, 24, 30, 40)** boasts 10 original blends including one co-created with Theo Chocolate. **Seattle Coffee Works (Map 3)** has an express bar for normal coffee consumption and a slow bar, which is more like an inclusive club for coffee nerds.

Hipster Country

If you like your coffee with a side of scene, try **Bauhaus (Map 4)** which is probably better known for its people watching than for the coffee it sells. At the Portland-based **Stumptown (Map 4)**, our frenemies from the south do a great job showing us up with their singular roasts and it feels as though Carrie and Fred could walk in any minute. **Victrola (Map 4, 18, 39)** is for the more high-end hipsters, **Analog Coffee (Map 17)** for the mustachioed pseudo-luddite and **Zeitgeist Kunst & Kaffee (Map 7)** for the revolution-through-philosophy-degree types.

Entertain Me

Sometimes you don't just want to sit quietly on your laptop. For live music, **Cafe Racer (Map 31)**, **Forza (Map 31)** and **Sureshot (Map 26)** have got you covered. Exercise the pop culture lobe of your brain with trivia nights at **Neptune Coffee (Map 30)**.

Take a Load Off, Annie

Say you're on rugrat duty but you also need to get some work done or catch up with your long-lost friend. These places have decked-out play areas that will keep your offspring distracted while you enjoy some adult conversation and sneak that extra cookie. **Mosaic (Map 25)** has the mother of play areas with a clubhouse, slide and a blocked off corner for accident-prone crawlers. **Twirl's (Map 13)** play area is also pretty sick and features a giant treehouse and an epic train table. The play corners at **Tougo (Map 5)**, **Cloud City (Map 34)**, **Green Bean Coffeehouse (Map 30)**, and **Ballard Coffee Works (Map 23)** pale in comparison, but still get the job done.

Two for Tea

Preferring tea to coffee won't get you voted out of the Emerald City. Overachievers that we are, we have to do it TO THE MAX. At **Panama Hotel Tea & Coffeehouse (Map 8)**, they serve their large international selection of loose-leaf teas with an hourglass timer so you know exactly how long to steep. At **Pearl's Tea & Coffee (Map 35)**, you can get all the usual bubble tea flavors plus house-created flavors like Taro and Avocado. **Roy Street Coffee & Tea (Map 17)** treats their tea like their coffee, using flowery language to describe their flavors which, fortunately, live up to their own hype.

Flavor Country

If you're tired of the same-old-same-old, you should head to the **Moore Coffee Shop (Map 3)** for their Nutella Latte, which is exactly as delicious as it sounds and comes with some of the best foam art around. **El Diablo's (Map 13)** Cubano espresso is a must try as is their Mexican Hot Chocolate. **Kitanda's (Map 48, 49)** Brazilian Latte is one of the better reasons to visit Kirkland or Redmond.

With such an embarrassment of riches in the coffee department, we hope you'll forgive us a little discernment. We're not trying to be dicks. But when you're born with a silver coffee stir in your mouth, it's hard to abide whatever it is that passes for joe at Dunkin' Donuts. You'll be one of us soon enough (gobble gobble).

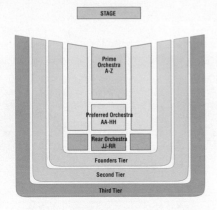

General Information

NFT Map: 3
Address: 200 University St, Seattle WA 98101
Website: www.seattlesymphony.org or @benaroyahall
Phone: 206-215-4800
Tickets: 206-215-4747

Overview

Rising up out of an entire city block in the heart of downtown, Benaroya Hall, home to the Seattle Symphony, opened in September 1998. The $118.1 million venue matches elegant architecture with state-of-the-art acoustics. (Taking full advantage of the astounding acoustics, local rock juggernaut Pearl Jam recorded *Live at Benaroya Hall* here in 2003.) In addition to the symphony, other performances and lectures take place throughout the year. There are also two smaller halls: the S. Mark Taper Foundation Auditorium (capacity 2,500) and the Illsley Ball Nordstrom Recital Hall (capacity 540).

Great glass flows of light and color fashioned by the renowned Dale Chihuly are featured in the lobby, which also houses a small cafe and a surprisingly good gift shop. Be forewarned when choosing your seat location—the front row seats in the upper tiers give the sensation that absolutely nothing is between you and the performance, including any protection from plunging over the edge. Nearby parking is plentiful, but if you arrive late, you can sip a glass of wine while you whisper to your fellow latecomers about the increasingly horrible Seattle traffic and watch the concert on a large screen television in the lobby until being seated at an appropriate break.

If you're interested in the nuts and bolts of Benaroya Hall, free public tours are held on a handful of dates during the year. In addition, free recital-demonstrations of the Symphony's 4,490-pipe Watjen Concert Organ are held on a few days each year. Check website for details on both.

How to Get Tickets

Avoid ticket fees and buy your tickets directly from the Benaroya Box Office at the corner of Third Avenue and Union. The ticket office is open 10 am to 6 pm weekdays, Saturday 1 pm to 6 pm, and before performances. Ticket buyers can park for free in the Benaroya Hall parking lot for 15 minutes.

How to Get There

Driving
Benaroya Hall occupies the block between 2nd and 3rd Avenue, and Union and University Streets. The main public entrances are on 3rd Avenue.

Southbound I-5: Take the Union Street exit (#165B) and proceed five blocks to 2nd Avenue. Turn left onto 2nd Avenue. The Benaroya Hall parking garage will be on your immediate left, with the garage entrance on 2nd Avenue just south of Union Street.

Northbound I-5: Exit left onto Seneca Street (exit #165). Proceed two blocks and turn right onto 4th Avenue. Continue two blocks and turn left onto Union Street. Continue two blocks and turn left onto 2nd Avenue. The Benaroya Hall parking garage will be on your immediate left, with the garage entrance on 2nd Avenue just south of Union Street.

When parking your best bet is the 430-car garage located beneath Benaroya Hall. The entrance is off of 2nd Avenue. If it is full, there is metered street parking and more garages nearby.

Public Transportation
Numerous bus routes serve Benaroya Hall, including RapidRide lines C, D, and E. The University Street Link light rail station is just a block from Benaroya Hall.

General Information

NFT Map: 15
Address: 321 Mercer St, Seattle WA 98109
Website: www.mccawhall.com or @McCawHall
Phone: 206-733-9725
Seattle Opera: www.seattleopera.org or @SeattleOpera
Pacific Northwest Ballet: www.pnb.org or @PNBallet

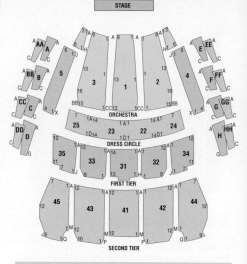

Overview

Marion Oliver McCaw Hall at Seattle Center, the state-of-the-art performance hall our reliance on cell phones helped finance. The facility opened in 2003 as the third venue on this spot. The first, the Civic Auditorium, was completed in 1928 and began hosting symphony concerts in the 1930s. The second iteration was built for the World's Fair and was in business from 1962 until 2001, when work began on McCaw Hall.

McCaw Hall houses a 2,900-seat auditorium, a 400-seat Lecture Hall, a cafe, a five-story serpentine glass Grand Lobby, and a 17,800-square-foot public plaza (the Kreielsheimer Promenade) that serves as an entry into McCaw Hall and the Seattle Center Campus. True to the eco-sensibilities of Seattle, McCaw Hall was built with green technology, featuring the use of recycled materials and energy-efficient theatrical lighting. Seattle opera – and ballet-goers keep up the green theme—Dansko clogs are more common than Jimmy Choos, polar fleece wins out over cashmere.

Besides being the home of the Pacific Northwest Ballet and Seattle Opera, McCaw Hall hosts various conventions, receptions, and even weddings if you have a pretty penny and need over-the-top accommodations. Even if you aren't an opera or ballet buff, it's worth a stroll through the promenade to experience just what money can buy, but if you want to be blown away by lavish productions in the extreme, splurge on the ballet and an opera and dress up—at least once. You might fall in love.

Free public tours are given on the third Tuesday of each month, schedule permitting. See the McCaw Hall website for details.

How to Get Tickets

Tickets for Pacific Northwest Ballet and Seattle Opera are sold through Ticketmaster or the individual companies. Tickets are also available at the the McCaw Hall box office and the KeyArena west plaza box office located just off of 1st Avenue North. Regular box office hours are Monday through Saturday, 10 am to 6 pm. Both ticket offices sell tickets without the extortionate fees.

How to Get There

Driving
From I-5: Take the Mercer Street exit. At the first light, turn right. At the next light turn left on to Valley Street. Follow Valley Street as it turns into Broad Street, turn right immediately after the underpass. Take a right on 5th Avenue. Turn left on Roy Street, and then turn left onto 2nd Avenue. Turn left onto Mercer Street. McCaw Hall is directly on your right at 321 Mercer Street (Mercer & 3rd Ave N). If you think these directions sound confusing—you've understood them perfectly, it can be tricky to navigate around the perimeter of the Seattle Center. If you get lost, just head toward the Space Needle—McCaw Hall is located just north of the Space Needle on the grounds of the Seattle Center.

If parking, your best bet is the parking garage located across Mercer Street from McCaw Hall. A skybridge connects the garage to the Hall. Or you can park in one of the several open-air lots surrounding the Seattle Center. Street parking is scarce and at night, Queen Anne neighborhood streets are reserved for residents with zone passes.

Public Transportation
Metro Transit bus routes provide service close to McCaw Hall, which is located on the north edge of Seattle Center. Many frequent routes run north via 1st Ave N and south via Queen Anne Ave N. Routes 3 and 4 travel on 5th Ave N. Then of course there's the Monorail, which will forever putter back and forth between Seattle center and Westlake Center, just waiting for you to finally look its way.

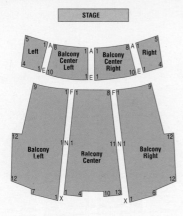

BALCONY

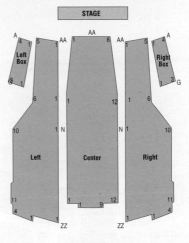

MAIN FLOOR

General Information

NFT Map: 3
Address: 1932 Second Ave, Seattle, WA 98101
Website: www.stgpresents.org/moore or @stgpresents
Phone: 206-682-1414

Overview

Seattle's oldest continuously operating theater opened in 1907 in the boom years following the Klondike Gold Rush. The culmination of effort and vision by developer James A. Moore, a Canadian who arrived in Seattle in the 1880s, its deceptively shoddy exterior and tacky marquee belie the grandeur and opulence within its walls, embellished with chandeliers, frescoes, mosaics, and marble. Its foyer was once noted for being the largest of any theater in the country. The Moore was on the vaudeville circuit in the 1920s, was the original home of the Seattle Symphony, and hosted the first annual Seattle International Film Festival (SIFF) in 1976. The majestic hall retains its striking elegance while continuing to be a relevant venue for music and other performances. Over the years, some of the most celebrated and talented actors, musicians, and entertainers have played the Moore—from Ethel Barrymore, Vaslav Najinsky, the Marx Brothers, and Harry Houdini, to Sonic Youth, Nirvana, and Pearl Jam. The non-profit Seattle Theatre Group operates the venue, along with the Paramount and the Neptune Theatres, and hosts free tours on the second Saturday of each month.

How to Get Tickets

Advance ticket sales are handled via the ticket kiosk at the corner of 2nd and Virginia (open 24 hours, seven days a week) or the Paramount Theatre box office at 9th Avenue & Pine Street (open Monday through Friday from 10 am to 6 pm). Tickets are also available online, and include the associated convenience charges. Day-of sales and will-call tickets are handled at the Moore Theatre box office, which opens 90 minutes before the start of the show.

How to Get There

Driving
From I-5 North, take the Seneca Street exit; from I-5 South take the Stewart Street exit. Turn right onto First Avenue and head north to Virginia Street. Turn right onto Virginia Street and go one block to Second Avenue. Cross your fingers and hope to find parking. From I-90 take the Madison Street exit. Turn left onto Madison, turn right onto Sixth Avenue, and head north to Stewart Street. Turn left onto Stewart Street, go down to First Avenue, turn right on First. Go north one block to Virginia Street, turn right onto Virginia, and go one block to Second Avenue.

The Moore Theatre is located downtown at the corner of Second Avenue and Virginia Street, four blocks from Pike Place Market. Parking is available in nearby pay lots and metered parking along the street, but is nearly impossible to find on a Friday or Saturday night. If you really must park, do your best to find street parking northeast of Fourth Avenue.

Public Transportation
Numerous bus routes serve Moore Theatre, including RapidRide lines C, D, and E. The Westlake Link light rail station is located just a few blocks from the venue.

Arts & Entertainment • **Paramount Theatre**

BALCONY

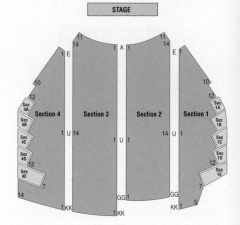

MAIN FLOOR

STAGE

| A9 A7 A5 A3 A1 A A2 A4 A6 A8 A10 |
| B7 B5 B3 B1 B B2 B4 B6 B8 |
| C9 C7 C5 C3 C1 C C2 C4 C6 C8 C10 |
| D11 D9 D7 D5 D3 D1 D D2 D4 D6 D8 D10 D12 |
| E13 E11 E9 E7 E5 E3 E1 E E2 E4 E6 E8 E10 E12 E14 |
| F15 F13 F11 F9 F7 F5 F3 F1 F F2 F4 F6 F8 F10 F12 F14 F16 |
| G9 G7 G5 G3 G1 G G2 G4 G6 G8 G10 |
| H15 H13 H11 H9 H7 H5 H3 H1 H H2 H4 H6 H8 H10 H12 H14 H16 |
| J15 J13 J11 J9 J7 J5 J3 J1 J J2 J4 J6 J8 J10 J12 J14 J16 |
| K13 K11 K9 K7 K5 K3 K1 K K2 K4 K6 K8 K10 K12 K14 |
| L15 L13 L11 L9 L7 L5 L3 L1 L L2 L4 L6 L8 L10 L12 L14 L16 |

CABARET

General Information

NFT Map: 3
Address: 911 Pine St, Seattle, WA 98101
Website: www.stgpresents.org/paramount
or @stgpresents
Phone: 206-682-1414

Overview

In the 1920s, Paramount Pictures built a movie house in nearly every major city, and Seattle was no exception. To make up for the fact that the land they bought was less than prime, Paramount Pictures built the grandest movie house Seattle had ever seen. Modeled after the Palace of Versailles, it boasted a four-tiered lobby, a player piano, grand chandeliers, and original paintings in gilded frames. Those paintings have since been stolen, but nothing could steal the Paramount's dignity. Even after the Depression when people couldn't afford luxuries like movies, The Paramount employed ushers, including famous Seattle native Bruce Lee. In the early days, The Paramount hosted movies and vaudeville, then just first run movies, then second run movies and eventually, it was barely scraping by. It wasn't until 1971 when the Clise Corporation came along and recognized its potential as a live performance hall that things started to pick up again. After changing hands a few more times and undergoing some serious renovations, the Paramount stands again as a Seattle jewel. It even has a fully automated convertible floor system that can turn the theater into a ballroom—the first in the country to do so. The non-profit Seattle Theatre Group operates the venue, along with the Moore and the Neptune Theatres, and hosts free tours on the first Saturday of each month.

How to Get Tickets

Advance ticket sales are available at the Paramount Theatre box office at 9th Avenue & Pine Street (open Monday through Friday from 10 am to 6 pm). Tickets are also available 24 hours a day via the ticket kiosk directly outside, as well as online (including the associated convenience charges for online ticket purchases). Day-of sales and will-call tickets are also available at the box office, which opens 90 minutes before the start of the show.

How to Get There

Driving
Coming north on I-5, take the Olive-Denny exit. Go one block to Melrose Street and turn right. The Paramount will be three blocks down on the corner of 9th Avenue and Pine Street.

Coming south on I-5, take the Stewart Street exit. Take Stewart to 9th Avenue and turn left. Follow 9th two blocks to Pine Street. The Paramount will be on your left.

The Paramount Theatre does not have its own parking lot, so you are stuck with paying for an expensive lot or trying to find street parking (free on Sundays). If you don't have that kind of patience, try Pacific Place Mall parking (7th Ave & Pine St), the Washington State Convention Center, or the Grand Hyatt's garage (7th & Pike St). There is a loading zone on 9th Avenue and Pine Street to drop off passengers.

Public Transportation
Because the Paramount Theatre is so close to the Washington State Convention Center, and in a prime downtown location, many bus routes will get you very close to the theater. From downtown, take the 10, 11, 43, or 49 buses. From the University District, the 43 or 44. From Capitol Hill, the 10. From Northgate, take the express 66. The Westlake Link light rail station is about a 5 – to 10-minute walk down Pine Street from Paramount Theatre.

No doubt about it, Seattle is a cinephile's city. Cutting edge film from around the world screens daily, and even chain video stores stock adventurous fare. Each spring since 1976 the Seattle International Film Festival has summoned the best and brightest talent from Hollywood and beyond for a month-long movie binge to rival Sundance and Cannes. The non-profit organization Northwest Film Forum offers film production workshops, equipment rentals, and funding grants to local filmmakers. And while there's no shortage of mainstream multiplexes for the latest big-budget snooze, Seattle also boasts many moviehouses that are exceptional not only in architecture and ambiance but also in their programming choices. The result is a consistent flow of cult favorites, foreign cinema, and rarely screened classics from the past.

Over in Capitol Hill, exciting, obscure cinema is the norm at **Northwest Film Forum (Map 4)**. In the University District, **Seven Gables (Map 26)** welcomes foreign film buffs with a bit of romantic atmosphere, aided and abetted by downstairs neighbor **Mamma Melina Ristorante**—a perfect first date package. The **Varsity (Map 26)** isn't as glamorous, but the sixty-year-old theater offers three screens on three floors connected by a staircase that claustrophobics should avoid. Employee-owned non-profit **The Grand Illusion (Map 26)** (a dentist's office in a former life) only seats 70, but it's one of the best movie-going experience in the city—a cozy, intimate space to enjoy films handpicked by the cineastes on staff.

There are only two places left in the world equipped to properly show films shot in the Cinerama three-screen format, and we got one. A local billionaire (his name escapes us) saved **Cinerama (Map 1)** from extinction in 1998 by kicking in for much-needed technological upgrades while preserving the retro charms of the house itself. Along with rare showings of 70mm classics, this is the place to experience big Hollywood special-effect spectaculars and wide-screen classics.

By contrast, the tiny **Jewel Box Theatre (Map 1)** seats even fewer than The Grand Illusion, but the advantage (or disadvantage, depending on one's attitude toward alcohol) is its location within Belltown's **Rendezvous**—a speakeasy and burlesque stage during Prohibition. Now the Jewel Box features live bands and fringe theater events, as well as occasional special film presentations. Centrally located in the Central District, **Central Cinema (Map 5)** gives pizza, beer, and movies equal weight, serving hungry film fans who love their themed programs, making it a better choice for regular drunken cinema binges. Central's more sophisticated sister is **Big Picture (Map 1)**, which pairs first-run films with classy cocktails. When you purchase your tickets, you can order a drink (or several) to be brought to you mid-movie.

Last, but not least, is the Seattle International Film Festival's year-round commitment to Seattle filmgoers. Their three venues fill a full docket of indie, foreign film, documentaries, and classics. **SIFF Cinema Uptown (Map 15)** in Lower Queen Anne has three screens, including a 500-seat auditorium. Down the street, the **SIFF Film Center, (Map 15)** located on the Seattle Center campus in what was formerly the Alki Room; it's got state-of-the-art equipment in an intimate 95-seat theater with retro seats salvaged from Cinerama's balcony. SIFF also rescued Capitol Hill's much-loved Egyptian, pulling the **SIFF Cinema Egyptian (Map 4)** into its cinematic constellation in 2014.

Movie Theaters

	Address	Phone	Map
Admiral Theater	2343 California Ave SW	206-938-0360	35
AMC Cinerama 1	2100 4th Ave	206-441-3080	1
AMC Loews Factoria 8	3505 Factoria Blvd SE	425-641-9206	43
AMC Loews Oak Tree 6	10006 Aurora Ave N	206-527-3117	33
AMC Loews Uptown 3	511 Queen Anne Ave N	206-285-1022	15
AMC Pacific Place 11	600 Pine St	206-652-8908	3
Big Picture Seattle	2505 1st Ave	206-256-0566	1
Broadway Performance Hall	1625 Broadway	206-325-3113	4
Central Cinema	1411 21st Ave	206-328-3230	5
Cinemark Lincoln Square Cinemas	700 Bellevue Wy NE	425-454-9100	45
Cinerama	2100 4th Ave	206-448-6680	1
Fremont Outdoor Movies	3501 Phinney Ave N	206-767-2593	24
The Grand Illusion	1403 NE 50th St	206-523-3935	26
iPic Theatre	16451 NE 74th St	425-636-5601	49
Jewel Box Theatre	2322 2nd Ave	206-441-5823	1
Kenyon Hall	7904 35th Ave SW	206-937-3613	37
King Cat Theatre	2130 6th Ave	206-448-2829	1
Kirkland Parkplace Cinema 6	404 Park Pl	425-827-9000	48
Landmark Guild 45th	2115 N 45th St	206-547-2127	25
Landmark Harvard Exit	807 E Roy St	206-323-0587	17
Landmark Metro Cinemas	4500 9th Ave NE	206-781-5755	26
Landmark Seven Gables	911 NE 50th St	206-632-8821	26
Landmark Varsity	4329 University Wy NE	206-632-6412	26
Majestic Bay Theatres	2044 NW Market St	206-781-2229	23
Movies at Marymoor	6046 W Lake Sammamish Pkwy NE	360-733-2682	49
Movies at the Mural	305 Harrison St	206-684-7200	15
Northwest Film Forum	1515 12th Ave	206-829-7863	4
Pacific Science Center IMAX	200 2nd Ave N	206-443-4629	15
Regal Bella Bottega Stadium 11	8890 161st Ave NE	425-861-6880	49
Regal Crossroads Stadium 8	1200 156th Ave NE	425-562-6596	47
Regal Meridian 16	1501 7th Ave	206-622-2434	3
SIFF Cinema	321 Mercer St	206-324-9996	15
SIFF Cinema Egyptian	805 E Pine St	206-324-9996	4
SIFF Cinema Uptown	511 Queen Anne Ave	206-285-1022	15
SIFF Film Center	305 Harrison St	206-464-5830	15
Totem Lake Cinemas	12232 NE Totem Lake Wy	425-820-5929	48

Art

The **Seattle Art Museum (SAM) (Map 3)** traces its beginnings to the early 20th century, and has grown and expanded as the city came into its own. In 2007 the museum's main downtown space was renovated, adding 70 percent more gallery space to show off its extensive collections of Pacific Northwest art. It also opened a new and improved museum store along First Avenue. Its sister gallery, the **Seattle Asian Art Museum (SAAM) (Map 17)** is located in idyllic Volunteer Park, with its sweeping city, water, and mountain views, and bad-boy reputation. The **Olympic Sculpture Park (Map 1)**, also a SAM project, showcases 22 monumental sculptures in a nine-acre park located on Seattle's waterfront. The **Frye Museum (Map 4)**, founded by a former meat packing executive, shows fairly traditional late 19th-, early 20th-century art in its elegant and contemporary building, although new curators have pushed the institution in a more cutting edge direction. Oh, and since Mr. Frye sold so much meat, it's always free admission.

The **Henry Art Gallery (Map 26)** is the University of Washington's gallery-cum-museum (or the other way around). On permanent display is James Turrell's Skyspace, a very cool enclosed light chamber. **Bellevue Art Museum (Map 45)** was once housed in a chi-chi mall, until it moved across the street into Steven Holl's architectural wonder where it promptly folded. BAM only reopened after reinventing itself as a crafts museum.

Historic Seattle

Wing Luke Museum (Map 8), located in the heart of the International District, is better than ever after its fantastic renovation. Its primary emphasis is on the cultural history of Asian Pacific Islanders, and the museum invites the community to participate in its exhibitions. The **Burke Museum (Map 26)** is the University of Washington's archaeological and ethnographic museum. Here you can see the notorious Kennewick man. The **Nordic Heritage Museum (Map 28)** is dedicated to the history of immigrant Scandinavians—free your inner Norwegian. The **Museum of History and Industry (Map 16)** is a city history museum for Seattle aficionados.

Allentown

Ever wonder what billionaires keep in the basements of their mansions? Paul Allen puts his personal collection on display at two museums in the giant titanium blob at Seattle Center. The **Experience Music Project (Map 15)** invites you to free your inner Jimi with lots of interactive music exhibits; it almost justifies the inflated admission when you get a little percussion or guitar time in. Right next to EMP, the **Science Fiction & Fantasy Hall of Fame (Map 15)** houses *Planet of the Apes* memorabilia and appeals to Seattle's geek-chic set (read: former Microsoft executives).

Plane Fun

In Boeing-obsessed Seattle, airplanes are serious business and **The Museum of Flight (Map 41)** has this topic covered. This is the place to tour the now-defunct Concorde and JFK's Air Force One.

Museums	Address	Phone	Map
Bellevue Art Museum	510 Bellevue Way NE	425-519-0770	45
Burke Museum	17th Ave NE & NE 45th St	206-543-5590	26
The Center for Wooden Boats	1010 Valley St	206-382-2628	16
Center on Contemporary Art (CoCA)	6413 Seaview Ave NW	206-728-1980	2
Chihuly Garden and Glass	305 Harrison St	206-753-4940	15
The Children's Museum	305 Harrison St	206-441-1768	15
Experience Music Project (EMP)	325 5th Ave N	206-367-5483	15
Frye Art Museum	704 Terry Ave	206-622-9250	4
The Henry Art Gallery	15th Ave NE & NE 41st St	206-543-2280	26
Klondike Gold Rush Museum	319 Second Ave S	206-220-4240	7
Log House Museum	3003 61st Ave SW	206-938-5293	35
Museum of Flight	9404 E Marginal Wy S	206-764-5720	41
Nordic Heritage Museum	3014 NW 67th St	206-789-5707	28
Pacific Science Center	200 2nd Ave N	206-443-2001	15
Science Fiction Museum & Hall of Fame	325 5th Ave N	206-770-2700	15
Seattle Art Museum Downtown	1300 1st Ave	206-654-3100	3
Seattle Asian Art Museum	1400 E Prospect St	206-654-3100	17
Seattle Metropolitan Police Museum	317 3rd Ave S	206-748-9991	7
Seattle's Museum of History & Industry	860 Terry Ave	206-324-1126	16
Wing Luke Asian Museum	719 S King St	206-623-5124	8

Seattle may be small by metropolis standards, but we use our space very efficiently. From quaint dives to swanky Belltown wine bars, punk rock to hipster kitsch, in Seattle, anyone can find their scene.

Find Your Thrill on the Hill

If you don't know what kind of vibe you're in the mood for, Capitol Hill has a wide range of destinations, from the sexy red lighting of **Cha Cha (Map 4)** to the hunting lodge chic of **Redwood (Map 4)**, you'll find a cool place to hang out. The Hill is often pigeon-holed as a hipster/homo ghetto, but as long as you're open minded, it really can be all things to all people. At **Pony (Map 4)** every day is Pride Day, meaning you're probably going to see a lot of genitalia and party your ass off. The wing to Pony's wang is the **Wild Rose (Map 4)**, a fun and inclusive lesbian bar with plenty of love for both genders and a haunted bathroom. **Smith (Map 4)** is another hunting lodge-style bar with an enterprising gastropub menu. Seattle loves its speakeasy-style bars what with cagey entrances and enthusiastic cocktails. They're like well-decorated clubhouses. **Knee High Stocking Co (Map 4)** is in an unmarked building on a weird triangular island between two busy streets. But if you feel like making the effort, your palette is richly rewarded. There are only a handful of tables so reservations (by text) are recommended. **Tavern Law (Map 4)** has a speakeasy-within-a-speakeasy called Needle & Thread with extra hoops to jump through for entry. **Pie Bar (Map 4)** wants you to have your pie and drink it too. **Sun Liquor (Map 17)** and **Sun Liquor Distillery (Map 4)** will serve you the greatest cocktails of your life using fresh squeezed juices and their own hooch and they are more than happy to customize. The **Unicorn (Map 4)** is a carnival-themed den of iniquity with an adult arcade called Narwhal in the basement. Both floors serve sugary beverages, an array of corn dogs (with veg options) and more deep-fried junk food than you can shake meat on a stick at. Experience Steampunk salvage chic at **Grim's (Map 4)** and soak up your mason jar cocktails with inventive and reasonably-priced sandwiches. After last call, on the weekends, find the Off the Rez food truck squeezed into a doorway on Pike and they will hook you up with some incredible hangover prevention in the form of frybread tacos.

It's a Live!

The grunge days of flannel and hype may be long gone (thank goodness), but Seattle still has a thriving live music scene. Ground zero for alt-country and twang fans can be found at the **Tractor Tavern (Map 23)**, but if you prefer turntables over pedal steel, then make it over to **Chop Suey (Map 4)** for "live" music. Nearby, **Neumo's (Map 4)** rivals the **Showbox (Map 3, 39)** for booking the latest indie rock sensations, but their sound is definitely more on the dirty side. **The Crocodile (Map 1)** features shows small in size but big in rock. **The Sunset Tavern (Map 23)** is Seattle's best small venue, a friendly joint with red velvet interior that consistently books great up and coming local acts plus a succession of superior touring rockers from abroad. Try **Shadowland**'s **(Map 35)** Tuesday open-mic night to be the first to discover the next Bon Iver. The bands at **Slim's Last Chance (Map 39)** are eclectic and smalltime but usually play something to get you up and dancing off that bowl of chili. **Blue Moon Tavern (Map 25)** conveys a down-and-dirty vibe, booking punk, honky tonk and everything in between. Fremont's **High Dive (Map 24)** is another good spot to check out new (though not necessarily stellar) local talent.

Dive On In

Whether ironic or earnest, one thing Seattle excels in is dive bars. We really know how to make the best of a dark drink hole. Coney Island-themed pinball bar, **Shorty's (Map 1)**, is on the NFT shortlist. Its hot dogs and boozy slushies have the Anthony Bourdain stamp of approval. **The Kraken Bar & Lounge (Map 26)** is very metal, very dirty and your best bet on the Ave for avoiding students. Ballardites would love to keep the **Tin Hat (Map 30)** to themselves, but the word is out about this marvelously mellow bar home to a handful of regulars and some of Sea-town's best tater tots. **The Comet (Map 4)** has been the Prom King of dives since 1948. They have live music and karaoke, but the real show comes from the customers. The only thing you can expect there is a memorable night. **Eastlake Zoo (Map 20)** is perhaps so called because of the eclectic clientele it attracts. Every inch of this vast space is covered in kitch, making it the perfect place for a smashed scavenger hunt. Georgetown's diamond in the rough is the **9lb. Hammer (Map 39)** offering free pool and a peanut shell-covered floor for added authenticity. The same owner also graced South Park with **Loretta's (Map 38)**, a cozy, friendly and economical restaurant and bar with an air of grandpa's rec room. West Seattle's best kept secret is the pirate/nautical themed **Benbow Room (Map 35)** which is tucked into the back of a mid-western comfort food restaurant.

Make Your Own Kind of Music

Seattle is filled with wannabe rock stars, some of which lack the wherewithal to form a band. That's where karaoke comes in handy. And we're not talking about that Gwyneth Paltrow "Duets" crap. Our karaoke is balls out. Some folks even occasionally don costumes add a little choreography to the mix. Often, this sort of dedication makes even the most tone-deaf performances entertaining as hell. Bachelorette parties and other karaoke dabblers usually start at **Ozzie's (Map 15)** or **Hula Hula (Map 1)**. Capitol Hill's **Crescent Lounge (Map 4)** has one of the more colorful crowds and sings it loud and proud every damn night of the week, much to their neighbors' chagrin. Everybody loves a karaoke room, but **Rock Box (Map 4)** takes it to the next level with their clean and classy rooms to accommodate nearly any party size from a huge birthday gathering to a single, solitary crooner. Whet your whistle with their Japanese-themed food and drink menu and don't forget to make advanced reservations, especially on the weekends. West Seattle's go-to is **Tug Inn (Map 37)**. Sing at **Monkey Pub (Map 26)** every Tuesday, Friday and Sunday. This beloved dive has a gritty, punk rock vibe and is refreshingly light on student infiltration. **The Twilight Exit (Map 5)** has moved their 70s dive shtick three times and their loyal patrons have always moved with them, singing their hearts out every Sunday night. Greenwood's **Baranof (Map 33)** has karaoke every night of the week, attracting ironic amateurs, intense regulars and everyone in between. If you get hungry, they have jello shots.

Pleased to Meat You

Do you love waiting in line while a power-mad bouncer hold the fate of your evening in his hands? Does your idea of a good time involve bumping genitals with strangers and rolling the dice on roofied drinks? In that case, you'll want to head straight to the breeding grounds of Pioneer Square where any bar can turn into a club at the drop of a white baseball cap. For those who prefer dancing on a bar or table top, check out **Cowgirls, Inc (Map 7)** or any number of bars in the dude-happy Pioneer Square triangle. The other white stretch-hummer lined strip is along 1st Avenue in Belltown. **Tia Lou (Map 1)** and **Foundation Nightclub (Map 1)** will make sure you don't go home alone, even if you want to. **Aston Manor (Map 39)** brings Vegas nightclub elitism to SoDo.

Come Dancing

If the frat party annex isn't your scene, but you still have happy feet, join the welcoming party scene at **Neighbours (Map 4)** This captain of the Capitol Hill Old Guard breaks out 80s, house, funk and mashups providing the opportunity to get your freak on any night of the week. **ReBar (Map 2)** has some very sexy dance nights in addition to cabaret, fringe theater and other alternative variety shows so check their calendar for details. **Mercury @ Machinewerks (Map 4)** is a private, invite-only goth club. So if your feet only get happy to Joy Division or Skinny Puppy, you might want to strike up a conversation with that pierced-up guy on the bus who wears his black trench coat year-round. **Lo-Fi (Map 2)** has a non-exclusive goth night on occasion but is best known for its super fun Emerald City Soul Club on second Saturdays. Want to hone your skills before hitting the town? You can take tango or swing lessons at the **Century Ballroom (Map 4)**.

The Kids Are Alright

When your old uncle NFT was a youth, there wasn't much in the way of an all-ages scene. But thanks to the efforts of **The Vera Project** (www.theveraproject.org), the oppressive Teen Dance Ordinance was repealed in 2002 and since then, the under 21 crowd has been able to enjoy a nightlife outside of their dorm room or house party. **The Vera Project (Map 15)** has its own venue with shows as well as arts programs and plenty of other activities that keep little hands from getting idle. Major venues like **Key Arena (Map 15)** and the **CenturyLink Field Event Center (Map 7)** are always open to all ages as are **The Moore Theatre (Map 3)** and **Paramount Theatre (Map 3)**, but their calendar isn't always geared toward a younger crowd. **Bumbershoot** (bumbershoot. org) is an annual music and arts fest that allows you to get in a year's worth of live music over Labor Day weekend. **El Corazon (Map 2)**, **Neumo's (Map 4)** and the **Showbox (Map 3, 39)** have loads of all ages shows, putting the grumpy legal drinkers in booze-dispensing bullpens while the kids have direct access to the stage. **The Crocodile (Map 1)**, **Dimitriou's Jazz Alley (Map 2)**, and **Skylark (Map 36)** have occasional all-ages shows as well. **Neptune Theatre (Map 26)** adds alternative comedy shows to their terrific entertainment calendar. Of course there's always a wealth of good cinema, make-out opportunities at the **Seattle Laser Dome (Map 15)** and allowance squandering at **GameWorks (Map 3)** to make keeping curfew a challenge.

24-Hour Party People

Seattle can be tough on night owls. But if you're still raring to go at three am, there are a few options, most of which involve greasy spoon grub. The **5 Point (Map 1)** has a solid 24-hour breakfast menu as well as a famous view of the Space Needle from the men's room urinal. The **Mecca (Map 15)** is the 5 Point's nearby little sister. Georgetown's **Square Knot Diner (Map 39)** isn't the best breakfast food you can get at 3 a.m., but it'll do in a pinch. **Beth's (Map 30)** 12-egg omelets and bottomless hash browns might make you sicker than the booze you're trying to soak up, but you'll have fun drawing dirty pictures on their paper tablecloths. For a classier after-hours meal, try **13 Coins (Map 2)** for some surf-and-turf that is guaranteed to bring on weird dreams. **Lost Lake Cafe & Lounge (Map 4)** is Capitol Hill's long overdue replacement to Minnie's, serving an incredibly diverse menu with a Twin Peaksian ambiance.

It's safe to say that Seattle has comfortably settled into its Big Boy Britches when it comes to restaurants. We have nationally recognized (and respected) chefs, many of whom have cultivated their own empires. One could argue that our food scene has begun to outshine our music scene (sorry, Macklemore). We specialize in the casually upscale affair and, while not everyone succeeds with the business model, many of our restaurateurs manage to knock it out of thepark. Tom Douglas (**Dahlia Lounge (Map 1); Lola (Map 1); Serious Pie (Map 1, 2); Cuoco (Map 2); Palace Kitchen (Map 1)**; ad infinitum) is the Coen Brothers of chefs. Each of his restaurants is a complete departure from his other work, yet there's a pleasing familiarity to them. The ones that succeed are so good, you forget there were every any bad ones. Ruling at his side are Ethan Stowell (**How to Cook a Wolf (Map 13); Tavolata (Map 1); Staple & Fancy (Map 23)**), Maria Hines (**Agrodolce (Map 24); Tilth (Map 24); Golden Beetle (Map 23)**) and Matt Dillon (**Sitka & Spruce (Map 4); Bar Sajor (Map 7); Bar Ferd'nand (Map 4)**). Linda Derschang (**Smith (Map 18); Oddfellows (Map 4); Bait Shop (Map 17)**) stands apart with her hipster restaurant kingdom, but you'll get your best meal at **Tallulah's (Map 18)** with meat-accented vegetables for dinner and sophisticated toasts at brunch. There are also plenty of successful one-offs, like the farm-to-plate genius of **Terra Plata (Map 4)** and the cozy, inventive flavors of Belltown's **Tilikum Place Cafe (Map 1)**. The national eco-friendly sustainable, free-range organic craze has long been a founding principle of Northwest cuisine, which relies on and reveres locally sourced ingredients. Flavor profiles range from New American (whatever that means) to Pan-Asian flair to rustic Italian to provincial French. But often, it's a pick n' mix of vivacious victuals. With all this awesome grub around, you might want to start biking to work.

Seafood

Because of Seattle's proximity to the Pacific, there's no wonder seafood seems to pop up on every menu in town. But selectivity is key. **Ray's Boathouse (Map 28)** is a venerable waterfront landmark that's been nailing it for decades, with a prime location and a slightly older crowd (including, yes, lots of tourists). **Ivar's Salmon House (Map 25)** is the classic place to take out of town guests because the only thing better than the chowder is the view. For a true taste of Pike Place, go straight to **Matt's in the Market (Map 3)**. If you get a jonesing for lubrication by fish and chips, **Spud on Alki (Map 35)** is traditional, but **Pike Street Fish Fry (Map 4)** ups the ante with late-night hours, jars of homemade pickles, and fancy-schmancy sauces. **The Walrus and the Carpenter (Map 23)** has garnered many a devoted follower, not unlike the subjects of Lewis Carroll's famous poem. If you'd like to spite the locavore movement, **RockCreek (Map 24)** is in your corner, flying their offerings in from all around the world like aquatic, edible rock stars.

Seafood, Nippon-style

Hardcore pescatarians like their fish raw and there's no shortage of sushi restaurants to accommodate them. It's rumored that Trey Parker bought a condo in Belltown just so he could take sushi-eating mini vacations whenever he wanted. Purists swear by **Nishino (Map 19)**, the eponymous establishment of Tatsu Nishino (a former disciple of famed Nobu Matuhisa). Put your meal in his skilled hands omakase-style for a spectacular experience. **Kisaku (Map 31)** is where the sushi chefs eat. In West Seattle, try the chef specials at **Mashiko (Map 35)**. **Chiso (Map 24)** and **Liberty (Map 18)** take sushi for a spin in hip, modern settings, inventing new rolls that are, more often than not, very oishii indeed. The ID offers more traditional sushi experiences, particularly at **Maneki (Map 8)**, Seattle's oldest sushi bar. The U District's **Village Sushi (Map 26)** gives a solid performance on the cheap, complete with an on-the-ball sake sommelier. For the newly initiated, **Blue C Sushi (Map 24, 26)** rolls out cheap and crowd-pleasing dishes on a gimmicky (though admittedly fun) conveyor belt system. They love experimenting with tempura batter, cream cheese, and vegetables, making it a great place to bring picky eaters and vegetarians alike. The proprietor of the eponymous **Shiro's (Map 1)** literally wrote the book on sushi (it's titled *Shiro: Wit, Wisdom and Recipes from a Sushi Pioneer*) and the dude knows his shoyu.

Classy Joints

Seattle is infamous for its constant state of casual dress. But you can still find establishments that request a bit more refinement from their diners. Sometimes, it feels good to step out of the yoga pants and into the lap of luxury. The Grande Dame is **Canlis (Map 13)**, a Seattle fixture since 1950 with a view to die for, impeccable formal service (crumb brush, bro), and spectacular food. Canlis is the ultimate Treat Yo Self. At **Art of the Table (Map 24)**, what started as a weekend supper club has grown into a hospitable and unforgettable celebration of all things edible. **Miyabi 45th (Map 25)** is a fine dining soba noodle house where you can feel comforted and pampered simultaneously. **Palisade (Map 11)** is breathtaking inside and out with the meals to match. **Cascina Spinasse (Map 4)** is extremely hyped Italian but it's all true, and worth the considerable money and effort required to eat there. **La Medusa (Map 40)** is the crown jewel of Columbia City. If you want an elegant meal but can't find a sitter, bring the kiddos and give them a taste of the high life. **Le Pichet (Map 3)** is all class without the cost and about as French as you can get without feeling like an asshole.

No Animals, Please

If your dietary preferences don't involve any fuzzy animals, or even their byproducts, we've got you covered. Seattle does meat-free so well, even the carnivorous have been known to relish the cruelty-free options. The cream of the crop is the fine dining at **Plum Vegan Bistro (Map 4)**. Their creamy mac & yease could only be the result of a nefarious supernatural bargain. **Cafe Flora (Map 19)** is slightly less polished, but nonetheless a very pleasant place to take your veggie-skeptical great aunt for brunch (they also cater to the gluten-free crowd). The U District is an oasis for the penny-pinching vegan. <u>**Wayward Vegan Cafe**</u> **(Map 31)** (no relation to **Roosevelt's vegan-friendly coffee shop**) is run by semi-militants, but if you can get past the gruesome pamphlets, they will treat you to the best tofu scramble and biscuits n' gravy in the city. They also sell an array of mind-blowing pies by the slice or whole. The college crowd loves **Araya's Vegetarian Place (Map 26)**, a tasty faux-meat Thai joint with an excellent lunch buffet and Asian-inspired breakfast pastries. Vegans needn't be deprived of the late-night joys of pizza: **Pizza Pi (Map 32)** has somehow cracked the dairy-free pizza code. The vegan donuts at **Mighty-O (Map 31)** rival anything on the **Top Pot** roster. Find them at their flagship store or in pastry cases around the city. For the comfort that only bar food provides, head to the gritty **Georgetown Liquor Company (Map 39)**, where you can dig into flavor-packed meatless sandwiches and Super Nintendo, quite literally, on the wrong side of the tracks.

More Meat, Please

If you find yourself agreeing with Ted Nugent on food matters, Seattle has your back there too. If you aren't lucky enough to work downtown, it's worth a personal day to grab a glorious sandwich and stock up on Armando Batali's amazing pork products at **Salumi (Map 7)**. West Seattle's **The Swinery (Map 35)** adds burgers and brunch to the shop-and-dine business model. **Quinn's (Map 4)** was at the forefront of the foie gras revival. To help you reach artery blockage bliss, order the double bacon deluxe at **Red Mill Burgers (Map 11, 30)**. **Rancho Bravo (Map 4, 25)** makes the most delicious brain, tripe, or tongue tacos this side of the border (though if you're in mixed company,

they have a terrific veggie menu too). **Ezell's Famous Chicken (Map 5)** is so good that Oprah literally has it flown from the Emerald City straight to her constantly fluctuating waistline. It doesn't really get any more Seattle than **Damn the Weather (Map 7)**—a gastropub housed inside a historical Pioneer Square building, where a former Fleet Fox serves cheeky cocktails alongside cured meats galore and fried pig skins for dessert. **Ma'ono Fried Chicken & Whiskey (Map 35)** offers just that, but with a Pacific Islands twist. Don't tell Ezell, but some say it's the best fried chicken in Seattle.

Palate Passport

Like most U.S. metropolitan cities, the cuisines of Mexico, Italy, Thailand, China, Vietnam, and Japan are well represented. However, the adventurous foodie can find plenty of other cultures from which to sample. At **Vostok Dumpling House (Map 4)**, you'll feel like you're back in the USSR (minus the oppressive influence of Putin). **Mamnoon (Map 4)** will get you hooked on their Syrian and Lebanese flavors. Dress up and dine in or do takeaway to enjoy in your pajamas. For more casual (and exceedingly vegetarian friendly) Lebanese bites, stop by **Cafe Munir (Map 23)**. People lost their shinola when Caribbean sandwich institution, **Paseo (Map 24)**, closed unexpectedly. Some super fans took over and did a decent job copying the menu, but the flavors will never live up to the original. Fortunately, you don't have to settle, because the former owners took their celebrated recipes with them to their new joint,**Un Bien (Map 29)**. In West Seattle, the **Salvadorean Bakery (Map 37)** specializes in fast food from waaaay south of the border. Save room for their decadent tres leches cake. Fans of Malaysian fare will be pleased as punch about **Malay Satay Hut (Map 46)**. Cambodian food is all about the noodles at **Phnom Penh (Map 8)**. Inside the dusty-pink, windowless walls of the mysterious**Marrakesh Moroccan Restaurant (Map 1)**, all the romance and intrigue of Morocco comes alive. There are numerous Ethiopian spots clustered around Seattle University, but two places stand well above the rest: **Enat Ethiopian (Map 34)** is widely considered the city's best but **Cafe Selam (Map 5)** has rightfully earned a legion of devotees including a disproportionate number of cabbies.

Cheap Eats

A high concentration of higher learning institutions means droves of intoxicated and hungry students prowling for food they can buy with their Coinstar winnings and leftover laundry change. Good thing there's an endless supply of local restaurants for the hard up, hungry, or hung over—with no unnecessary sacrifice in taste. At **Aladdin Gyro-Cery (Map 26)**, soak up booze the British way with a lovely kebab or falafel. (Be leery of the inferior imposter **Aladdin Falafel Corner**, a couple blocks north.) Hill trolls swear by **Hot Mama's Pizza (Map 4)**, where a gargantuan, foldable slice costs less than a bus ride. Even in Seattle, pizza proprietors endeavor to be the most New York-style, and **Big Mario's (Map 4)** makes a strong case. A native Neapolitan, the Vellotti family business gained notoriety in the Big Apple before bringing their bona fide pies westward. On the lighter side, Pho (pronounced "fuh") is one of the most mouthwatering meals you can get for a fiver. Seattleites couldn't face the winter without this eminently filling and fragrant Vietnamese noodle soup. **Pho Cyclo (Map 17, 39)** ladles out a most intriguingly flavored version, but the ubiquitous **Than Brothers (Map 17, 23, 26, 30, 35)** chain undercuts the rest and throws in a free cream puff with every bowl). For gourmet sandwiches on the cheap, pick up a Brown Box lunch from **Le Fournil (Map 20)**, which includes an expertly brewed espresso and one of their amazing French pastries. If a late-night craving for the lovably limp burgers you downed as a kid proves unshakable, local staple, **Dick's (Map 15, 17, 25, 33, 34)**, will sling you a paper sack full for not much more than your leftover change from that evening's bar-hopping.

Take Out

For a city averaging 140 days of rain each year, Seattle has woefully few food options. East Coasters are often appalled. Given the limitations, we usually just sigh and order a pizza. **Pagliacci (Map 15, 17, 26, 35, 45)** or **Flying Squirrel (Map 31, 40)** are your best bets there. If you want something else, you'll need to muster up enough energy to pick it up yourself. In the U District **Thai Tom (Map 26)** is usually packed, but you can always call in an order. The crack-like sauces at **Taste of India (Map 31)** will make you a regular. **Kedai Makan's (Map 4)** Malaysian street food is one of the best meat and carb based alcohol sponges in the city (and open till 2 am on weekends). However, Seattle isn't completely devoid of delivery. Some of Seattle's best Thai restaurants will provide dinner without the need for pants. A lot of Thai food is created equal, but **Savatdee (Map 31)**, serving the U District and surrounding areas, is unmatched in its awesomeness and even has a special Laotian menu to expand your horizons. **Judy Fu's Snappy Dragon (Map 34)** will bring UD and Maple Leaf residents their divine dumplings and hand-shave noodles, but be prepared to wait as long as 90 minutes for your food (pick-up is faster). **In the Bowl (Map 4)** will also deliver its delectable vegetarian noodle bowls to those not willing to vie for one of their scant seats.

Food Trucks

Time was, some silly law made it prohibitive as hell to open a food truck in Seattle. Until 2011, sidewalk vendors could sell only hot dogs, popcorn and espresso unless they wanted to shell out a ton of cash and jump through some daunting hoops. But thanks to new regulations, our very own mobile food scene has emerged and now there are so many trucks (over 180) that someone had to make a **website** (www. seattlefoodtruck.com) to keep track of them all. We've got sweets, savories and every kind of taco and sandwich imaginable. Some of the more successful trucks have opened brick-and-mortar restaurants to keep up with the demand (**Skillet**, **El Camion**, **Marination Mobile**) while several popular and established restaurants (**Plum**, **Ezell's**, **Top Pot**) have taken to the streets to spread the love around. Other favorites include the life-changing fry bread tacos of **Off the Rez** (available for lunch or the perfect weekend drunk snack). **314 Pie** bakes locally sourced ingredients into savory pies with cinnamon sugar "fries" (more pie crust!) for dessert. **Where Ya At** peddles authentic and lovingly made Cajun cuisine. My Sweet Lil Cakes takes chicken and waffles to the next level (it involves a stick and maple butter dipping sauce). There are two meat and two veggie options each day. Save room for more waffles for dessert.

Essential Mobile Food Trucks

BeanFish (Taiyaki) www.beanfish.net

Beloved Mexico (Mexican) www.belovedmexico.com

Bread and Circuses (Ecelectic/Gastropub)
eatbreadandcircuses.com

Brown Bag Baguette (Vietnamese Sandwiches)
brownbagbaguette.com

Caravan Crepes (Crepes) caravanseattle.com

Cheese Wizards (Sandwiches) wizardsofcheese.com

Cotigo (Mexican) www.contigoseattle.com

Dante's Inferno Hot Dogs (Hot Dogs)
dantesinfernodogs.com

Ezell's Express (Fried Chicken)
twitter.com/EzellsExpress1

Fez! (Mediterranean) twitter.com/fezonwheels

Fish Basket (Fish & Chips) www.fishbasketnw.com

Hallava Falafel (Mediterranean)
www.hallavafalafel.com

Happy Grillmore (Sandwiches)
www.happygrillmore.com

I Love My GFF (Gluten Free) www.ilovemygff.com

Jemil's Big Easy (Cajun) jemilsbigeasy.com

Marination Mobile (Hawaiian/Korean)
www.marinationmobile.com

My Sweet Lil Cakes (Sweet and Savory Waffles)
mysweetlilcakes.com

No Bones About It (Vegan) nobonestruck.com

Nosh (Eclectic) www.noshthetruck.com

Now Make Me a Sandwich (Sandwiches)
www.nowmakemeasandwich.com

Off the Rez (Native American)
www.offthereztruck.com

Outside the Box (Paleo) www.eat-otb.com

Papa Bois (Carribean) www.papaboisfood.com

Pinky's Kitchen (BBQ) www.pinkyskitchen.com

Plum Vegan Burgers + More (Vegan)
www.plumbistro.com

Snout & Co (Cuban) www.snoutandco.com

Skillet (Seasonal) skilletstreetfood.com

Street Treats (Sweets) www.streettreatswa.com

Streetzeria (Pizza) www.streetzeria.com

Tat's Truck (Sandwiches) tatstruck.com

Where Ya At Matt (Cajun) www.whereyaatmatt.com

Xplosive Truck (Vietnamese/Filipino)
www.xplosivemobilefoodtruck.com

Seattle is nothing if not eclectic, and that's good news for all you shopaholics. Whether you're named in the Gates family trust or scrounging for dollars, Seattle provides plenty of opportunities for retail therapy. If you're looking to do some one-stop shopping, but can't stand the soul-killing atmosphere of a mall, there are a number of funky and/or chic commercial strips in Seattle. Get yourself to: the Pike/ Pine Corridor (**Map 4**), Broadway on Capitol Hill (**Map 17**), Ballard Avenue (**Map 23**), 36th Street & Fremont Avenue (**Map 24**), University Way ("The Ave") in the U District (**Map 26**), and pretty much anywhere in Belltown (**Map 1**).

Look Sharp

Some people think Seattle dresses too casually and perhaps they're correct. But what we lack in formality, we make up for in style. No matter where you are in this city, you will never be far from a cute boutique or funky thrift shop. If money is no object, you'll find some hip duds at **Mishu Boutique (Map 17, 24)** and **Ian (Map 3)**. Fellas will want to check out the post-mod threads **Kuhlman (Map 1)** and **Recess (Map 32)**. It's **Leroy Men's Wear (Map 3)** all the way for fedoras and Zoot suits in every color of the rainbow. Rebels without a cause will not want to miss the jackets and boots at **Insurrection (Map 30)**. For a more mainstream look, it's all about the original **Nordstrom (Map 3)**. Do moths fly out of your wallet whenever you open it? Try **Buffalo Exchange (Map 23, 26)** and **Crossroads Trading Company (Map 17, 26)**, where you can buy and sell used, fashionable clothes from name brand designers. It's never too early to get your baby into Johnny Cash. You can score hipster-themed clothing in baby and toddler sizes at **Bootyland (Map 4)** and the slightly more affordable **Boston St (Map 1)**.

Play that Funky Music

Some cities have let the Internet render their music stores obsolete. But in Seattle, independent record shops are thriving. Maybe that whole grunge thing wasn't so bad after all. Those who know the sound of a record scratch outside of movie trailers may be interested in **Spin Cycle (Map 17)**, **Georgetown Records (Map 39)** and **Jive Time Records** Records (**Map 24**). **Bop Street Records (Map 23)** is known for its amazing selection at exorbitant prices. Discover further relics at **Golden Oldies Records Tapes and CDs (Map 25)**. **Sonic Boom (Map 23)** and **Easy Street Records (Map 35)** are great places to see a live band and buy their music simultaneously. **Singles Going Steady (Map 1)** and **Everyday Music (Map 20)** specialize in bands from a time when things like record labels and "selling out" mattered. If you prefer to make your own music, you can get your gear cheap at **Trading Musician (Map 31)**.

Don't Toy With Me

We take a lot of things seriously in the Emerald City, but we're never too old for fun and games. Quality baubles and gadgets for the pre-pubescent crowd are easy to score in Seattle, thanks to progressively minded toy stores like **Magic Mouse (Map 7)** and **Top Ten Toys (Map 3, 30)**, where cheap plastic crap is an endangered species. If you dream of space exploration but Huntsville, AL seems impossibly far, **Greenwood Space Travel Supply (Map 30)** is a fine substitute. Providing all of your tiny cosmonaut needs are an enthusiastic crew of folks still sore about that whole Pluto demotion thing. Best of all, proceeds go entirely to tutoring non-profit, 826 Seattle. If you think toys were better in the past, **Max and Quinn's Atomic Boy's Shop-O-Rama (Map 35)** agree with you. Stock up on potato guns, slingshots and other wholesome toys for the child in your life, instead of that iPad they asked for. But forget about those unappreciative money drains. This is a city full of adults in various stages of arrested development and they demand to be catered to. Enter **Schmancy (Map 3)**, a cozy boutique for vinyl and plush toys made for whimsical folk of voting age who need a cuddly T-bone steak doll or a sock monkey to get them through the night. Head out to Wallingford to **Archie McPhee's (Map 24)**, a veritable supermarket of kitschy gag gifts and other wacky wares for adults who miss the thrill that only whoopee cushions and potato guns can provide. **Card Kingdom (Map 23)**—"the ultimate in lawful good times"—is the ultimate for anyone who owns dice with more than six sides. You can test any game in their adjacent Cafe Mox or become King of the Elves in a D &D tournament in their back room. Speaking of adults and toys, **Babeland (Map 4)** up on Capitol Hill offers an utterly shame-free zone to casually shop for all manner of stimulating marital (or otherwise) aids—dildos, vibrators, leather whips, silicone sleeves, and how-to books are available in a clean, well-lit atmosphere with helpful sex-positive salespeople. Oh, didn't think we'd go there, did you?

Eat, Drink, and Spend Money

Pike Place Market (Map 3) is unbeatable when it comes to fresh seafood; just don't go to the guys throwing fish around. That's for tourists, which you are not. Go to Harry at **Pure Food Fish (Map 3)**. While you're down in the market load up on cheese at **Beecher's (Map 3)** and the myriad fresh dairy products at **Pike Place Creamery (Map 3)**. Save room for a craft soda (with or without booze) from **Rachel's Ginger Beer (Map 3)**. If you don't eat your meat, you can't have any pudding. **Salumi Artisan Cured Meats (Map 7)** does a fine job of keeping your carnivorous cravings at bay. Around here, we like to keep our fridges and cellars stocked with alcohol to get us through the long, wet winters. **Vino Verite (Map 17)** has the best wine selection. **Bottleworks (Map 25)** specializes in beer, filling every nook and cranny of their small store with international options. **Wine World and Spirits (Map 25)** is your one-stop shop for all things inebriating including an impressive locally distilled liquor section and all the accoutrements you can shake a swizzle stick at. Got a sweet tooth? **The**

Confectionary (Map 26) in U Village is your upscale candy boutique with a mouthwatering hand-made chocolate case, the underrated joys of salted black licorice and even some lowbrow favorites. That long line at Molly Moon's isn't worth it, especially when some of the best gelato in town is just up the road at Fainting Goat (Map 25). They do gelato the Turkish way. Don't knock their signature flavor, made from goat milk, until you try it. Pig's Peace Sanctuary owns Vegan Haven (Map 32) a small store that is packed to the gills with cruelty-free goods from frozen pizza to lip balm and even the means to enforce your beliefs onto your pets. Uwajimaya (Map 8, 46) is a wonderland of Asian food and gifts that can't be missed. Rising Sun Farms (Map 32) brings the rural roadside produce stand to the big city. Speaking of farms, there's a farmer's market in pretty much every neighborhood but the standouts are the University District Farmers Market (Map 26) on Saturdays and the Ballard Farmers Market (Map 23) on Sundays. Both happen year-round, rain or shine. Melrose Market (Map 4) made the smart play and put a roof over their vendors. Among those keeping the residents of Capitol Hill stocked up on locally sourced, organic foodstuffs: The Calf and Kid, Rain Shadow Meats, Marigold and Mint flowers and produce.

Pot

In 2014, Washington made history as one of the first states (along with Colorado) to end marijuana prohibition. The journey from legalization to retail has been a lengthy and grueling and the cannabis landscape will no doubt continue to morph (hopefully for the better), but here's the rundown on the retail experience in its current incarnation: Adults 21+ show ID to a guy at the door who resembles an extra from Road House. You then enter a windowless building where you are greeted by a "budtender" (seriously), who gives you the lay of the land. You may purchase up to 1 ounce of "flower" (née weed), 16 ounces of infused edibles, 72 ounces of liquid, and 7 grams of marijuana concentrates. You pay your 37% sales tax on a $12-20 per gram base price. They place your goodies in a paper bag, and you proceed directly to the exit. The process retains an air of sordidness, made more so by the ruling that stores can't be within 1000 feet of a school, public transit center, public park, day care, arcade, or library. In other words, most of the stores are in sketchy or desolate areas. Now, you'll probably want to toke up. As Vincent Vega would say, "it's legal, but it's not 100% legal." The law bans "public consumption," meaning the only place you can smoke is in your residence—so long as your name is on the deed. Also, it's illegal to take it out of state.

The lines at the stores have subsided and supply and demand has leveled so buying weed legally has actually started to become the rather pleasant experience we were promised. People can afford to be picky about where they shop and even get uppity about the little things on that website that rhymes with "help." Uncle Ike's Pot Shop (Map 5) is the best bet for the cost-conscious everyman. They update their menu daily online and the budtenders know their stuff. It reads like a wine list at a cool bistro. Ganja Goddess (Map 39) is for the folks looking for the shopping "experience". The all-female budtender staff is renowned for its savvy and savior faire alike. The space itself has a very hipster, gastropub feel to it with exposed brick and low lights. Their edibles include high-end items like macaroons and sea salt chocolates. Cannabis City (Map 39) was the first retail store in the city, which ended up being a curse as much as a blessing for them. Now, with other places shouldering some of the demand, they've become a decent little shop; prices include tax so you're not surprised by a huge gouging at checkout. Eastsiders wanna get high, too. At BelMar (Map 46) they can do it without having to drive into icky Seattle and shop with the common people.

They Don't Make 'Em Like They Used To

Let's face it. Things were better in the past. Fortunately, many Seattle shop owners agree with you. Find Formica galore and your new favorite old easy chair at Fremont Vintage Mall (Map 24) or Space Oddity Vintage Furniture (Map 23). If Mad Men has got you longing for golden age fashions, try Pretty Parlor (Map 17), carefully curated by Ms. Anna Banana with a bonus section for the men folk. She supplements her always-impressive inventory with clothes from some of Seattle's best vintage-style designers. Diva Dollz (Map 3) is where Bettie Page would have shopped and they also have cute designs in plus sizes. Valley of Roses (Map 26) has threads for men and women, and frequently cycles through their inventory. The customer service oriented owner hides treasures all over the store, including the clearance rack. Vintage Angel Company (Map 24) spans several decades. Try not to get too depressed about the 90s section. If you prefer quantity to quality or are looking for pieces for a Halloween costume, Atlas Clothing Co (Map 4) or Red Light (Map 26) are your best bets.

Mallrats

If you must patronize a mall, it's good to know which to hit and which to avoid. Let's start with the malls to avoid. Westlake Center (Map 3) is well known as the most useless mall in Seattle. It is one of the two stops on the monorail, which makes it a bona fide tourist trap. Pacific Place is your other downtown option, but with all the Tiffanys, Club Monacos, and J. Jills, really only Amazon and Microsoft executives can afford to shop there. The mall for the masses is Northgate (Map 34), appealing to the simple folk who enjoy the mainstream pleasures of The Gap, Macy's, JC Penney, and Express. Somewhere in between Northgate and Pacific Place is University Village (Map 26) with shops like the Apple Store, Eileen Fisher, and Lululemon. It is outdoors, but they provide shoppers with free yellow umbrellas while they stroll around.

Street Index

Street Index

Street	Page	Grid
NE 107th Ln	48	B2
107th Pl NE	48	A1/B1
107th Pl SE	43	B1
NE 107th Pl		
(10600-12899)	48	B1/B2
(16400-16499)	49	B2
SW 107th Pl	37	C2
N 107th St	33	B2
NE 107th St		
(1200-4899)	34	B1/B2
(12100-12399)	48	B2
(16500-18399)	49	B2
NW 107th St	33	B1/B2
S 107th St		
(1-2198)	38	C1/C2
(4640-5099)	41	C2
SW 107th St		
(600-1399)	38	C1
(1400-4299)	37	C1/C2
NE 107th Way	49	B2
SW 107th Way	37	C2
108th Ave NE		
(1-5999)	45	A2/B2/C2
(6000-13337)	48	A1/B1/C1
108th Ave SE		
(1-277)	45	C2
(278-6499)	43	A1/B1/C1
108th Ct NE	48	A1
NE 108th Ct	49	B2
NE 108th Ln	48	B2
108th Pl NE		
(3400-3599)	45	A2
(6200-11199)	48	A1/C1
NE 108th Pl		
(2500-2699)	34	B1
(12400-12899)	48	B2
(15100-16699)	49	B1/B2
S 108th Pl	38	C1
NE 108th St		
(1000-2399)	34	B1
(10500-13199)	48	B1/B2
NW 108th St	33	B1
S 108th St	38	C1/C2
SW 108th St		
(1-1199)	38	C1
(3000-4199)	37	C1/C2
NE 108th Way	49	B2
109th Ave	45	C2
109th Ave NE		
(900-5899)	45	A2/B2/C2
(11200-13298)	48	A1
109th Ave SE		
(100-919)	45	C2
(933-6628)	43	A1/B1/C1
109th Ct NE	48	A1
NE 109th Ct	49	B2
NE 109th Ln	48	B2
109th Pl NE		
(2400-4733)	45	A2/B2
(11100-11199)	48	A1
NE 109th Pl	48	B2
SW 109th Pl	38	C1
N 109th St	33	B2
NE 109th St		
(3900-4099)	34	B2
(10400-12699)	48	B1/B2
(15400-18633)	49	B1/B2
S 109th St	41	C2
SW 109th St		
(400-499)	38	C1
(2500-4399)	37	C1/C2
NE 109th Way	49	B2
110th Ave NE		
(1-5999)	45	A2/B2/C2
(6200-13099)	48	A1/B1/C1
110th Ave SE		
(1-599)	45	C2
(900-6199)	43	A1/B1/C1
NE 110th Ct	48	B2
110th Ln NE	48	A1
NE 110th Ln	48	B2
110th Pl NE		
(900-3899)	45	A2/C2
(9400-9429)	48	B2
110th Pl SE	45	C2
NE 110th Pl		
(12400-13199)	48	A2/B2
(15100-15499)	49	B1
S 110th Pl	38	C2
SW 110th Pl		
(400-799)	38	C1
(2800-2999)	37	C2
N 110th St	33	B2
NE 110th St		
(2500-4699)	34	B1/B2
(10000-12699)	48	B1/B2
(15600-16516)	49	B1/B2
NW 110th St	33	B2
S 110th St		
(100-199)	38	C1
(2400-2649)	41	C1
SW 110th St		
(100-798)	38	C1
(1601-3799)	37	C1/C2
NE 110th Way	49	B2
111th Ave NE		
(200-5299)	45	A2/B2/C2
(6000-13249)	48	—
111th Ave SE		
(100-813)	45	C2
(2500-5849)	43	A1/B1/C1
111th Ct NE	48	B2
NE 111th Ct	49	B1
111th Ln NE	48	A2
NE 111th Ln	48	A2
111th Pl NE	48	A2/C2
111th Pl SE	43	A1/C1
NE 111th Pl	48	A1/A2
S 111th Pl	41	C1
SW 111th Pl		
(400-499)	38	C1
(2800-2899)	37	C2
NE 111th St		
(1000-1199)	34	B1
(11600-11699)	48	A2
(15700-16599)	49	B1/B2
S 111th St		
(500-599)	38	C2
(4800-4899)	41	C2
SW 111th St	37	C1/C2
112th Ave NE		
(1-5299)	45	A2/B2/C2
(6000-13289)	48	A2/B2/C2
112th Ave SE		
(1-699)	45	C2
(700-6799)	43	A1/B1/C1
112th Ct NE	48	B2
NE 112th Ct	49	B2
112th Pl NE		
(5800-5999)	46	A1
(11400-12899)	48	A2
NE 112th Pl	48	A1/A2
SW 112th Pl		
(400-499)	38	C1
(3300-3449)	37	C2
N 112th St	33	B2
NE 112th St		
(100-4999)	34	B1/B2
(10001-13199)	48	A1/A2
(15600-16299)	49	B1/B2
NW 112th St	33	B2
S 112th St		
(1-2099)	38	C1/C2
(2200-5099)	41	C1/C2
SW 112th St		
(1-1399)	38	C1
(1400-3799)	37	C1/C2
112th Way NE	48	A2
NE 112th Way	49	B2
113th Ave NE		
(3600-3999)	46	A1
(6100-12399)	48	A2/C2
113th Ave SE	43	B1
113th Ct NE	48	B2
NE 113th Ct		
(12600-12699)	48	A2
(15600-16299)	49	A1/A2
113th Ln NE	48	B2
SW 113th Ln	38	C1
113th Pl NE		
(5300-5399)	46	A1
(8800-13199)	48	A2/B2
113th Pl SE	43	C1
N 113th Pl	33	B2
NE 113th Pl	48	A1/A2
NW 113th Pl	33	B2
SW 113th Pl	38	C1
N 113th St	33	B2
NE 113th St		
(900-4799)	34	B1/B2
(10000-13199)	48	A1/A2
(16500-16699)	49	B2
NW 113th St	33	B2
S 113th St		
(2000-2099)	38	C2
(3900-5099)	41	C1/C2
SW 113th St		
(1300-1399)	38	C1
(3200-3399)	37	C2
113th Way NE	48	B2
NE 113th Way	49	B2
114th Ave NE		
(200-5999)	46	A1/B1/C1
(6100-11798)	48	A2/B2/C2
114th Ave SE	43	A1/C1
114th Ct NE	48	A2
NE 114th Ct		
(11500-11529)	48	A2
(15800-15899)	49	A1
114th Dr NE	48	A2
114th Ln NE	48	A2
114th Pl NE	48	A2/B2
114th Pl SE	43	C1
NE 114th Pl	48	A1/A2
NW 114th Pl	33	B1
S 114th Pl	38	C2
SW 114th Pl	38	C1
N 114th St	33	B2
NE 114th St		
(901-1199)	34	B1
(10400-12799)	48	A1/A2
S 114th St	41	C1/C2
SW 114th St		
(1-1399)	38	C1
(1400-3499)	37	C1/C2
115th Ave NE		
(100-1899)	46	B1/C1
(11100-11199)	48	A2
NE 115th Ave	48	A2
115th Ct NE	48	B2
115th Ct SE	43	C1
NE 115th Ct		
(11413-11519)	48	A2
(13200-13499)	49	A1
115th Ln NE	48	A2
NE 115th Ln	48	A1
115th Pl NE		
(5800-5999)	46	A1/B1
(7400-11299)	48	A2/B2/C2
115th Pl SE	43	C1
N 115th St		
(100-2335)	33	B2
(2336-2499)	34	B1
NE 115th St	34	B1/B2
NW 115th St	33	B2
S 115th St		
(1000-1399)	38	C2
(3998-4299)	41	C1
SW 115th St		
(1-399)	38	C1
(2100-3026)	37	C2
116th Ave NE		
(1-5999)	46	A1/B1/C1
(6000-13251)	48	A2/B2/C2
116th Ave SE		
(2-599)	46	C1
(4500-6499)	43	B1/C1
116th Ct NE	48	A2
NE 116th Ln	48	A2
116th Pl NE	48	A2/B2/C2
116th Pl SE	43	C1
NE 116th Pl	48	A1/A2
SW 116th Pl	37	C2
N 116th St	33	B2
NE 116th St		
(100-299)	34	B1
(9800-12799)	48	A1/A2
(14200-18714)	49	A1/A2
NW 116th St	33	B1/B2
S 116th St		
(1-2048)	38	C1/C2
(2049-4299)	41	C1/C2
SW 116th St		
(1-1449)	38	C1
(1450-3049)	37	C2
116th Way NE	48	A2
S 116th Way	41	C1

Street Index

Street	Range	Page	Grid
117th Ave NE	(4100-4829)	46	A1
	(6700-7599)	48	C2
117th Ave SE		43	C1
NE 117th Ct		48	A1
117th Dr NE		48	C2
NE 117th Ln		48	A1
117th Pl NE		48	A2/B2
NE 117th Pl		48	A1/A2
N 117th St		33	B2
NE 117th St	(151-3999)	34	B1/B2
	(11326-13162)	48	A2
NW 117th St		33	B1/B2
S 117th St		41	C1/C2
NE 117th Way		49	A1
118 Ct NE		48	C2
118th Ave NE	(800-4836)	46	A1/C1
	(7500-13299)	48	A2/C2
118th Ave SE	(100-599)	46	C1
	(900-6199)	43	—
NE 118th Ln		46	A1
118th Pl NE		48	A2/B2/C2
NE 118th Pl	(10200-10399)	48	A1
	(13200-13399)	49	A1
NE 118th St	(3100-3999)	34	B2
	(10900-12799)	48	A1/A2
NW 118th St		33	B1
119th Ave NE	(400-3499)	46	B1/C1
	(6700-10399)	48	B2/C2
119th Ave SE		48	B2/C2
NE 119th Ct		48	A1
119th Pl NE	(4800-4999)	46	A1
	(13000-13199)	48	A2
119th Pl SE		43	C2
NE 119th Pl		48	A1
NE 119th St		48	A1/A2
NW 119th St		33	B1
NE 119th Way		49	A1
120th Ave NE	(100-3199)	46	B1/C1
	(6001-13199)	48	A2/B2/C2
120th Ave SE		43	B2/C2
NE 120th Ln		48	A1/A2
120th Pl NE		48	A2/C2
120th Pl SE		43	A2
NE 120th Pl		48	A1
N 120th St		33	B2
NE 120th St	(100-4299)	34	B1/B2
	(9165-13199)	48	A1/A2
NW 120th St		33	B1/B2
121st Ave NE		48	A1
121st Ave SE		43	A2/B2/C2
NE 121st Ct		48	A1
121st Ln NE		48	C2
NE 121st Ln		48	A1/A2
121st Pl NE		46	C1
121st Pl SE		43	C2
NE 121st Pl		48	A1
N 121st St		33	B2
NE 121st St		48	A1
NW 121st St		33	B1
121st Way NE		48	A2
NE 122 Ln		48	A2
122 Pl NE		48	C2
122nd Ave NE	(600-5949)	46	A1/C1
	(5950-8999)	48	B2/C2
122nd Ave SE		43	A2/B2/C2
122nd Ct NE		48	B2
122nd Ln NE		48	A2/B2
122nd Pl NE	(300-3799)	46	A1/B1/C1
	(13200-13238)	48	A2
122nd Pl SE		43	C2
N 122nd Pl		34	B1
NE 122nd Pl		48	A1
N 122nd St	(100-2248)	33	B2
	(2251-2399)	34	B1
NE 122nd St	(900-1799)	34	B1
	(10000-10599)	48	A1
	(16400-17199)	49	A2
NW 122nd St		33	B1/B2
NE 122nd Way		48	A2
123rd Ave NE	(500-799)	46	C1
	(6100-10799)	48	B2/C2
123rd Ave SE	(400-499)	46	C1
	(1200-6399)	43	A2/B2/C2
NE 123rd Ct		48	A1
123rd Ln NE		48	A2/B2
NE 123rd Ln		48	A2
123rd Pl NE		46	C1
123rd Pl SE		43	A2/C2
NE 123rd Pl		48	A1
NE 123rd St	(200-4599)	34	B1/B2
	(10000-13299)	48	A1/A2
	(18000-18099)	49	A2
124th Ave NE	(100-5599)	46	A1/B1/C1
	(6400-13499)	48	A2/B2/C2
124th Ave SE	(400-499)	46	C1
	(2300-4499)	43	A2/B2
NE 124th Ct		46	A1
NE 124th Ct		48	A1
124th Ln NE		48	A2
NE 124th Ln		48	A1/A2
124th Pl NE	(301-2999)	46	B1/C1
	(7500-7599)	48	C2
NE 124th Pl		48	A1
NE 124th St	(500-4599)	34	B1/B2
	(9313-13323)	48	A1/A2
	(13324-17717)	49	A1/A2
NE 124th St NE		49	A1
125th Ave NE	(2500-3199)	46	B1
	(6400-13399)	48	A2/B2/C2
125th Ave SE	(400-499)	46	C1
	(1400-12549)	43	A2/B2/C2
NE 125th Ct		48	A1
125th Dr NE		48	A2
NE 125th Dr		48	A1
125th Ln NE	(5601-5805)	46	A1
	(7900-12899)	48	A2/C2
NE 125th Ln		48	A1/A2
125th Pl SE		43	C2
NE 125th Pl		48	A1
N 125th St		33	B2
NE 125th St	(100-4299)	34	B1/B2
	(9272-9399)	48	A1
	(17200-18399)	49	A2
NW 125th St		33	B1/B2
NE 125th Way		48	A2
126th Ave NE	(100-3699)	46	A1/B1/C1
	(6000-11399)	48	A2/B2/C2
126th Ave SE	(400-499)	46	C1
	(1700-6449)	43	A2/C2
126th Ct NE		48	A2
NE 126th Ct		49	A2
126th Ln NE		46	A1
126th Pl NE	(800-999)	46	C1
	(8100-13299)	48	A2/B2/C2
126th Pl SE		43	C2
NE 126th Pl	(9200-13199)	48	A1/A2
	(13500-17499)	49	A1/A2
NW 126th Pl		33	B2
NE 126th St	(530-1099)	34	B1/B2
	(9900-10199)	48	A1
NW 126th St		33	B1
126th Way NE		48	A2
127th Ave NE	(2300-5899)	46	A1/B1
	(7000-11499)	48	A2/B2/C2
127th Ave SE		43	A2/C2
NE 127th Ct		48	A2
127th Dr NE		48	A2
127th Ln NE		48	A2/C2
127th Pl NE	(1400-1499)	46	B1
	(7900-11399)	48	A2/B2/C2
127th Pl SE		43	A2/B2/C2
NE 127th Pl		48	A1
N 127th St		33	B2
NE 127th St	(500-3999)	34	A1/A2/B2
	(17900-18299)	49	A2
NW 127th St		33	B1/B2
128th Ave NE	(1-3199)	46	B1/C1
	(6000-13226)	48	A2/B2/C2
128th Ave SE	(1-425)	46	C1
	(426-5999)	43	A2/B2/C2
NE 128th Ct		49	A2
128th Ln NE		48	A2
128th Pl NE	(1450-1549)	46	B1
	(7500-11099)	48	B2/C2
NE 128th Pl	(12900-13199)	48	A2
	(17600-17742)	49	A2
N 128th St	(700-2166)	33	B2
	(2167-2399)	34	A1
NE 128th St	(800-2499)	34	A1
	(9400-12299)	48	A1/A2
	(12600-18099)	49	A1/A2
128th Way NE		48	A2
NE 128th Way	(12584-12699)	48	A2
	(18100-18799)	49	A2
129th Ave NE	(100-3599)	46	B1/C1
	(7300-13199)	48	A2/B2/C2
129th Ave SE	(1-529)	46	C1
	(530-6460)	43	A2/B2/C2
129th Ct NE		48	A2
NE 129th Ct	(11300-12799)	48	A2
	(17000-17022)	49	A2
NE 129th Dr		48	A2
129th Ln NE		48	A2
129th Ln SE		43	C2
NE 129th Ln		48	A1
129th Pl NE	(300-999)	46	C1
	(9900-13299)	48	A2/B2
129th Pl SE		43	A2/B2/C2
NE 129th Pl	(9469-10099)	48	A1
	(13200-18199)	49	A1/A2
129th St SE		43	B2
NE 129th St	(11100-13199)	48	A2
	(13499-17915)	49	A1/A2
130th Ave NE	(100-3899)	46	A1/B1/C1
	(6100-12899)	48	A2/B2/C2
130th Ave SE	(1-499)	46	C1
	(1900-4899)	43	A2/B2/C2
130th Ct NE		48	A2
NE 130th Ct	(12400-12799)	48	A2
	(17600-18099)	49	A2
130th Ln NE		48	A2
130th Ln SE		43	B2
NE 130th Ln		48	A1/A2
130th Pl NE	(100-3199)	46	B1/C1
	(13200-13230)	48	A2
130th Pl SE	(400-640)	46	C1
	(700-4834)	43	A2/B2/C2
NE 130th Pl	(1500-1999)	34	A1
	(9400-11899)	48	A1/A2
	(13200-18144)	49	A1/A2
N 130th St	(100-2334)	33	A2/B2
	(2335-2399)	34	A1

Street / Range	Page	Grid
SW Atlantic St		
(4000-4099)	36	A1
(4100-4599)	35	A2
Atlas Pl SW	35	C2
Auburn Pl E	21	C1
Augusta Pl S	39	B2
S Augusta St	41	C2
Aurora Ave N		
(100-173)	1	A2
(174-499)	2	A1/B1
(500-1699)	16	A1/B1/C1
(1700-2599)	13	B2/C2
(3300-5599)	24	A2/B2/C2
(5600-8499)	30	A2/B2/C2
(8500-14899)	33	A2/B2/C2
SW Austin Pl	38	A1
Austin St	41	A1
S Austin St		
(200-1299)	38	A1/A2
(2800-5099)	41	A1/A2
SW Austin St		
(700-1099)	38	A1
(1600-4699)	37	A1/A2
Autumn Ln SW	35	C1
Avalon Dr	42	C2
Avalon Pl	42	C2
SW Avalon Way	36	B1
S Avon St	41	C2
S Avon Crest Pl	39	C2
Avondale Pl NE	49	A2
Avondale Rd NE	49	A2/B2/C2
Avondale Way NE	49	C2
Bagley Ave N		
(3400-4699)	25	A1/B1/C1
(7400-8499)	31	A1/B1
(10600-14499)	33	A2/B2
S Bailey St	39	C1/C2
Bainbridge Pl SW	37	A1
Baker Ave NW	24	A1/B1
Ballard Ave NW	23	B1
NW Ballard Way	23	B1/B2/C2
S Bangor St	41	C2
NE Banner Pl	31	B2
Banner Way NE	31	A1/B2
Barberry Ct S	40	B1
E Barclay Ct	4	C2
Barnes Ave NW	23	B1
W Barrett Ln	11	B1
W Barrett St		
(300-1399)	12	B1/B2
(1600-4499)	11	B1/B2
Bartlett Ave NE	34	B2
Barton Pl S	41	B2
SW Barton Pl	37	B2
S Barton St		
(200-1199)	38	B1/B2
(3600-4999)	41	B1/B2
SW Barton St		
(800-1399)	38	B1
(1400-4899)	37	B1/B2
Bataan Pl SW	37	A2
S Bateman St		
(2300-2331)	39	C2
(2800-5099)	40	C1/C2
Battery St	1	A2/B1/B2
Bay St	1	A1/B1
Bayard Ave NW	33	C1
S Bayview St		
(500-2599)	39	A1/A2
(2600-3399)	40	A1
Beach Dr SW		
(3300-6399)	35	B1/C1
(6400-7399)	37	A1
SW Beach Dr Ter	35	C1
Beacon Ave S		
(1900-7024)	39	A2/B2/C2
(7025-11698)	41	—
Bedford Ct NW	33	B1
Belfair Ln	45	C2
Belfair Rd	45	C2
Belgrove Ct NW	33	B1
Bell St		
(1-499)	1	B2
(500-899)	2	B1
Bellavista Ave S	40	A1/B1
Bellefield Park Ln	43	A1
Bellevue Ave	4	A1
Bellevue Ave E	17	B1/C1
Bellevue Ct E	17	B1
Bellevue Pl	45	C2
Bellevue Pl E	17	A1/B1
Bellevue Way NE	45	A2/B2/C2
Bellevue Way SE		
(1-799)	45	C2
(800-3499)	43	A1/B1
Bellevue Redmond Rd		
(2000-2499)	46	B2
(2500-4598)	47	A1/A1/B1
(11800-15299)*	46	—
Belmont Ave	4	A1
Belmont Ave E	17	A1/B1/C1
Belmont Pl E	17	A1/B1
Belvidere Ave SW	36	A1/B1
NE Belvoir Pl	27	C1
S Benefit St	41	B1
S Bennett St		
(100-2499)	39	C1/C2
(2900-4799)	40	C1
Benotho Pl	42	C2
Benton Pl SW	35	B1
SW Bernice Pl	37	B1
W Bertona St		
(1-99)	13	A1
(100-1499)	12	B1/B2
(1500-4799)	11	B1/B2
Beveridge Pl SW	37	A1
SW Beveridge Pl	37	A1
Bigelow Ave N		
(1100-1499)	15	A1/A2
(1500-2450)	13	B2/C2
Birch Ave N	13	B2
Bishop Pl W	11	B1
Bitter Pl N	33	A2
Blackford Ln	42	C1
Blaine Pl	19	C2
Blaine St	13	C1
E Blaine St		
(100-1099)	20	C1/C2
(1900-2299)	21	B1
(3700-4299)	22	C2
W Blaine St		
(1-99)	13	C1
(100-1499)	14	A1/A2
(2600-3599)	11	C1/C2
Blair Ter S	40	C2
Blake Pl SW	37	A1
NE Blakeley St		
(2200-3499)	26	A2/B2
(3500-3699)	27	C1
NW Blakely Ct	33	A1/B1
Blakely Pl NW	33	B1
Blanchard St		
(1-599)	1	B2
(600-899)	2	B1
Blarney Pl	43	A1
Blarney Pl SE	43	A1
Blenheim Dr E	22	B1/C1
NW Blue Ridge Dr	33	B1
NE Boat St	26	B1/C1
Bonair Dr SW	35	A1/A2
Bonair Pl SW	35	A1
S Bond St	41	B2
Bonney St	42	B1
Boren Ave		
(100-249)	8	A2
(250-1599)	4	—
(1700-2099)	2	B2/C2
Boren Ave N		
(100-499)	2	A2/B2
(500-799)	16	C2
Boren Ave S	8	A2/B2
Boston St	13	B1/B2
E Boston St		
(1-1499)	20	B1/B2/C2
(1500-2499)	21	B1/B2
(3849-3999)	22	B2
W Boston St		
(1-99)	13	B1
(100-1499)	12	C1/C2
(2300-2999)	11	C2
E Boston Ter	21	B1/C1
Bothell Way NE	34	A2
W Bothell St	12	C1/C2
Boulevard Pl	42	B1
Boundary Ln	33	A2
N Bowdoin Pl	24	B1/B2
NW Bowdoin Pl	24	B1
Bowen Pl S	40	B1
Bowlyn Pl S	41	A2
Boyd Pl SW	35	B1
Boyer Ave E		
(1500-2424)	21	B1/C1/C2
(2425-2899)	20	A2/B2
Boylston Ave	4	A1/B1/B2
Boylston Ave E		
(100-1123)	17	A1/B1/C1
(2000-2899)	20	A1/B1/C1
S Bozeman St	41	A1/A2
SW Brace Point Dr	37	B1
S Bradford Pl	40	B1
S Bradford St		
(700-1399)	39	B1/B2
(2500-4699)	40	B1
SW Bradford St		
(3000-3999)	36	B1
(4000-5799)	35	B1/B2
Bradner Pl S		
(1120-1699)	10	C1
(1700-1899)	40	A1
S Brandon Ct	39	C2
S Brandon St		
(1-2599)	39	C1/C2
(2600-5699)	40	C1/C2
SW Brandon St		
(1400-3999)	36	C1/C2
(4000-4899)	35	C2
Briarwood Ln	42	A2
Bridge Way N	24	B2/C2
Bridlewood Cir	46	A1
NW Bright St		
(500-599)	24	B1
(600-899)	23	C2
Brighton Ln S	40	C2
S Brighton St		
(400-2699)	39	C1/C2
(2700-5299)	40	C1/C2
Broad St		
(1-399)	1	A1/B1
(401-599)	15	C2
(900-999)	16	C1
Broadmoor Dr E		
(1200-1799)	19	A1/A2
(1800-2399)	22	B1/C1
Broadway		
(100-349)	8	A1
(350-1899)	4	A2/B2/C2
Broadway E		
(100-1199)	17	—
(1500-3199)	20	—
Broadway Ct	4	B2
NE Brockman Pl	34	A1
Brook Ave SW	36	A1
Brook Bay Rd	42	B1
Brooklyn Ave NE		
(3700-5199)	26	A1/B1
(5200-8199)	32	A1/B1/C1
Brown St	49	C2
SW Bruce St	35	C2
Brygger Dr	11	A2
W Brygger Dr	11	A2
NW Brygger Pl	28	C2
S Budd Ct	41	A2
Burke Ave N		
(3300-4999)	25	A1/B1/C1
(8000-8799)	31	A1
(8800-14499)	33	A2/B2/C2
Burke Gilman Trl	24	C1
S Burns St	41	B1
Burton Pl W	11	B2
S Bush Pl	9	C1
Butterworth Rd	42	B2
S Byron St	40	A1
E Calhoun St	21	B1/B2
California Ave SW		
(1100-5999)	35	A2/B2/C2
(6000-10799)	37	A1/B1/C1
California Dr SW	37	B1
California Ln SW	35	A2
SW California Pl	36	A1
California Way SW	36	A1
S Camano Pl	41	A2
S Cambridge St		
(800-899)	38	B2
(3700-5098)	41	B1/B2
SW Cambridge St		
(500-1399)	38	B1
(1400-4399)	37	B1/B2

Street Index

Street Index

Street Index

Street Index

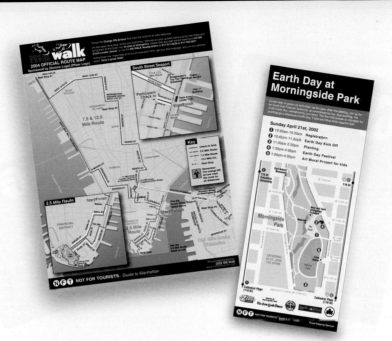